HOUSTON AND THE PERMANENCE OF SEGREGATION

Jack and Doris Smothers Series in Texas History, Life, and Culture

HOUSTON AND THE PERMANENCE OF SEGREGATION

An Afropessimist Approach to Urban History

DAVID PONTON III

University of Texas Press Austin

Publication of this work was made possible in part by support from the J. E. Smothers, Sr., Memorial Foundation and the National Endowment for the Humanities.

Historical GIS data used by the author to create the maps was provided by Steven Manson, Jonathan Schroeder, David Van Riper, Tracy Kugler, and Steven Ruggles. IPUMS National Historical Geographic Information System: Version 17.0 [dataset]. Minneapolis, MN: IPUMS. 2022. http://doi.org/10.18128/D050.V17.0

Copyright © 2024 by the University of Texas Press
All rights reserved
Printed in the United States of America
First edition, 2024

Requests for permission to reproduce material from this work should be sent to:
  Permissions
  University of Texas Press
  P.O. Box 7819
  Austin, TX 78713-7819
  utpress.utexas.edu

∞ The paper used in this book meets the minimum requirements of ANSI/NISO Z39.48-1992 (R1997) (Permanence of Paper).

Library of Congress Cataloging-in-Publication Data

Names: Ponton, David, III, author.
Title: Houston and the permanence of segregation : an Afropessimist approach to urban history / David Ponton III.
Description: First edition. | Austin : University of Texas Press, 2023. | Includes bibliographical references and index.
Identifiers: LCCN 2023009335 (print) | LCCN 2023009336 (ebook)
  ISBN 978-1-4773-2847-7 (hardcover)
  ISBN 978-1-4773-2848-4 (pdf)
  ISBN 978-1-4773-2849-1 (epub)
Subjects: LCSH: Black people—Segregation—Texas—Houston—History. | Black people—Segregation—Texas—Houston—Historiography. | Black people—Civil rights—Texas—Houston—History. | Racism against Black people—Texas—Houston—History. | Black people—Segregation—United States—Cases. | Black people—Civil rights—United States—Cases. | Black people—Texas—Houston—Social conditions—History. | Afropessimism (Philosophy) | Houston (Tex.)—Social conditions—History.
Classification: LCC F394.H89 B5366 2023 (print) | LCC F394.H89 (ebook) | DDC 976.4/141100496073—dc23/eng/20230331
LC record available at https://lccn.loc.gov/2023009335
LC ebook record available at https://lccn.loc.gov/2023009336

doi:10.7560/328477

CONTENTS

Acknowledgments *vii*

Introduction
Decades of Capture *1*

1. Captured by Gender Roles
Christia Adair's Fight for Inclusion *31*

2. Captured by the Rule of Law
Johnnie Lee Morris's Trouble on the Bus *57*

3. Captured in the Impossible American Dream
Dorothy and Jack Caesar Buy a Home *93*

4. Captured by the Role of Gender
Carter Wesley's "Frustrating Compromises" and the Establishment of Texas Southern University *131*

5. Captured by Blackness
Prior Tortures and Law Enforcement's Reign of Terror at Texas Southern University *163*

Coda
Why Not Dream Impossible Dreams? *205*

Notes *217*

Index *267*

ACKNOWLEDGMENTS

If this book represents nothing else, it is a reminder that I have been deeply loved. Every keystroke on these pages reflects the people who have cherished me, challenged me, inspired me, fed me, encouraged me, believed in me, lifted me, and sustained me. Despite appearances to the contrary, this book is autobiographical. As such, it is a testament to what these people have taught me about the possibilities of life beyond the constraints of *this world*.

To those who have cherished me—my parents, Sandra and David Jr. (life-giving and love-sustaining through-and-through); my siblings, Jermaine, Kiyana, and Daiquan (a brother, a friend, and my heart); my first nephew and niece, Najee and Kiara; my aunts, Sylvia (a living monument to love), Doris, and Monique; my uncles, Robert and Bo—I can only speak from my experience, but I have difficulty imagining how love could be any greater than what you have shown me. To you I have been Jun Jun, Big Red, "the Third," and sometimes simply "nephew." To me, you are my earth, wind, and fire.

To those who have challenged me—my advisor and mentor, Alex Byrd, for whom I have *absolute* admiration and respect; the members of my dissertation and comps committees, Lora Wildenthal, Brian Riedel, Randal Hall, and Michael Emerson; my inspiration at the *Journal of Southern History*, Bethany Johnson; faculty at Rice University in the Department of Sociology and the Center for the Study of Women, Gender, and Sexuality, some of whom may not be fully aware of just how much they helped me grow as a theorist, including Susan Lurie, Helena Michie, Jenifer Bratter, and Erin Cech—thank you for allowing me to pursue all the lines of flight that tickled my interests and brought me here, a place where I am living a dream I did not even know was possible to dream.

To those who have inspired me from my days at Rice and beyond—Elizabeth Korver-Glenn and Junia Howell (both very dear graduate school compatriots, colleagues, and friends who have been beyond generous, kind, thoughtful, and affirming); Keith and Ana, Maria, Miller, Eddie and Lauren, Ben and Whitney, Wright, John, Kelly and Tim, Kim, and the indomitable Zora Hamsa—your ideas, your words, your careful reading, your questions, and your casual conversations live throughout these pages. And Emily Straus, who sat with me week-to-week during my first semester as a graduate student and put me on the path to becoming a historian, there is no way to repay the debt I owe you. And to my most recent master's student, Jordan Battle, your mind, diligence, and integrity reflect so much of what I continue to aspire to be.

To those who have fed me—Tommy Curry, Walter Greason, Venetria Patton, Ethan Kleinberg, and Malcolm McGlaughlin, some of whom I have gotten to know closely and others whom I have taken from by way of your scholarship—thank you for your intellectual nourishment. Additionally, the Humanities Institute at the University of South Florida (USF), the Texas State Historical Association, the Center for Engaged Research and Collaborative Learning (CERCL), the Florida Education Fund, the National Endowment for the Humanities, and the Fondren Library at Rice, have provided funding that made it possible for me to travel, research, and write without ever going hungry. And I would be remiss not to try, even if I fail, to remember the librarians and archivists who spent hours, days, weeks, and sometimes months retrieving dusty boxes, guiding me down new paths, and watching over my personal items as I crawled outdoors to the Texas sun to escape the air conditioned halls that left me shivering and numb: thank you to the brilliant staff at the African American Library at the Gregory School; the Houston Metropolitan Research Center; the Harris County Archives; the Harris County District Clerk's Office; the Briscoe Center for American History; the McGovern Historical Center at the Texas Medical Center Library; Texas Southern University special collections; the Museum of Fine Arts, Houston; Southern Methodist University; Texas Tech University Southwest Collection; the Texas State Library and Archives Commission; the University of Houston libraries; the special collections at the University of Texas, Arlington; and the Woodson Research Center and Kelley Center for Government Information, Data and Geospatial Services.

To those who have encouraged me—my colleagues at USF, Scott Solomon and Cheryl Hall (true mentors and inspiring leaders); Cheryl Rodriguez and Daphne; Laurie Lahey, Manu Samnotra; Nick Thompson; Ed Kissi; Steve Tauber and Meghan; Bernd Reiter; and Tayo Jolaosho—thank you for all of the kind words, advice, checking in, meals, and casual moments that have made the School of Interdisciplinary Global Studies (SIGS) a dream department to call home. To Magali Michael, Liz Kicak, and my colleagues in the Department of Women's Gender, and Sexuality Studes, Michelle, Kim, and David, thank you for helping make USF, in big and small ways, a great university to call home. Tangela Serls, McArthur Freeman, and Elizabeth Hordge-Freeman, I am constantly in awe of how amazing and talented and hard-working and real you all are. I am beyond honored to know you.

To those who have believed in me—my editors at the University of Texas Press, Robert Devens and Dawn Durante—you had an early faith in this project that remains, in my view, unjustified by where it began, and I am forever thankful for what you have done to facilitate this journey.

To those who have lifted me—all the way from childhood to early adulthood, including Tameka Blackshir, Elizabeth Emmanuel, Roy Dean Johnson Jr., Anthony Harris, Richard Hutchinson, Fonz Ford, LaTasha Riddick (PharmD!), and Jorge Loaiza; from Ewing, including Danielle, Kelly and Sean, and Mary (I wish I had more space for the four of you, but know that you mean the world to me); from Houston, including Isaiah, Brandon, Disha and Rebecca, Brandon, Jaison, Jermaine Thibodoeux, Lisa, Marie Kunthara, David and Megan, Morgan, Willie, and Richard Prather; from Princeton, Jason Klugman, Jasmine Helen Wade, and Samantha Hyacinth; and from Tampa, including Reggie, Marco, Ron, Mike, Nate, Toya, David and Marlon, and Shaunette—your friendships were and remain the condition of possibility for my ongoing process of becoming.

And to those who have sustained me—Michael Koch, whose love remains an undeserved, unmeasurable gift; Cecilia Oyediran (and *our* dear mother Funlola), who showed me what it means to live beyond fear; Malcolm Pyles, who is nothing less than a brother; Shamelle Ribeiro-Yemofio, who is nothing less than a sister; and Brandee Nicole Tate, who remains the rubric by which I measure what it means to be a friend—you are my chosen family, through and through.

I tend to write too much. In my effort to curb this tendency, I have surely left names unnamed. To those remaining who have cherished me, challenged me, inspired me, fed me, encouraged me, believed in me, lifted me, and sustained me in various ways—Rosemary Leonard-Bethea, Raymond and Myrna, Korey, Tilisia, among so many others—please know that your imprint on this book and on me are felt and deeply appreciated.

To readers near and far, thank you in advance for affording me patience through this book. I have grown wary and weary of *this world*. It's suffocating. But I grew up Pentecostal, so I know something of pneumatology—the study of the spirit, of its breath, of the air. I'm ready for all of us, somehow, to finally be able to breathe the air of a world-yet-to-come, but a world that I know is possible because of the people whose names grace these pages.

HOUSTON AND THE PERMANENCE OF SEGREGATION

INTRODUCTION
Decades of Capture

Black people will never gain full equality in this country. Even those herculean efforts we hail as successful will produce no more than temporary "peaks of progress," short-lived victories that slide into irrelevance as racial patterns adapt in ways that maintain white dominance. This is a hard-to-accept fact that all history verifies. We must acknowledge it, not as a sign of submission, but as an act of ultimate defiance.

Derrick Bell, *Faces at the Bottom of the Well: The Permanence of Racism*

Houston and the Permanence of Segregation is a historical study of race and racism in the city of Houston, where residential segregation made and makes concrete the structural relationship between whiteness and blackness. In some ways, this means the contours of the story may be familiar when juxtaposed to mid-twentieth-century Philadelphia, Chicago, or Los Angeles, even if the local players were different. Of course, material differences exist between these metropolitan areas, and historians have rightfully called our attention to them. Local differences elucidate the significance of the racialization of space to the maintenance of the social, political, economic, and psychological relations that structure American life and hold together the nation's democracy as it is. Notably, historians suggest diverse but overlapping processes for maintaining racialized space across geographies: white flight in Atlanta, the suburbanization of work in Pittsburgh, and the collapsed tax structure in Detroit in the mid-twentieth century have been represented elsewhere by scholars as local processes that redrew and deepened lines of segregation in the postwar period. These local differences notwithstanding, the structural outcome was the same.[1]

Plainly, historians have proffered various explanations for the persistence of residential segregation, including those that are sometimes labeled race-reductionist (i.e., all roads lead to racism).² Others start from the premise that individuals are rational beings seeking to maximize their economic potential—that seemingly racist decisions were really economic ones with inadvertent racial consequences.³ Still others offer a hybrid of racial and economic explanations for the persistence of residential segregation in the twentieth century.⁴ The content of these debates appears inconsequential vis-à-vis the thesis of this book. Suffice it to say that race and economy are inseparable in US history: "Historically, white Americans have accumulated advantages in housing, education, and security based solely on the color of their skin. Being white, as a consequence, literally has value."⁵ As the "old history of capitalism" makes clear, there has never been a capitalism without racism.⁶

Houston can be instructive because it is both unique and typical, at times parallel and at other times perpendicular to the economic, demographic, and administrative processes taking place contemporaneously in comparable cities in the postwar era. However, Houston is conspicuously absent in urban history. For instance, Kenneth L. Kusmer and Joe W. Trotter's *African American Urban History since World War II* aims to be the "first source consulted by the next generation of scholars and students on this subject." Despite gathering the work of some of the most prominent scholars in the field as well as several brilliant junior scholars, none of the chapters address Houston directly.⁷ This omission reflects a pattern. Matthew Lassiter's history of the postwar Sunbelt only cursorily mentions Houston, and prominent studies of black suburbanization do the same, if they provide any treatment of Houston at all.⁸

After much neglect, Houston's past is generating excitement among historians.⁹ Historians like Tom Sugrue and Kevin Kruse have warned that their studies of Detroit and Atlanta, respectively, are not generalizable ones and that local histories still need to be told—that attention to the differences between cities can illuminate the ways race and place were made in the twentieth century. Their scholarship, alongside other work such as Robert Self's on the California Bay Area, demonstrates how those metropolitan areas evince that the federal subsidization of suburbia, the phenomenon of white flight, the divestment of industry from central cities, black migration, and conservative politics precipitated the racialized distinction of the chocolate city and the vanilla suburb, the former as ghetto and the latter as a safe haven from black encroachment. This generated a racial stigmatization of the inner city, and through heavy federal investment, local and national leaders built these cities into "architectures of confinement" and "defensible space."¹⁰

While these local variants of anti-black racism were mechanisms for maintaining segregation in the aforementioned cities, the end result of a racially bifurcated city-suburb was not necessary for maintaining or hardening the lines of segregation. And the history of Houston's black suburbs demonstrates the fallacy of any history of segregation that relies fully or predominantly on arguments about the "primarily economic" considerations of white Americans. Indeed, postwar urban historians have debated the causes of segregation's shifting but deepening lines in the middle of the twentieth century. Houston's distinctive development as a major city challenges the argument that postwar urban-suburban geographical bifurcation as well as the "suburban exodus" provide the most compelling *explanations* for the consolidation of black ghettos in the latter half of the twentieth century, even if they are *mechanisms* by which such spaces were consolidated.[11]

We can more clearly see the intransigence of anti-black segregation in hindsight. However, during the mid-twentieth century, editors at the black-owned *Houston Informer* lauded US Supreme Court decisions that they believed would precipitate a break in the ideological war for democracy, writing, "When the full history of this peculiar struggle is finally written, the school segregation opinion may easily go down as a turning point in the struggle."[12] To wit, in 1948 the Supreme Court ruled in *Shelley v. Kraemer* that racial restrictions in property deeds were no longer enforceable by law. White Houstonians thereby lost their primary remaining legal means for maintaining racial ownership of their neighborhoods. In 1950 the same court unanimously ruled in favor of Heman Sweatt, a black Houstonian seeking admission to the all-white University of Texas Law School, in *Sweatt v. Painter* and desegregated trains involved in interstate travel in *Henderson v. United States*; in 1954 it affirmed that the Fourteenth Amendment proscribed ethnic discrimination by the state in *Hernandez v. United States* and also decided *Brown v. Board of Education*, which defined racial segregation in public schools as inimical to the principle of equality. The following year in its *Brown II* decision, the court ordered the nation's public schools to desegregate "with all deliberate speed." Through the rest of the decade and following, the court continued to issue decisions that appeared to provide immediate civil rights protections to racially subordinated groups as it pushed Jim Crow into its shallow grave. For black Houstonians who had been hoping and actively fighting for what they called a "raceless democracy," the 1940s, 1950s, and 1960s were decades of promise. I contend otherwise; like the centuries before them and the years after them, these were decades of capture.

"Capture" functions in three related ways throughout this book. It refers to the various ways historical subjects, their actions, and their thoughts were always constrained by the worlds in which they lived: constricted by ideologies like gender and race, by faith in the law, and by hegemonic narratives. I refer to this in shorthand as subjective or narrative capture. In lieu of applying a rubric of "agency" to these subjects, I emphasize constraint, which refocuses analysis toward the structural rather than phenomena like identity and individual experience.[13]

A second use of capture, racial capture, implicates anti-blackness as a violence that is constitutive of the modern world. *This world* has relied on antiblack violence since its inauguration, and thus it appears impossible for *this world* to survive without such violence. Anti-blackness traps people who are marked as black into a stubborn antagonism with the world: one in which insecurity and death always loom over them.[14]

Racial capture is the product of violence, and such violence inevitably produces archival sources that can only fail to fully reveal the subjects they claim to represent or give voice to.[15] Subjective and racial capture also constrain the historian. Therefore, subsidiary to these is the challenge of disciplinary capture—the methodological dictates, unquestioned theoretical assumptions, and conventions of writing and presentation that delimit what and how scholars can acceptably argue within our fields. While calling attention to my own subjective, racial, and disciplinary capture, I make a case for privileging perspective over method—a perspective that, in turn, values the structural over the empirical. I do this not assuming I can escape capture entirely, but to provide a convincing justification for the need to experiment with thought and method in anti-disciplinary and anti-ethical ways, experiments I attempt herein and that I appreciate as part of the legacy of the ancestors of black freedom struggles, passed on and alive.

Thus, in large part, this book concerns the ways historians think about and do history. For instance, urban historiography has sometimes pivoted on disagreements about the roles racial prejudice versus economic rationalizations have played in the continuation of segregation in the twentieth century. I am not convinced these debates are ethical toward black people, laden as they are with social constructions like "agency" and "contingency" which eschew the problem that capture presents for such notions and for the grammars with which historians narrate the pasts we invent. I draw on the rich philosophies of black thinkers, answering the Afropessimist critique of history, in an effort to expose rather than rearticulate *this world*'s hold on the discipline of history and on black political thought.

HOUSTON AND THE CASE FOR HISTORIOGRAPHICAL REVISION

Economists Trevon D. Logan and John M. Parman have upended scholarly assumptions concerning residential segregation in the United States from 1880 to 1940, using newly released census manuscript files to develop a segregation index based on individual households rather than census tracts. Contrary to previous studies, Logan and Parman found that southern cities, not northern ones, "were the most segregated in the country and remained so over time." In the South, black and white Americans "were the least likely to be neighbors," even if they lived in "the same wards and districts." Additionally, and in contradistinction to much of the urban historiography, they conclude that "increasing segregation . . . was not driven by black migratory patterns, nor was urbanization the sole force behind increasing segregation." Moreover, white flight and mass suburbanization, phenomena that picked up rapidly in the post-World War II period, cannot possibly explain the dramatic increases in racial residential segregation that Logan and Parman found in urban areas and offer no explanatory power for the increases in segregation they documented in rural areas.[16] With these compelling findings in mind, Houston's story, which has been left out of general studies of the Sunbelt and black suburbanization "because of its peculiar demographic distribution," offers an opportunity to rethink the assumptions underlying this historiography.[17]

Leaving aside the suburbs for a moment, differences within Houston's racialized inner-core neighborhoods show that if white neighborhoods were considered the American norm, black neighborhoods were decidedly aberrant. Census tracts in the city where white people were likely to live shared a number of favored qualities—and many of these qualities were covariates (i.e., greater education, higher median incomes, white-collar professions, low unemployment, and low poverty, for example, were likely to be related in the whole population). In these predominantly white or all-white tracts, residents above the age of twenty-five tended to have at least a high school diploma. The people who lived in these tracts often had careers in management, sales, office work, and crafts, while they were highly unlikely to do domestic work for pay. Male and female unemployment were negatively correlated with these highly segregated white tracts, as was the overall poverty rate of the community within the tract. The whiteness of a census tract correlated with a relatively higher proportion of homes in "sound condition," as opposed to those that were "deteriorating" or "dilapidated." Residents living in these tracts were likely to own a car and unlikely to have neighbors who lived in cramped accommodations.[18]

In the 1960 census, the evidence suggests black Houstonians at all income levels simply lacked the residential choices that their white counterparts had. As the proportion of black residents in a census tract grew, each of the aforementioned variables often exhibited *reverse* directionality in its correlations. Nationally, unemployment and poverty rates rose as levels of education and housing quality fell. However, apart from demonstrating that white Houstonians tended to have—on average—higher levels of completed formal education and its concomitant benefits in jobs and housing, these correlations reveal little about the socioeconomic diversities within these broad racial groups and whether that diversity mattered when it came to housing. For example, they do not reveal that as the rate of high school completion among white Houstonians rose, unemployment rates fell, while as the rate of high school completion among black Houstonians rose, unemployment rates remained unaffected. They do not show the stronger positive correlation between the proportion of white residents with college degrees and the proportion of white people with professional careers relative to nonwhite college degree earners with professional careers (0.896 versus 0.603). That is, highly educated black people were less likely to find jobs and live around neighbors with careers that were commensurate with their years of completed schooling. And these correlations do not make clear that lower-middle-class black families were more likely to live in census tracts with higher proportions of poverty than were lower-middle-class white families *and* white families who were impoverished themselves. These were differences *within* the city itself.[19]

The distinctions between Houston and the cities on which much of urban history has focused are immediately apparent in demography. In 1950, both Detroit and Atlanta each had one large pocket of majority black areas near their central business districts. Over the course of the next two decades, there was an unmistakable exodus of white folks from the inner core of both cities as the suburbs filled in. In Houston, this pattern did not hold. In 1950, the central business district was abutted on all sides by segregated black and white communities, with most of the black communities to the east and northeast of downtown, but with four suburban enclaves, including Independence Heights and Acres Homes northwest of the city, the Clinton Park tri-community out toward the east, and Sunnyside directly south. Over the next two decades, Houston's black inner-core neighborhoods expanded as some white Houstonians fled east for the suburbs. However, the inner core never emptied of white people, and white urbanites living west of downtown never abandoned their neighborhoods. Thus, the white-suburb versus black-city bifurcation that developed elsewhere did not occur in Houston, and suburbanization

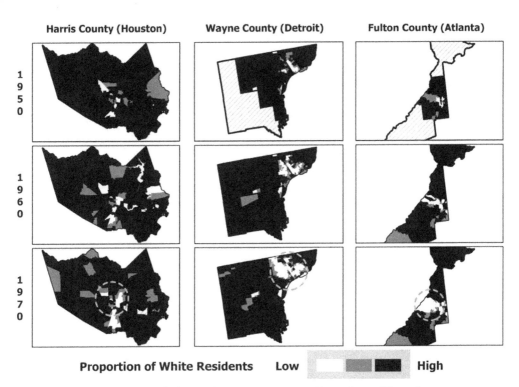

Map 1 *The proportion of white residents per census tract in Harris County, Wayne County, and Fulton County with central business districts indicated.*

therefore does little to explain white racial attitudes or postwar segregation there. Atlanta and Detroit became *black* cities, and everyone knew it. Houston never carried such a reputation.[20]

Population decline or very slow growth also characterized many cities of the Rust Belt and the West, where the movement of industry out of central cities encouraged further flight from these hubs of increasing unemployment. Comparing the number of vacant residences while controlling for differences in the number of residential units between 1950 and 1960, I found dramatic increases in vacant homes in central Detroit and Oakland, while Houston's central city remained almost void of vacancies. Indeed, eighteen of the twenty-five largest cities in the nation lost population numbers in the postwar period, while suburbs multiplied with new residents. Of the fifteen largest cities, only Houston had a majority—55 percent—still living in the boundaries of the city proper, albeit boundaries that were expanding through annexation.[21] Houston did lose some density from its core between 1950 and 1970, specifically in tracts where new highway construction decimated black neighborhoods, but when juxtaposed with the loss faced in Detroit, especially between 1960 and 1970, Houston mostly shifted populations *within* its core as opposed to witnessing an evacuation of its core.

Finally, one pattern holds true for Houston, Detroit, and Atlanta: the census tracts where black people clustered were also the tracts that registered the highest proportion of families living below the median income for the area. However, in 1950, the families in areas outside of the core of the cities were not noticeably better off than those who lived closer in. By 1960, Detroit and Atlanta suburbs were remarkably better off than they had been in the previous decade, and by 1970 both places evinced a clear distinction between the poorer inner city and the affluent suburbs. Thus, Sugrue and Kruse's contention about economic divestment from the cities concurrent with white flight holds true. However, while Houston's suburbs attracted more middle-income and wealthy families, its socioeconomic map did not demonstrate the same stark delineation as its counterparts. Indeed, while the greatest cluster of lower-income families lived in the more densely populated census tracts of the city's inner core, sparsely populated suburban enclaves to the north and south and especially the east of downtown also housed lower-income families. Moreover, many of its wealthiest neighborhoods remained in the center city.

By 1970 Atlanta was more than 50 percent black and Detroit was well on its way to becoming a majority black city, rising from 43 to 63 percent black between 1970 and 1980. Houston actually witnessed a stability of the black proportion of the total city population, despite its ballooning population and continued in-migration of large numbers of black people. Black Houstonians were 21 percent of the population of the city in 1950, 20 percent in 1960, and 19 percent in 1970, notwithstanding consistent growth in the absolute number of black residents.[22]

That is to say: although there was white flight in parts of Houston, the city's development did not mirror Detroit's, Oakland's, or Atlanta's. Although black unemployment was about double white unemployment in each city, Houston and Atlanta did not see unemployment rates skyrocket as they did in Oakland and Detroit. And, although white folks certainly dominated Houston's suburbs, a stark distinction between the chocolate city and the vanilla suburbs never emerged, as many white people remained in the city center and many black Houstonians made their homes in all-black suburbs.

These realizations compel reconsideration of the assumptions of what might be considered the urban history canon. While city politics, conflicts over infrastructure, and demographic shifts remain important in the histories of Houston and its counterpart cities, a shift in perspective might yield histories that more fully account for race, not as a matter of demography, but as the

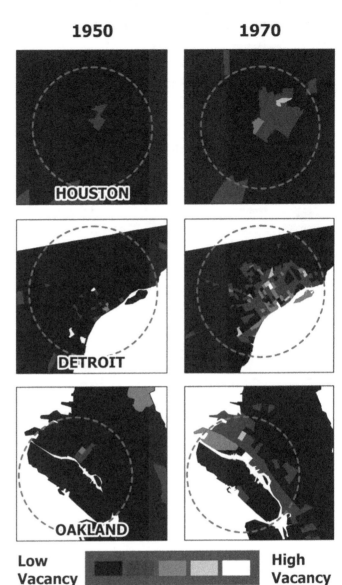

Map 2 *The proportion of vacancies normalized by the number of housing units in and around the central business districts of Houston, Detroit, and Oakland.*

consequence of racial terror. Racism always precedes race. Therefore, blackness is always precipitated by racial violence. Regardless of their particular local situation, people marked as black would always be captured within a racial construct that they did not make for themselves—a construct that justified black people's poverty, dispossession, unemployment, over-policing, and general dishonor and legitimated the racist mechanisms deployed to keep black people in their proscribed economic, political, and geographic place.

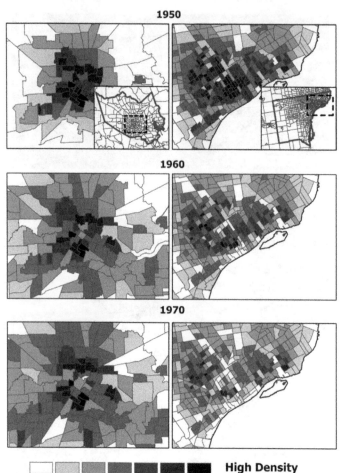

Map 3 *The changes in population density in the central business districts of Houston and Detroit.*

This book focuses on anti-blackness in lieu of the more generic term racism, since the conceit of white racial purity was based specifically on the "biological" and social exceptionality of blackness, and the sociopolitical superiority of other so-called "people of color" required their participation in the abasement of blackness.[23] Indeed, still in the third decade of the twenty-first century, black people remain outliers on all segregation metrics. Not only do white Americans avoid living in neighborhoods with them, but so do Asian and Latinx Americans insofar as they have the choice, a pattern observable in Houston itself.[24] (Thus, while Mexican-descended Houstonians did live in Houston during the mid-twentieth century and experienced forms of racial subjugation, their experiences were distinct from those of black Houstonians.[25] Their stories are beyond the scope of this project for a number of

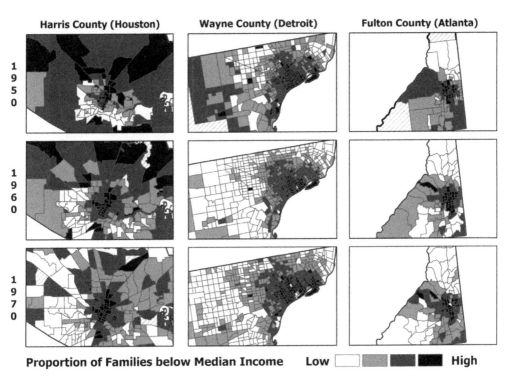

Map 4 *The proportion of families living below the Standard Metropolitan Statistical Area's median income.*

additional reasons. For most of the time period covered in this book, people of Mexican descent remained a relatively small and, in terms of the US Census, poorly accounted for population group in Houston. Moreover, they often identified as white and strategically identified otherwise in moments where it was politically expedient to do so, such as during the 1960s and 1970s school desegregation movements.[26] This is not to say that Latinx people in Houston were not racialized, did not face discrimination, did not live in segregated communities, or were simply not present; it is to say, however, that until the late 1960s, Houstonians by and large understood their city as a *bi-racial* one, where the problem of the color line was one of a bifurcation of black versus white. As Tyina Steptoe demonstrates, despite their ethnic identities as Mexican, Mexican-descended Houstonians "consistently asserted that they were racially white."[27] And somewhat ironically, while the experience of Latinx Houstonians demonstrates that race is socially constructed and that the meanings of racial categories can change over time, this "change" also demonstrates the static nature of anti-blackness. Even as Mexican Houstonians became white, or brown, or indeterminate, black Houstonians remained relegated to the bottom of the social structure, exposed to

11 | Introduction: Decades of Capture

violence that other groups could negotiate reprieve from through the strategic manipulation of "race.")

Inspired by Saidiya Hartman's *Scenes of Subjection*, with the stories I tell in these chapters, I intend "to bring into view the ordinary terror and habitual violence that structured everyday life and inhabited the most mundane and quotidian practices," exposing how violence, on registers including and beyond the spectacular, characterized Houston's desegregation era.[28] Nevertheless, framed as nonevents, these stories do not inaugurate novelty into history or measure "change," but rather indicate the stubborn structural relationship that divides the world into humans and less-than-humans. What we learn about "the past" is incidental to what we learn about history (the discipline). Importantly, this demands a departure from the kind of writing typical of urban historiography. Sylvia Wynter identifies conventional history as "ethnoculturally coded narrated history" whereby the world of Man is sustained. Therefore, "if we are to be able to reimagine the human in terms of a new history whose narrative will enable us to co-identify ourselves with each other . . . we would have to begin by taking our present history, as narrated by historians, as empirical data for the study" of how the ways we construct/invent the past perpetuate "our present Western world system."[29] In other words, if we do not account for *how* we account the past, then history (including urban history) is mere "endless self-creation" that "can only be extended as a servile representation . . . always already trapped inside a predefined meaning of what counts as history."[30] To oppose "*history* for Man," this text experiments with trying to make urban history a history *of* Man.[31]

As Michel-Rolph Trouillot explains, "History is the fruit of power, but power itself is never so transparent that its analysis becomes superfluous."[32] Throughout the book, I reckon with how anti-blackness, as a form of power, works through the historical discipline, for while urban historians are deeply concerned with social, political, and economic power in "the city," we have made scant contributions to understanding how urban historiography rests on and traffics in the same ideologies that we lament in our work. In *Houston and the Permanence of Segregation*, I note how Houston's lines of segregation hardened after World War II alongside other recent works concerning the city.[33] Domestic racial terrorism, the racialized criminalization of space, processes of annexation and underbounding, and so on helped concretize Houston's racial geography even in Jim Crow's demise. White flight, suburbanization, deindustrialization, highway construction, and urban renewal were neither linear processes nor essential to segregation, even if they were common tools for building and maintaining it. And liberal projects, including efforts at interracial gender solidarity, could only fail to account for the power of gender and sexuality as central discourses in the subordination of black people.

However, my call is not simply that we make Houston part of the urban history canon, though its near absence from this canon is quite remarkable. Historians must also consider how urban history reproduces existing power relations and imagine how it might be deployed to invert them. For instance, concerning Nashville's public school system, Ansley Erickson explains how state actors, compelled by individually and collectively held racist ideas, sidestepped integration. Following a 1971 school order, Nashville adopted a busing program that would yield "statistical desegregation," which actually "remade . . . educational inequality." When Erickson concludes that "inequality shifted form," she gestures toward a key contention in *Houston and the Permanence of Segregation*, namely that anti-blackness disrupts the narrative device of change over time. Still, Erickson also concludes that the nation must now "ask how a robust democracy might define and realize the schooling it needs."[34] After nearly 250 years of American democracy, it would seem more prudent to ask whether democracy is inherently as virtuous, progressive, and inclusive in fact as it is articulated in theory. Philosopher Lewis Gordon suggests that there will be no answer to the problem of anti-blackness, no arrival at a racial or raceless democracy "without a dialectic in which humanity experiences the blackened world."[35] Existence as experienced by black people under slavery and its afterlives—the blackened world—reveals democracy as a project of racial subordination and exclusion. Erickson's work is symptomatic of what I call subjective/narrative capture.

Each of the chapters in *Houston and the Permanence of Segregation* is an experiment against the powerful appeal of prevailing narratives. How can we write a story that honors the struggles, failures, and successes of those we find in the archive without relying on a grammar of "agency" that functions, in the end, to reinforce the idea of the (anti-black) liberal individual (chapter 1)? How might we write about American democracy as a vehicle for rather than an impediment to racism and racist futures (chapter 2)? How might we question the hegemony of the narrative of progress to reshape how we think about change, contingency, power, and resistance (chapter 3)? How can we expose gender, not as a category of being or identity nor as a mere analytic, but as a technology of race that constrains rather than enhances what we can understand about black political activity (chapter 4)? What practices of invention can we draw on to do history differently (chapter 5)?

Urban history currently functions under an education paradigm—the more we learn about the past, the more contempt we will have for historical discrimination and the more we can understand about how to redress it. Urban history that shifts perspective might function under a consciousness-raising paradigm—the more we understand about who *we* are through our narrative construction of the past as its contemporaries, the more inventive we can be with our methodologies.

DEFYING THE COMMITMENT TO CHANGE OVER TIME

The underlying reason these debates matter to historians at all is less academic than it is moral and affective. At the core is the matter of contingency, which is central to the ways historians tell stories. Often, to maintain narrative coherence, historians resort to practices of identifying causal relationships and deconstructing taken-for-granted categories ad infinitum, emphasizing the experiential at the expense of the structural. However, throughout urban historiography, despite the many local differences historians focus on to make their contributions to the field, the structural antagonism between whiteness and blackness is a constant across geographies and time. Empirical, positivist explanations for local histories of segregation focus attention on specific mechanisms that produced and maintained segregation rather than the underlying structure that guaranteed anti-black outcomes.[36] Contingency, then, is implied throughout historiography. It is a concept that traverses all time and space: historians accept it as a universal truth—as a condition of *being*. This concept, while tacit in most historical writing, does not compel scholars to "engage" or "reflect" on black suffering, but rather allows us to "parade . . . black suffering," providing ourselves relief from the terror by way of a superficial but satisfying "voyeuristic gaze."[37]

In her groundbreaking work, religious studies scholar Liane Carlson traced the historical lineage of the idea of contingency and its import, saying that academics employ it for two types of opposed reasons. They either attempt to "domesticate contingency in teleological narratives of progress" or, by suggesting alternative pasts, weaponize contingency to use "its disruptive power as an opportunity for social critique." I would add that although apparently incongruous, both these approaches to contingency encourage impenetrable optimism. Carlson then deftly demonstrates the origins of the idea of contingency in theology—particularly Christian theodicy—and the purpose this idea serves philosophically, even today, for historians: "A successful theodicy is one that allows the reader to trust that one day she will understand every miserable stroke of bad luck she ever experienced as contingent, as, in fact, necessary, orderly, and congruent with a higher good when viewed from the proper perspective. *Contingency would become an illusion of perspective.*"[38] I write, therefore, suspicious of the very idea of contingency, aware that historical knowledge production is an act of power that can work to disrupt or affirm the status quo. The status quo is one in which the history of black Americans—the suffering of black Americans—is consistently written as the unfinished but ongoing project toward fully realized democracy in an age to come. This is one component of what I call disciplinary capture, which *Houston and the Permanence of Segregation* attempts to consciously confront.

Like all historical studies, this study of Houston is necessarily concerned with context. Context and contingency are not synonymous. Context is not merely what we can know and how we can represent the past, but also consists of our relative awareness of and confrontations with our own as historians—as researchers whose approaches to the archives are shaped by the epistemologies of our day.[39] Contingency has no place here. When I ask the questions that guide this project—namely, why/how did segregation persist in Houston through and beyond the 1940s, 1950s, and 1960s, decades of apparent promise, and what were its consequences on the lives of black Houstonians—I am neither searching to give meaning to black suffering or endurance, nor am I wondering how the nation could have done things differently, which is, to be honest, an anxiety rooted in present concerns about how we (historians, this writer, the readers) and our world might be redeemable even as we bear witness to the continued and unique segregation experienced by black Americans today. Instead, I ask these questions much more pessimistically and maintain, implicitly, that there are no alternative pasts to comfort us.[40]

By meditating on the meaning of history detached from the idea of contingency, historians can see how the stories of Houston, Detroit, Miami, and so on are not particularistic, but rather congeal into collective narratives about who we are (and not merely who we *have been*). Specifically, when the depravity and intransigence of American racism are fully accounted for, the bread and butter of history—"change over time"—collapses. What emerges in its place is critical race theorist Derrick Bell's thesis that racism is a permanent feature in *this world*.[41]

Within Black Studies, *this world* is the world of modern Man. The concept of "humanity" has changed over time. *This world* is one in which humanity is generally understood, not in purely theological terms, but as a matter of biological evolution. Within this episteme, *we* humans are a distinct species. This understanding of human as biological makes it categorical—essential, both prior to and beyond social construction. It is upon this belief that humans have erected monuments to abstract equality: "We are all born equal." Yet as philosopher Sylvia Wynter has argued and helped situate at the core of Black

Studies, "the human" is an object of knowledge, not a foreclosed biological unit. She writes, "[T]he human species . . . realizes itself *as human* only by coming to regulate its behaviors, no longer *primarily*, by the genetic programs specific to its genome, but by means of its narratively instituted conceptions of itself; and therefore, by the *culture-specific discursive programs* to which these conceptions give rise."[42] *This world*, which is "nothing less than the past millennium-plus in which one particular cultural conception of humanity has forcibly, steadily, and increasingly occupied global space as if it were the only way of understanding human beings and life," is thus a violent epistemological imposition that prohibits imagining alternative worlds by way of a positivist definition of "humanity" in biological terms.[43]

However, in a society where race has historically delimited who counted as persons and who counted as property, the idea of the unitary biological human actually obscures what it means to *be* human. Therefore, "the human" is not an issue of genetic code but one of political ontology; that is, society is structured such that *to be/come* human requires the negation of blackness. The biological notion "we are all human" obscures this structural antagonism.

Throughout this book, blackness should not be understood as *being* black, nor as a matter of identity, culture, or ethnicity.[44] "[B]lackness is not identity," Calvin Warren writes, and to treat it as such "is the error of identity politics." Thus, when I refer to race, I do not mean racial categories or phenotype. Instead, blackness (as understood and assigned in *this world*) is a sign, representing "ugliness, sin, darkness, immorality," and all that is evil "in the collective unconscious," according to Frantz Fanon. But this sign has no material referent. It does not refer to the people we call black. Indeed, this sign participates in the very making of people as black. Rather, it refers to nothing. Following Warren, I mean this literally.[45]

Nothing—the absence of substance, meaning, and presence—terrifies Western epistemology because nothing exposes the limits of metaphysics and reveals "value" as a social construction rather than something that inheres in matter. If value obtains meaning on nothing but social relations—not on biology, superior culture, or how hard a person or group works, but rather on the meanings ascribed to categories of race, gender, and class via the violence that sedimented the historical relations between the categories therein—then the Western episteme, which presupposes value as a fact, loses coherence. What if there is no agency, no merit, no guaranteed right to life or liberty, no justification for suffering? This threatens the denizens of the Western world with an existential crisis. For Warren, this crisis is what is avoided by the invention of blackness, the attempted corporealization of nothingness. And blackness is invented by way of anti-black violence, which, as Saidiya Hartman notes, defines "the very foundation of the settler state." Thus, what is at stake—the reason for blackness's creation and anti-blackness's intractability—is the modern world's justifications for and meanings ascribed to its laws, its imperialism, its markets, its being, and its facilitation of black suffering.[46]

Hearkening back to Derrick Bell, racism is not permanent because it is ahistorical, but racism is permanent in *this world* because it is constitutive of it: insofar as *this world* remains committed to its metaphysical project of dominating everything and nothing. The discipline of history demands change over time, but this demand is not an end to itself. Rather, it serves a fundamental paradigm of thought in *this world*—the implicit doctrine of the Enlightenment and the disciplines that emerged from it, including history, which maintains that "the suffering of a people, [and] in fact, their possible extermination, was part and parcel of the forward march of human history."[47] However, as philosopher Frank Wilderson III argues, "The narrative arc of the slave who is Black . . . is *not an arc at all*, but a flat line, what Hortense Spillers calls 'historical stillness': a flat line that moves from disequilibrium, to faux-equilibrium, to disequilibrium restored and/or rearticulated."[48]

Many historians of slavery have been much more adept than urban historians at accounting for such philosophical interventions out of Black Studies. They consider the material depravity of racial slavery as it pushed blackened bodies to the survivable limits of labor exploitation and sexual subjugation. In doing so, they have written groundbreaking works concerning the displacement of Afro-descendant peoples that have further supported the political claims of critical theorists. Walter Johnson found that he could not write a book "organized around change over time" as he counted, soul by soul, the material consequences of capitalism's consumption of blackened people. Indeed, a world constituted by the violent processes of making people into property renders "complete confusion" to temporality and thereby disrupts narratives of "transformation."[49] Likewise, as Stephanie Smallwood demonstrated, "The individual stories of saltwater slavery form the antithesis of historical narrative, for they feature not the evolving plot of change over time but rather a tale of endless repetition that allows no temporal progression."[50] Yes, political economies have changed from chattel slavery, to Jim Crow, to the postracial, Anthropocenic era. However, the structural antagonism between whiteness and blackness remained constant across these systems, and as Houston's history attests, residential segregation has been at the center for over a century.

AN AFROPESSIMIST CRITIQUE OF HISTORY

Thus far, I have made the case that we historians must chronically reckon with the ways we are captured by the rules of our academic discipline—rules that lend themselves to linear narrativity despite that the structure of this world defies such a temporality while it also relies on the illusion of progress to sustain the theodicy of black suffering and anti-black violence.[51] Moving forward, I suggest that Afropessimism offers a clear justification for resisting disciplinary capture. Acknowledging the inescapability of this capture by any tools created or strategies articulated from within it, Afropessimism eschews the epistemological hubris of disciplinary methodology and encourages wayward practices of invention.

Afropessimism offers a countervailing force that I grip onto to attempt to circumnavigate disciplinarity's gravitational pull, even if I cannot obtain full escape. By exposing ontology as political rather than the mere fact of *Being*, Afropessimism displays the vacuity of the academic disciplines' epistemological commitments, opening space for methodological experimentation, reorientations of perspective, and polemics that may be read as anti-ethical. It is only by admitting my own disciplinary capture that I have been able to resolutely defy the urge to affirm the fictional agency of black people and to rest easier with the idea that decades had passed while time had remained still.[52] With disciplinary mandates thusly unsettled, Afropessimism justifies practices of invention that attend to the abyss of meaninglessness avoided by anti-black ontologies. This book is such an experiment.

While it is often mistaken as a theory, Afropessimism is a meta-theory—an attempt to make sense of how thought is constructed in the modern world and the consequences of that construction on people who are marked as black within *this world*. Afropessimism commits to the historical fact that blackness is a consequence of racial slavery and that as long as blackness exists as a collective formation, and in whatever form it has or will come to take, it does so from the position of being first posited as synonymous with the slave.[53] This is not an ontological claim that black people *are* inherently slaves. Rather, it is a claim about ontology: that ontology itself is political and that in the grammar of *this world*, a world in which the modern human historically emerged as a political distinction opposed to the enslaved/enslavable Black, it remains "impermissible" to develop an epistemology (that is, we are unallowed to think) of blackness apart from its emergence as the subordinate collective under the regime of slavery.[54]

As such, blackness throws ontology itself into relief, revealing that ontology is not an account of *being*, but rather that it, like all other *-ologies*, is knowledge constructed in time and space. In other words, no matter how well ontology appears to be an objective account of being, it is a science.[55] This science provides the originary codes for all knowledge production—codes like humanity, agency, race, gender, and liberty. These codes, in turn, provide us, among other things, with the language of "blackness," telling us, indeed, that "blackness," if only because it can be uttered, is something that *be*.[56] Calvin Warren reminds us that blackness refers to nothing, and thus writes in terms of black ~~being~~, a typographical emphasis I adopt in this text at times. Indeed, within this grammar, blackness must always *be* defined in relation to its historical emergence with slavery. (It might be worth the reader pausing here to try to define blackness apart from slavery. It is, in the end, a tautological effort.) Therefore, Afropessimism comments, ontology is ill-equipped to sever blackness from slavery because whenever blackness is considered, slavery is always there.[57]

History, which is colloquially understood as the study of or telling of the past, is also an *-ology*, a method of metaphysics. "'Modern' Western historiography" emerged as a "set of practices adopted and modified in the historical discipline as it has evolved since its emergence after the French Revolution."[58] While often considered a harbinger of slave revolutions, the French Revolution's "idea of freedom was frequently cast in racialized terms" and participated in the philosophical construction of freedom as being a property of whiteness and whiteness as the defining limit of humanity.[59] Thus, the discipline of history emerged as a liberal humanist project. It is no surprise, then, that it *disciplines* scholars into a limited way of thinking, writing, and asking questions that appears to be universal and testable, even as it traffics in its own ahistoricism.

Sylvia Wynter and others have already made this case. If modern historiography developed in the wake of the French Revolution, its dedication to the "agency" of white revolutionaries and its complete disavowal of the same to black revolutionaries and maroon communities indicates that "agency," and the "human" itself, were defined against the irrational, nonhuman black object.[60] This problem is fundamental to the discipline, since history's subject matter is "the human," not "the past," and the historical production of "the human" was bought with a price: the production and negation of black people who became objects of gratuitous violence.[61] Historians, in turn, occlude this violence and negation, offering tales of human agency in order to redeem "the human" from its repulsive origins: "the human emerges as an object of knowledge, as a by-product, so to speak, in the quest to ascertain black people's humanity because western humanity necessitates recalibration once black folks . . . become part of its conceptual protectorate."[62]

The framework of change over time allows historians to redeem humanity—to make its past appear as mistakes that can be understood and prevented from reoccurring. Without this practice of human redemption, history might very well lose its coherence, though it is precisely this investment in "the human" and its codes by which the discipline constructs "new" knowledge—much of which is now avowedly "anti-racist"—and thereby obscures its investment in the selfsame social and political categories that rendered black people nonbeings.[63]

The unrelenting investment in redeeming "the human," by narrating black people as humans despite their historical and juridical treatment as nonhumans, betrays not only ongoing intellectual violence against black people, but also exposes the discipline of history to damning critique. Scholar and literary critic David Marriott notes:

> Now, insofar as what cannot be historicized are the codes or genres that make History itself "historical," history is in some senses the least historical of discourses. It also seems reasonable to suppose that these codes, which are "historical" while being themselves never simply historical, are in some sense more originary than the narratives of history which they ground, and are thus the origin and possibility of History itself.[64]

Proudly, historians identify the significance of the discipline as "the study of man and his environment, of the effects of man on his environment and of his environment on man" toward the end of improving "human awareness . . . by the contemplation of vanished eras."[65] What then does history do with the "no humans"—not just the enslaved chattel but also the contemporaneously free black folks denied entry into the juridical category "human" by way of the denial of their rights to vote, to own property, and to do so of their own accord, free of intimidation and terror? History compulsively rewrites them into the category "human," and in doing so disappears these "no humans" from archives, archives where they were already dismembered, and replaces their corpses with lifelike effigies of—even monuments to—the universal, liberal human subject.[66] In effect, as Saidiya Hartman puts it, "[T]he kind of social revisionist history undertaken by many leftists in the 1970s, who were trying to locate the agency of dominated groups, resulted in celebratory narratives of the oppressed. Ultimately, it bled into this celebration, as if there was a space you could carve out of the terrorizing state apparatus in order to exist outside its clutches and form some autonomy."[67]

This is the guaranteed outcome of fashioning nonhuman corpses into humans, postmortem: the valorization of "the human," which, despite its evident depravity, has learned how to make its moral universe more perfect with lessons learned from those black objects forced, in "vanished eras," to live/die at its margins. Even as historians deny the tradition of Whiggish narration and protest against teleology, the underlying and comforting lesson is that history will inexorably inform "the human" of its promise. History itself comes to take on a life of its own, or in the words of Michael Hawkins: "By letting history speak for itself rather than coercing insights from it that must speak on behalf of a particularly urgent present, scholars can gain more accurate and revealing insights, messages, and representations of the human condition as it unfolded in its own discursive temporality." Accordingly, the lesson Hawkins learns from this theoretical exercise is that history so conceived "reveals human agency in its purest form."[68] Even in his denials of inevitable progress, Hawkins implies that history, when done right, is necessarily revelatory concerning the fact of being human, and in doing so, can make humans better.

This kind of disciplinary self-deception is patently ahistorical: history cannot speak for itself. There are many interrelated and obvious reasons why this is so. One, the historian *creates* history. History is nothing if not a form of knowledge production.[69] Two, knowledge production happens within culture and, therefore, history speaks only the words, thoughts, and narrative structures permissible within a given culture.[70] Third, what is permissible today is rooted in what has already been sanctified as the biological universality of "the human." This biological "human" is also understood in terms beyond the physiological and through codes such as sovereignty and agency. Thus, before the project of historical investigation even begins, its epistemological limits have already been set. Hawkins argues that allowing history to unfold without the prying hands of presentism means there is "no telling what one might turn up," an unconvincing take since he is sure that "human agency in its purest form" is what history ultimately uncovers.[71]

The consequences are more dire than theoretical disagreement. The approach to history described above does nothing less than "serve the police power against blackness by delimiting the permissible questions, debates, perspectives, and paradigms as the price of the ticket for participating in the conversation itself."[72] It reinscribes black people as fungible material, capable of being dismembered (and disremembered) such that their muted screams against the tyranny of "the human" become reconfigured as evidence of the righteousness of anti-racist projects that seek black "inclusion into liberal humanist conceptions of 'the human'" as, within this historical discourse, "the black body is an essential index for the calculation of degree of humanity and the measure of human progress."[73] The lesson of this subtending historiographical narrative is that the black suffers, but at least out of that suffering humanity may be made whole.

AN AFROPESSIMIST EXPERIMENT FOR HISTORY

How, then, can a history that is accountable to black subjects be written? It is, perhaps, an impossible task.[74] The narrative in these pages was written by a historian who has been trained in a diverse but still delimited range of methods that are viable for the field. Traditional archival and quantitative data collection and analysis, alongside geographic information systems (GIS), constitute much of the material foundation of this project. My process of archival digging began haphazardly as I read through every page of the *Houston Informer* from 1950–1959, from which I began to see the ways space, race, criminalization, and violence were interrelated. Census data helped me quantify and visualize the consequences of segregation, while personal papers, letters, civil rights organization records and literature, and so on allowed me to feel their meaning. I relied significantly on critical race theory, assemblage theory, black feminist thought, black male studies, and narrative theory to read the archives with fealty to social constructivism.

Nevertheless, *Houston and the Permanence of Segregation* plants some seeds for anti-disciplinarity, and I attempt to remain suspicious of both my tools and grammar throughout the work. First, I avoid investment in the codes of "the human." My goal in pushing against the constraints of history as a discipline and its imposed narrative structures of contingency and change over time is to provide a reading of the archives void of "agency" that still honors the lives lived and lost therein.[75] Likewise, following Tryon P. Woods, I present the modern idea of gender as one of humanity's codes and a means by which black revolutionary thought is "quarantined."[76] Whereas historians of slavery have contended with this question for decades, twentieth-century urban historiography lacks thorough grappling with it. In this way, the former serve as more immediate interlocutors throughout this project.

Early histories of racialized slavery depicted enslaved property as mere victims, uninvolved in their own fates.[77] Revisionist histories have elegantly and convincingly argued the opposite; enslaved people actively resisted their conditions and at other times ironically helped establish social, legal, and economic lattices upon which slavery grew and flourished.[78] Historians no longer debate whether enslaved people acted efficaciously. However, being an actor is not quite the same as having agency, and as Walter Johnson has pointed out, it has not been so much the actions of the enslaved that many social historians have been trying to "recover" as an attempt to "give the slaves back their agency." Johnson continues, "Historians' use of 'agency' as a framing device has reduced historically and culturally situated acts of resistance to manifestations of a larger, abstract human capacity—'agency'—thus obscuring important questions."[79] Such historical projects ultimately rest on a philosophical understanding of "agency" and "humanity" as being the same thing; but it is an odd project to try to restore humanity to people who were not humans—indeed, to restore humanity to people who were violently constructed as props against which this very genre of "the human" was created. Agency is the lexicon of Man; rather than restoring something of value to enslaved subjects, imposing the term on them may in fact diminish the severe violence of racial slavery (and later Jim Crow) while affirming the rightfulness and naturalness of the modern construction of "humanity."

Instead of avoiding the consequences of eschewing agency (the most feared of which is descent into determinism), I embrace them to write a different kind of narrative, void as it may be of a simple linear chronology. The first consequence is that I understand the historical subjects in the archive as captured subjects. As a historian, the best I can hope to do is recapture them through archival glimpses, to re-present them but never to fully know them.[80] I am offering an interpretation of Houston's history, acknowledging that I can only re-present and not reproduce or resurrect the subjects herein as they knew themselves. Actually, and more accurately, I am providing a presentation of *the world* wherein I am captured and whence I re-present, by way of narrative invention, these subjects and their world. In Afropessimist terms, I eschew any fealty to "static positivism" through which scholars may approach the archive. Rather, following Giorgio Agamben, Afropessimism appreciates that the "paradigm is not merely a particular phenomenon, nor is it a universal, but is rather a singular case that is isolated from its context only insofar as, by exhibiting its own singularity, makes intelligible a new ensemble." Thus, I understand the subjects I have co-created with the archive as re-presentations (as opposed to representations); rather than making an authorial claim that I can unearth the internal lives, feelings, or self-images of these subjects, let alone their self-conscious motivations and intentions, I have reimaged the persons whose names I've found in these archives as paradigmatic figures that elucidate the sociopolitical structure of their world toward the end of exposing the epistemological structure of my own.[81]

The second consequence is that I appreciate, rather than elide, each subject's capture in subjectivity. Race, gender, class, and sexuality figure significantly in the lives of the people in these pages. These are not essential categories of being, but rather are shorthand for processes that have historically organized the modern world and American society hierarchically. This social organization manifested as a result of state policy, legal practices, formal education, informal socialization, and of course, violence and subjugation. Historical subjects had no choice but to be raced, gendered, classed, and sexualized. There was no pure liberal individual subject *prior* to these processes; there is nothing for the historian to hold onto or try to redeem underneath. All persons *be/come* through socialization, and thus identity, as a consequence of these processes, is the result of narrative contests over naming, belonging, and exclusion.[82] In short, because I have no allegiance to agency or the human, I present a history where we need not feel uneasy about understanding human action, even those of resistance and reform, as coerced by identity-making schemes out of which there was no escape.

Indeed, I interpret the archive while thinking of identity as "narratively constituted."[83] All narratives are matters of contest—that is, they are highly political because they are the terms by which actors understand the world and understand in what ways it is possible to act in the world.[84] Narratives, then, are inherently limiting. They capture historical subjects, past and present. For example, narratives (propaganda, even) of "the human," of the sanctity of property, of the indivisibility of the liberal individual subject, and of Houston's special progressiveness bound the actors in this book who resisted their world to the selfsame philosophical orientations that undergirded that world. In no uncertain terms, then, I argue that, since its emergence, segregation has been a permanent and not a contingent feature of the landscape of Houston and, indeed, of the United States. This is where the theoretical rubber meets the methodological road.

To wrestle against the constraints of narrative, I employ tools developed by scholars like Saidiya Hartman, David Kazanjian, and Frank Wilderson.[85] Hartman offers critical fabulation as a means of writing a history of an unrecoverable past (i.e., a story about *why* we cannot tell the stories we seek to tell). This is not my goal, though the tools of this methodology still prove useful. Like Hartman, I begin by acknowledging that archival sources are opaque, that the archives of the modern world were producible as a result of the energy extracted from black slave labor, and that archives were a tool in the production of slavery and race. A full acknowledgment of this means that the veracity of the archives is always contestable, that the elements of the stories they tell can be rearranged and flattened. It also means that my project is not to "fill in the gaps" or allow closure, but rather to write about the unverifiable that exceeds what the archive permits. Because black people are absented from the world of Man, it seems unlikely to find them as mere "people" in the archive, as they are always politically modified by the condition of blackness. However, these unrecoverable persons leave an indelible mark in the archives because it is their negation that makes the human legible. Like Hartman, at times I exploit the subjunctive to write a story or build an argument. I also lean heavily into the fact of unrecoverability. Generally, I do not use the subjunctive as a hedge, for while I cannot impute motives to past actors whose interior lives remain inaccessible, I also have little interest in "preconscious interests" and "unconscious identification." Rather, I am most concerned with "structural positionality," which W. E. B. Du Bois pioneered as a more appropriate perspective from which to do history.[86]

For instance, resistance against segregation was always constrained by the narrative terms of *this world*. Despite what they considered small victories against the system of racism that exposed them to premature death, black Houstonians articulated their collective visions for a raceless Houston on the basis of liberal individualism, Americanism, property rights, and legal legitimacy. They employed this lexicon to demand change and, as I mentioned earlier, circumstances did change at an immediate level of analysis. However, this selfsame lexicon was instantiated by the very world that had restricted black life in the first place. The self-possessing liberal subject was white and remained so through these decades of capture. The self-possessing liberal subject as black was narrative illusion, illusion that captured black freedom dreams in temporal, epistemological, and moral stasis. As intellectual historian Nahum Chandler elegantly explains, "the *historical situation* of the African American" appears unable to be apprehended: "that there is not now nor has there ever been a free zone or quiet place from which the discourse of so-called Africanist figures, intellectuals, writers, thinkers or scholars, might issue." They (we) "cannot *simply* choose, even if [we] *must* choose."[87] This book is not about choices, though choices, coerced as they were, are at every turn in the book. Choices, when written alongside a grammar of agency, allow for narrative development and thereby offer the illusion of movement, perhaps even of progress. This book is instead about the "*must* choose"—the capture of subjects in structural positions and what this reveals about the history of racism in Houston and the United States, namely that it has been unyielding. I, too, *must* choose, to write with or against my disciplinary training, with or against the anti-blackness that is tacit in and foundational to the metaphysics of *this world*.

TRAVERSING *HOUSTON AND THE PERMANENCE OF SEGREGATION*

What follows in these pages is an experiment in thought. Attempting to write a history about a people who have been racially constructed as having no history requires confronting the terrible truth that the discipline of history likely has inadequate tools for telling their stories. Always, it seems, I am confronted with options to maintain fealty to the codes of liberal humanism, like agency and personal responsibility, or faithfulness to blackened subjects whose predicaments necessarily destabilize those codes. I have consciously chosen to do the latter—to do work that appears anti-disciplinary and anti-ethical in *this world* precisely because that work is committed to a full exposure of anti-blackness at the expense of humanism's codes and a positivist approach to the archives.

The first chapter follows the life of Houston NAACP executive secretary Christia Adair in order to demonstrate the ways gender roles constrained thought in black freedom movements. Where the first chapter demonstrates subjective capture at the individual level, the second chapter demonstrates this phenomenon at the group level. It tells the story of Johnnie Lee Morris, convicted of killing a white bus driver, but spared the death penalty to show how the "rule of law" compelled black Americans to view injustice as a sign of progress. Subjective capture at the group level indicates the presence of hegemony, and in the case of Jim Crow Houston, a hegemony that was always hostile to black people's freedom dreams. Yet black people's understanding of the law and their political organization around it was always and already informed and constrained by the anti-black ideas and ideals of their day. Thus, the third chapter begins with the bombing of the home of Dorothy and Jack Caesar to reveal the ways Houston's narrative about itself as a "heavenly" place for race relations functioned to occlude quotidian anti-black terror and convince black Houstonians to have faith in the abstract rather than take full account of their material deprivation. Significantly, then, the capturing of subjectivity is never just an individual or group phenomenon, but an institutional one as well. The fourth chapter returns to a sustained meditation on gender but, following the work of *Houston Informer* owner Carter Wesley, demonstrates how gender, *as an ideology of race*, rather than gender roles, kept black people invested in projects of inclusion into the world of Man rather than its dissolution. Echoing sentiments of black nineteenth-century writers, Wesley looked for the Negro race to achieve "manhood," despite that the Negro race was an invention without a referent, created as that which was not Man and could not be Man.

Thus, the first four chapters contend that black freedom dreams have themselves been captured in ways that may only be perceptible by fully accepting how anti-blackness is always and already imposed upon and embedded in black people's own senses of identity and politics of reform and inclusion. I find no evidence of what might be called an ethical solution to capture, and thus I appreciate the anti-ethical ideas and actions of those archival subjects who rejected *this world*'s rules of engagement, albeit with an uneasiness that exposes my own remaining capture in anti-blackness. In the fifth chapter, placing the case of the 1967 police riot at Texas Southern University in the context of the "prior tortures" endured by black Houstonians, I mine the archives for speculative and critical thought, arguing that if the previous chapters seem to suggest an impossible escape from *this world*, an unchecked pessimism and nihilism, we can locate in the archives a tradition of black optimism—a violent movement of thought and action toward apocalypse.

This is not merely apocalypse in a vulgar eschatological sense, for "Afro-pessimism's apocalyptic thought is not reducible to its demand for the end of the World," but rather apocalypse in terms of its etymological roots, which "primarily means to *un-cover*." I endeavor to "un-veil" the emptiness of a world that exists with and depends on making meaning of black suffering in order to "direct [our collective] gaze from *this world*" and toward the abyss where identity (chapter 1), individualist notions of crime (chapter 2), law and property (chapter 3), and gender itself (chapter 4) have no presumption of value. In a black hole where nothing is settled, the possibilities for invention are infinite—unpredictable in their outcome—but necessary for introducing change to time.

Admittedly, from an Afropessimist perspective, the stories in this book are "nonevents," for as I present them, they compelled no break in *this world*. Indeed, this conclusion is central to my argument. Still, these particular stories are not without merit if we want to learn something specifically about Houston and the age of desegregation. They bring the pessimism of critical race theory to urban historiography, demonstrating specifically how the Houston civil rights movement was constrained by dominant, hegemonic narratives, terrorist and state violence, and municipal decision-making. Adair (chapter 1) matters as the paradigmatic figure of Houston's NAACP branch during the mid-twentieth century, and her investments in gender and interracial coalition-building offer pertinent lessons for the limits of racial democracy. Despite her efforts, Houston's NAACP was largely ineffective by the end of the 1950s. Johnnie Lee Morris's travails (chapter 2) were as consequential for black and white Houstonians as the cases of Trayvon Martin or George Floyd have been for Americans more recently. In the latter, as was true in the former, the "rule of law" constrained what Americans understood as ethical responses to anti-black violence, and the case reinforced that, despite ongoing racial terror and brutal treatment by police, black Texans had no right to self-defense. Dorothy and

Jack Caesar (chapter 3) understood this but maintained that as property owners they had a more fundamental right to protect their home with arms. What they learned, as did hundreds of other black families, was that violence did not always take the form of a direct physical attack on persons or property. It could be the consequence of government decisions that undervalued black communities, allowed them to be cleared for urban renewal or highway development, and left them displaced. By the end of the third chapter, we see multiple ways Houston's black neighborhoods were exploited and subordinated through political, economic, and terrorist means with the consequence of hardened lines of residential segregation. Along the way, black Houstonians tallied what they understood as small victories, including the establishment of Texas State University for Negroes (TSUN) in Third Ward (chapter 4). TSUN functioned as a "bribe," but for Carter Wesley, who was an important mouthpiece for middle-class black Houston through much of the twentieth century, the realization of this truth came too late.[88] He lamented, in retrospect, that black self-governance and self-sufficiency under Jim Crow were illusions. The consequences of this bribe would be realized in the fifth chapter, where I emphasize the "prior tortures" endured by black Houstonians to expose the depravity of the police assault at what was, by then, Texas Southern University (TSU).

In addition to bringing national attention to Houston's racial violence and extracting major leaders from the city's student movements, the assault at TSU indicated that Houston was very much like other American cities, despite its protests otherwise. Desegregation would be met by anti-black violence there and everywhere else. These stories reject the historiographical trope that Houston desegregated peacefully and maintains that where there is race, there has been and continues to be violence. They demonstrate this at the levels of ideology, subjective identity, collective action, social interaction, and state-level decision-making.

Finally, each chapter begins with the words of Saidiya Hartman, functioning as a moment to pause—a moment to meditate on this book as a project speaking on multiple registers. It is a project *of* Houston's history. It is also a philosophy of the historical discipline and its relationship to black existence. And it is history *as* the present, where perspective supersedes method. It is one additional attempt to resist, as a writer, the limits of linear time, which presses historians to think and write about change over time, sometimes while mourning the past and other times while celebrating the not-yet. I invite you to join me in staying present—because, in Hartman's words, "it mattered little" the details of the story for their own sake; rather, "[w]hat mattered was that" even now, "the reverberations of what happened in the hold," what happened through anti-blackness, "would touch us; we too would experience its intensities."[89]

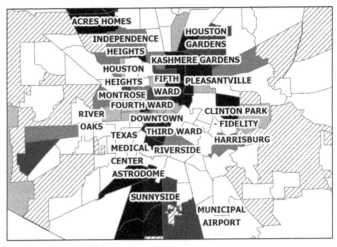

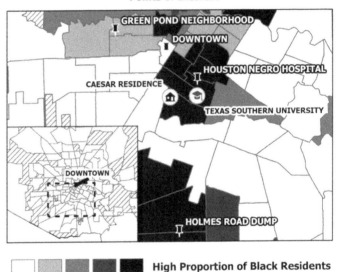

Map 5 *The proportional distribution of black residents across Houston neighborhoods in 1960 with a focus on the Third Ward, Fourth Ward, and Sunnyside.*

CODA

Spoiler alert: there is no plot twist here. The Kinder Institute for Urban Research has measured Houston's social landscape for decades, and it consistently releases the same finding in its measures of segregation as they relate to the *unique* segregation patterns that affect black residents. As the institute's research methods become more sophisticated over time, a truth has remained. While Houston and its surrounding municipalities repeatedly garner the top spots as the most racially diverse cities in the United States, and while the region has witnessed "an overall trend" of a "slight decline in segregation," black Houstonians remain the exception to the rule. The Kinder Institute considers black Houstonians' degree of segregation "extreme": "What is known is that African Americans continue to live substantially apart from Anglos and Asians." And studies have repeatedly shown that white, Asian, and Latinx Americans express high levels of dissmell for black neighborhoods and, importantly, make real choices to avoid having black neighbors.[90] Challenges to residential segregation have been historically captured and rendered ineffective by hegemonic narratives wrapped in racial and gender socialization, discourses of black criminality, and the sanctity of the liberal individual and (his white) property. Simply, segregation has been and will be a permanent feature of *this world*. Thus, this is not a story strictly about Houston, but rather a claim about a world that Houston reflects.

1
CAPTURED BY GENDER ROLES
Christia Adair's Fight for Inclusion

[I]s the very notion of being outside the hold a kind of fiction, a myth of progress, the price of admission to the welcome table? If the matrix of death and dispossession constitute the black ordinary, even if not solely or exclusively, then how are we to think about practice in the hold? I believe it requires us to rethink the meaning of abolition . . . as the daily practice of refusal and waywardness and care in the space of captivity, enclosure, and incarceration.

Saidiya Hartman, "The Dead Book Revisited," *History of the Present*

If, as Saidiya Hartman suggests, abolition was a "daily practice," Christia Adair's existence was emblematic of that truth. As a leader of black Houstonians' mid-twentieth-century civil rights struggles, Adair lived a politics that refused the social and political relegation of black people to a subhuman class. However, abolition politics were not free-floating or abstractions. Adair's politics were also constrained by the norms of her day. They remained moored to notions of proper gender embodiment and expression that the myth of black subhumanity was predicated on.[1] Adair was not unique in this regard. Fealty to normative gender ideologies has long constrained the freedom dreams of black folk. Thus, while Adair serves as an anchor for this chapter and her life as a lens through which to see, hear, and feel Jim Crow Texas in the late nineteenth and early twentieth centuries, the Christia Adair that I am capable of constituting by way of the archive should be thought of as synecdoche. That is, this is not a biography of Christia Adair, but rather an analysis of a collective biography of contemporaneous black freedom fighters. Simply, as a figure that grounds the chapter, Adair demonstrates how gender ideologies suffused the life course of black folks and forbade alternative ways of understanding the world and its troubles for black people.

Herein, I invite a protracted meditation on Hartman's suggestion that "the very notion of being outside the hold" may be a "kind of fiction, a myth of progress."[2] This may seem a bit more obvious if we think of the hold literally as the bowels of the slave ship; can it be convincingly argued that the "black cook" on the slave ship was somehow outside the hold, somehow less enslaved than the cook's counterparts below?[3] Can marronage in the Atlantic world be conceptualized as "outside the hold," if the precondition for marronage was racial slavery, if maroons practiced all manner of deceit to conceal themselves, and if their landscape remained "a contested terrain that slaveholders, overseers, drivers, slave hunters, dogs, militias, and patrollers strove to control and frequently invaded"?[4] Likewise, in slavery's afterlives, and in this chapter that specific afterlife known as the political economy of Jim Crow, the very notion of a freedom dream was preconditioned on a desire to escape the hold. The hold was Jim Crow—the laws and customs that mandated and governed segregation—but the hold was also constituted by the ideologies and practices that upheld Jim Crow, and ideologies and practices about gender were pivotal to the structural integrity of the hold.

The hold refers to the very material conditions that constrained the life chances of black folk. When Adair arrived in Houston in 1925, she bore witness to the hold. Acres Homes, an unincorporated black town on the outskirts of the city, evinced this condition. It was emblematic of the economic and political negligence black Houstonians endured even within the city limits. And Acres Homes' meager resources in the shadow of metropolitan economic excess mirrored the condition of the Dorcas Home, a juvenile detention camp for black girls, that was plotted there. In this sense, this chapter is about the sociopolitical landscape of Jim Crow Houston.

The hold also refers to the discursive capture at the center of this chapter: gender ideology. In Adair's world, gender was treated as an essential fact rather than the cumulative effect of exclusions and expectations regarding the proper constitution of the self; an essential fact rather than a technology by which racism and fear of the full breadth of human sexuality degraded black people—recognition of which would undermine myths of white racial purity. Indeed, gender functioned (and continues to function) as a hold that captured thought and imagination, trapping civil rights discourse into a conversation predicated on the terms of liberal humanism. If gender was the technique by which Adair and others hoped they would insert themselves into civil society and the human family, it remained an ideology through which white Americans articulated their basic and necessary biological, historical, and spiritual distinction from the Negro. In this sense, this chapter is also about the violent exclusion of black people from liberalism's notions of universal humanity and how that selfsame liberalism surreptitiously guided black liberation politics, a theme that will return repeatedly throughout the book.

No less important, the hold also refers to the black image in the white mind. Where I conceptualize the hold as the material and discursive apparatuses that limited black people's geographic, economic, and sociopolitical mobility, in the two senses described above, Adair and her contemporaries thought of the hold in the lexicon of "the Negro problem." Black thinkers have pointed out since at least W. E. B. Du Bois's turn-of-the-century ruminations on it that "the Negro problem" is a misnomer, for while black people have endured many problems, "the Negro" was a fantastical creature with no referent in the material world.[5] Still, this creature had significant purchase in the minds of white folk. It was the sign in which they deposited their anxieties and desires about themselves and about others. Here was the body splayed that could be murdered without criminal offense, that could be sexually assaulted without a sense of guilt, that could be economically exploited without offending liberal humanism, that could be an object to service the emotional needs of white folk but with little or no capacity for human emotion itself. This object, "the Negro," was sexually overdeveloped and therefore a species characterized by the underdevelopment of proper gender, unable and unwilling to properly organize the world by way of gender bifurcation and thereby establish civilization.

This sign, "the Negro," was the hold Adair and others sought to escape. They endeavored to do so by destabilizing the relationship between blackness and gender "development" that established the Negro as the "feminine race of the world" by acquiescing to normative notions of gender and its embodiment.[6] The "price of admission to the welcome table," to borrow from Hartman, was investment in the very idea that human dignity could be earned by demonstrating command of the master's tools. In this sense, this chapter is fundamentally about the simultaneous dizzying and inert methods upon which a politics of liberal, civil inclusion is predicated—dizzying because the methods of liberation remained the tools of black degradation and inert because the pursuit of normative gender role expression promised no reprieve from racism's grasp on the lives of black folk.

The chapter proceeds as follows. I introduce Christia Adair as the young Christia Daniels, focusing on the details of her early life that indicate the ubiquity of gender socialization that would shape her worldview for the remainder of her life. As a married young adult, she would develop and employ a sense of gender affinity with white women in order to advance the kind of moral causes that defined early-twentieth-century women's activism—moral entrepreneuring meant to protect children and the nuclear family. Faced with contradictions within the movement for women's suffrage, Adair would recognize the limits of but not give up on the project of a gender-based interracial movement for black civil rights. When she arrived in Houston from rural Texas, Adair would see anti-blackness on a much larger scale. In those early days as a Houstonian, Adair would register feelings of regret for her inability to rescue "delinquent" black girls from their non-normative gender waywardness, an attitude and mission not uncommon for black clubwomen in the twentieth century.[7] The condition of Acres Homes as well as the Dorcas Home and its inability to service its inmates in the ways Adair saw fit was a microcosm of the systemic neglect and dearth of resources endured by black Houstonians. Ever resilient, she eventually became a sustaining figure of Houston's NAACP branch, helping to keep the organization alive after near-death-dealing blows to its constitution by Texas's successful legal prosecutions of the organization. As one of the branch's unfailing mouthpieces, Adair investigated instances of regular discrimination endured by black women, supported fundraising efforts to defend black men from rape accusations, and publicly debated white women who promulgated notions of sexuality-based essential differences between white and black people. These challenges brought her face-to-face with the vacuity of normative gender ideologies, and thus she attacked notions of racial purity and black sexual excess by recasting the history of black enslavement as one of white men's sexual exploitation of black women. Still, she made her appeal to the public, based not on the deconstruction of gender and the attendant moral values given to it in relation to race, but rather by emphasizing the shared womanhood of black and white women as an indicator of their shared humanity.

If abolition can be thought of as "daily refusal and waywardness," it nevertheless took place within the hold. The centripetal force that we call gender captured black freedom dreams in orbit around liberal humanism. By the end of the chapter, despite Adair's hard work, the structural position of black Houstonians vis-à-vis white Houstonians, and indeed blackness vis-à-vis whiteness, remained unchanged. The appearance of movement—what I visualize as an orbital movement—occludes the gravitational pull of anti-blackness, or more directly, the refusal of racists to unmoor black people from the image of the Negro and to obliterate that image by way of real material commitment and investment in the well-being of black folks despite how well or not black folks have conformed to their racist notions of gender. In short, this is a chapter about the ways black freedom dreams have been captured by investments in gender roles.

CULTIVATING A PROPER BLACK GIRLHOOD

Christia Daniels's childhood in the small town of Edna, Texas, had been about discipline. Both her parents were children of the Reconstruction era and gave birth to Christia on October 22, 1893, in Victoria, Texas. Her father, Handy Daniels, inherited his father's hauling business after he, Augustus Daniels, passed in 1895.[8] Using a two-wheeled dray and a single horse, Handy was Jackson County's unofficial transporter of goods, engineering and modifying his cart as needed to move items between destinations. Taking on jobs as they came, "he hauled everything from bales of cotton to pianos, moving people with furniture and everything." Over time he became credentialed to move flammable materials from inbound trains to local customers. His business was steady and successful enough over time that he hired teams of men who kept Jackson County moving, although like most black families in the rural South, the Danielses continued to live with meager financial resources.[9]

Christia's life would be shaped by race before she was even conceived. Both she and her mother had light brown skin. Her maternal grandfather had been a white man who "must have been in love" with Christia's grandmother. She had died in childbirth with their third child. Rather than abandon their two daughters, Christia's biological grandfather kept four-year-old Ada and her sister until he found a loving home for them. Ada had not been welcomed by her own kin, suffering verbal and physical taunts for her skin color, hair texture, and parentage. Ada eventually found a home after her baptism in a Methodist church, adopted by her new godparents. Her father remained an active part of her life, supporting her financially with what little money he had, but after his death another family member—"a cousin or brother or something"—took possession of whatever he had left her with the help of lawyers.[10] Ada was not unique in this regard; it was a common enough practice for white people to strip black people of their inheritances and properties through legal and extralegal means in Texas and throughout the South, and increasingly so after Reconstruction.[11]

The Daniels parents expected their children at the dinner table each night "around eight o'clock." The devout Methodist family joined together in prayer before eating. Handy told the family news he had learned about politics, law enforcement, and race. Even through their boredom, the Daniels children acquired a sense of community responsibility through these discussions, becoming more attuned to the issues that did and would continue to shape their lives and life outcomes. They learned to aspire, not to personal greatness, but to community uplift, and this started with bringing honor to their home.

"Girls don't get whipped by other people," Ada warned Christia and her sister. "Nobody whips you. Your daddy don't whip you, so I am the only person to whip you." For his part, if Handy learned that either daughter had been corporally punished by Ada, he would express "disgrace" at "the very fact that his daughter got a whipping."[12]

The lessons Christia learned at home and at church compelled her to live within the strict confines of respectable black womanhood. As a black girl, she was inescapably moored to the white supremacist cultural representation of black women—the jezebel, the sapphire, the wench, the negress—as sexually available and aggressive. As an emancipatory scheme, many black women in the late nineteenth and through much of the twentieth centuries preached a doctrine of sexual chastity and general moral respectability to their daughters. However, more than just a means of patriarchal discipline of "women"—for black women were not legally or culturally understood as women outside of black sociality—"respectability was a way for black women to reclaim themselves, for it required taking ownership and control over one's body" and "[f]orged a sense of self preservation" in a society that maliciously maligned, marginalized, and masticated the flesh and souls of black folk.[13]

Recent scholarship has emphasized the "fungibility" of black people as a consequence of global racial slavery. This word is meant to abbreviate the material fact that the Negro was an object for white consumption; that any negro could be exchanged or bought to replace any other negro; that this "any other" exchangeability indicated a political economy that saw "sex and gender as mutable" as they pertained to the Negro; and that the Negro was therefore a not-human object, for Western philosophy had determined that gender differentiation was an achievement of human civilization.[14] The evidence supporting the fungibility thesis is substantial, and still we know that sex differentiation remained a tangible part of the experiences of black people during slavery and through its afterlives. That is, black people were not genderless. Rather, gender functioned as a technique of race-making, allowing for some differentiation in training, labor, and mobility between male and female slaves, but differentiated by categories outside those recognized in Man's episteme as rights-bearing subjects. The negro male was not simply a man, but a boy, or a buck, or a "negro man." Likewise, the negro female was a wench, a bitch, or a "negro woman."[15]

Still, even as the structurally antagonistic relationship between blackness and whiteness banished black people to gender categories defined as deviant within the epistemic regime of Man, Christia nevertheless understood herself as a girl and eventually as a woman. That is, gender has multiple, mutually reinforcing, but functionally differentiated meanings in US history. It is, at least, a disciplinary cultural mechanism, a social structure, and a subjectivity. Culturally, gender is "the discursive means . . . by which 'sexed nature' or 'natural sex' is produced and established as 'prediscursive.'"[16] That is, gender functions to naturalize the differential and hierarchical treatment of the *racialized* sexes within society: white men deserve superior access to natural, symbolic, spatial, and natural resources because biology has decreed it so. This is not to simplify gender as how Americans have culturally interpreted (anatomical) sex, but rather it is to say that gender functions to direct how a society collectively assigns hierarchical meaning to perceived sex differences (often dimorphically) and that this is a tool of racialization. This hierarchy has been institutionalized by the state through the instantiation of rigid sex markers (e.g., through the US Census) and, for example, sex segregation in education, legal discourse, religious practice, and sports. In short, gender has historically structured life and life chances in the United States. Gender thereby suffuses social life, operating as a technique of subjection to the order of things, a consequence of which is also a sense of gender as a mere fact of existence and critical component of subjective identity.

Christia, then, learned her place in the world within gendered regimes. Like the members of the National Association of Colored Women, she would always be constrained by the specter of the Negress—compelled to live a life that disproved black inferiority by assimilating into the very "true womanhood" that attained value precisely through the specter of the Negress. This often meant a conciliatory approach toward potential white allies and an emphasis on making black women proper custodians of the domestic— sexually chaste, moral educators, and sanitation experts. Women like Ida B. Wells-Barnett abhorred these "petty" politics, rejected facile notions of gender respectability as a means of racial uplift, and exposed white male and female sexualities as predatory and cannibalistic. For her part, Wells did not gain popularity for her critiques of the politics of gender-conservative black clubwomen, and her approach was the minority view of her time within the black leadership class. Wells attempted to explode the sophistry whereby gender appeared to be primarily a matter of identity but was actually a matter of political organization. Indeed, gender as identity tended to obscure the fact that the conditions of black communal life and gender organization should register as "a symptom, not a cause," and that the alternative ways of life and doing gender that black people had developed were not malignant, but evidence of "striving."[17] Christia, however, remained captured by gender. For her, advancement for black people from racialization required submission to the behavioral and sexual norms associated with womanhood, where womanhood is a property of whiteness.

As a young girl, Christia developed an affinity for dolls while her brother was attracted to baseball; she arranged her toys and taught them Sunday School lessons as she observed the women at her church do the same. In 1908, when she reached fifteen years old, Christia's godfather, Professor John W. Frazier, convinced the Daniels to send Christia to Samuel Huston College (now Huston-Tillotson College) in Austin to complete her secondary schooling. While the boys learned shop, the girls studied sewing, cooking, and home economics. She continued her schooling at Prairie View State Normal and Industrial College (now Prairie View A&M) as a junior, where, as was true for black women at black schools throughout the South, she learned her place in society as an educated woman. This lesson was succinctly stated by Reuben Shannon Lovinggood, the first president of Samuel Huston College, at a commencement speech he delivered to Prairie View students in 1907:

> A mother artist has a tender flower upon her veranda. Three times a day she waters it, nurses it, watches it. How she loves it! It blooms. She calls in her neighbors. How they rejoice! But her own darling son, blood of her blood, flesh of her flesh, within him an immortal soul—does she care for him? . . . And the daughter—I pity the Negro girl with beautiful form and face. I must enter this field in euphemistic terms. Often without the watchful care of father or mother she is hounded from pillar to post by demons.[18]

Lovinggood emphasized, as did educators across what would become historically black colleges and universities, women's duties as mothers and wives and nurturers of "the race" more broadly, responsibilities that required regular conformity to the disciplinary demands of the gendered order. The black woman must be trained to de-sexualize herself, lest she fall prey to the predations of white men and her own carnal desires.[19]

The irony for young black women like Christia, of course, was that they were socialized as women in a society that largely denied them this category, "woman," as an existential certainty. This irony was embedded in Lovinggood's very proclamation: his "pity" for the "Negro girl" had just as much to do with the "Negro" as with the "girl," two ineluctable and interlocking statuses foisted upon her by the co-constituted structures of race and gender. Christia would repeatedly confront this irony throughout her life, condemned as she was to the dual existence of both banishment from and capture within the category "woman." Reflecting on this irony much later in her life, Adair opined concerning second-wave feminism and the women's liberation movement: "I don't particularly care about woman lib because the Negro woman has always had to work. I don't think we had to get laws and bills passed for her to get a job, she could always work."[20] In short, black women's experiences did not configure, politically, as "women's" experiences. And yet Christia was made a woman in her own mind and in the eyes of the community that loved her. This identity would inform her politics throughout her life.

WOMANHOOD'S RACIST BETRAYAL

Ada Crosby Daniels, Christia's mother, worked alongside her husband. She cared for their home as well as their business. All the men in Handy's employ ate breakfast and dinner with the Daniels family, which included a young Christia and her three siblings. Using cotton gingham, Ada sewed together the jumpers the men wore for work and cleaned and ironed them regularly. From both her parents, then, a young Christia learned the value of community—of sharing her home and her life with her community. "The one thing that impressed me as a child," she recalled, "was that my father and mother had a lot of influence in our little town. Nobody set them aside or looked up to them or put them on a pedestal or anything like that, but Mama always could get the hearing of other women and my daddy could get the hearing of other people."[21]

Christia carried the weight of community responsibility learned at home and in her formal education back to Edna, where she taught for two years after completing her studies at Prairie View. Afterward, she accepted an offer to teach in Kleburg County. There, about 130 miles southwest of Edna, in the small town of Kingsville, she met her husband, Elbert Adair, whom she wed in May 1918. They remained in Kingsville for eight years where he worked as a brakeman at a Missouri Pacific railroad junction. In her own words, the new Mrs. Christia Adair "became a woman" during her time in the segregated "little town." She remembered, "It had what they called Negro Town, White Town, and Mexican Town. And it looked like never the twain shall meet." As a teacher and missionary for respectable moral standing, she immediately recognized challenges to the project of racial uplift in Kingsville, specifically the presence of a "big gambling house" that seemed poised to steal away the livelihoods of local families, the prevalence of "common-law marriage," and the absence of religious leadership. "[T]he Methodist minister was capitalizing on the fact that the money was easy," she lamented, "and whoever got to the men first would get their money. The gambler, the bootlegger, the preacher, the whatnot. So, he was making a good stab at it and he was getting to them first and he was just taking advantage, I thought, of people."[22]

In response, Adair started a nondenominational Sunday School in the fall of 1918, pulling in children from around town and using the children's involvement to recruit parents to the church. She convinced the Methodist bishop to replace the unscrupulous minister, and when the local Baptist church established a new leader, she worked with both churches to build community through spiritual regeneration and childhood education. She credited the women of Kingsville collectively with the successes she witnessed, particularly watching these children grow up to attend secondary schools and colleges. These women, she said, had "fine ideals" but lacked a civic outlet.[23]

She found her "war-fire" one day when she saw a teenaged Sunday School student leaving the town gambling house. Calling this her "last straw," she interrogated the student and learned that he and several peers had been hired to work at the tables. This was a women's issue—all women, she understood, had a maternal obligation to the well-being of all children in her community. Recognizing that black women alone would never gain an audience before the local sheriff's department, she decided to build an interracial coalition with the president of the local Mothers Club (predecessor to Parent-Teacher Associations), a white woman with whom she was acquainted. "So we went to this woman," Adair recounted, "and told her what was what and she just became fired up with it too. She said, 'Well, no, you wouldn't have no business trying to do it by yourself, because we can help.'" Negro Town organized its own Mothers Club, formally segregated but interracial in practice, insofar as both Mothers Clubs worked collaboratively to tackle the gambling house problem.[24]

Alarmed at the political organizing among the women of Kingsville, the local sheriff "subpoenaed a lot of women to come to his office" where he "held court." Elbert Adair informed his wife that the sheriff had no legal right to call them in but recommended that his wife and the other women comply by attending his office and while there deny any knowledge of the organizing activities. After allaying the sheriff's fears with its feigned ignorance, Adair's interracial coalition reached out to the district attorney. The D.A. swiftly ordered the sheriff to "nail up the building himself" as the women of Kingsville stood "on the sidelines rejoicing and praising God."[25]

The jubilation was short-lived. The year 1919 promised to be a political watershed for civil rights, but the women's suffragist movement in Kingsville did not inspire Adair, who recognized that if the right to vote were extended to women it would not include her, given that black women, socially apprehended as not-quite-women, could not claim ownership to the political demarcation "woman." Legal and extralegal racism prevented black men in Texas from voting in primaries in the one-party state. Even though a scant few black men had managed to salvage their right to the franchise from the aftermath of Reconstruction's dissolution, they practiced it only if they dared face the threat of maiming and murder. A group could only lay claim to civil rights if they were members of civil society; according to the Houston branch of the NAACP, the fourteen million black people that sustained the nation had been emancipated "in name" but never "in fact."[26]

Adair's suspicions of women's suffrage and her understanding of the limits of the term "woman" to do equally politically liberatory work for black women as it did for white women was confirmed when presidential candidate William Harding came to town. Elbert informed his wife that Harding would be arriving by train at the station where he worked. He told her that white teachers were taking their students down to the junction to meet the candidate, and so Adair took her dozen with her to the train station. She was familiar with the architecture of the depot because of her frequent presence there to meet Elbert after work, and thus found the perfect spot that would earn her students "the best attention." Harding's mistreatment of the group disgusted her:

> And when the train stopped, well, my husband was the rear brakeman, and he came out to open the observation gates so the candidate could get out to talk with the people. And so, my children were right at the steps. And some white children were there by white teachers or parents, and he—Mr. Harding—reached over my children's head to shake hands with the white children and never did pay any attention to my children. And I pulled my children out, hurt, disappointed, and sorry for the children. But in my own heart, I said, "If that's what Republicans do, I cannot be Republican. I'll have to change parties. From here on out I'll have to work for Democrat presidents."[27]

She refused Lincoln's party and dedicated herself to a project of diversifying the Democratic Party by voting in the state primary, perhaps with the consequence of also forcing the Republican Party to renew its former "radical" racial agenda.

Primary day arrived in Kingsville in July 1920.[28] Adair and the other black women of the town donned their best clothes with the hope of reshaping the future of electoral politics in Texas. Their hope was deferred. "They gave us all kinds of excuses," she said, echoing and presaging the voices of so many black southerners who would experience the same, "but we just stayed." They pressed for answers and, unsatisfied, a Mrs. Simmons asked, "Are you saying that we can't vote because we're Negroes?" The clerk's deadpan response remained with Adair throughout her life: "Yes. Negroes don't vote in primary in Texas." She lamented, "There was nothing we could do about that but just take it."²⁹ In response to challenges like these, the National Equal Rights League pressed the National American Woman Suffrage Association, the National Woman Association, and the National Woman's Party to remember that "Colored men . . . were devoted champions of freedom and equality of rights without distinction because of race or color. . . . [I]n the dark days, when your champions were few and the cause weak and unpopular, the gifted orators of the Colored race came to its rescue with their genius, and Frederick Douglass was a friend prized by Mrs. Stanton and Miss Anthony till his death."³⁰ Adair would continue her fight for the franchise, but circumstance would lead her to do so in the big city.

PUTTING GENDER ROLES TO WORK FOR RACIAL UPLIFT

Five years later, after learning Elbert was diabetic and needed a less-taxing job, the Adairs moved to Houston. Christia immediately became involved with a local Methodist church and joined a woman's club that was "concerned with . . . a home for delinquent girls located in the Acreage Home area."³¹ The Dorcas Home for Colored Girls was emblematic of the condition of Acres Homes. Dorcas Home had been established by private citizens because the state of Texas had refused to fund a training school for black girls. The justification for homes for delinquent youth was that they would function as more than detention centers; they would be reformist institutions that "provided schooling along with medical treatment" to their "inmates." However, as historian Courtney Shah notes, "Inmates" at Dorcas Home "received limited 'prevocational' training in cooking and domestic service, but they did not receive any education, outdoor recreation, or books." Therefore, Shah concludes, "Dorcas Home emulated a prison more than a rehabilitation facility." Acres Homes, where the Dorcas Home was situated, reflected this pattern of state neglect toward the needs of black Americans at the level of the census tract.³²

The Wright Land Company had established Acres Homes as an unincorporated town on the outskirts of Houston to meet the growing demand for home ownership among black residents. By 1957, these 631 acres had become "the largest all-Negro community in the United States." There, black residents could remain close enough to the city for urban labor opportunities while also taking advantage of the chance to escape high rents, grow their own food, and raise their own livestock.³³

Although the majority of black people in America have never owned their own homes, urban studies scholars at times gloss over the reality that in more-spacious and less-developed cities in the South, investors, developers, and real estate brokers had been interested in the financing mortgages for black folk long before "fair housing" became national policy.[34] Developing unincorporated land was cheap and promised high profits while maintaining the custom of residential segregation. This kind of development was predatory, pushing off the costs of building basic infrastructure to the new residents. Indeed, like other Houston-area subdivisions marketed to black communities, Acres Homes' profit margin was so attractive because it was not master-planned for modern conveniences. Even in 1950, it remained devoid of a central water system, a police force, sewage, and a fire department. Its roads, save for the major thoroughfares of West Montgomery and West Little York, remained unpaved.[35] With much to be desired, Acres Homes stayed attractive for urbanites looking to "escape high rents" and rural migrants hoping to evade the vagaries of white terrorists. Black Houstonians moved to Acres Homes not to build wealth, but for security of a different kind, or in the words of "old time resident" Mrs. Abe Grabenheimer, to "live isolated from fear of meeting the rent man in older years."[36]

Despite its marketing to black people specifically, Acres Homes attracted European immigrants as well, and families from "Germany, Italy, Mexico, Holland, Prussia, Switzerland, and Sweden" bought homes in the mixed-income neighborhood. This was, of course, before the post-World War II ascendancy of these European groups into the category "white." It resembled what sociologists like Du Bois had been documenting since the turn of the century—black folks and immigrant groups living in proximity to each other, even sharing the same neighborhoods, but still living generally segregated lives. The landscape of the Acres Homes census tracts reflected the diversity in income and wealth, "dotted" as it was "with homes varying in size from incomplete one-room huts to state[ly] and magnificent two-story homes equipped in every detail with the latest modern conveniences." From 1950 to 1960, as the city of Houston experienced explosive population growth, so did Acres Homes, doubling in size from ten thousand to twenty thousand residents. Greater population density enabled residents to build strong local businesses to serve their community's daily needs. Established on West Montgomery and West Little York Roads, these "stores and shops," as well as "filling stations, tailors, grocery stores, amusement places, drug stores, cab lines, [and] undertakers," met "almost every human need" and provided opportunities for employment, making it so that "many of the inhabitants [left] the community only on rare occasions." The residents prided themselves on building an autonomous community onto the bare scaffolding they now possessed through mortgage.[37]

However, autonomy was not so simple to achieve or maintain. Acres

Homes was not without financial, infrastructural, or demographic challenges. Five decades after its development, census enumerators recorded homes in Acres Homes as being in much better condition than those in Houston's black urban core neighborhoods of Third Ward, Fourth Ward, and Fifth Ward. And despite having fewer average years of formal schooling, Acres Homes residents also had higher rates of employment than folks in the inner city—a phenomenon probably reflecting the city's greater likelihood to attract and house newcomers and transients as well as the initial relative economic stability of those families that were able to take advantage of home ownership in Acres Homes in the 1910s. Still, more than half of Acres Homes residents lived below the poverty level, and by the late 1950s, residents realized they faced a Sisyphean task of attempting to incorporate the town as a municipality that could serve all their needs with the meager tax base that it had. Residents feverishly debated whether they would seek annexation by the City of Houston, with the major objection being that incorporation into a segregated city that already neglected the needs of its black sections would guarantee an increase in taxes without any commensurate increase in services.[38] The needs of residents were immediate, for while they fashioned their own electric pumps to provide water to the community, the lack of sewage lines and treatment remained an environmental hazard—exacerbated by the siting of nine privately owned dumps in the community that contaminated the neighborhood through the late 1960s.[39]

Even if they were not themselves economically impoverished, all Acres Homes residents paid more to live there because their community was underfunded. For example, working black folk in Acres Homes took the Yale Street bus line, operated by Pioneer Bus Company, into Houston to work throughout the week until 1958 after the relationship between residents and Pioneer ruptured over the company's segregation policies and exorbitant prices. Until then, the average weekly cost of bus rides into the city for work could take 10 percent of the average black family's earnings. Residents began organizing a boycott in July 1952 and survived the lack of bus service by upstarting and patronizing their own jitney services. The jitneys could neither meet the demand of the large community, nor were they always convenient. Houston police harassed the drivers and charged them "with operating conveyances without a license." But the service worked as a stopgap until residents successfully established the Acres Homes Transit Company with a fleet of seven buses and twelve drivers as the first black-owned bus company in the South. The service ran from 1959 until 1968 with the financing of Acres Homes residents, who participated as shareholders and received dividends out of the company profits.[40]

The financial needs of the town did not abate, though. Therefore, in October 1957, Acres Homes residents approved the first step toward annexation by a "landslide" of 90 percent of voters shooting down the alternative proposal to incorporate Acres Homes as the city of Accra.[41] For its part, Houston avoided annexing Acres Homes's parts until the late 1960s and mid-1970s, as was its pattern with other predominantly black subdivisions. While it made fiscal sense for Houston to avoid annexing a town that would require such expensive efforts to improve the quality of life, this could not explain its avoidance of Acres Homes. The city frequently "incurred additional public costs not entirely offset by addition to its tax resources" when it annexed white subdivisions throughout contemporary decades. Indeed, in 1956 Houston annexed "a number of water districts and private utilities for which the city paid $10 million and assumed $39 million in debt," leaving Houston with an "annual deficit of $1.5 million."[42] This process of "underbounding" black areas was common practice not unique to Houston, for what appeared to be fiscal was always and already racial.[43] Acres Homes was a town captured socially, economically, and politically by the racial organization of residential space.

This is the town, then, where several of black Houston's business and community leaders, including Columbia University-educated social worker and professor Ellie Alma Walls Montgomery and school principal Nathaniel Q. Henderson, sited the Dorcas Home for Delinquent Negro Girls.[44] Though the recipient of some charity, the Dorcas Home relied on public appropriations to operate. These financial provisions could not meet the demands, as editorialists at the *Informer* lamented in 1921:

> Did you ever hear the story of the rotten apple in the barrel? We can't throw these girls out of our group—they are human beings and of our own blood. We can't afford to let them disintegrate by vitiating it. We've got to reclaim and reform them. What, then are you going to do about Dorcas home? . . . [T]he institution has never had a fair chance. It has received a total of $2,700 a year appropriation from the city and county combined, plus private, club and church contributions totaling not over $2,300—a sum total of $5,000, to house, clothe, feed and teach from fourteen to twenty girls and young women and maintain a matron and assistant. It has never had a good location, it has never had proper attention from its own people, it has never had proper support.[45]

Adair admitted she had never interacted with girls who faced legal challenges like those who resided at Dorcas. The home, rather than "reforming" the girls, transmogrified them from children to criminals: they "were dressed like prisoners and treated like prisoners." With other clubwomen, she would visit Dorcas to deliver "nice little goodies" to the girls, but she had no opportunity to do the kind of moral entrepreneuring she accomplished in Kingsville. Back there, she relied on the community of women and mothers to rear children in the direction of respectability.[46] Black Houstonians' social challenges were exponentially greater, considering the geographic and demographic expanse of the city, lower community cohesion given that there was no single "Negro town," and the interference of the state into community life through a more robust criminal and juvenile legal system. What had once been an effort of benevolence by community-minded black leaders became a cesspool. Indeed, as was the tradition of American penology, the Dorcas Home warehoused black girls, alienating them from their social worlds and limiting their capacity for personal growth.[47] Notably, as historian Sarah Haley has documented was true in Georgia in the aftermath of Reconstruction's destruction, the girls condemned to the Dorcas Home were "paroled as domestics in white families," effectively prolonging the detention of black girls by deputizing private citizens to train them for a life of service to white people. If disobedient, inmates could be returned to serve a longer sentence.[48]

The Dorcas Home was swiftly condemned in 1932 after years of underfunding by Harris County. One grand jury noted that it was not "a decent place in which humans can live." The sanitary conditions threatened their health, as did the spread of venereal diseases. The sleeping arrangements abridged their privacy. Indeed, this was no home for humans, a category, after all, which the residents of Dorcas had no legal or cultural ability to claim for themselves. Once heralded as a one-of-a-kind institution, the shuttering of Dorcas meant that Harris County no longer had any home for juveniles that served black children in need. Adair regretted her failure to do more to save the home, or perhaps even more her inability to save the girls.[49]

Adair's regrets notwithstanding, she became one of the most well-known, well-connected, and well-intentioned civil rights activists in Houston. A year after her arrival in the city, she became the assistant to the first recording secretary of the city's NAACP branch and shortly thereafter replaced her predecessor to become the "first volunteer secretary of the branch here." However, "Heavenly Houston" was far more hellish than the city's boosters wanted publicized. Black folks came to Houston for economic opportunity, but after folks like Adair settled in, they realized they "did not know that people could be treated like people in Houston were being treated."[50]

Black Houstonians' ability to fight what they perceived to be civil rights violations and what white Houstonians appeared to understand as mere conceit on black people's part was stymied by repeated and successful legal attacks against the operation of the NAACP in Texas. Throughout the 1940s, a public campaign to discredit the NAACP as an anti-American Communist operation coupled with broader Red Scare intimidations severely limited the numerical and financial health of Houston's branch. By 1949 it could no longer afford to employ Adair or Lulu B. White, the organization's executive secretary. Board members Ernest Ollington Smith, Sid Hilliard, and Lee Haywood Simpson asked Adair if she might continue as an unpaid volunteer, which she did in February 1950. The board could only guarantee that her personal bills would be paid and that her quality of life would not be compromised. Board members hoped that one day they would be able to offer her a salary. She would continue in this role for twelve years, though after 1956 the capacity of the NAACP to work in Texas was almost fully amputated in Judge Otis Dunagan's courtroom when he declared the organization a foreign entity illegally operating in the state in *Texas v. NAACP* (1956).[51]

Like other black women leaders in Houston, Adair "struggled against Jim Crow," including mundane indignities in downtown department stores and discrimination at the Municipal Airport (today the 1940 Air Terminal Museum at Hobby Airport).[52] The world of Jim Crow obsessively surveilled black women. People—black and white and across genders—fixated upon black women's bodies, their clothes, their scents, and their comportments. Adair and the black women of Houston encountered this obsession when they went clothes shopping in downtown Houston.

Drawing on Frantz Fanon's analysis of white racism and its consequences for black people's own psyches, Black Studies scholars have pointed to this obsession and discursively described "the Negro" as "phobogenic." The phobogenic object is that which arouses irrational anxiety, fear, and hatred but also attraction and desire. Indeed, white women and men both demanded the intimate uses of black women's bodies—for sex, for breastfeeding their children, for laboring in their homes—as they simultaneously expressed revulsion for these same women. During a World War I tuberculosis outbreak in Jim Crow Atlanta, white Atlantans targeted black washerwomen "not only because of their preponderance in white households, but also because of the stereotypes of libidinous women and the connotations of TB." Without a hint of irony, one white physician warned: "Many negro women have gonorrhea, and pay little attention to it. This is a very real menace to our white boys, and through them, after marriage, to our innocent daughters also. For despite our best efforts, many boys are going to sow wild oats." Historian Tera Hunter succinctly describes black women's place as a phobic object: "If disease constituted a metaphor for evil, dread, and pollution, the black female servant was a metaphor for disease."[53]

However, the language of phobogenesis may leave the responsibility of this irrational fear and hatred at the feet of black people. I maintain that black people did not generate or even activate white revulsion. The Negro, as George Fredrickson rightly notes, was invented in the white imagination—via the tools and discourses of science, mathematics, politics, philosophy, and economics, and materially by way of slavery, incarceration, convict leasing, employment discrimination, and segregation. This ideological invention was and is still treated as a corporeal fact.[54] This fact was that, according to medical physician William Lee Howard in 1903, "[T]he African as a distinct race is not immoral, he is un-moral, and no amount of education or training is going to change a non-existent element."[55] White racists tasked black people's bodies with giving physical form to this invention. Calvin Warren argues that the function of this corporealization was always to make it appear possible for Western metaphysics to turn nothing (where nothing is the best way that we can describe nonexistence and meaninglessness) "into an object of knowledge," something that science can "dominate, analyze, calculate, and schematize." Nothing, Warren argues, terrifies Western epistemology and philosophy, its notions of freedom, its already existing supposition that human life is inherently valuable, indeed its assumption that the human is an "ontological *fait accompli*" rather than a historical and political construction. Thus, the Negro is both necessary for Western epistemology to maintain its own coherence and the embodiment of nothing, which terrifies Western thought. The Negro's existence, as imaginary as it is, is as necessary as it is hated. Thus, what Fanon means by phobogenis is not that black people are the source of white fear, but rather that "the Negro"—the black image in the white mind and not "black people," though the Negro appears to be black people because these real people are thought to be the empirical referents for "the Negro"—is "a stimulus to anxiety." Fanon diagnoses this as Negrophobia.[56]

Therefore, historical analysis should not treat racism as rational or not—though historians debate whether race, and therefore racism, can be apprehended as an "unthinking decision" derivative of the exigencies of black chattel slavery.[57] In contrast, I maintain that black people and their bodies did not generate or catalyze Negrophobia. Negrophobia can only be described as irrational by adopting the "logics" of a psychoanalytic framework and presuming the inherent goodness of white people.[58] Scholars have already critiqued Freud's psychoanalytics as predicated on an ontological erasure of blackness and black people.[59] Elsewhere, they have argued that attempts to shoehorn racism into binary categories of the rational versus irrational rely on a Eurocentric understanding of human thought, behavior, and consequences—effectively "leaving uncontested and so seemingly legitimate any racist expressions not clearly irrational."[60] In this way, social psychological definitions of racism generally understate or ignore racism as a social structure upon which the world as we know it is predicated. Indeed, "analyses of racism seem to be struck dumb when confronted with the insatiable specter of black historical struggle."[61] Fanon prefers to see "the phobic [as] a person who is governed by the laws of rational prelogic and affective prelogic."[62] Quite simply, when black women in Houston suffered the indignity of being treated as objects of fear, this hatred preceded their arrival and was not irrational within the episteme and ethics of the world in which they were so treated. Like Fanon, they were "locked" in their own bodies, "the slave of the past." If we consider an alternative definition of capture, where an object is made inert by way of painting or photography—the capturing of an image—we find black people captured by/as the Negro.

However, racism is most often conceived as a matter of ignorance.[63] Accordingly, in the minds of many racial reformers, if racism could be apprehended as irrational by the standards of Enlightenment philosophy, the solution to racism would ultimately be moral education. Adair and the women she worked with believed this—indeed, they were inheritors of Enlightenment and Protestant Christian thought. Sometimes education required pressure and not simply discursive appeals, but the motivation was always to teach racists the ways their beliefs were incommensurate with idealized notions of equality. So, when black women came to Adair at the NAACP and reported that they were disallowed from trying on hats, girdles, and other garments in downtown clothing stores like Sakowitz, at the corner of Main and Dallas Streets, Adair went to "try it out myself to see if this is really fact" and then proceeded to act. For such investigations, she practiced taking a witness who could testify to explicit declarations of discrimination. At Sakowitz, she forced the issue by demanding to try on a girdle. Store personnel attempted to push her into the alteration room when she asked to have it fitted. Adair protested until she convinced a manager to have an employee take her to a fitting room. Then, she pressed further. As the clerk walked away, Adair told the worker that she was required to stay to help customers fit their girdles—that she could not hide away from this black body today. "And she sort of fumbled with me, my body, and I know she felt like her little hands were becoming contaminated, but that's what had to happen." Adair tried on two more girdles with the clerk's help, and when she found one that fit well, despite not needing a girdle, she paid the twenty-nine dollars for it.[64] It is unlikely that the woman's phobia of blackness was changed by this interaction; this was a significant sum of money to assert a humanity that was supposedly naturally endowed.

Adair admitted that she bought the girdle because not doing so "would be carrying it too far," and she did not want to confirm the white woman's stereotypes about black people. This indicated the capture she remained trapped in as "the Negro" object, in Adair's case a biological body signified by the category "female" (or "Negro woman") but without the attendant social privileges of being a woman and lacking the political rights and bodily capital that women were due within the gendered hegemony of the United States. This moment itself captured the limits of civil rights discourse—a righteous demand for black people to be included as full members of society, but a society that was a "society" built and dependent upon the scaffold of anti-black exclusion. Thus, Adair saw herself through the lens of black sociality—a full person worthy of dignity, honor, and the presumption of goodness. Simultaneously, she saw herself through the lens of the world as it was—perhaps a person, but certainly an object, both necessary for the continued regeneration of society and an omnipresent risk to its health. This (im)possible paradox, predicated as it was on the "objective" biological unity of "the human" as a species and the inalienable rights afforded humans—not through divine decree, but by philosophical and legal constructions, to be sure—chained Adair and her contemporaries to a civil rights discourse founded on liberal individualism.[65]

This was evident in private correspondences and a public argument she had with two white women, G. McDonald of Houston and A. McFarland of Oletha, Texas, some of which was published in the *Houston Post* and some stored in Adair's personal papers. McDonald began the tiff by accusing the NAACP of being "trouble makers" influenced by outside agitators. McDonald claimed that "our colored folks" in Houston were satisfied with race relations and that black Americans should express more gratitude for their nation. Adair rejected McDonald's claims, to McFarland's disgust. Writing to Adair, the latter asked, "If the colored people . . . feel that they are equal to the whites, why do the[y] try to force themselves on the whites?" Adair wasted no ink and aimed for the jugular: "Do you know that the white men who were slave holders . . . left their wives' bedrooms, went to the slaves quarters, ran the Negro men from their beds and their wives and there would spend as much time with her as he desired, many times he left his offsprings right there?" If McFarland opposed desegregation, perhaps she did not recognize that "all this," by which Adair meant the sexual assault of Afro-descendant women, "was forced integration." As far as being appreciative, Adair maintained, Negro-Americans' civil rights demands were perhaps the most American claim any group had ever made in the nation's history. She was, as her ancestors had been, the most "loyal" of Americans—the only ones consistently committed to compelling the nation to realize its ostensible ideals.[66]

This commitment to inclusion within the world of humans was also why Adair rejected the term "black," for black was a color that did not reflect the varied skin colors of Negroes and occluded the interzones of cross-racial sexual liaisons omnipresent in American history. While a proud "Negro-American"—for Adair a signifier of America's ethnic diversity rather than a claim to race as biologically essential—she argued that she would "never, never, never accept the word" black. For her, "black" served as a semiotic device through which white Americans had managed to strip Negroes of their Americanness, inscribed as it was on Jim Crow signage, slathered as it was on the faces of minstrel performers. In rejecting both color and the ontological status of blackness (and therefore black people) as a void, she hoped to salvage the liberal individual subject—each Negro person as a citizen in their own right—from a color caste system and introduce them to a "color blind" future.[67]

Indeed, Adair's subjectivity, which was captured in the hold of normative gender ideology, as a woman and an individual shaped her appeals to McFarland, whom she addressed as a "sister." She appealed to McFarland's sense of moral respectability, placing contemporary black suffering in the context of not only the bold-faced discriminations that black folks faced in the twentieth century, but also the "wicked" degradations enslaved black grandmothers experienced at the whims of men that they surely "hated." She called on McFarland to join in solidarity with her, as a woman and as a Christian, to move beyond criminations of black folks' morality, arguing that any perceived moral depravity among them was a consequence of the limits placed on their upward mobility by white supremacy. For Adair, white women's failures to act against racism were an affront to "the true worth of womanhood," which hinged on "justice."[68] But these ideas—of justice, of American promise, of the possibility of inclusion—were narratives that would fail to convince women like McFarland of Adair's claim to humanity, and which would limit the range of options available for Houston civil rights struggle in the coming years.

Necessarily, Adair's struggle against Jim Crow echoed the existential fault lines expressed differently by Du Bois: "How does it feel to be a problem?"[69] How does it feel, the white contemporaries of Du Bois and Adair wondered, to be a Negro—members of the biological unity called "human" but violently positioned as the antithesis of the "human?" But Adair did not feel like a problem—she took actions to fix what she saw was the "problem" as she helped force the city of Houston to desegregate its airport and buses.[70] And yet she also viewed herself intersubjectively—that is, she could see the distorted version of herself that white people saw when they looked at her. She accepted that there was a problem to be solved—what she saw as a contradiction at the center of the American project and in the heart of her white interlocutors that could be unraveled through the kind of moralizing education she practiced in her letters to McDonald and McFarland. She wrestled against the duality that constricted her, wherein she understood herself as a woman but recognized that the white world did not allow her any security in that self-recognition. Rather than challenge the meaning and function of gender, however, Adair sought to solve this duality by being incorporated into a gender schematic.

Thus, Adair's civil rights work can be described as a politics of inclusion and incorporation: she raised hell at Houston's Veterans Administration hospital until they changed their segregation policies; she threatened to publicize the degraded conditions at the Carnegie Library in Fourth Ward with its limited capacity and inaccessibility to most black Houstonians, compelling the mayor, Roy Hofheinz, to personally call her, saying, "Mrs. Adair, this is not healthy news for publication, so I would like for you . . . to notify the high school principals and your reading public to go to the [city] library and get their library cards." Certainly, Adair's work improved the quotidian life experiences of black Houstonians on average, earning her the honor of being remembered as the "Rosa Parks of Houston."[71] Simultaneously, it contributed to a discourse of racial liberalism that would only have limited purchase in a world predicated upon anti-black exclusions—the evidence of which can be found throughout American history and is succinctly stated by critical race theorist Derrick Bell as "the permanence of racism."[72] In short, Adair's faith in the political category "human," in part actualized through her gendered subjection, was also her prison, for even as she helped bring Jim Crow to its knees in terms of public accommodations, white Houstonians redrew and hardened the lines of segregation in the realms of residence and jurisprudence using the same frameworks that shaped her demands for inclusion.

SEX: THE PRINCIPLE AROUND WHICH SEGREGATION IS ORGANIZED

Like Ida B. Wells-Barnett who came before her and Rosa Parks, her contemporary, Adair quickly learned that doing the work of racial justice inevitably required engagement with sex. Gunnar Myrdal made the same observation in *An American Dilemma*, writing, "Sex becomes . . . the principle around which the whole structure of segregation" is organized.[73] More than merely suggesting a difference between universal "male" and "female" types, gender roles were racialized for and to the exclusion of black people from politics and civil society. Rather than providing a pathway into the human family for black people, gender roles justified their perpetual exclusion.

Wells-Barnett knew intuitively and proved emphatically that the specter of the ever-looming black male rapist that haunted white imaginaries was just that—an imagined specter. Under the threat of death, she courageously published indictments of lynching not only by proving this myth as a myth but also by historizing interracial sex, and especially interracial rape, as white men's prerogative. Likewise, Parks risked her safety by traveling throughout the Deep South to investigate black women's claims of sexual assault for the NAACP.[74]

Issues of sex and sexuality effectively raised the rancor of white Americans. Politicians animated their constituents by preaching a gospel of segregation justified by the need to protect white girls and women from black men's sexual excesses. Entire black communities were demolished by ravenous mobs under the belief or pretending to be under the belief that a black man had raped a white woman, even when medical evidence proved otherwise. The 1943 race riot in nearby Beaumont, Texas, for example, was allegedly the result of a rape accusation of a white woman by a never-identified black man. The "irrational" fear of the black male object would remain the excuse for mob violence, even as evidence pointed toward other motivations. In Beaumont, two medical practitioners found no evidence of rape on the woman. And increased racial hostility against black voters and war industry workers had been evident in the weeks leading up to the riot. Moreover, the riot itself manifested in the destruction of black homes and the blatant robbery of black possessions, not a hunt for a rapist. White bystanders testified, "It was like hell. The mob would beat the few Negroes who stuck by their homes. Many of the mob carted off valuables of the Negroes." And the *Chicago Defender* reported, "Many women lost diamond rings which were torn from their fingers." Countering the early narrative set forth in white newspapers and mainstream national papers, the black press excoriated white Beaumonters as American Nazis—"the fifth column of pure, unadulterated prejudice and jealousy over workers who have been putting their war earnings to good use, improving their businesses and their economic progress."[75] Indeed, the violence black communities across the country faced in the wake of singular rape accusations was not contingent but gratuitous. They were not looted, ejected, and murdered in cold blood *because* a white woman had been raped; they were looted, ejected, and murdered in cold blood because such violence was the prerogative of whiteness against its nonhuman Other.

Thus, much of Adair's work focused on "rape cases where white people used to become dissatisfied and disgruntled about a thing." She explained, "The best way they could do, some white woman would holler that she'd been raped by a Negro or ventured to rape . . . and of course that meant a burned or lynched Negro." One high-profile case happened in the nearby town of Conroe, which black Houstonians and their NAACP took interest in. Bob White, a black Houston plantation worker, was coerced into a false confession that he raped a white woman in August 1937. Adair and the Houston NAACP helped him acquire a lawyer. In a rare set of decisions, White won several appeals, including one which challenged the prosecution's racial prejudice and one which acknowledged his forced confession was inadmissible as evidence. Close to having his innocence declared, White's life was stolen from him by the alleged victim's husband, who shot White in the back of the head in a Montgomery County courtroom.[76] White's death indicated, again, that institutions designed to preserve the rights of those people legally recognized as humans would fail to protect black lives.

Conroe may bear the historical stain of this blatant racial assassination, but when black persons committed crimes against Jim Crow, Houston also rejected their claims to be recognized as human. The high-profile case of Johnnie Lee Morris threatened to expose the severity of Jim Crow's indignities against black people in Houston and black Houstonians' indignant responses to it on a national stage, and it all started with a charge of miscegenation. Accused of murdering a white bus driver during a racial spat with a white passenger, Morris's cause garnered Adair's attention, and her fundraising efforts helped afford him some of the city's best and upcoming criminal defense attorneys. In the end, black Houstonians cheered the disposition in Morris's case: Morris managed to avoid a death sentence by the end of his legal travails, notable and rare for homicide victims with a black defendant and white victim. However, the lexicon of civil rights, equal protection, due process, and self-defense that underpinned this "victory" for Morris also legitimated the apparatuses, logics, and institutions that violated his person, ripped him out of his social world, threatened him with symbolic and material death, and continued to terrorize black Houstonians during and after his trial. This is the subject of the following chapter.

The significance of Adair's work on Morris's behalf and in civil rights activism throughout her life cannot be diminished. She helped make the mundane a bit more bearable for black Houston. Still, Adair's life as a self-identified Negro-American woman demonstrated that gender for people racialized as black was both material and fungible—material at the level of individual subjectivity and social interaction but indeterminate and violable structurally. She recognized this as a tension to be reconciled, a problem worth revisiting, an injustice to be redressed. That is, Adair's life from girlhood to womanhood stands as an example of the inescapable capture of gender in *this world*. And gender, English scholar Zakiyyah Iman Jackson reminds us, was central in the marking of Man's negated Other (i.e., blackness) "from the earliest days of the invention of 'the human.'"[77] Thus, Adair's projects of moral education and racial democratization, situated as they were within the subjecthood of the human and gender, were indeed efficacious, demonstrating what some might term "agency" (but which I maintain was itself "a social creation"). This "resistance registered by social actors . . . occur[red] within the manifold forces that both call[ed] the social actor into existence and shape[d] the resistance of that social actor against these same forces."[78]

That is, a critical approach to making sense out of Adair's world and the onerous task of defeating Jim Crow elucidates both an immediate and broader point: Adair did not meet the limits of liberalism in Houston, for liberalism was accomplishing its hegemonic dominance even through her acts of resistance. Moreover, Adair's life did not demonstrate this alone; rather she serves here as a paradigmatic figure emblematic of Houston's civil rights struggles, struggles which certainly mattered for making everyday life a bit less vexing and a bit more comfortable for black folks, but which were constrained in their capacity to dismember the structural antagonisms that made those struggles unending. Where Adair helps us see how subjective capture might constrain thought for an individual, the trial of Johnnie Lee Morris illustrates that such capture is never an individual process, but always simultaneously functions at a macrosocial level where ideas about sex and gender, the sacredness of the law and legal proceedings, the obviousness of what counts as "crime," the universal fact of "individual responsibility," and the morality of nonviolence and respectability are taken for granted and thereby predetermine the limits of acceptable and popular black political action. Such limits coerce black politics to affirm rather than antagonize *this world* and thus participate in sustaining decades of capture.

2
CAPTURED BY THE RULE OF LAW
Johnnie Lee Morris's Trouble on the Bus

> We still bear the mark of the commodity: the lockdown of the hold, the chokehold, arms in the air, walk backwards, makes it impossible to breathe. The state transforms us into nobody, no human involved, disposable through the exercise of violence, by enclosure and abandonment, and by measuring "safety in chains and corpses."
>
> Saidiya Hartman, "The Dead Book Revisited," *History of the Present*

Walking unknowingly into the thick of it all, Bessie Pavlicek and her seven-year-old daughter Kathryn prepared to board a bus at the corner of Main and Preston on their way to the Foley's department store. It was October 11, 1951, a cool autumn Thursday in downtown Houston, nearly ten degrees below the average high for that time of year. Jim Crow, both in law and in custom, was still in season, though, and as was true throughout the segregated South, public conveyances were often hot with racial tensions.[1] Following her daughter onto the Houston Transit Company bus, Pavlicek attempted to ask the bus driver, Florian Antone Nowak, if this route would take them to Foley's, but he was distracted. "Then at that time I saw a negro standing [in] the aisle talking to a big white man."

Trouble.

Nowak demanded that the black man, later identified as Johnnie Lee Morris, sit down.

Morris refused.

So, the driver "handed him a transfer, and told him to get off the back way." And then time seemed to speed up.

The black man refused the indignity of being told to leave the bus from its rear and made his way toward the front. The driver pushed toward Morris. Another white customer joined in. Pavlicek caught the white light reflecting off a sharp tool in Morris's black hand as he pulled it from his pocket. He "raised his hand" at the "big white man" and before she knew it the object "brushed the side" of her face. The woman grabbed her daughter and "stepped back down to the sidewalk." From there she watched for a moment as three men struggled on the bus, Nowak and the other white man against the conceit of Negro defiance and Morris against the intransigence of Jim Crow's conceit. Panicked, she ran into a nearby business and asked store personnel to call the police. Pavlicek never saw the stabbing. By the time police arrived, bus driver Nowak had been fatally wounded and Morris had left the scene.[2]

As a witness, Pavlicek was not privy to whatever precipitated the fight between Nowak and Morris, nor could she testify to its end. The relevant details were "a negro," a "white man," and "a knife." This was true for white Houstonians generally, who upon hearing the news of Nowak's death, charged the yet unidentified assailant as "a murderer."[3] District attorney Sam Davis, with the support of the Houston Transit Company and the local bus drivers' union, confirmed that a Negro murderer was on the run and that he would, in the end, be indicted for his crime.[4] Whatever legal fictions legitimated the criminal court system, the presumption of innocence did not exist for "a negro" with "a knife" who left behind a "white man's" corpse. This is not a matter of scholarly editorialization on my part. During Morris's eventual trial, several veniremen (and they were all men) had been dismissed because they could not offer an acceptable answer to the question: "Do you believe a Negro has a right to defend himself against a white man to the extent of taking the white man's life if the Negro believes that his life is in danger or that he will suffer serious bodily injury from the white man?"[5] The legally acceptable answer, "yes," was at odds with the culturally and tacitly understood answer, "not at all." Their dismissal from the venire jury was not to ensure Morris stood before an unbiased jury, but to ensure against claims of explicit racial bias that could be raised on appeal.

Houston police eventually found and arrested Morris, but not because he had been successfully identified and traced in relation to Nowak's stabbing. He and his wife, Christine, a white woman he had married in Nevada, now lived in Houston and shared a small apartment at 416 Saulnier Street, one of many residences in the historically black Fourth Ward that would eventually be razed to make way for Interstate 45.[6] In 1951, Texas's antimiscegenation statutes were still legally enforceable. Though interracial liaisons and relationships were bountiful enough in Houston, prosecutors avoided taking such cases to court in the interest of preserving Houston's image as a happily segregated city and a heavenly southern environ in which to establish business without the economic risks associated with racial upheavals. In fact, prosecutors in Houston had not tried a miscegenation case in almost thirty years, and in their last attempt had not won a conviction. Trying a white man was a violation of his sexual prerogative and trying a white woman would make public that white women could and did desire consensual sexual and romantic relationships with black people.[7]

Indeed, Christia Adair interpreted the case in precisely this way. The trial would present an opportunity for Houstonians to not only reckon with segregation on public transportation, but also acknowledge the ways Jim Crow allowed white men to regulate—or attempt to regulate by way of legislation—the sexual behaviors and desires of white women and black men who had sex with them.[8] (White men's efforts to sexually dominate black women and queer black men were also a feature of white men's prerogatives, but often manifested as sexual assault or as financial exchange in the illicit sex economy.)[9] With a competent defense team, Adair believed the Morris case could deliver several victories for Houston's black community. By dramatizing a case wherein "a white woman" was "happy with him [a black man] and wanting him," Morris's defense could undermine white men's—and white women's—claims that black men had unrequited and insatiable demands for white women and were therefore a risk to those women. The case might also force an equal protection appeal, since Harris County's criminal courts practiced a pattern of excluding black people from petit juries and considered them "not qualified" to serve in cases of interracial violence. If the rest of Houston could understand the significance of Morris's case as a righteous transgression against Jim Crow segregation, Adair believed the NAACP would "prove that we had people in all walks of life that could not only serve on juries, but [who] could do anything."[10]

Contrasting Adair's hopefulness, the trial would affirm that black men like Morris who resisted Jim Crow's abuses by practicing violations of their own had no right to self-defense, because as a not-human, Morris had no claim to his "self" as property. In the minds of white Houston, Morris was only a Negro—any Negro, every Negro. White people's physical and discursive violence against him simultaneously constituted Morris as a subject (responsible for his own actions) and object (inert and incapable of redemption). As such, Morris—again, any Negro, every Negro—was their intellectual property incarnate. In other words, their violence produced a political, social, and economic capture that society often abbreviates as "race."

Race is not reducible to "epiphenomenon, to superstructure, [or] to particular example," but is rather a result of the birth of racial capitalism itself through the transatlantic slave trade.[11] That is, race is the historical consequence of the violence deployed by Europeans to differentiate what kinds of people were reducible to chattel and what kinds were eligible for at least some cover under the umbrella of humanism to benefit from the extraction of energy from property.[12] In a parallel case, the conviction of the Green Pond Seven, black boys accused of the rape and murder of a young white boy—a crime of which none of the boys were guilty—we see that they were not eligible for legal protections. Their travails help elucidate the ways the law itself functioned to constitute black people as non-rights-bearing subjects.

Legal scholar Nirej Sekhon's articulation of "the limit of the law" is helpful here. Arguing that "criminal procedure's failure to adequately constrain police is not a correctable defect but rather a design feature," Sekhon demonstrates that the law itself is the precondition *and* justification for its own exemption. Ostensibly, the function of the law is in part to limit the excesses of the state-market, thereby justifying its own existence. More accurately, according to Sekhon, the function of the law is to *appear* to limit the excesses of the state-market. The law actually functions to determine who or what has the right to declare a state of emergency/state of exception. This is sovereignty. Note, then, that the law determines who or what has the right to declare when the law itself can be suspended. The police torture of the Green Pond Seven and their subsequent convictions demonstrated again how black people were forced to live outside the umbrella of humanism, outside the law's "zone of validity," always subject to the emergency powers not just of the police, but of white civil society.[13] The law was the precondition for the torture of black folks, not the means by which they could seek protection from that torture, because the protective cover of the law only extended to humans, and humanity was constructed racially as the absence of blackness. W. E. B. Du Bois opined on this in 1940, writing that the past and/as the present exposed the fact that liberalism's "mythical Humanity," which supposedly covered "every featherless biped," functioned to occlude the phenomenon that "those of any nation who can be called Men and endowed with rights are few."[14]

Black Houstonians were well aware of their exclusion from the world of Man and the law's inconsistent, ambivalent relationship to their well-being. But as the case of Johnnie Lee Morris makes clear, they also remained captured by the idea of the law and its ability to guarantee their inclusion into American democracy. If capture signifies an impairment of ability and mobility, this chapter takes a critical view of the idea of resistance in black civil rights struggles. It does not argue that resistance is inconsequential but does demonstrate how black efforts to be included in American democracy and therefore transform it functioned to legitimize American democracy itself, which was defined historically and politically by the exclusion of black people from citizenship and its attendant rights. Though not meaningless, resistance might often (and necessarily) be inclusive of negotiation and accommodation.

Lastly, after elaborating on these ideas of *racial capture* and *capture in democracy*, the chapter offers a meditation on the methods used to construct the narrative herein. To tell an honest story about Johnnie Lee Morris and the very little we can know about him given the limits of the archive, I follow Tryon P. Woods's argument that perspective supersedes method.[15] Thus, I endeavor to acknowledge *disciplinary capture*, articulate some means by which historians can challenge their own disciplining, and admit that such challenges remain constrained by disciplinary mandates. In the white spaces between the texts on the pages that follow, I welcome readers to join my meditation on the notion that resistance may be an inadequate language for thinking about the long black civil rights movement. For some scholars this may be an impermissible claim, since resistance seems ubiquitous in the archive—it appears to be an empirical fact—but this is a matter of perspective. By demonstrating the workings and outcomes of criminal court procedure in Morris's case, this chapter presses against the claim of the empirical and toward the structural, attempting its own escape from disciplinary capture in order to develop a structuralist's-eye view of democracy and the ways it functions to fortify rather than weaken the anti-black power that made race and the modern world.

THE (RACIAL) APPREHENSION OF JOHNNIE LEE MORRIS

Three days after the Nowak stabbing, Johnnie Lee and Christine Morris rested in their marriage bed. That night, October 14, at 10:30 p.m., Harris County sheriff C. V. "Buster" Kern, captain Lloyd Frazier, and deputies Paul Anderson and Alvin Baker entered their home, "made them dress," and arrested them on suspicion of miscegenation and vagrancy. The two had been reported to the sheriff by Deputy Baker, who was black. There is no evidence of any prior connection between the couple and Baker. The deputy and his partner Leo Busby had only just become the Harris County Sheriff's Department's first black deputies on November 16 of the previous year.[16] Baker and his black comrades in the Houston Police Department (HPD) understood their "vital and useful function as overseers of the black community." The analogy to plantation overseers was metaphor and material. Their job was to control and contain the presumptive black criminal—that is, all black persons—in the interest of "the elite."[17] Indeed, if Adair's life and Morris's circumstances demonstrated black people resisting vacillation between the capture of liberal humanism and the material realities of racialization, folks like Baker and Busby were castigated as race traitors whose consciousnesses had been nearly wholly colonized by the black *imago* in the white mind. In other words, black Houstonians suspected that Baker and Busby did not simply understand how white people viewed black people; to them, these deputies accepted white perspectives, attitudes, and ethics as objectively true. The two deputies, along with later black HPD officers, garnered unsavory reputations among black Houstonians throughout their service. In particular, Morris claimed he had been "whipped, beat and struck" by Baker and deputy Red Williams in the early morning hours before sunrise on October 15 in order to force the suspect to reveal the location of his weapon.[18]

It was a coincidence that officers found a ticket stub from a movie theater in San Francisco in Johnnie Lee's coat pocket. A hat that police had found at the scene had been purchased in San Francisco. Soon they extracted a signed statement from Morris "saying he had stabbed the bus driver," and on October 17, without having had any opportunity to consult with an attorney, he admitted to the stabbing before Judge A. C. Winborn, arguing that he had acted in self-defense. After indictment and prior to trial, officers searched his apartment, where they found a bloody undershirt, and with Morris's directions, a jack-knife hidden "in a hole in the floor under the shower bath."[19]

Johnnie Lee was indicted for murder, officially charged with killing Florian Nowak "with malice aforethought . . . by cutting and stabbing him with a knife." Christine was charged on a separate offense of miscegenation, despite her husband's claim that she was "part Negro and part Czechoslovakian." Officers denied that Christine was anything but white. Sheriff Kern made sure that Mrs. Morris remained unavailable to reporters from the black-owned *Houston Informer* and NAACP representatives, including Christia Adair, all of whom continued to press county jail officials for the opportunity to talk with the incarcerated woman. Denied legal representation and a sympathetic press by a Jim Crow sheriff's department, the Morris couple's narrative remained shaped by the city's white media, who did have direct access to Christine.[20]

In fact, Houston's white newspapers had been in a frenzy since the stabbing. Prior to Morris's arrest, the *Houston Post* ran several front-page stories about the killing. They wrote that Nowak had only been on the job for about three months when he was killed by "a 'smart aleck' Negro [who] was fired from a South End drive-in grocery because of his attitude, who then went to work for an attorney as a yard man." The newspaper claimed that the unnamed attorney's wife said that she gave the employee "a shirt similar to the one the slayer was reported wearing." Despite this matter-of-fact description of the "slayer," the *Post* did not have a name. It turned out that these reports were inaccurate; Morris was a longshoreman.[21] Despite not having much evidence about the suspect, white Houstonians and the white press had already been cultivated to see him as a working-class Negro who refused to stay in his place, complete with a sour disposition and a chip on his shoulder.[22] Indeed, disposable and interchangeable, black men remain captured—racially apprehended—in white imaginaries as always criminal.

During their Harris County grand jury hearings, both Christine and Johnnie Lee Morris were no-billed on the miscegenation charges after the district attorney's office "made a verbal request that the charges against Mrs. Morris be dismissed." District attorney Sam Davis wanted to avoid "agitat[ing] the racial angle of Morris who is married to a white woman." Meanwhile, Davis commenced a public press campaign meant to foment white anxieties outside of the courtroom by spreading unfounded rumors that black Houstonians were threatening violence against white witnesses to the Nowak murder. Editors at the *Informer* found this laughable; racial intimidation in cases of this type had always been the monopolized prerogative of white people.[23] The nature of the case was obviously racial—and materially so in the courtroom, where all the decision makers were white. But Christine Morris's indeterminate racial background promised prosecutorial failure; indeed, such cases had a long history of bewildering American courts to the point of aphasia.[24] The real win would be a murder conviction. Nevertheless, despite the no-bill, white Houstonians' anxieties around race, gender, economic class, and sexuality did not have to be on display in the courtroom for these co-articulated social structures to have significant purchase there.

THE GREEN POND SEVEN'S INTERLUDE: THE COERCIVE IDEA OF DEMOCRACY UNDER THE LAW

Those same anxieties were still on full display at the end of the decade. In 1959, twelve-year-old Billy Bodenheimer was robbed, raped, and murdered near his home in Montrose, a collection of mostly or all-white small urban core neighborhoods that had previously been suburbs, situated between the heavily black Fourth Ward and deeply wealthy and white River Oaks. The Houston Police Department arrested seven black teenagers and young adults for the crime, many of them residents of the Green Pond area. Green Pond was a small majority-black enclave nestled between River Oaks and Montrose. The residents were disproportionately employed as domestics or service workers, an accessible labor pool which had been an important consideration prior to River Oaks's development. Despite that they had resided in the area long

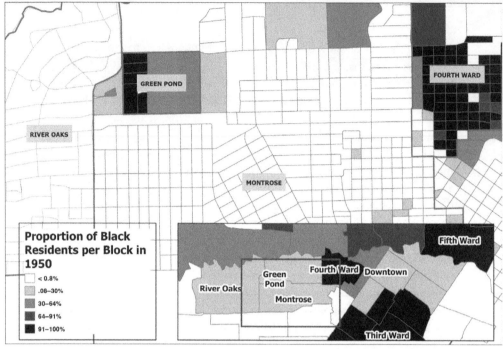

Map 6 *The Green Pond was a small majority black community established in the wake of the Civil War. River Oaks, which was developed in the early twentieth century, was intentionally placed in proximity to underpaid black workers in Green Pond and the Fourth Ward who would be exploited as domestic laborers, childcare providers, cooks, and chauffeurs. Today, Green Pond is no longer known by this name; it is majority-white with single homes generally valued between $300,000 and $700,000, and condominium units valued at more than $500,000.*

before many of the surrounding white families, Green Pond residents were still recognizable as "out of place" when they traversed neighboring communities.

Their proximity to white residential spaces actually increased their visibility and vulnerability during the brief Bodenheimer investigation; the supposed depravity and sexual excess of Green Pond's residents was always a threat in need of containment. Such containment was possible through quotidian anti-black violence and punctuated by notable moments such as Bodenheimer's murder. In this case, the brutality began with HPD officers A. C. Hopper, Herman Clyde Mackey, and Leroy Mouser's descent into the neighborhood and their treatment of their suspects. Instead of taking the black teens to the police station for booking, the officers drove them to the old shack where Billy Bodenheimer had been killed and forced each into the icebox where the body had been found because they "wanted these niggers to see the ghost of that white boy." Under duress, each young man made a false confession.[25]

Seventeen-year-old Adrian Johnson was convicted of murder, his appeals were denied, and he was executed by electrocution after his final words: "I want to pray. I pray that this will be the last time something like this will happen."[26] (It would not be; it had happened the same way in the notable case of Willie McGree in 1951 and continues through the first decades of the twenty-first century.)[27] Despite overwhelming evidence of police misconduct, falsified evidence, and corroborating alibis for each of the young men, none escaped the bloodlust of the criminal legal system to locate, condemn, and snatch black lives.

The other defendants included David Arthur Clemons, who was sent to Gatesville School for Boys—essentially a juvenile prison where, ironically, some white professionals raped minors; Charles Archer, who was sent to Rusk State Hospital for mental illness; Robert Miller, who was convicted of sodomy and sentenced to prison; Roy Miller, a minor, who was convicted of the same charge, sent to Gatesville, and then charged and found guilty of Bodenheimer's murder after his seventeenth birthday and sentenced to fifteen years in prison; Joe Edward Smith, who was sentenced to death but earned parole after the Supreme Court temporarily ended the death penalty in the United States in *Furman v. Georgia* (1972); and Ira Lee Salder, only thirteen years old, who was sent to Gatesville without a trial for eight years.[28] For white Houston, the young men got "what's coming for them." Their involvement was statistically unlikely given that the majority of violent crimes in Houston were intraracial, with more than 94 percent of all homicide victims in Houston between 1958 and 1961 killed by someone of the same racial categorization. Nonetheless, the understanding of blackness as criminal compelled many people to demand a hardening of the lines that divided black space from white space.[29]

Before trial, doubt had settled into black Houstonians' minds quickly. At least one postal service worker, a white man, hinted that the confessions were likely untrue. Residential segregation and Jim Crow customs made it unlikely that young black men could traverse a white neighborhood unnoticed: "I just don't see how that many Negroes could do anything in this neighborhood and not be seen." This would have been especially true on the traffic-heavy West Gray Street where Bodenheimer was initially abducted.[30] Additionally, skeptics pointed out that in recent weeks a white man who had been previously charged with attempted rape was suspected of recently raping a twelve-year-old boy in the neighborhood. Recently and nearby, a young black girl had been found too, "raped, strangled, and beaten" in a park in similar condition to Bodenheimer. Moreover, just a few days prior, a twenty-five-year-old white man reportedly attempted to abduct two or three young white girls in the area.[31] However, these facts, which pointed to a young, white, serial pedophilic rapist, seemed immaterial to the Houston Police Department.

Black Houstonians rebuffed the police department and sided with the young men as they recanted their earlier confessions and pleaded innocence. In fact, black residents were already predisposed to distrust the HPD, given their failure to investigate, with any semblance of care, the murder of Mattie Louis Mitchell, a young black girl who had been killed a month prior in similar circumstances. And information quickly spread that four residents of Green Pond had already gone on record to provide the young men's alibis, each claiming they saw the young men boxing in the yard of another teenager until "it was almost dark," and thus could not have been responsible for a murder that occurred in daylight more than half a mile away. Indeed, nearly thirty people were involved in or were spectators of the neighborhood boxing match and could corroborate their alibis. Confessing that she "positively saw the boys boxing," Mrs. Frances Hollins believed "the boys are a victim of circumstance." Additionally, Arthur Breitkreaux, a white man, assured police that he too "positively saw" at least two of the young men boxing where they claimed.[32]

Some white Houstonians agreed that the HPD had manufactured the prior confessions. The census tract where Bodenheimer was killed was 90 percent white, and the string of rapes and attempted child abductions by a white man suggested the same white man was still terrorizing their neighborhoods. In a public letter, Bodenheimer's own mother cautioned that she was not convinced at all that the seven black suspects were guilty. Nevertheless, many white Houstonians, predisposed toward believing that black people were especially prone to criminality and the depravity of child rape, remained confident that the young men had commited the crime. Some anonymously promised the Bodenheimer family that the "niggers will get what's coming for them," as they swore to go on a bludgeoning campaign against any and all of black Houston. They demanded "more segregation," "stricter laws," and "greater punishments" as they "condemn[ed] the whole Negro race" as ravenous and murderous.[33]

We cannot know for sure all of what happened to the Green Pond Seven when police took them to that ice shack, but we have enough evidence from similar situations to critically speculate.[34] While David Kazanjian's method of "speculative work" or "overreading" was conceived as a way to "read documents of subalternity as offering philosophical reflection as well as data or description," it can also be useful for elucidating the philosophies of nonsubaltern subjects.[35] And Saidiya Hartman's method of "critical fabulation" encourages interrogation of the unrecoverable past, an interrogation wherein the end is not recovery, but narrative. Particularly useful here are Hartman's suggestions to imagine the unverifiable and trouble the idea of narrative authority by attending to the fraught relationship between narrators and speakers.[36]

The only record of what the police officers said as they forced the Miller brothers into the icebox are Roy and Robert Miller's memories of them, spoken to a journalist in the early 2000s. Again, they recalled that officers wanted them to see the "ghost of that white boy" and "asked if they [the Millers] wanted to die in the electric chair. Dead charcoal niggers." Hartman might encourage questions here: how did these officers understand the world, the relationship of blackness to civil and *human* rights, and their relationship as officers to the idea of the law and the written law? She might also suggest exploitation of the subjunctive: as one brother watched the other confined to the ice box, did his heart sink? Did he hold his own breath as he imagined his brother suffocating inside the dank enclosure? Did his mind race: was he imagining how to escape, how to run home fast enough to hide under a porch or a mattress in hopes that someone could save him? Or did he know that domestic space was no guarantee of safety from public violence if you were Negro? Did he give up hope in that moment, well before he too was placed in the icebox, knowing the only way to make it out of the shack alive was to tell the officers what they wanted to hear? Did he know that so-called resistance would literally be a dead end?

The officers' exact words were not recorded anywhere, but it need not matter. The Millers' memory of their words suffices as an imprint of their psychosocial power. They remembered the slurs. They remembered the gravity. They remembered the threat subtending the words. The words, but more importantly the memory of the words, participated in the (re)constitution of the Miller brothers' subjectivities. To the officers, the Millers were "niggers," and so to themselves they were "everything that the wishful shameless fantasies of culture want [them] to be, an enigma of inversion and hate." David Marriott sighs, "And this is our existence as men, as black men."[37]

The officers expressed a foundational philosophy of their world. Their first duty was to a concept of justice in Billy Bodenheimer's name, where the young boy was synecdoche for whiteness. Their idea of justice did not extend to "the nigger," conceived by them as sexual and murderous subhuman types with no rights worthy of their respect. Indeed, they unilaterally suspended the *legislated* rights of the young men—which is not to say that these rights were in any way *material*—creating a localized state of exception which necessarily existed outside of the law's zone of validity. The officers were empowered by the law, but their power exceeded the law.[38] Their duty was not to the written word but to white civil society's beliefs about the violent libidinal nature of "the nigger" and its demands that this threat be handled through whatever means necessary, legally sanctioned or not. The shared philosophy of white Houston was one wherein "the Negro" was reducible to biology. This subhuman entity represented the state of nature, chaos which always threatened encroachment on the *demos*, the "people" by which and for whom democracy was made. As such, though superficially protected by the law's letter, black people's political condition as "black" rendered them always outside of the law's humanist grammar and therefore always vulnerable to the exercise of police power beyond the law.

To wit, the prevailing faith in the modern world that the rule of law establishes an objective standard by which all people can be treated justly is untenable. Whatever else the law may accomplish, it remains the precondition for its own dismissal, because liberal legalism maintains that legal rules must necessarily "define the proper sphere of their own application."[39] In other words, the idea of the "rule of law" homogenizes difference under the rubric of liberal equality and declares legal subjects as free from capricious, arbitrary decision-making by despotic rulers, insofar as those subjects remain within what the law has announced as its own jurisdiction. If the law creates its own jurisdiction, it declares in the same utterance that there is a place in which the law does not apply—a place where despotism may reign free. And here it is helpful to be more precise because "the law" is a social construction and the outcome of politics, and thus my use of active verbs in relation to the subject, "the law," is an abstraction. Rather, powerful political actors create laws and the idea of "the law," establish their jurisdiction, and thereby also determine their finitude, thus allowing themselves power and justification to do things both lawless and unlawful.[40] The supposed limits the law is thought to place on sovereign actors then obscures that the law is essentially political and that American democracy, rather than approximating popular self-rule, *is* a racial oligarchic plutocracy. Despite the diurnal countervailing evidence of Jim Crow and notwithstanding a steady tradition of skepticism, black Americans remained bewitched by the promise of a truer democracy fortified by the law.

Johnnie Lee Morris and the Green Pond Seven would receive the help of black Americans and Houstonians because these supporters believed it was possible to leverage the law and jurisprudence in ways that would integrate them into the world of Man. For them, this was democracy in action. Over the course of the twentieth century, this faith manifested into grassroots organizing that yielded significant quantitative changes for black people via successful desegregation suits and new civil rights legislation, but the qualitative relationship of blackness to whiteness remained fixed. Indeed, desegregation did not yield integration. Today black and first nation peoples remain the most segregated groups in the United States.[41] Civil rights legislation, from the

Fourteenth Amendment through the Civil Rights Act of 1964, has been used to reinforce white prerogatives.[42] And, as of the time of this writing, while the Voting Rights Act of 1965 has been effectively stripped of its power by judicial decree, racial animus remains the strongest predictor of a population's support of voter identification laws and a state's likelihood to legislate more voter suppression.[43] This philosophy of the Negro as non-rights-bearing was and remains a feature of American society.

Black efforts to make democracy "more democratic" by way of their inclusion in civil society unwittingly contributed to the perception that democracy was inherently progressive rather than a material expression of white civil society's will. It was unwitting not because black people were naïve, but because the democracy that was conditioned on racial slavery, genocide, and legal exclusion was (and remains) a convincing promise.[44]

It is important to maintain a distinction here between democracy *as an idea* and democracy as it has been experienced by black people in the United States, not because the distinction means there is a truer democracy to be attained in the future, but because the dissonance between these two is where black people and black politics have been captured. An Afropessimist approach demands an investigation of the relationship between the idea and the material. Here, the idea's function is to obscure the material—to suggest that democracy is an unfinished project, and therefore the solution to society's dilemmas is to finish that project rather than to imagine a different one entirely. The distance between idea and material need not always be a point of contention, but in the case of American democracy, the price of maintaining the fiction has been the regular murder of black people under the color of law *and* black people's historical struggle against their murder. Johnnie Lee Morris's criminal case, which was conceived as a legitimate expression of democracy at work, was guaranteed to demonstrate that democracy did not mean governance of the people by the people, but rather domination of the not-human by the human.

THE TRAP OF AMERICAN DEMOCRACY

Following Johnnie Lee Morris's arrest, police officers questioned him "continuously" for three or four hours until about three o'clock in the morning and beat a confession out of him. He signed "some form of written instrument" without knowledge of "the contents" of the document, neither during his trial nor when he signed the papers themselves. His attorneys would argue, in short, that Morris's "free agency had been destroyed and his will power over come" by the police officers. Morris's confession to murder contradicted his narrative of what actually happened on the bus with Nowak.⁴⁵

Two hundred sixty-five pound white car salesman Frank Morrison of Houston's East End had been boarding the bus alongside Morris, shoving along with other passengers to get through the doors, when he snarled, "Get back nigger." (Pause. The shared philosophy of white Houston was one wherein "the Negro" was reducible to biology. Rinse. Repeat.) Morris stepped aside and boarded after Morrison. Making his way toward the rear of the bus, Morris stopped when he heard Morrison, who was seated near the front door, mutter something to him from his seat along the lines of, "Watch it, boy." Defiantly, Morris asked Morrison, "What you mean by calling me 'boy'?" The irate Morrison responded, "Nevermind; move on."⁴⁶

The significance of Morris's defiance should not be understated; he was a black man on a Jim Crow bus in a city with a penchant for anti-black brutality, even if publication of those acts was suppressed through image-conscious collusions between city leaders and the mass media. As Robin D. G. Kelley has elucidated in the Jim Crow South, working-class black individuals and communities did not consent to such degradations when they appeared to oblige white demands. They had developed a tradition of "hidden transcripts," "infrapolitics"—quotidian acts of rebellion generally invisible to white observers but detectable in their effects and well-known among black people.⁴⁷ Many historians have explored the ways the intimate spaces of buses and other public conveyances were particularly fertile spaces for both invisible and observable small political conflicts between white and black people. Kelley writes, "The design and function of buses and streetcars rendered them unique sites of contest." He signifies them as "moving theaters," gesturing toward the ways that public transit was a "site of performance" and "site of military conflict." The constant "readjustments" of the color line—by which I mean the actual line moved by bus operators to accommodate different racial ratios at different times of service—added to the frustrations that accompanied acts of disrespect, humiliation, mis-recognition.⁴⁸

I am not describing Morris's act of self-defense as infrapolitics, but merely noting, as Kelley does, that it is no mere accident that so many violent interracial incidents boiled over on the selfsame public conveyances where black folks regularly gritted their teeth and bore racial indignities. The difference here is that, for Kelley, infrapolitics indicate a resistance against the imperfect democratic order and thereby a vehicle toward black political mobilization in the interest of perfecting that democratic order. In my understanding, infrapolitics are *constitutive* of the democratic order. An act of defiance might include an enslaved mother's resistance against dehumanization by nurturing her child, but that resistance also required her to endure the indignity of having her reproductive labor provide "increase" for the institution of slavery.[49] Likewise, the cultures of dissemblance practiced by black people throughout the long abolitionist struggle have been directed against the incursions of the white gaze into black interior life, but they have also looked like archival absence that fails to fully subvert the ever-present white gaze and white voice that predominates the archives.[50] Johnnie Lee Morris's defense could not resist but to manifest the same paradox.

Houston Informer editorialists offered their own commentary on the implications of the Morris case: "The street-cars, buses, and trains of the South have long been the arena for a large percentage of racial incidents." They noted that these incidents always involved some disagreement between black passengers and either white passengers or transportation officials. "Of equal importance," the writers stressed, "is the fact that incidents involving violence almost never occur between white passengers and company employees." *Informer* staff believed that the sheer statistical improbability of this pattern occurring randomly raised suspicion worthy of investigation. First, the editorial staff questioned the "rationalization [of] white people" who blamed such events on "'smart-aleck' or 'uppity Negroes' (whatever that means)." They argued that "millions" of interracial contacts "occur hourly, every day" in both public and private spaces. These contacts occurred "without incident." Thus, it appeared "rather foolish" to blame violent interracial clashes on public transportation "on Negro aggressiveness, intractability, or resentment." Therefore, the *Informer* concluded, the problem was in the lack of "indoctrination and training" for public transportation employees, who were "costing transportation companies of the South millions of dollars a year in lost revenues." In Houston, the editors claimed, "literally thousands of Negroes . . . refuse to ride the buses under any circumstance, [and] other thousands . . . limit their use of this public utility."[51]

The solutions proffered by the *Informer*—"training and indoctrination"—appear incomplete given the depth of the problem. Public transit operators were conveyers of the will of white civil society, corporations, and the state. The *Informer* did not suggest that racist bus drivers should be fired from their jobs, nor that corporations should be penalized for racial capitalism, nor that the state should create a competing service that strictly employed black people, nor that white civil society needed to relinquish any of its rights. The solution of the editors was to fix what they understood was an aberration in the system. Even the informal, unorganized boycott of buses as an act of resistance, meaningful as it was, came at a price for black people: they "limited their use of this public utility" in part by constraining their own mobility and ability to partake in a public service. This condition was precisely what Morrison demanded of Morris. Damned if they did or did not, the Negro was captured by democracy.

While Kelley and others see what is possible in these "seemingly innocuous, individualistic acts of survival and opposition" on public transit, including their potential for broader political mobilization, Johnnie Lee Morris's travails also indicate stagnation over time. For while folks like Adair would marshal together a biracial-funded defense for Morris and though black Houstonians would show up en masse to support Morris at trial, their activities would not ultimately change the structurally antagonistic relationship between black and white Houstonians. That is, while Kelley's preferred analytic of infrapolitics concludes that "African Americans . . . did not *experience* a liberal democracy" but rather "a fascist or, more appropriately, a colonial situation," by the end of Morris's trial black Houstonians concluded that he had a "fair trial." This *was* liberal democracy, despite ideological and academic contestations otherwise.[52]

Rather than speculate what a liberal democracy *could* be, I suggest that in our meditation on the meaning of history, all we have as evidence of the content of liberal democracy is "the archive," a body of material produced at the intersection of Morris's life with the regimes of violence that documented his fate. At the risk of belaboring the point, "infrapolitics," and even the institutionalized political activities that they generated, can obscure the material fact: Morris had no right to self-defense against a white man (and this I can assert as materially true because of the guilty verdict he received) and, therefore, his trial could never challenge and always legitimated the "structure of antagonisms" that defined the United States's racial order. The antagonism is, in simple terms, the blackening of people of African descent such that they are marked for and condemned to premature death for the purpose of valorizing white life.[53] This antagonism, rather than being an impediment to the realization of democracy, has been historically constitutive of liberal democracy. Opposing the tacit racial optimism whereby most historians seem to interpret the past and project into the future, P. Khalil Saucier and Tryon P. Woods explain that democracy is not "an unfinished project." They write:

> [W]e see in "democracy" the same intrinsic fatal flaw that we find in "emancipation," "sovereignty," "inclusion," "rights," "justice," or any of the rest of modern society's nomenclature. While [sociologists Michael Omi and Howard Winant] understand democracy as "the heart of the racial formation process," we follow black radical thought in viewing legal abstractions like "democracy" in relation to material political practices. As such, democracy proves to be embedded within

enslavement, rooted in captivity, and a leitmotif for social parasitism. Democracy first emerges as a political value only among the Western European societies that were already deeply invested in the slave trade, and struggles internal to these societies for democratic inclusion were premised upon the concomitant expansion of slaveholding. . . . To be ruthlessly critical directs us to the social fact that blackness enables democracy, mass incarceration is the prerequisite for democracy, and democracy is therefore the internal limit to the black freedom struggle. Consequently, racial theory's apprehension of "democracy" is something of a litmus test for conceptual aphasia.[54]

In short, it is important to apprehend the courage of Morris's act of defiance given the material constraints on his self-expression in a Jim Crow society without overstating the consequences of the capacity of that defiance through mass political mobilization to change the structure of that society, insofar as those people so mobilized understand their efforts through a grammar of democratic inclusion. Ultimately, justice and Morris's fate would be determined by a legal system that did not register him as a *being*, and moreover, he had no choice but to participate in that legal system. He was captured, and democracy itself—resting on the Manichean opposition of white to black, of human to nonhuman, of being to nonbeing—was his captor.

If laid out linearly, this was the trouble on the bus: the argument between Morris and Morrison escalated such that W. M. Grant, a twenty-six-year-old bus driver who was on board as a passenger, intervened and advised that both Morris and Morrison vacate the bus "if they wanted to fight." According to Grant, Morrison said, "Nevermind, just move to the back of the bus." Morris, offended and probably irate, made no effort to deescalate. Nowak intervened, bringing Morris a transfer and commanding him "to get off and catch another bus." Still defiant, Morris refused Nowak's order to exit out of the back of the bus and insisted, "I'm going out this [the front] door." Nowak then "stood up and took hold of the Negro's arm." Morrison joined in. In battle with two white men for his defiance against the rule of law and custom, Morris reacted. He whipped out his pocket knife, probably in an adrenaline-induced frenzy, and scraped Bessie Pavlicek's cheek as he attempted to orient himself toward his attackers. He drove his knife into Nowak's chest and then again on his neck near his left jaw. He squeezed through the crowd of people, "jumped out the door," and walked away from the scene.[55]

This was the trouble on the bus: Jim Crow, in law and in custom, had relegated black Houstonians to an inferior sociopolitical status. It was the duty and prerogative of Frank Morrison to enforce this hierarchy, remind black

Houstonians of their ontological displacement: they were not Man, but rather the Negro, the nigger, the "nothing," the fungible, formless form which "the Wolf, the Devil, the Evil Spirit, the Bad Man," and "the Savage" haunted the world of Man and threatened its dissolution.[56]

Morris inched toward the bus entrance, an act innocuous enough to himself, but the concretization of civilization's very doom in the eyes of Morrison. With all the eloquence of a parrot, Morrison lobbed two prescribed words at Morris: "boy" and "nigger," a stern reminder of Morris's lack of "ontological resistance in the eyes of the white man."[57] These words were meant to pierce Morris's soul—if he had one. But if he were not a "man" in the grammar of the world that enslaved him, Morris had all the capacities associated with that category, including a will for whatever he defined as dignity. And if he were the object of violent projectiles—both those discursive attacks by Morrison and Grant and their physical advance against his person—that violence met, flowed through, and exceeded Morris's body. That is, the work of Jim Crow through Morris and Grant was to rip Morris's subjectivity from his person and re-create him as the foundational "tool" for Man's domination and ownership of everything (and nothing, according to Calvin Warren), manifested not only as the attempts to cage Morris nor as simply the physical blows against his body.[58] But rupturing what Du Bois called the "souls of black folk" was an impossible feat, and so the violence used against Morris exceeded the capacity of two white men to contain it and direct its purpose. That violence, then, manifested at the tip of Morris's knife—white supremacist violence turning on itself as it tore into the flesh, not of a black man this time, but of a white man.

This, however, was not freedom for Morris. It was not noble resistance. It did not claim or reclaim dignity for him, for dignity required not merely "an ontological state of freedom," but also "recognition and regard." Even if "dignity does indeed refer to 'instrinsic human worth,'" English scholar Nick Bromell writes, "this very sense of intrinsic arises within—and is dependent upon—a social matrix of interpersonal relations."[59] Morris cooly walked away from the scene as the "madness" that was and remains insatiable "White Imperial Industry" fed on the remains of yet another body, a body soon to be resurrected as a martyr for whiteness, as a symbol of Negro depravity, as the necessary barrier preventing "social equality" on buses and trains and at lunch counters, as the levy keeping the floodwaters of Negro blood out of the stream of white purity. Jim Crow was the political economic manifestation of an enduring structural antagonism predicated on anti-blackness. It necessitated violence. It presaged death. Most often, the corpses left behind were black, but these deaths were the fault of the Negroes themselves. Sometimes, those corpses were white. These deaths, too, were the fault of the Negroes. And so, death was always the outcome, the Negro always and already guilty. Johnnie Lee Morris was death walking.

The Anti-Communist Trap: Captured in the American Way

Black Houstonians did not question the veracity of Morris's story as he told it, nor did they doubt that he had killed Nowak. Before the trial, many had already determined that he acted out of self-defense. The only question remaining was whether he would get a fair trial. A bit more context is helpful to understand their disposition. While the NAACP raised money for Morris's defense, the *Informer* also alerted the public that some of the funds might be used to investigate the beating of Dorothy Johnson Simon.[60] Deputies suspected that her husband, thirty-three-year-old Felogen Simon, had stolen over one thousand dollars in cash from the Buccaneer Drive-in restaurant in the city's Fourth Ward. Violence workers were also sure that Simon "shot and wounded" a deputy. His wife charged Harris County's deputies "with beating her in an attempt to make her reveal the hiding place of [her husband] which she claims she did not know." Predictably, the sheriff's department denied those allegations.[61]

On the same day that the *Informer* announced the initial successes of the fundraising effort for Morris, the newspaper also featured a front-page story about the beating of John Broussard. Police had arrested the black Houstonian on suspicion of car theft. Officers claimed that they shot Broussard in the back after the arrested man "jumped out of the [police] car and ran." In a confounding revision to the plot, officers later claimed that the running man was threatening because "he had come up to them with a grass scythe." An anonymous witness told the *Informer* that Broussard was shot and then beaten by police afterward. Another witness said she watched and heard as Broussard pleaded to the officers, "Please don't kill me, I was just trying to help my sister." No matter. The "gang of police" handcuffed him and told the frightened man, "Shut up, boy." The officers attempted to coax a confession from Broussard on the scene, but he refused to admit that he had ever tried to attack these violence workers. "Both witnesses said that Broussard lay for a long time before an ambulance was called," the *Informer* lamented, adding it was also possible emergency medical personnel had been present on the scene without treating the injured man because the ambulance was reserved for white people.[62]

Such acts of brutality, of course, were familiar enough to black Americans, and Broussard and Simon's stories were only local manifestations of a nationwide problem. Less than a month after the alleged attacks on these two Houstonians, "Word reached Houston . . . that Samuel Shepherd was slain and his co-defendant in the Groveland, Florida, case, Walter Irvin was critically wounded by Sheriff Willis McCall who allegedly shot the men while taking them, handcuffed, from the jail to the courthouse for a new hearing." (The evidence against McCall, presented by Gilbert King, is unassailable.) Such stories were ongoing and redundant, scripted by centuries of white terrorism in practice. Mistrust of police officers, the white people they protected, and the white people who protected them in the media and in courtrooms was therefore a regular disposition within black communities in Houston and throughout the United States.[63]

Thus, Morris's account of the bus slaying seemed likely and familiar to black Houstonians. "Negro interest" was in the question of whether Morris could receive "a fair and impartial trial." "In the meantime," *Informer* editorialists hoped, "the bus drivers (and the police) could better address themselves to the elimination of the basis that underlie altercations on the buses between drivers and Negro patrons," which they identified as a racially biased "lack of courtesy." The injustice, then, for those black people who were interested in Morris's defense, even without hearing the details of the case, was in the unequal treatment they received regularly under Houston's Jim Crow regime. Morris, in stabbing Nowak, had defended them all against this injustice. Now they had to do their part to defend Morris and force the court to render him dignity.[64]

Their contributions would have to be as courageous as Morris's. Outside of the courtroom, black Houstonians reported "numerous incidents" of police officers "threatening [them] with the Morris case in their minds and the Morris case on their lips." To attend Christia Adair's "public meeting . . . for all interested persons" meant facing the possibility of police harassment.[65] Still, the case remained on the minds of Houstonians, black and white; it was the most sensational murder case of the year in the city, and thus it was unavoidable for many. In fact, it garnered the attention of the Communist Party. *Political Affairs*, the Communist magazine, asserted that Morris was caught in a "'frame up' after defend[ing] himself against a white bus driver."[66] The interest of the Communist Party in Morris's case added more risk for Morris's sympathizers should they become associated with un-Americanism. Indeed, during the Red Scare, the repeated attempts of Texas law enforcement officials to implicate the NAACP as a cover for Communists and anarchists could mean involvement in Morris's defense risked personal investigation, harassment, jail time, and unemployment.[67]

Thus Christia Adair's NAACP and black Houstonians had a fight on two fronts: Morris's defense and the defense of black people's "Americanness." This was another narrative capture, compounding those of gender and the human. The editorialists at the *Informer* stridently endorsed Americanism and condemned communism, writing, "All endorse Americanism as long as it is a broad term meaning love of the country and belief in the merit and righteousness of the nation's ideals."[68] Loyalty to the nation was necessary for institutional legitimacy for the NAACP, especially in post-World War II racial politics. And the "poison" of liberal utopianism served as an effective "decoy" from recognizing the "price" of this fantastic dream of American inclusivity: the selfsame American system they looked to for racial justice was sustained by anti-black exclusions.[69]

In the same year as Morris's trial, the Supreme Court's decision in *Dennis v. United States* (1951) made it seemingly necessary for black Houston's leaders to assert their fealty to the nation in order to hedge against allegations of sedition. Ruling in favor of the constitutonality of the 1940 Alien Registration Act, the court decided the eleven petititoners in *Dennis* did not have a First Amendment right to speech that "advocated the overthrow or destruction of the Government of the United States by force or violence, to organize or help to organize any group which does so, or to conspire to do so."[70] Concurrently, black Houstonians were alert to the travails of W. E. B. Du Bois, by now a proponent of socialism, who had been ensnared by the Justice Department and the House Un-American Activities Commission. That same year, he appeared before the Supreme Court, defending himself against claims that he failed to register his Peace Information Center "as an agent of a foreign principal." The *Informer* published an open letter that had been printed in the *Ashanti Pioneer*, a Ghanaian newspaper in which the writer noted that Du Bois, "the most outstanding of all the intellectual leaders produced by the Negro people of the United States" was undoubtedly a "native American." The letter continued: "That such a man at such an age should be regarded as a foreign agent is a pathetic token of the hysteria to which, increasingly, we are being exposed." Du Bois and his codefendents were eventually found not guilty under the Foreign Agent Registration Act.[71]

The NAACP in Houston remained vigilant toward the threat posed by accusations of any involvement in communism and refused to display anything but absolute loyalty to the ideals abbreviated as "Americanism," even as the organization tactfully critiqued racist impediments to the realization of those ideals. In support of Morris, the Communist Party warned that there could be no justice for the defendant insofar as the legal system was structured to maintain racial capitalism. The NAACP interpreted these as attacks on the legal system itself—which, the organization was sure, needed reform, but which was fundamentally sound because, voided of biases, it could treat all parties before the court as equal (e.g., via the allowance of prosecutorial and defense teams, the rules and procedures of questioning and procuring and presenting evidence, the use of precedent, etc.). To suggest the impossibility of the *ideas* of fairness, justice, and reform within American democracy was understood as an attack on America itself, because America, if it was anything to Houston's mainstream black leaders, was a conglomerate of such *ideas*, even if yet unrealized. For them, America was not democracy now, but it was, prayerfully, democracy to come. One black Houstonian wrote to the *Informer*, "Negroes have learned Communism, whether to be in Korea, China, or the U.S. is neither desirable nor acceptable democracy. The American Negro has once again made clear that our goal is first-class citizenship, here in America."[72] Thus, black Houstonians dismissed the Communist Party's pessimism and its disbelief in the legitimacy of the criminal legal system, blaming the bus slaying incident on "white 'arrogance,'" and naming "segregation as the cause of it all."[73] Thus they obscured the foundational, ontological issue of anti-blackness by implicating one of its many manifestations—the political economy of Jim Crow segregation—instead.

Executive Secretary Adair made it clear that "if the [NAACP] heads the fund raising for Morris, contributors and solicitors would be safeguarded from the brand of Communism through the use of NAACP receipt books and a careful screening of solicitors." This was all the more pressing because Sam Davis, district attorney, had already implied that he "expect[ed] a group of Communists out of New York" to get involved with raising funds for Morris's defense. The *Informer* reported that it was "swamped" with interest in the nascent defense fund by "people of both races who are known not to be Communists." The paper proposed that the extraordinary attention resulted from "the increasing number of reports that Negro men riding some of the buses had been beaten on the buses and some had been taken off in cars and beaten before the arrest of Morris."[74]

Together, black Houstonians mounted Morris's defense. Lulu B. White, responsible for "revitalizing the Houston NAACP" in the late 1930s, and her businessman husband, Julius White, were central to the fund-raising effort. Julius White asserted, "We believe there is more behind the scenes of this case than the newspapers are telling." He speculated, "Johnny Lee was jumped on that bus," and concluded, "We are going to get a lawyer who will represent him fairly." Over the next two weeks, the fund, which was officially set up to assure that Morris received his "fair trial," was "steadily on the increase." Black and white Houstonians donated funds, and NAACP solicitors claimed "every area in the county is responding overwhelmingly."[75]

With more than $5,000 raised, the NAACP retained the services of Houston lawyers Henry Doyle, William J. Durham, and Thomas H. Dent, a trio that would come to be known as the "3 Ds" for their cooperative efforts in Houston's civil rights movement. Dent was a graduate of Howard University's law school and "the first Negro ever to be admitted to a southern bar group." He was known for successfully obtaining a reversal of the death sentence of Herman Lee Ross of Galveston County in 1949. Dent successfully argued that Ross had been denied due process because of systematic racial discrimination in the process of grand jury selection. (The Supreme Court's ruling in Ross's case was quite narrow, guaranteeing no right to a diverse jury, but rather instructing lower courts on how to satisfy the veneer of democratic inclusivity. Ross was eventually executed. Even at a mere one hundred pounds, he was described in familiar anti-black tropes of superhuman monstrosity at the scene of his own execution by the state of Texas: "At the railing in the death chamber, the gnome-sized man broke free of his guards and lunged at [Don] Reid [a man who watched 129 executions], grabbing with tremendous, powerful arms.")[76]

Durham, coming from his practice in Dallas, worked with Thurgood Marshall to successfully convince the Supreme Court of the unconstitutionality of the University of Texas's segregated law school. Durham's win in *Sweatt v. Painter* (1950) gained him significant notoriety. Doyle had just graduated from the law school at Texas State University for Negroes the previous year as its first graduate and as "the first black graduate of any Texas law school," and it became primarily his responsibility to "ensure that Morris's constitutional rights to due process and equal protection under the law . . . were enforced." Morris's case would be a springboard for Doyle's distinguished career as an attorney and a judge. For now, however, this newly hired defense team had to ensure that Morris received his "fair trial."[77]

The Trappings of Legal Procedure
What made a trial "fair" was whether it followed proper procedure, gave a hearing to all defense complaints, and avoided explicit appeals to race. This had been a standard, colloquial understanding of fairness among black Houstonians and, by the 1950s, was also Supreme Court precedent following the infamous Scottsboro cases. Judge A. C. Winborn, presiding over Morris's trial, was unwilling to have his decisions remanded or cases successfully appealed, and so was adept at meeting these procedural standards.[78]

Morris's defense team first attempted to implicate the police in his unlawful detainment, complaining that he had been kept in custody by Sheriff Kern without bond since October 14. With one witness testifying that Nowak began the physical confrontation by pushing Morris, albeit "not hard," Doyle believed there was enough to reasonably doubt that Morris had acted with malice aforethought. Winborn decided against the protest.[79] In an effort to have Morris's confession and the recovered knife thrown from evidence, attorney Dent tried another equal protection tactic, arguing that Houston police illegally took evidence from the Morris residence "some time between 9:30 P.M. and 10:30 P.M." on the night of his arrest while Morris "was in his home . . . conducting himself in a peaceable and law-abiding manner and not violating any laws of the State of Texas." (Of course, Morris was violating anti-miscegenation laws, which, according to Texas criminal statute, was an "offense against public peace" akin to conspiracy to murder, polgyamy, incest, and beastiality. Dent dared the court to make this an issue.)[80] Following his arrest, police questioned Morris "continuously" for three or four hours until about three o'clock in the morning. Dent claimed that police subjected him to threats of "physical violence," that two officers, Alvin Baker and Red Williams, did physically assault Morris, and that investigators ultimately forced him to sign confessions that he neither wrote nor understood. Winborn denied these protests as well.[81]

Hoping to acquire a jury more representative of Houston's demography, Dent pointed out that the all-white Grand Jury Commission appointed by Winborn himself fit historical and statistical evidence of the "purposeful, systematic, and intentional" exclusion of black residents in Harris County from the commission over the course of more than forty years. Drawing on the Supreme Court's decision in *Norris v. Alabama* (1935), Dent presented that of the "31000 [black] male citizens" above twenty-one years old in the county, "more than seventy-five percent . . . were intelligent citizens, and were able to read and write the English language." He continued, noting that these men were all "eligible to vote" and had never been indicted or convicted of any felonies "at any time." In conclusion, he argued, "But, notwithstanding all of the foregoing facts, [Judge Winborn] in the selection of said Grand Jury Commissioners included only white citizens . . . and excluded from the [Commission] all members of the Negro race and of African descent on account of race and color." Indeed, within the forty years preceding Morris's trial, only four black men had been selected as grand jury commissioners, and as a result of this "deliberate . . . exclusion and limitation" of black grand jurors in criminal cases involving black defendants, Morris's indictment was necessarily a violaton of the equal protection clause of the Fourteenth Amendment according to precedent set in *Carter v. Texas* (1900).[82]

Criminal district attorney Sam W. Davis denied all of Dent's allegations and conclusions. The D.A. argued that "at all times the District Judges of Harris County" have been aware "that a great proportion of the population" of the county "was composed of members of the negro race," and that the judges' decisions in appointing grand jury commissioners were based solely on the judges' collective desire "to have a fair, honorable, representative group of qualified citizens." He also noted that all members of the jury commission were "instructed" that they "not discriminate" when it came to the selection of grand jury members, but instead create a grand jury that was representative of "a cross-section of the qualified citizens of Harris County." Davis also noted that since May 1939, "[P]ractically every grand jury has contained a member or members of the colored race." He also recorded that there were "two members of the colored race" on the grand jury that true-billed Morris's indictment.[83]

Winborn decided in the prosecution's favor by inventing a technicality, saying that the Scottsboro cases did not address historical discrimination in the selection of grand jury *commissioners*: "We are aware of no case from the Supreme Court of the United States holding that an indictment in a state court may be invalidated solely because racial discrimination, within the meaning of the 14th Amendment, had entered into the selection and organization of the jury commissioners." Judge Winborn and his two predecessors, Langston King and Frank Williford, all of whom were called as witnesses before the appellate court, testified that "it had never been [their] purpose" to "discriminate against any particular race or in favor of any particular race" in selecting their grand jury commissioners. Nevertheless, neither King nor Winborn were able to certify that they had ever chosen black citizens to sit on their grand jury commissions. Williford had appointed all of the four black men who had served as commissioners since 1928. When Morris appealed to the Supreme Court, Texas attorney general John Ben Shepherd argued that there was no precedent regarding racially biased selection of grand jury commissions and opined that if they allowed for a reversal of the lower court's decision based on discrimination by judges, a slippery slope of racial discrimination lawsuits at every level of the trial would bombard the courts. The Supreme Court sided with Shepherd, and the purpose was not justice, but rather the containment of justice, lest its realization lay bare the depravity and chicanery of the whole criminal legal system.[84]

Despite what many viewed as victories in the Supreme Court's Scottsboro decisions, the relationship between blackness and whiteness remained in stasis. The fate of the Scottsboro boys testified to this fact, and so did Morris's trial. Morris had no right to a demographically representative grand or petit jury. But more important than that—given that he very well may have been convicted by a jury that included the kind of Negro who could survive a prosecutor's peremptory challenge because of internalized anti-blackness and a fealty to whiteness—Morris also had no right to a jury that was ideologically representative of the will of the majority of black Houstonians. To rule in his favor would cause great inconvenience to the court because, to infer from Shepherd's argument, the practice of racial exclusions in the selection of grand jury commissioners must have been standard judicial behavior.

With no success in having Morris's indictments quashed, the attorneys proceeded to jury selection on December 10 and continued for two days.[85] The court summoned two hundred Harris County residents from the voter roles. At the time, both the defense and prosecution were entitled to fifteen peremptory challenges.[86] By the morning of December 13, the jury was ready to be seated but the result skewed in the prosecution's favor. Of the two hundred called to the jury pool, only twelve had been black. Willie Johnson was immediately struck; the note left next to her name in red ink indicated that she was "female colored." District Attorney Davis exercised eleven of his peremptory strikes to remove all remaining members of "the Negro race" from the jury. Davis could have justified some of his strikes because some of the potential black jurors opposed the death penalty, but he was never compelled to explain to the court why he removed all the black citizens. Meanwhile, out of the remaining 188 white jurors, the prosecution used no peremptory strikes and only excused two with cause: one for admitting having a fixed opinion on the case and the other for opposing the death penalty.[87]

Dent immediately filed a motion to quash the trial jury. He argued that Sam Davis and special prosecutor Spurgeon Bell, both white men, had "deliberately, intentionally, purposefully, and systematically" excluded the possibility of having any black jurors "on account of race and color" alone. The defense attorney pressed that the district attorney and all attorneys working with him were "performing a governmental function," and were therefore especially beholden to constitutional provisions of equal protection and due process. Dent maintained that this was not an isolated event: the exclusion of black people from the petit jury in Morris's case "was done under a custom, system and practice inaugurated, promulgated and followed by Sam Davis . . . and his predecessors in office" for "more than forty (40) years." The motion narrowed the claim, specifying that Dent was only interested in looking at petit juries in criminal cases where black persons were the alleged assailants in cases with white victims. The systematic exclusion of black men from a given list of veniremen manifested in the fact that even after certain black veniremen disqualified themselves from a jury for reasons such as conscientious objection to the death penalty, the state nevertheless excluded "members of the Negro race on [the] special venire who had met all of the qualifications for jury service and had given no answer or answers to any questions . . . which gave [Davis] the right to challenge said prospective juror or jurors for cause." The result was an all-white, all-male jury of twelve every time.[88]

Anticipating the arguments that black jurors had been both summoned and interrogated, that mixed-race juries were not a legal requirement, and that the peremptory strike relieved attorneys of the burden of justifying their potential juror dismissals, Dent countered with a historical argument. He pointed out that until the 1940 *Smith v. Texas* Supreme Court decision, Harris County criminal district attorneys "pursued a custom and practice of excluding every member of the Negro race . . . called for jury service in a criminal case." The Supreme Court found that such a practice was a violation of the Fourteenth Amendment. Nevertheless, Dent pointed out, the custom had not been changed; the all-white jury outcome remained a central feature in these criminal proceedings with alleged black assailants and white victims. The interrogations of black veniremen was "token compliance," or better, "a semblance of compliance" to the Supreme Court's ruling—a "formality" meant to circumvent what Dent viewed as the substance of the equal protection clause.[89]

Morris's defense team also pointed to direct evidence of discrimination in the selection of his jury. One example was the examination of Jesse Mills, a fifty-six-year-old Harris County resident who swore before the court that he had no fixed opinion of Morris's guilt or innocence, that the race of the defendant would not sway his opinion, and that he had no conscientious scruples with the death penalty. Black Houstonian Sherman Holmes also swore before the court that he would not oppose consigning a deserving man to death. Both of these men and others like them were excused by Davis without cause.[90]

Davis swiftly dismissed the charges against himself, saying that eight of the black veniremen opposed the death penalty and the remaining were dismissed "through the exercise of peremptory challenges," which required no defense. He snorted at the accusation that he worked to "intentionaly exclude members of the negro race from service on the jury" and claimed that several "members of the negro race" had served on juries in criminal cases over the past ten years, "though the exact number is not recalled at this time." Of course, Dent had not asserted that *no* black men had served in *any* criminal cases, but rather that no black men had served on cases involving alleged black assailants and white victims. Nevertheless, with nothing more than a scribbled sentence on Dent's documentation, Winborn overruled the defense's motion. And so the sun set on the thirteenth day of December.[91]

Morris's trial was swift. The charge of the court was given to the jury on December 14, and they returned the verdict on the same day. Specifically, the charge ordered the jury to determine if "Johnny Lee Morris, did with malice aforethought kill Florian Antone Nowak by cutting and stabbing him with a knife." If the jury was convinced that Morris's testimony did "excuse or justify the killing," the defendant was not guilty of murder. Murder was a voluntary act that required a sentence of death or imprisonment for not less than two years. To determine if murder was committed with "malice aforethought," the jury would have to be convinced that Morris was of sound mind and intended to kill Nowak. If the jury believed that Morris was guilty of murder but not with malice aforethought, then they could not assess a penalty of more than five years of imprisonment. Murder without malice aforethought came about from the "immediate influence of sudden passion arising from an adequate cause, by which is meant, such cause as would commonly produce a degree of anger, rage, resentment or terror in a person of ordinary temper sufficient to render the mind incapable of cool reflection." Thus, if the jury believed or had reasonable doubt to believe that Morris was, first, "ordinary," and second, provoked to the point of having his emotional and mental state altered, he would not be guilty of murder with malice aforethought and should receive the lesser sentence.[92]

The court's charge to the jury also specified the circumstances for acquittal. If the jury was convinced of Morris's recounting of the events on the bus or maintained doubts about the circumstances which led to the stabbing, Morris could not be found guilty. In particular, if the jury was compelled by the testimony that Morris had been or was about to be unlawfully assaulted by Nowak, with or without the assistance of Morrison, so much so that Morris believed, regardless of the actual circumstances, that his life or body were at risk, he was to be found not guilty of murder at all. The jury would have to be convinced "beyond a reasonable doubt" that Morris did not have a sensible plea of self-defense in order for the murder charge to stand.[93]

Foreman of the jury H. E. Logan signed his signature under the handwritten verdict and the jury returned to court. They had found Morris guilty of murder with malice aforethought and assessed life in prison.[94] Morris would take appeals all the way to the United States Supreme Court, but to no avail. Practically, the criminal legal system had determined again that it was unreasonable for black Americans to defend themselves against white terror.

Still, black Houstonians, and indeed black Americans, considered the outcome a win. Morris's attorneys had defended him admirably. The prosecutorial team had avoided explicit racial epithets, even as racism was legally permissible during jury selection and in the public campaign against Morris. Most importantly for his peers, Morris's life had been spared despite that he had been convicted of murdering a white man. In fact, the NAACP often considered it a "win" if they could have a black defendant's life spared in a case where the victim was white. For example, in the 1924 case of black Houstonian Luther Collins, the Houston branch of the NAACP was able to win Collins a reversal of his capital sentence. He had been accused of criminal assault of a white woman. Discord among the jurors, fueled by doubt, resulted in a retrial in which he avoided the death penalty, but was sentenced to ninety-nine years in prison—death penalty by another name. This success gave Collins's supporters opportunities to continue the struggle to prove his innocence. By 1926, the state decided there was not enough evidence for further litigation and Collins was released from prison.[95] Still, as historian Lisa Lindquist Dorr discovered through her meticulous analysis of twentieth-century rape cases in Virginia, the ultimate disposition of "not guilty" in Collins's case should not be simplified as an example of justice:

> White southerners' need to achieve equilibrium among the mandates of segregation, white patriarchy, and all kinds of personal interactions created a gap between rhetoric and reality. Not every black man who previously "knew his place" immediately transmogrified into the stereotypical black beast. Not every white woman who made an accusation was a paragon of white female virtue. . . . At the same time, the ability of white elites to show mercy to accused black men through the legal system could be a powerful means of control over the black community, as well as a means of reassuring whites that southern society was just.[96]

Dorr recognized that, over the course of the twentieth century, elite white men sought to unmoor themselves from their social contract with white women—a contract in which white women acquiesced to patriarchal rule to secure protection and provision. White women conjured this contract each time they charged rape, and white men grew weary of having their power co-opted by white women, or, as Dorr articulates it, "[W]hite men no longer believed it their duty to lay down their lives to protect white women from black men."[97] Dorr saw in this development the legal reinforcement of what is commonly abbreviated as rape culture. However, whereas rape culture is often understood to be a matter of patriarchy and misogyny, scholars have documented "an age-old rhetorical technology of sexual racism and power that is often ignored; white female rape of black men."[98] Far from benefiting from patriarchy's prerogatives, black men were still most often found guilty of white women's rape accusations, remained the primary victims of state execution, and meanwhile were paradigmatic invisible victims of sexual assault themselves under white supremacist political economies.⁹⁹ And while Collins eventually was emancipated from prison, I maintain that his ordeal as a prisoner should be understood as a sexual violation.¹⁰⁰

Even then, Collins's successful appeal was anomalous. In 1932, Charles Hamilton Houston and his student, Thurgood Marshall, defended George Crawford, a black man charged with the murder of a white woman, and "won" for him life imprisonment, thereby avoiding the electric chair. This indicated to the attorneys "that there was reasonable doubt sufficient enough to save Crawford's life." George Davis, another black man accused of attempted sexual assault of a white woman in 1932, also avoided the death penalty after a three-judge panel expressed doubt about the evidence. "So twisted was the justice system when black men were accused of crimes against white women," Sherrilyn Ifill writes, "that Davis's sixteen-year sentence was perceived as a victory for the defense, and in a way it was."¹⁰¹

As bailiffs escorted Johnnie Lee Morris out of the courtroom, he passed by his wife, Christine. She kept her gaze straight ahead. When asked by the press about the verdict, she replied, "It was a fair trial. The verdict didn't surprise me. I thought he might even get death." Sid Hilliard, the well-respected black leader representing the Harris County Council of Organizations (HCCO), a meeting ground for the varied civil rights organizations in Houston, responded, "The Southern people showed less prejudice during this trial, and they showed a definite tendency to be fair. But I didn't expect the sentence to be that severe after hearing the testimony."¹⁰²

Morris's case indicated the unchanging structurally antagonistic relationship between blackness and whiteness. Despite the decisions in the Scottsboro trials that preceded his own, Morris still had no equal protection claim recognizable to the US court system at any level of his trial. The practice of legal procedure suggested a standardization of treatment for all persons entering into the court system. Yet the performance of this procedure was trappings—ornamentation that hypnotized onlookers into a reality where the distance between the idea of democratic inclusion was more material than mere dream. Critical race scholars, recognizing that racial disparities still inhere in the American criminal court system, despite the rulings in the interwar-period cases, argue that each was limited in its scope and that while none guaranteed that black Americans would receive equal protections, they did prime white Americans to "hide" racial discrimination "in the criminal justice system . . . behind discretion." Indeed, constitutional law scholar Susan N. Herman argues that "fairness" was a standard manufactured by the courts and that the decisions in the Scottsboro cases eschewed the question of "equality," which, in a liberal humanist utopia, would critically consider the historical consequences of racial discrimination in court proceedings and case law as pivotal to ensuring due process. Contrary to this fantasy, in the late twentieth century, the Supreme Court decided in *McCleskey v. Kemp* (1987) that empirical evidence of racial discrimination against black defendants in death penalty sentences was not enough to prove that the defendant, Warren McCleskey, had been personally discriminated against when he too was sentenced to death in Georgia after killing a white Atlanta police officer. If anything, legal scholar Michael J. Klarman contends, the Scottsboro cases helped mobilize black communities to become active participants in an increasingly noisy civil rights agenda in the mid-twentieth century. However, insofar as legal impact was concerned, the cases did not necessarily yield greater procedural or civil rights for black Americans. "The most that *Norris* seems to have accomplished anywhere—and even then only large cities in the peripheral South," Klarman wrote, "was place a single black person onto an occasional jury."[103]

The Supreme Court continued to wrestle with—perhaps "against," but not impressively or uncompromisingly so—explicit racial discrimination in the nation's lower courts through the following decades to excise procedural errors that violated their interpretations of the Fourteenth Amendment. Of course, getting prosecutors and attorneys to avoid making errors was not the same thing as ensuring justice or redefining due process, even if the trial was deemed "fair." The courts thereby beckoned the postracial era and its practices of anti-black denialism. In pursuit of this future, already taking shape within the political economy of Jim Crow, the agents of the court had learned to hide any *intent* to discriminate against Morris on the basis of race. In this way, for Communist sympathizers in such racially charged criminal cases, the Supreme Court was responsible for taking "great care to instruct" lower courts on how to legally execute "lynch schemes" while restoring faith in the moral authority of the criminal court system. By the time of Morris's trial, then, he was still subject to the racialized machinations of the Harris County criminal courts—a system that had adapted to the new normal in the Supreme Court's application of the equal protection clause. In other words, fairness as material (rather than a mere idea) simply meant following procedures that understood racism as a matter of intent rather than anti-black violence that can be conscious and not, material and discursive, explicit and implicit, and apparent and concealed all at once. Fairness did not require the absence of racial motivation, nor did it engender any challenges to the legitimacy of the legal system itself.[104]

Finally, it is also significant that Morris's trial took place in Houston, a city obsessed with promoting itself as the seat of racial tolerance in the South. Black Houstonians imagined their home to be the Chicago of tomorrow, the next great metropolis, and a city where even black people could realize their economic dreams. They pointed to tumultuous Little Rock and battle-scarred Dallas as Houston's antithesis; Houston was the region's "leader in moral integrity and courage." That is, if Morris was going to receive a procedurally fair trial in Texas, Houston was perhaps his best option. Heavenly Houston's narrative of itself functioned as an additional kind of capture that easily lent to confirmation bias. Black supporters lauded what they saw as their city's relative propensity for civility and race-blind justice and banked their vision for a raceless, liberal democratic future on that perception.[105]

This vision belied the capture that defined Morris's life and rested on a progressivist assumption of the ultimate deracialization of the United States, an assumption that his case ultimately refuted, but a refutation that was occluded by the narrative of progress. Even now, syntactically, the words that name my argument seem redundant and always folding into each other, denying disentanglement. In Houston, bound in a body blackened by the legal and customary violences that produce race and racial subjectivity, Morris was relegated to a low-paying job as a longshoreman, was unable to legally remain married to his wife, was compelled to live in a small apartment in the economically declining Fourth Ward, was denigrated while trying to board a bus, was apprehended by the general public as a person without a right to self-defense against a white man, was unlawfully but apparently legally detained by violence workers without access to counsel, was placed on trial before an all-white jury with no legal recourse to challenge this blatant racial discrimination, and was sentenced to life in prison in a trial that signified for his supporters that fair justice had been accomplished.

CODA: DISCIPLINARY CAPTURE AND THE METHODS TRAP

As did Morris's contemporaries, some historians might prefer to interpret the evidence herein as proof of what was possible. Hannu Salmi provides a compelling argument for "the possible and the principle of plenitude," arguing that respect for contingency is critical to the historian's job. Salmi's argument hinges on a dichotomy between "'historical realism,' the view that history is composed entirely of observable actions that actually occurred," and "anti-realist" history that emphasizes, either singularly or alongside more realist narrative accounts, "many abandoned possibilities" if this or that thing, person, or motivation had been different. Histories, especially of civil rights struggles, tend to be anti-realist in this sense, much like Morris's supporters, who, despite not securing any recognition of black people's right to self-defense, considered his life sentence a win. For them it pointed to future possibilities in Houston's racial system. Indeed, scholars have argued, "What was won must be judged by what was possible." Therefore, "small victories" count. In narrating those victories, historians have convinced themselves that they "have indeed been successful in restoring the 'humanity and agency of working-class black men and women' in the longer freedom struggle of the twentieth century."[106]

I argue otherwise, not situating this chapter as realist or anti-realist. Against the notions of realism and objectivity, I understand history as a narrative liberal art—a *"literary"* form."[107] More to the point, alongside Hayden White, I understand history as fiction.[108] This is not to say that this story of Johnnie Lee Morris that I have reconstructed is false or that it is a lie, but rather that the act of historical narration required that I necessarily meet an already narratively constituted archive with an already constituted political position. If I were a realist, for example, I could not impute racist intent to Davis's striking of all the black veniremen without explicit evidence of said motivation. I nevertheless infer this from the material facts that given Davis's history as a prosecutor and what he practiced in Morris's trial, he and his actions were racist. And throughout the chapter I have made plain my refusal to engage in speculations that seek to elide the severity of the white terrorist violence that is required for the production of blackness. Rather, I approached these archives through Afropessimism—namely, its insistence on "moving conceptually from the empirical to the structural or, more precisely, from the experiential to the political ontological."[109] Understanding that *"perspective* is more vital than *method* for confronting the order of knowledge on which slaveholding rests," my gaze has been focused by the paradigmatic relationship between whiteness and blackness that was evidenced in Morris's case and continues to manifest in the twenty-first century: from George Floyd's murder, to mass mobilization in his name, to legislative reform, and to white racist retrenchment once again.[110]

Method did not play an inconsequential part in the construction of this narrative. I employed the quasi-antidisciplinary tools of Hartman's critical fabulation and Kazanjian's critical speculation alongside disciplinary archival narrative and citation practices.[111] But the twofold purpose of method is to legitimate the authority of the academic disciplines and to discipline academics, making certain ways of thinking and writing impermissible and justifying this impermissibility through a grammar of testability, replicability, and authority.

My theoretical orientation is such that method is subsidiary to perspective, so I am nonplussed by the historical discipline's creed against presentism. The Morris case *should* make us think about the ways democracy still captures the long civil rights movement and its most recent offspring, the Movement for

Black Lives. And inasmuch as this is not a criticism of Morris, his attorneys, or his supporters, it is not an indictment of anti-racist struggle today. Rather, it is an invitation to consider the ways anti-racist thought and action are produced within a racist system and therefore unwittingly rely on the grammars of the racist system in order to articulate grievance and mobilize action.

As I interpret Morris's travails as a man who lost his life to an intransigent racist judicial system—but moreover, who lived his life in a society fundamentally structured by intractable racial categories—to name his avoidance of the death penalty a win or to suggest his defiance on the bus and his attorney's work as agency would amount to professional hubris. Even his defense team was bound by the procedural rules, the definitions of fairness, and the conceit of written law itself within the selfsame racist institutions that captured Morris.

This is not a denial of the significance of context. Morris may have avoided capital punishment because his trial took place in Houston. *That was significant for him.* But this chapter is not precisely about Morris the person; it is about Morris's case as a paradigmatic example. Houstonians' ability to reject explicit appeals to race in criminal proceedings did not fundamentally alter the structural relationship that relegated Morris to the status "black" in the first place. Indeed, the whole of Morris's case was structured and captured by the stubborn relationship between whiteness and blackness and through appeals to "human" equality through the lexicon and self-asserted power of the law. Speculating about contingencies is not critical work. Wondering what could have altered the outcome would not alter the outcome. But imagining what was "possible" *does* serve as an attractive distraction from the viciousness of what was and what remains. So, instead, if we think about the critical work of history of/as the present, speculating about contingency only renders visible what historians wish was possible *then* to avoid recognizing the foundational anti-blackness of the social structure that persists even *now*.[112] This is the disciplinary capture I attempt to avoid in order to tell the truth about the present as we (historians) do the very political work of acknowledging a past that has not yet passed away. Indeed, Morris's travails continue to have purchase on the present not as a specter haunting the historian, but rather because those travails indicate the gravitational pull of anti-blackness on the lives of the no-humans-involved who remain the blood sacrifice, even through their faithful struggles for "equality," that sustains the tenuous claims of liberal democracy and Americanness itself: that we are all human and the law makes us or has the capacity to make us equal.

While black and white Houstonians existed in a structurally antagonistic relationship, they were still bound together in the material world. They certainly depended on each other economically. However, at an ontological level, whiteness also acquired its value only in contrast to the devaluation of people marked as black. (Is this any less true at the moment you read this than it was in 1951?) This was the underlying conflict that locked Morris, as it did Adair, in temporal stasis. As we have seen, both these figures in black Houston's history resisted their devaluation. But in each case they could only do so by relying on the same logics they held together with white folks as Americans: a faith in the inherent progressiveness of liberal humanism. This faith would also undergird the claims of Dorothy and Jack Caesar, a black couple who ventured to buy a home in a white Houston neighborhood. Like Morris, they would "win" this fight—sort of. Ultimately, however, their struggles revealed a material linchpin of the structural relationship between whiteness and blackness— indeed, the problem that inaugurated my encounter with Houston's archives: residential segregation. The power of the law and the seeming indisputability of property holding as a human right wed black political imagination to the very institutions that made them eligible to become possessions while negating their capacity to properly own themselves or to possess objects of their own.

3
CAPTURED IN THE IMPOSSIBLE AMERICAN DREAM
Dorothy and Jack Caesar Buy a Home

> Anti-black violence and stolen life define the very foundation of the settler state. Captivity, whether understood as slavery or debt peonage or the enclosure of the ghetto or incarceration, continues to be the prevailing schema.
>
> Saidiya Hartman, "The Dead Book Revisited," *History of the Present*

On April 17, 1953, Carl Dewey "Red" Davis ignited four sticks of dynamite on the front porch of Jack and Dorothy Caesar's home. Since the Caesars had moved into the neighborhood in 1952, white residents had been fighting to return the neighborhood to a white-only residential enclave. Aside from an incident on New Year's Eve when the Caesars' roof was littered with fireworks, the family lived without physical attacks on their property until April 1953. According to fifty-one-year-old Davis, George Howell, a fifty-six-year-old insurance company owner and vice president of the Greater Riverside Terrace Homeowners Association, had been hiring him for various jobs for about three weeks. Howell, an ex-convict who had been in federal prison for committing fraud, called Davis, also an ex-convict with a five-year suspended sentence for attempted murder, into his office one afternoon and instructed him, "I want you to blast that nigger house across the street" for five hundred dollars. Three weeks prior to the attack on the Caesars' home, Davis went to Rosenburg to buy dynamite. He turned over the material to Howell, who prepared the four sticks for detonation. On the week of the twelfth of April, Howell announced that he was ready to go through with the plan. On April 16, Davis left his room at the Standard Hotel, located downtown, caught a bus toward Riverside, and then slept in the back seat of a car until about four o'clock on Friday morning. He explained, "I took the dynamite out of the car and walked across the street (Hutchins Street) from the Howells' house to the niggers' house. I stopped on the steps of the niggers' house and lit the fuse. I set the dynamite near the pillar and walked off."[1] Christia Adair, executive secretary of the Houston NAACP, received a call in the darkness of the early morning. The voice on the other side frantically alerted her: "Mrs. Adair, they have burned down Jack Caesar's home."[2]

This chapter is about black Houstonians' dreams—dreams that seemed to inevitably yield to nightmares. The Caesars had done everything they were supposed to: they had built wealth in a capitalist society, and they used their economic resources to try to secure what they imagined was a better life for their family. However, their dreams were incommensurate with their political condition: they remained captured in blackness, incarcerated by race.

Following Calvin Warren, blackness was not about identity, but rather the sign given to nothingness. An animating research question might be, "Why was the Caesar house bombed?" The answer, "because they were black," is troubling. Their skin color did not *cause* the bombing; this interpretation, which appears like racecraft, is incorrect in one sense. However, in a different reading, because blackness refers to nothing, "because they were black" means they were bombed for nothing—for no reason. There is no meaning to be uncovered here, no great plotting of a historical arc toward justice or racial democracy to be found. This answer is terrifying because it commands a reckoning with the senselessness of the whole social context—a reckoning that compels us to admit that "the law" is a political construct, based not on some greater or natural Law, but rather on the whims and will of people who wield incommensurate power. Thus, the notion of being made equal under the law, because that is simply what the rule of law means, is revealed as a decoy. The outcome of the Caesar case, like the outcome of the Johnnie Lee Morris case, demonstrated empirically that the law did not place limits on the prerogatives of white supremacy, but rather white supremacy dictated the meaning and execution of the law toward its own interests. In other words, there is nothing inherent in the law that makes people equal.

Rather than actually referring to some universal law that can be objectively obtained, the "rule of law" refers to itself for its own legitimacy: it claims itself as justification for its own rule on the basis of being nonarbitrary (as, say, opposed to autocracy). The law both delineates a sphere in which it applies and can be enforced and defines its own limit, establishing a zone outside of its own jurisdiction—a "zone of exception"—so as to appear to be nonarbitrary. Out there (no-where) is the world of lawlessness, where morality, responsibility, recognition, and meaning itself are suspended. There takes place the rape of the slave, the selling away of their kin, the lynching of the black voter, the bombing of the black home and church, the segregation of the black soldier in a war for democracy, the torture of the black body in a jail cell, the knee on the neck until death. There is plenty of violence in that formless void (no-where), but death alone does not inhere with meaning. The violence does not register as a crisis for the law, because despite the law's self-justification through the discourse of liberal universalism, it is a universalism proscribed by political borders, racial signification, and economic markets.[3]

Thus, the bombing of the Caesar home "because they were black" *can* shift attention away from the meaninglessness of the law, but it should compel us to recognize and grapple with that meaninglessness. Despite that bombing another's home was legally codified as a criminal violation, white Americans bombed the homes of black Americans with impunity throughout the twentieth century, whether in acts of individual terror such as the bombing of the Anderson home in Berkeley, California, in 1918, the 1923 mob destruction of black homes and businesses in Rosewood, Florida, or the attacking of black homes by the state itself, as happened in 1985 when the Philadelphia police dropped a bomb of Tovex and C-4 on a residential neighborhood.[4] Indeed, the Supreme Court has interpreted and sustained its precedents in cases like *U.S. v. Cruickshank* (1876) and *Monell v. Dept. of Social Services* (1978) regarding the immunity of individual and state entities from federal prosecution of blatant acts of anti-black terror and other civil rights violations.[5] The losses of life and property, usually sacred under the law, were of no consequence. Indeed, that "life" and "property" could be voided of meaning when the victims were black and when the perpetrators worked in service of white supremacy demonstrated the emptiness of those terms, which are hegemonically understood as if they inhere with irreducible value. Anti-black violence, then, was "gratuitous, without reason or constraint."[6] And its justifications, "because they were black," or because they moved into a white neighborhood, or because their presence depreciated home values, or insert whatever justification ad nauseam, serve as the decoy from the fact of its gratuitousness, lest this lack of reason undermine the foundational ideas and ideals of the rule of law, democracy, and value itself.

Thus black Houstonians, including the Caesars, remained deracinated people, trapped in a permanent zone of indistinction, responsible to the dictates of the law but guaranteed no protection under the law. The order of racial slavery that ushered in the modern world "established permanent and hereditary slavery of the most onerous sort," which Robin Blackburn calls the "Great Captivity."[7] Living the afterlife of racialized chattel slavery, the Caesars' circumstances revealed the continuity between their own political status and those of their ancestors: a people counterposed to modernity's dominant genre of the human and ineligible for the rights, protections, and value ascribed to Man. In this way, the Caesars' story is one among millions that have already been told and that expose the long-lived depravity of anti-blackness and the deprivation suffered by black people as its price.[8]

The Caesars' story can be instructive in an additional way because of the peculiarity of Houston's local identity. The narratives Houstonians told themselves about their city shaped what they imagined was possible. Houstonians, black and white, understood themselves as exceptional, and their city as an aberration from "the South" and Texas. "Heavenly Houston" was a city of progress, a leader in business, the arts, and race relations, they would often argue. Whether Houston's uniqueness was real or imagined, mainstream black Houstonians shared with their white counterparts a perception that their city challenged what it meant to be of and to live in "the South." If the arbitrary racial terror of "the South" threatened to expose the meaninglessness of the law and to reveal that value was socially and politically constructed, then Houston's self-image served to restore meaningfulness to the law and secure value as a mere fact of existence. If Houston could appear to integrate its schools without one incident of "newsworthy" mass violence, if house bombers could be prosecuted and convicted in court by an all-white jury, if a similar jury could spare the life of a black man who killed a white man, and if economic interests could trump racial antipathies, then so too could Houston realize a future where color did not restrict life outcomes, black Houstonians dreamed, because for them humanity held within it intrinsic value that could not be forever circumscribed.[9]

As middling and self-identified middle-class women and men, socialized to believe in the possibilities of economic mobility afforded by American capitalism, the Caesars and like-minded black civil rights leaders remained invested in and captured by narratives of individual uplift, meritocracy, and democratic equality.[10] These were treated as if they inhered with value—as if a doctrine of democratic equality in the modern world was not preconditioned on racial slavery, which referred to racial categories that themselves referred to nothing real. Thus, theirs was not a vision of a new way of life, but rather a desire to assimilate—to transmogrify the black object into a human subject, recognized by all other humans as such. We might call this the politics of recognition. Within the constraints of their world, this was an impossible task, for as Lewis Gordon argues, "Against the raceless credo . . . racism cannot be rejected without a dialectic in which humanity experiences a blackened world."[11] In other words, while the Caesars deployed a bourgeois politics of recognition to claim an unrestricted legal right to home ownership and thus demanded incorporation of black people into the white world, they did not develop a politics of redistribution, whereby white folks would have to become black. Becoming black would not be a change in racial identity, for this would not be about identity politics and recognition. Rather, becoming black would mean, among other things, experiencing the meaninglessness of dispossession and the insecurity of a freedom contingent on the whimsical racial organization of the world. Such a mandate necessarily inaugurates the end of *this world*.[12] But this was and remains an impermissible hypothetical. The Caesars' attempts to realize the assimilationist dream of black incorporation into a white world hypostatized the human as a biological and ontological fact, even as the absolute exclusion of black folks from this state of being was precisely the condition that made assimilation a desire *in the first place*. Indeed, it is worth repeating: what an impossible task.

The Impossible American Dream, however, was intoxicating. It beckoned the Caesars and other black Houstonians to white neighborhoods and new black suburbs where they imagined escape from the deprivations of black inner-city living: the violence, the congestion, the pollution, the economic heterogeneity, as well as the municipal neglect, the police brutality, and the underfunded schools.[13] But black Houstonians were not safe in the suburbs either.[14] Whereas other scholars have argued that postwar demographic shifts in the form of white flight and concurrent divestments of tax dollars and employment opportunities precipitated the dual urban crises of economic depression and hardening racial segregation, this chapter demonstrates that it was not the materiality of urban living, the blackening of urban spaces, or a "new" political conservatism that perpetuated an anti-black racialized political economy amid Jim Crow's demise. While urban historians have helped us understand the various mechanisms and politics that intensified the deprivations experienced by black Americans in the postwar era, theirs is an approach of analyzing relational contingencies that I endeavor to avoid.[15]

Following Foucault's call to genealogy, historians have searched for the "origins of the urban crisis," but for Tryon P. Woods, employing "Foucauldian methodology for the study of race is the multicultural academy's postracial quarantine of independent black thought."[16] The purpose, of course, is to contribute to thought, to intervene in the literature—in essence, to constitute meaning by way of historical narrative. But what if "the urban crisis" is meaningless? If the body of urban historiography has taught us anything, and if Houston's peculiar landscape in that body of work elucidates anything, it is that whether urban or suburban; located in the North, South, or West; working class or middling; before or after Jim Crow's legal defeats; concerning the Philadelphia Negro in the 1890s, Black Houstonians in the mid-twentieth century, or African American communities in the late twentieth century, anti-black racism sustained environmental, economic, and social crises within the cartographic boundaries of neighborhoods marked as black. If anti-blackness exceeds all these contingencies, then the violence is not contingent, but gratuitous, and gratuitousness lacks genealogy.

In turn, Afropessimism refuses genealogy, for while "Foucault's genealogy regards history as the organization and reorganization of power/knowledge regimes, with each new episteme signaling a break into a new order, from the millennium-plus paradigm of black struggle, these changes amount to quantitative disruptions that do not rise to the level of a qualitative transformation in how the world sees itself."[17] Indeed, when the Caesars and other black folks moved to Houston's suburbs, their quotidian living conditions may have improved in some ways, but when they pushed against the boundaries of racial segregation and when black suburbs sought municipal resources that had long been hoarded by white communities, they were reminded that they were still the wretched of the earth.[18] Terror preceded their claims for recognition. In fact, terror was their precondition. And, necessarily, terror also followed.

The Caesars' travails appear as a mere instance of spectacular anti-black violence within this chapter because this chapter is not about the Caesars per se. It is rather a meditation on the ways fascination with and capture by the narrative of the American Dream intersects with the racial capture of blackness to make it appear as if the daily nightmares of black existence are dreams deferred rather than fever dreams.

George Howell and Carl Davis were not the only terrorists in the Caesars' story. The family bought their home through a white liaison because they were already terrified. They moved into their home under the cover of night because they were already terrified. They kept their curtains closed and stayed inside their home because they were already terrified. But to rewind a bit more, they felt a compulsion to escape their Negro neighborhood because the racialization of residential space had been a terror for every black person. Indeed, a meditation on the history of Houston's Third Ward begs the question: under what pretense could black Houstonians have imagined a peaceful incorporation into the world that exacted so much terror against them in order to sustain its value for white people? Moreover, beyond the urbanized Third Ward, the experience of black suburbanites reveals that neither economic class nor levels of urbanity provided meaning to (that is, they could not explain away) the problems that burdened black communities.

It is a "sincere fiction," repeated still today, that Houston desegregated without racial violence.[19] The high rates of stress, anxiety, and trauma that

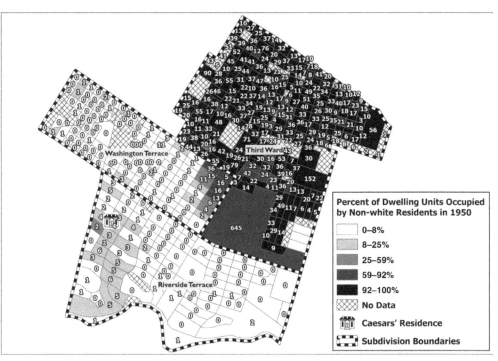

Map 7 *The Third Ward, Washington Terrace, and Riverside Terrace boundaries and blocks, labeled by the total number of nonwhite-occupied dwelling units per block in 1950. Those small numbers of black residences outside of the black Third Ward were nearly all servants' quarters until after* Shelley v. Kraemer.

black Americans expressed as a result of *everyday* racism cannot be overstated. Racism was the violence that produced race—the violence that constituted what it meant to be made black in the first place. And blackness signaled a political condition well before it was taken on as an identity.[20] If terrorism is defined by the threat of or use of violence to meet political ends, in this case the end being race itself, then this *everyday* racism was terrorism. The Caesars sought to escape the terrors of living as black in a black neighborhood, only to find that it was not the demography of the neighborhood that constrained their life chances. Rather, they were chained to blackness, and remained moored to this political status regardless of how high they climbed economically or how far they moved geographically. But their faith in Americanism did not diminish, because to allow its dissolution would command a reckoning with the possibility that there was nothing of value in the dream. To be captured in the dream of a (racial) democracy allowed black and white Americans alike to avoid the empirical reality: that anti-black terror allowed the world to secure meaning for itself at a price that exceeded all moral reason.

Captured in the Impossible American Dream

THE IMPOSSIBLE AMERICAN DREAM

Riverside Terrace had only been "white-only" in the sense that only people defined as "white" could own or rent property in the subdivision due to racially restrictive covenants developers had placed in property deeds—restrictions enforceable until *Shelley v. Kraemer* (1948). However, since its development, the community of Riverside Terrace had benefited from the movement of black domestic workers and servants across Blodgett Street, the thoroughfare that marked its northern border with the predominantly black section of Third Ward. Some white residents even had black workers live in servants' quarters on their families' lots. This necessary proximity to black laborers was one indication that Houston's Jim Crow was not a project of complete racial separation, but one of "structured intimacies."[21] It was indicative of the paradox of existing as black: both negated and necessary, stripped of *human* value but full of extractable *inhuman* potential, black as/like coal.[22] The presence of black Houstonians as servants in Riverside Terrace did not challenge that structure.

In 1952, Jack Caesar, who ran Caesar Brothers, a company that traded cattle out of the Port City Stockyards, asked his white male secretary to purchase a home in Riverside Terrace for him. The Caesars were actually not the first black family to move into the MacGregor area; the president of the Negro Chamber of Commerce, Rodney Hoggatt, had already moved his family onto Alabama Street in Washington Terrace, and several black families lived "unmolested in garage apartments" in Riverside Terrace's alleyways "for as many as ten years."[23] Despite this, despite having the capital, and despite that racial restrictions in deed covenants were no longer enforceable, the Caesars faced considerable obstacles in buying a home outside of the city's "black" neighborhoods. Nevertheless, Jack and Dorothy Caesar remained committed to moving into superior housing than that available to most black Houstonians. Mr. Caesar made it clear that he did not buy the home to gain proximity to white people, and Mrs. Caesar confirmed this sentiment, saying, "We had no interest in being neighbors to white people, we were only interested in finding a house we wanted. . . . This is the house we wanted."[24]

Jack Caesar's secretary purchased a home at 2202 Wichita Street in Riverside Terrace through a real estate agent, after which, for a fee, he transferred the papers to Caesar.[25] The Caesars moved into their new seven-room home on a spring night in 1952. One white neighbor remembered it was odd:

> Well, nobody normally moves into a new house or their new house in the middle of the night . . . It did provide a lot of panic and it

immediately started people worrying about the value of their homes going down, et cetera et cetera, and would it be safe to continue living there. . . . It came up so fast, and you know—in the panic and the excitement of the moment the reaction is violence. Violence. They shouldn't do that. They should move in the daytime like everybody else does, you know.²⁶

Another woman who lived directly across the street from the Caesars remembered how quickly rumors spread: Riverside Terrace residents assumed the Caesars were "very wealthy," that they "owned some nightclubs on Dowling Street," or that they were funded by the NAACP to force integration. The only things most Riverside residents could know for sure were that the Caesars were quiet and rarely made themselves visible. Still, "people were really miffed because they felt that the neighborhood would not be the same."²⁷

The interviewee's words are revealing. Although her words compel us to look to the normative—people move into their new homes while the sun is out—her literal phrasing, "nobody normally moves into a new house . . . in the middle of the night" revealed the lack of ontological standing the Caesars had in their world. They had, in fact, moved in the dead of night because they experienced the world as nobodies. They possessed *no body* guaranteed protection from white terrorism and *no body* that could purchase a home in this neighborhood without deceptively deploying (and paying) a somebody/a white body to act as cover. Simultaneously, the Caesars were corporeal, and this was undeniable. But rather than being self-possessed, these corporeal entities were empty vessels. Calvin Warren might call them accursed, entities "unintelligible within the field of ontology." English scholar Elizabeth Maddock Dillon provides additional language, looking to the Haitian vodou concept of the zombie, a ~~being~~ "without essence," "the reduction of the human, in the words of Sylvia Wynter, to 'so many units of labour power.'" Whether subject to the exploitative plantation economies of the Caribbean or those of the Jim Crow South, black people experienced ontological mutilation, reduced to juridical *nobodies* and reanimated as "living corpses" with two functions: to be available for material labor and to be containers of all the fears, anxieties, insecurities, and conflicts of the modern world.²⁸

Black servants had long lived in Riverside Terrace with no concomitant worry among white residents that their presence might diminish their home values because those servants properly occupied their status as laboring instruments. With no meaningful provocation, no evidence that the mere presence of black people necessitated a degraded quality of life in Riverside Terrace, the white community descended into panic as they made the Caesars the embodiment of their preexisting ontological insecurity. Violence followed, the interviewee noted, before a non sequitur that indicted the Caesars as responsible for their own victimization. Had they not moved in the night, she intimated, there would have been no violence. This was the absurd world into which the Caesars sought incorporation, the absurd world they would appeal to for protection in the wake of the bombing.

Ironically, while the residents of Riverside Terrace assumed that the Caesars were wealthy, they still viewed black home ownership in their neighborhood as a harbinger of community decline. No matter their economic standing, the Caesars could not escape the capture of the black image in the white mind. By the time the Caesars moved into the neighborhood, one out of every three housing units there was renter-occupied. Their presence as home owners, then, should have signified investment in the well-being of the neighborhood, but this assumes that the housing market is determined by "pure" economic considerations rather than an economic rationality that is always and already constituted by way of anti-black racism.[29]

Moreover, the Caesars paid a lofty premium for their new home, as did many black families moving into white neighborhoods. The average value of a house on the 2200 block of Wichita Street in 1950 was $18,166. The Caesars paid nearly $8,000 more than that average and invested an additional $3,000 into the home once it was transferred to them. In 1960, only about 15 percent of the homes in Riverside Terrace were worth as much or more than the Caesars's. Thus, their class status likely exceeded that of many of their white neighbors.

Concurrent with *Shelley*, the Supreme Court also decided *Hurd v. Hodge* in 1948, which allowed for racial restrictions to remain in private deeds in Washington, DC, but made them unenforceable by the nation's courts. One of the petitioners, Mrs. Frederic Hodge, requested that the Hurd family, which claimed to be Mohawk and not "Negro," be prevented from occupying property on Bryant Street. When asked if she would prefer an "untidy white person to a negro, no matter how educated or cultured" as a neighbor, Hodge plainly answered: "As long as they are white, I would prefer them." When asked, "Even if the white man just came from jail . . .?" She responded in the affirmative, "Because he is white and I am white."[30] In short, there was no reason that black occupancy might depress property values in formerly all-white neighborhoods.[31] Certainly, the Caesars did not bring crime with them to Riverside Terrace, but they did expose that criminals and racial terrorists, like Howell and Davis, convicted and not, were a ready feature of this white "idyllic" enclave. The problem was never fundamentally a fear of crime or housing values; it was always anti-blackness.

The MacGregor area remained mostly quiet during the initial months following the Caesar family's occupation of their new home, and Caesar opined that it might have been because their neighbors assumed they were live-in domestics for a white family that had not moved in yet. He believed the blatant acts of intimidation began once the neighbors realized he and his wife were permanent owners.[32] The Caesars had good reason to consider they might become victims of more than petty harassment, but they remained confident that Houstonians, white and black, would not tolerate mob violence. The narrative of Houston being a heavenly place for race "relations" was captivating. However, the evidence suggested it was a collective delusion.

In the same year that the Caesars moved to Riverside Terrace, a group of "hoodlums, or bigots, or just plain fools" threw stones into a black family's home, "and made threatening telephone calls to the owners." Houstonians responded swiftly: municipal authorities and law enforcement bluntly condemned the acts of hatred, and "more than five hundred persons, white and Negro, rushed to the aid of the victim, offering to stand around-the-clock watch over the property." The *Informer* praised Houston, believing the reaction was undoubtedly an exception in the "Southern pattern." As liberal humanists, the editors at the *Informer* declared that the "average white readers" of Houston's dailies "have more and more tendency to see their fellow Negro citizens and neighbors in much the same way they see themselves and resent unfairness practiced against them in the same way." Fair treatment based on individual merit, the editorialists at the *Informer* proclaimed, was "the American way—the better way." Houstonians appreciated their city's version of racial tolerance and bemoaned violent actions that threatened to destabilize what they viewed as harmony.[33]

Houston's self-adulation was itself the "decoy" that sold the "poison."[34] It made it seem as if there was nothing impossible, nothing impermissible to dream in the liberal world of Man. And it configured black people's suffering and their constant struggle as an indication of the possibilities that yet awaited them. For the faithful, the destiny of black folks was predetermined by the originary codes of American governance—liberty, democracy, capitalism, and freedom. But these codes were only attained *through* the establishment of racial slavery and maintained via unabating anti-black racism.[35] Historians, too, demonstrate fealty to these codes. Black resistance to slavery—and in this moment I do not mean the political economy of chattel slavery but the appropriation of black people within liberal humanist ontology as objects rather than subjects—gets translated through these codes as an indication of human agency. The Caesars' predicament suggests otherwise: racial capture compelled black people to resist *in the first place*. Liberty and its attendant grammars induce people to "believe that a thing called 'America' exists." So, the story of the Negro, which most often appears to be a teleological one about the accomplishment of a "true" democracy, makes it seem as if the American Dream is possible despite that the actual plot points of the narrative reiterate time and again that which has been and continues to be impossible for black people.[36] The cruelty of this irony showed up for the Caesars in the form of dynamite.

It should have been no surprise, then, that one month after the *Informer* lauded Houstonians for their ascension to racial democracy, the newspaper was again reporting on white terror against black home owners. Carter Wesley wrote that the Caesar family was "being systematically harassed by the white citizens" of Riverside Terrace. Neighbors played pranks on the family ("The Negro is a toy in the white man's hands," Fanon writes) and gathered in "milling groups of men and women around the property."[37] They also made "offers" to "buy the Caesars out" of their home. These incidents received little or no attention in the city's non-black press outlets, a real-time demonstration of the absenting of black people from the archive.[38]

Carter Wesley complained that the police allowed the harassment to continue and did "nothing to protect these people in their home."[39] And while Wesley probably believed home owners were justified in using deadly force to protect their property, he also understood that if the Caesars did "kill some of these people on their land," the act would precipitate police brutality and outrage on the part of white Houstonians, as officials "would be . . . blaming every Negro in the world for 'causing trouble.'" The nation had already witnessed this repeatedly. A prominent case involved black home owner Dr. Ossian Sweet after he bought into a "white" neighborhood in Michigan. Wesley warned Houstonians to proactively condemn the agitators before the city began to resemble Dallas, where white people had made a practice of bombing black homes.[40] The liberties, the democracy that white Americans enjoyed—including the right to protect those rights with armed force—remained unavailable to the Caesars.

With no other recourse and no faith that the Houston Police Department or city leaders would come to their aid, the Caesars entered negotiations with the Greater Riverside Terrace Homeowners Association, a group of white residents led by neighbor Sidney Smiley that offered to buy their house. The home owners' association was created after the Caesars moved in to "keep Negroes out of Riverside Terrace."[41] It managed to collect a little over $13,000 for the purchase of the home; the Caesars were asking for $30,000.[42] The Caesars' lawyer, Jack Ginsburg, who was negotiating with the white group, reported threats against his life and his home. He said that the "organized hoodlums" attacking the Caesars were "worse than Hitlerism or Communism." Ginsburg attempted to gain the support of several law enforcement agencies, including US district attorney Brian S. Odom, but Odom "white-washed the whole thing" and "failed in every respect" to "uphold the Constitution."[43] I follow Ginsburg's sentiment, but as an executioner of the law, Odom's (in)action should push us to think in terms not of the ostensible ideals of the Constitution, but instead of the lived realities under the Constitution. This originary legal document did not merely tolerate black subjugation for 150 years, but rather its very production was made possible by the energy extracted from enslaved people, and even in the wake of the Reconstruction amendments it did not rupture the political conditions that made black people black.

The Caesars were further demoralized when it appeared Rodney Hoggatt, president of Houston's Negro Chamber of Commerce, was attempting to get the family to reduce their asking price in favor of the white group. Mrs. Caesar explained that, in addition to the $26,000 ($308,000 in 2023 dollars) they had paid for the property—about $8,000 more ($95,000 in 2023) than the average value of homes on the block—the family had also invested money into the interior of the house and had ordered custom furniture made specifically for the home's architecture. These were among the expenses they would have to shoulder if they reduced their price.[44] The family eventually agreed to sell the home for $28,250. They bought their home at a premium, but the terror was so great that they were willing to accept a significant loss to escape. However, the Greater Riverside Terrace Homeowners Association failed to raise the money to buy it from them.[45]

The Caesars' troubles did not seem to discourage other black Houstonians with the means from searching for quality homes in formerly white-only neighborhoods. Mattie Marcher Hilliard, a nightclub owner, moved into 2412 Wichita Street and declared she had "no intentions of moving," despite the threats she and the Caesars received.[46] After moving in, Hilliard found the sidewalk in front of her house "lined" with "morbid, angry, anxious and even sympathetic stares from crowds of white people," some of whom prevented her furniture from being delivered. Smiley, of the home owners' association, believed that buying out both families was impossible, and thus stopped negotiations. He said, "Nature will take its course" regarding the future of Riverside Terrace, which in the context of his other remarks, the *Informer* interpreted as a promise of violence. Smiley, for his part, understood that inciting mob violence publicly was not socially acceptable in Houston. Indeed, he condemned the violence in other cities and said that the *Shelley* decision was "a good law," but held that black citizens "should not buy in neighborhoods where they are not wanted." Though he claimed to value the individual rights of the Caesars to own the property, he maintained that the will of the white majority superseded those rights.[47]

For Smiley, the issue was not "segregation or racial," but that "white people 'just don't want Negro neighbors.'" He also believed that the relationship between neighbors was an intimate one, and believed black folks should delay neighborhood integration, suggesting they wait until "the time comes when they can say, 'I can sit down beside you on the bus,' before they try to live door to door with whites." The *Informer* reporter, apparently befuddled by this statement, asked for clarification. Smiley reasoned that "white people do not want to live next door to Negroes [as] an issue of 'biological phenomena.'" While white residents explained that their greatest fear was whether their new black neighbors would have the wealth to maintain their homes and stay in the neighborhood, the *Informer* believed that Smiley's comments revealed a deeper libidinal concern: white fear of interracial sex and marriage—or more precisely, white fear that white daughters might have consensual, enduring relationships with black men and thereby threaten the racial order by undermining the myth of racial purity and, in turn, the notion of purity itself, which according to Calvin Warren "constitutes a metaphysical fiction (and a racial privilege).""[48]

For their part, white Houstonians did not submit easily to the revolution the Caesars' move threatened to precipitate. Forming a new organization, the Citizens Committee of Riverside Terrace and Other Areas, they called together the area's white residents to discuss how they might prevent "further encroachment and depreciation of property value." Of course, from Carter Wesley's perspective, there was no "encroachment," but rather financial transactions between home sellers and buyers. And while these black home buyers paid higher prices for their new homes than white buyers would have to—up to "two to three times the value of the property," according to Wesley—the value of homes in the neighborhood would eventually depreciate. This was not a market phenomenon based on the neighborhood's material condition, Wesley surmised, but rather a social and psychological one based on the social constructions of value and purity. "The only depreciation," he argued, "is in the mind of the guy who thinks that he is superior and imagines that his property depreciates because a Negro moves next door." Wesley dismissed such racism as "poppycock," as white Houstonians' failed to apprehend that, by paying such exorbitant prices for homes in their neighborhoods, black home buyers could raise the long-term market value of the communities they moved into. But loathing and dread on the part of white residents prevented this realization.[49]

This dread of black neighbors was prevalent and resonant. One woman who as a little girl had lived across the street from the Caesars remembered the bombing frightened her family so much that they moved away in response: "My family's reaction after the bombing was fear. My parents were very upset. And I know my mother was very frightened. And it was shortly after that that we moved." However, Jack Caesar told the press that even prior to the bombing, that selfsame family had been aiming to sell their home to a black family and real estate agents had been showing the home to potential black buyers daily.[50] The bombing had not motivated white flight; intransigent Negrophobia had. White Houstonians valued individualism and its relationship to property rights, but there was no Negro individual, only the Negro group. The Caesars threatened the white monopoly on individualism, and the white community responded. Davis and Howell, and perhaps other conspirators, reacted with violence. Most others, however, attempted to negotiate a buyout even as many fled.[51]

The dynamite exploded on the Caesars' front porch at 4:17 a.m. and resulted in about a thousand dollars' worth of damage ($12,000 in 2023), blowing out "chunks of concrete from the pillar," bursting through a French door, ripping apart windowpanes, and dislodging parts of the roof. Sleeping in two bedrooms at the rear of the home, the Caesars and their guests Ruth Phillips and Edith Johnson were unharmed. Startled from his sleep, Jack Caesar "snatched up a .38 caliber rifle" and inspected his house. Even as Dorothy Caesar called the police, two patrolmen who had been two miles away were already on their way. Patrolmen J. W. Biggs and A. J. Crow arrived to find a completely dark neighborhood and mostly vacant streets. Upon learning of the attack on the Caesar residence, Christia Adair called Mayor Hofheinz's house. Hofheinz quickly ventured to Wichita Street and told the chief of police that he wanted the case solved immediately.[52]

The *Informer* called the bombing "the seeds of a reign of terror" and "senseless hate," lambasting the perpetrators as "essentially psychopathic." Here, racism was reduced to irrational prejudice in service of preserving Heavenly Houston's self-image. Empathy, fertilized by moral education, could continue to push Houston toward its raceless destiny. Whereas the community had seemingly determined that it needed to be shielded from Negro encroachment, the *Informer* argued, "Society needs to be protected from the machinations of such human Satans so that it can outgrow the emotional roadblock standing in the way of the development of a just and Christian social order." Reserving no animus for the "warped minds" of white supremacists, the *Informer* maintained that "strict enforcement of law is the only answer" for all racial hate crimes—the self-same law that determined Morris had no right to self-defense.[53]

Donald Caesar, Jack and Dorothy's son, who always made a point to drive past his family's house when he was leaving work and heading back to Texas Southern University, where he lived and attended classes, learned about the attack when he arrived on Wichita Street and saw the commotion. He and the family seemed to have faith in law enforcement despite that the Houston Police Department had done nothing in the past when the family reported threats. But now, while the protection of a black family was not necessarily motivating, "Heavenly Houston's" image was at stake. "We knew that something had to happen for us to—for actually the climate in Houston to remain the same as it always had been," Donald Caesar said. "Houston, had always, fortunately enough, relent[ed] to blacks when they were repressed—and blacks would ask for something and put a lot of pressure—they would respond."[54] There was no historical evidence to support this assertion, and the Caesars' own experiences in Riverside Terrace to this point had indicated otherwise. Memory, again, as an act of self-preservation, revealed the narrative capture of "Heavenly Houston."

Night chief Hobson "Buddy" McGill interviewed the Caesar family, who shared with him details of suspicious activity they had noticed around the neighborhood. Assistant police chief George Seber called the FBI for assistance and instructed one of his detectives, John F. "Jack" Heard, to take charge of the case. Heard, who would eventually become police chief and sheriff, as well as a mayoral candidate whose campaign would not shy away from Negrophobic rhetoric, recalled of his part in the investigation and interpretation of what happened, "I think the purpose behind this, quite frankly, was just to scare the hell out of the Caesars, to intimidate them and run them out of the neighborhood."[55] Dynamite was one hell of a way to intimidate a family at rest.[56]

As night turned to day, with the neighborhood seemingly calm, even if blatantly unhelpful to investigators, Jack Caesar went to work. By nine o'clock in the morning, "the house was surrounded with whites—many whites," according to Donald. They mulled, "made threats," and, only after they grew weary, "disbursed." When he returned home, Jack Caesar made efforts to protect his family like other black families had done elsewhere, including Dr. Ossian Sweet. Sweet, his wife, Gladys, and his friends, who had holed up in the house with guns, ended up facing murder charges for fighting back against a mob that had terrorized them and stoned their house. In the process, he lost his health and his livelihood. Soon thereafter in 1926, Iva, the Sweets' two-year-old daughter, died from tuberculosis-related complications, which Gladys likely contracted during her wrongful imprisonment. Gladys passed from similar complications the same year.[57] This loss of health, livelihood, and family was a real possibility for the Caesars too, but without other resources they still anxiously hosted friends at their home who could help protect them against the white terrorists in their neighborhood. This was their immediate line of defense against white supremacist violence and a declaration of their individual rights to property.[58] Things played out differently in Houston than in Detroit. Although Caesar had several black cowboys around the perimeter of the house with firearms, Caesar and his neighbors did not fire their weapons.

Mayor Hofheinz's quick response, Adair believed, helped maintain the city's relative calm. He told chief of police L. D. Morrison Sr. that he "didn't want the sun to go down without the culprits apprehended," and Adair testified that "before sundown, three men were in jail." Lack of neighborhood cooperation notwithstanding, detectives searched the Howell residence, where Mrs. George Howell also denied hearing any explosion. There they found evidence of explosive materials and also found Davis's car title, which established the connection between the two men. They arrested Davis later that evening at his room at the Standard Hotel. Davis admitted his role, but Howell denied any involvement. "This whole situation is ridiculous," Howell claimed.[59] He refused to take a lie detector test and posted bail shortly after his arrest. When the press questioned him about his connection to the man from whom Davis purchased the dynamite, he responded, "It has to be a coincidence." Howell maintained, "I'm being framed on this. I've never heard of dynamite."[60] Facing off against Davis, Howell asked, "Red, did you tell these men that I told you to buy the dynamite?" Davis shrunk into himself, responding, "Well, you're one of the main ones," suggesting a larger conspiracy than anyone in Riverside cared to admit.[61]

Davis's prosecution was underwhelming. A state's witness, peddler Ocher Chumley, undermined the defense's claims, arguing that in December of 1952 Davis offered him one hundred dollars to help blow up the Caesar home. Davis received the minimum sentence of two years.[62] Howell's prosecution did not go as smoothly as some hoped either. He consistently denied his involvement throughout the investigation and after his indictment by the Harris County grand jury. He and Davis, if convicted, faced a maximum sentence of twenty years for charges of possession of a bomb, arson, and property damage. One official recalled the difficulty of convicting Howell based on the circumstantial evidence and Davis's testimony alone: "The rule in the state court is that you cannot convict a person upon the uncorroborated testimony of an accomplice." Even though Davis got the minimum sentence and Howell was not prosecuted, Wesley believed that Houston had proved itself different from its peer southern cities and argued that Houston's black residents need not fear future bombings against their homes.[63]

Wesley's hopes were based on an understanding of racial terror as spectacular rather than quotidian. I maintain that black Houstonians lived under the duress of racial terror constantly and perpetually. The conditions in black neighborhoods, whether terrible air quality, unpaved roads, or street violence, reflected their structural positioning as black spaces—political voids where anything could happen without registering as a crisis worthy of redress. The material conceit of segregation "transformed . . . collective problems" like poverty, unemployment, and crime "into . . . 'black problems.'"[64] Black problems were then pathologized as biologically predetermined or endemic and unchangeable cultural failings.

Ironically, even as Houstonians bought this argument which suggested the immutability of black criminality, the individual—the discrete self defined by their independent agency—was still responsible for their own condition. That is, in a swift sleight of hand, the discourse of criminality justified the choices of white "individuals" to segregate themselves from black "individuals" by eliding the structural violence that produced black spaces and instead pathologized black people. Saidiya Hartman describes this paradoxical existence as "burdened individuality," where the appearance of being free imbued black people with the veneer of individuality, a subject responsible for their own condition and punishable because they could be held responsible. This "ascribed responsibility of the liberal individual," Hartman writes, "served to displace the nation's responsibility for providing and ensuring the rights and privileges conferred by the Reconstruction Amendments and shifted the burden of duty onto the freed."[65] Thus, while white Houstonians' anxiety around residential desegregation was often expressed in economic terms, it was rooted in concerns about the Negro's sexuality and criminality. They had not yet proved to be responsible subjects under freedom.[66] If liberal individualism justified the Caesars' right to buy their home in Riverside Terrace, the same philosophy justified white people's efforts to exclude black people from such neighborhoods based on a claim of individual physical, economic, and psychological security. This was the epistemology of Wesley's Houston, and it occluded the everyday violence that could, if fully appreciated, expose the impossibility of the American Dream for the Negro.

The bombing of the Caesars' residence in Riverside Terrace presented a crisis for Houstonians, black and white. It challenged Houston's ostensible heavenliness and tested its residents' commitment to liberal individualism. Prior to the bombing, black Houston leaders, with Carter Wesley's *Informer* amplifying their concerns, argued that *Shelley v. Kraemer* (1948) had settled the issue of residential segregation and had affirmed the individual right to property ownership unrestricted by color. However, as law scholars Carol Rose and Richard Brooks demonstrate, the legal precedents upon which *Shelley* rested slyly "upheld the free sale of individual property while implicitly permitting white owners to exercise a group property right—exclusive white residency in the neighborhood as a whole."[67] Indeed, residential desegregation was never a legal or moral mandate; if black people had gained the right to move in, white people had certainly maintained their right to leave and to close ranks. Thus, at first, it seemed as if the Caesars had won a solid victory—and indeed, they were part of an early trickle of black Houstonians who found more desirable homes in Riverside Terrace than was available in much of Third Ward. However, as white residents accepted that black people would become permanent residents of the Riverside area, they abandoned the neighborhood in droves.[68] Between 1960 and 1970, Riverside Terrace grew from 74 percent black to 95 percent black and Riverside astoundingly transitioned from less than 1 percent black to 70 percent black during the same decade.

That is, while the Caesars and others experienced a quantitative change in their capacity to buy property where they wished, the two decades immediately following *Shelley* would demonstrate that the qualitative relationship between whiteness and blackness, between white governance and "black spaces," had not been altered. To wit, in 1959, city administrators and the Texas Department of Transportation altered plans they had put together for the construction of State Highway 288, the South Freeway, in 1953. Although the original plans for the freeway would have cut through some of Riverside Terrace, the new plan would "avoid an oil field" and "be situated closer to development in southeast Houston" while it would displace nearly three hundred families after construction began in 1968.[69]

At first glance it may have seemed as if the South Freeway was not very destructive to the increasingly black Riverside Terrace and Riverside neighborhoods. While Riverside lost about nine hundred residents between 1960 and 1970, Riverside Terrace gained about the same number. Home vacancies fell in Riverside Terrace and maintained at 14 percent in Riverside between 1950 and 1970. However, as historian Kyle Shelton has noted, I-45 and SH-288 demanded "the removal of over 2,000 homes" in Greater Third Ward, and black residents "absorbed a great deal of the impacts" of the South Freeway's construction, "losing what some families had fought for decades to achieve."[70]

The seeming paradox of residential demolition unaccompanied by demographic decline is solved by the changing composition of the housing stock in the neighborhoods, where in Riverside Terrace the share of single-family homes fell from 69 to 39 percent and in Riverside from 78 to 53 percent. Together with blockbusting efforts by realtors, highway construction precipitated the transformation of single-family houses in the MacGregor area into multi-family units, with a concomitant increase in transience and less incentive for home owners to maintain their properties. Although vacancy percentages seemed to indicate neighborhood desirability between 1960 and 1970 in Riverside Terrace, this was also due to the increase in the number of housing units per structure as opposed to a constant number of housing structures. That is, although vacancies decreased from 12 percent to 9 percent over the course of the decade, the number of vacant structures actually increased from 314 to 417. This was a consequence of the "ripple effects" of highway construction. As was true with the construction of I-45 for Houston's Fourth Ward, black residents who could afford to flee the path of destruction abandoned "many homes" adjacent to the highway's right-of-way, "changing the neighborhood from vibrant, livable space into a shell of its former self."[71]

White flight and municipal practices thereby produced another "black space" in Houston's inner core—a neighborhood that had once been of peak desirability for its location, its stately homes and small mansions, large lots, tree-lined streets, and easy access to the central business district and medical center transformed into a void, a negated nothing, redundancy notwithstanding. The Caesars' house would have been demolished for the highway had it not been taken from the ground and transplanted in south Houston. Home vacancies, overcrowding, noise, and increases in nightlife-related disturbances would quickly come to trouble some pockets of the Riverside neighborhoods. White property owners "neglected" what had been transformed into rental units, "waiting for the commercial takeover of the community."[72] The legal dignity apparently granted by *Shelley* was ephemeral, and black Houstonians' right to own property was curtailed yet again by the social and material construction of "black space." Indeed, liberalism would not guarantee black people's absolute right to property, nor did it curtail white people's exercise of their long-standing group right to racial alienation. And so, the American Dream remained an empirical impossibility.

RACIAL TERROR: EVERYDAY IN HEAVENLY HOUSTON

I began the previous section with the bombing of the Caesar residence as a spectacular act of terror. Another way to begin the Caesars' story is to visit Houston's Third Ward in the aftermath of the Civil War. Like their freshly emancipated counterparts in Freedmen's Town in Fourth Ward, the new black residents of Third Ward sought home ownership, and by 1880 a quarter of black Third Ward residents owned their homes. Growing increasingly popular to black residents of Houston through the early twentieth century, Third Ward "eclipsed" Fourth Ward in 1910 as a residential destination. The size of Fourth

Ward would diminish in the middle of the century through eminent domain seizures to construct I-45 and San Felipe Courts—an all-white housing project. In 1870, 35.6 percent of black Houstonians lived in Fourth Ward, and 29.1 percent and 15.7 percent lived in Third and Fifth Wards, the areas in the city with the highest proportions of black residents. In 1890, Fourth Ward's proportion remained about the same, while Fifth Ward's grew to 19.2 percent and Third Ward's declined to 25.6 percent. In a dramatic reversal of trends, by 1910, Third Ward accounted for 32 percent of Houston's black population as Fourth Ward's share declined and Fifth Ward's showed less-remarkable growth rates. "By the 1930s," journalist Alan Ehrenhalt notes, ". . . the Third Ward became the center of Houston's African American life."[73]

During Reconstruction, with the help of the Freedmen's Bureau and the American Missionary Association, black residents of Third Ward secured educational opportunities for their children in Frederick Douglass Elementary School. Jack Yates and his Antioch Church members bought land in Third Ward, establishing Emancipation Park in 1872—Houston and Texas's first public park. In 1916, Third Ward also housed Blackshear Elementary School, established as Emancipation School. Jack Yates High School, the second high school to serve black Houstonians, opened in 1926 on Elgin Street, about one city block from bustling Dowling Street and the lively Emancipation Park. In 1926, the Houston Negro Hospital (now Riverside Hospital) was built on Elgin as well, the next block east of Yates High School on a $25,000 plot of land with an $80,000 building donated by Joseph Stephen Cullinan, the oil magnate who founded Texaco. In 1885, Yates established Houston Baptist Academy (HBA), where the focus, like in many early black schools, was to make a literate population out of freedpeople and provide them with ministerial and vocational training. HBA survived until the 1920s, but the demand for professional education from black Houstonians did not subside. In 1927, the Houston school board established the Houston Colored Junior College, which evolved to become a four-year institution in 1934 under the new name Houston College for Negroes. Students attended evening classes for the college at Yates High School, until in 1947, in response to the Supreme Court's decision a year prior in *Sweatt v. Painter*, the state established the Texas State University for Negroes (now Texas Southern University) in Third Ward.[74]

Third Ward had the reputation, at least among the city's black populace, of being more "upscale" than its Fourth and Fifth Ward counterparts—the "brain" to Fifth Ward's working class "brawn," as one journalist put it. Indeed, historian Tyina Steptoe notes of Third Ward that while "[s]ome black residents of the neighborhood were certainly poor . . . Third Ward had enough well-to-do African Americans and black enterprises to give it the reputation of being Houston's most elite black community by World War II." Born in 1935, Donald P. Lee, who attended Douglass Elementary and Yates High schools, remembered that Third Ward "was a very nice community . . . it was a lot of nice homes, fairly upscale people that lived in that neighborhood," especially near his family's home at Tierwester and McGowen Streets. His parents "attached" his mother's beauty salon to their $5,000 house, and their neighbors "were kind of well-educated people." "It was nice," he recalled, "what you call middle-class and upper-middle-class homes—people that lived there kinda kept their homes up." His life there was entrenched in the neighborhood, its people, its traditions, and its institutions—the churches, the restaurants, and eventually the vibrant intellectual community of Texas Southern University: "It was a wonderful life."[75]

Commensurate with this middling-class reputation, Dowling Street housed some of black Houston's most enduring and influential institutions and commercial enterprises of the twentieth century. St. John's Baptist Church, located at the corner of Dowling and McGowen Streets, was the religious institution of choice for many of black Houston's business leaders. Churches like St. John's were the center of life for some residents, who, outside of schools, had few spaces to enjoy structured community and for whom transportation to other neighborhoods was often a luxury.[76] Other churches, funeral homes, several movie theaters, bars, eateries, and beauty shops dotted Dowling Street. Lee recalled the vibrancy of the street and the surrounding community:

> Black people didn't necessarily go downtown. Now, on the weekends we would probably go to Kress's or Grant's . . . but basically you would buy—we bought our stuff at Weiner's, or Reubenstein's—they would be like on Dowling Street which was the main vine for our neighborhood which was in Third Ward—was Dowling Street. And at that time they had mostly the black businesses. And that—kinda—the integration—uh, you went to, you stayed in your neighborhood. You didn't have to go downtown. Had good shoe stores and the rest of your haberdasheries, this, that, and the other was on Dowling Street. You could just go down there and buy what you need.[77]

Avoiding the indignities of shopping in segregated spaces, as well as, for some, the inconvenience of lugging heavy bags onto the LaBranch streetcar or the Dowling Street bus, Third Ward's residents shopped close to home. Lee recalled that the "Hig and Pig and Weingarten's [grocery stores] were downtown" near Prairie Street, but in general, "you didn't have to go to supermarkets." He noted, "Basically, you went to the neighborhood groceries, which was just about one on every corner." Likewise, Annabelle McMillon, born in 1913 in her family's home on Live Oak Street, recalled fulfilling most of her everyday needs by shopping at local area grocery stores and other businesses, at times venturing to the Pilgrim Auditorium in Fourth Ward or the Harlem Grill on Harlem Street in Fifth Ward for dancing and entertainment.[78]

Third Ward also offered its own entertainment venues, and they were among the city's most popular, fashionable, and well-known. The El Dorado Ballroom, built by wealthy black entrepreneurs and philanthropists Anna and Clarence Dupree on the corner of Dowling and Elgin Streets, became a destination venue for black musicians from across the United States. There, black Houstonians "could dance to the trendier sounds of big bands or urban 'jump blues,'" and on its most formal nights onlookers could catch sight of hundreds of guests in "colorful gowns [and] well-fitted tuxedos." The club "was top of the line," blues booking agent John Green recalled.[79] Attracting acts far and wide with its reputation for sophistication and elegance, the El Dorado Ballroom was a crowning jewel for Houston's Third Ward and a centerpiece of the Dupree commercial empire.[80] To borrow from Kevin Quashie, therein existed "aliveness," a black world that exceeded the dictates of anti-blackness and social death.[81]

In this take, life in Third Ward seemed grand, but the oral histories that seek to resuscitate it actually accomplish a different end. As is true with all archival sources, oral histories are mediated representations. Participants in these interviews do not just share facts, but narrate experiences, and this is an act of self-preservation. In other words, interviewees have a sense of "self" that they actively seek to stabilize and maintain through fabulation. Inheritors of Western philosophy generally and unquestioningly understand the "self" as a "discrete individual who is sufficiently autonomous" and who "can make self-conscious decisions and accept responsibility for them."[82] Scholars, then, should expect to find unknowing contradictions and pointed rhetorical choices in oral history interviews—contradictions that result from the difference between the ideals (such as "equality") people hold and the realities (such as persistent inequity) people face, expressed by their rhetorical choices that aim to hold the "self" together despite that dissonance. To meditate too long on the contradiction without resolving it is to risk tearing the "self" apart—to descend into the abyss of *meaninglessness*. (If "equality" is not real, then might there be *nothing* on which to anchor notions of individualism and responsibility? Might there be *nothing* at all, the black nihilist insistently asks?)[83]

"Our memories not only allow us to remember; they also allow us to forget," writes education scholar Antoinette Errante. Therefore, she continues, "At any given time, we may remember, forget, and re-invent certain aspects of our personal and collective past" because doing so "makes the present *meaningful* and also supports the present with a past that logically leads to a future that the individual or group now finds acceptable" [emphasis added].[84] In short, oral histories may be interpreted as memory, but perhaps are best understood as efforts to preserve the "self" that is present at the time of the interview and best used as evidence of the philosophical anxieties that organized the world in which these narratives are formed.

The nonchalance with which Lee and McMillon talked about navigating racialized space indicated the ways that black Houstonians were racially and spatially disciplined into understanding their place in Houston's social and economic landscape. "You didn't *have* to go downtown," surely, but black Houstonians also understood that white consumers did not *want* them downtown. This was true in southern cities like Houston and Norfolk, but also in shops, theaters, and nightlife establishments in the Northeast, Midwest, and West Coast.[85] These circumstances were fondly narrated in terms that emphasized black aliveness rather than the degradation that Jim Crow segregation imposed on black people by capturing them in certain geographies, physical and social, as a mechanism for delineating the limits of humanity. In other words, Lee and McMillon occluded the violent preconditions necessary for making coherent any adjoining of the concept "aliveness" with the racial marker "black." The pride expressed in these oral histories was certainly no illusion, but "to survive is not to live and to live is not to have one's *being* questioned."[86] This pride was an attempt to argue that black people *be*, too—in an ontological sense—an impossibility in the world of Man where blackness signified a lack of being. This "self"-preservation via narration-as-memory was an attempt to turn away from what Christina Sharpe calls "quotidian disasters."[87]

The very mundanity of racialized space, white people's policing of it, and black people's socialization in it illustrates the *void* of meaning of blackness in an anti-black society.[88] In his analysis of Frantz Fanon, political scientist Tendayi Sithole puts it this way:

> Arguably, Blacks are not humans because of the mere fact that their existence is that of survival. They are not humans as they are at ontological margins. Making Blacks believe that they are human and for them believing themselves to be such in the midst of injustice, cruelty, and horror that confront their daily existence (even if they do not perceive their existence as such) is the very act of self-deception. This self-deception stems from the very fact of making Blackness to be blind to the existential crisis it faces . . . The mode of survival is to put forward as if it is life, but in actual fact that in turn being, to invoke

Fanon, "moving from one life to another." . . . To live in the self-deception of being human while not being human means that Blackness lives the very construction of Whiteness.[89]

In other words, what we witness in the oral histories is not just a memory of how things were, but the disciplining of—the capture of—the person who remembers. Because it was philosophically *compulsory* to maintain the "self," they *compulsively* elided the violence of white supremacy by focusing on black "agency" in order to make an unspoken positivist claim for black humanity. This is the liberal humanist frame for understanding black existence in an unequal society, and it proved, in some cases, to be useful for black Houstonians, providing the foundational moral frame for the Caesars' right to buy their home in Riverside and Johnnie Lee Morris's claim for a right to self-defense. However, it ultimately proved ineffective for transforming black objects into human subjects. That is, the Caesars' newly gained legal right did not inoculate them from gratuitous violence.

While the oral histories focus on the vibrancy of Third Ward, racialization (in this case, the violent processes by which Third Ward became segregated and "black") had detrimental effects on its residents—the selfsame effects the Caesars sought to leave behind by buying their home in Riverside Terrace. Thus, I turn the attention of this chapter to those effects now.

Third Ward exhibited widely spread socioeconomic indicators that sometimes varied from block to block. A block with 75 percent owner occupancy abutted another with only 14 percent owner occupancy. The average home on one block was close to $20,000 while the homes on an adjacent block could hover somewhere around $6,500 in worth. The blocks on the northern fringes of Third Ward exhibited more "slum" characteristics than those closest to Texas Southern University. Those northern blocks had higher rates of overcrowding in housing units, greater residential density per block, and more deteriorating dwellings without running water. In some areas, residential crowding was so bad that one resident said, tongue-in-cheek, a person could "stand in one house and hear the inmate in the adjacent house change his mind."[90] Though said jokingly, the language of being inmates in prisons to refer to residential space indicated the feeling of capture, of suffocation, of unfreedom felt especially by low-income Third Warders. And this is not to say that higher-income people deserved to live in superior conditions, or that neighborhood economic heterogeneity is a negative condition. Rather, it is to highlight two manifestations of capture: the repression of black mobility despite economic means, and the depravity of racial capitalism that made the gap between the well-to-do and the rest of society so wide.

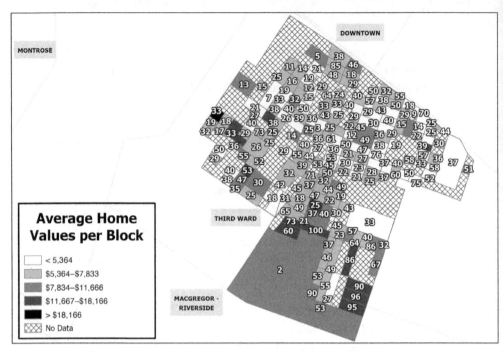

Map 8 *The rates of homeownership in the black Third Ward with blocks labeled by the percentage of owner-occupied housing units in 1950.*

For black Houstonians, segregation ensured that their schools would be overcrowded and underfunded. On March 10, 1954, the roof at Crawford Elementary School in Fifth Ward collapsed. "37 pupils at Crawford escaped injuries by only a few minutes," the *Informer* reported, as "concrete plaster and [the] steel wire ceiling of their classroom crashed five minutes before the 1st graders were scheduled to return from lunch Wednesday." The brick building, only twenty years old, was unmaintained and being used to "absorb the pupils of Dunbar Elementary," which had been demolished to make way for the Eastex Freeway—an infrastructural project that would subsidize suburban expansion. Parents were outraged and inundated the offices of the *Informer* with phone calls expressing their grief and anxiety. One father, Archie Stevens, called to say, "I had a look at the room this morning. It was a mess. Now something ought to be done about this terrible thing." The teacher, Thelma D. Thomas, reported that she had noticed cracks in the ceiling but didn't realize there was a structural risk because other classrooms were in similar condition. Her classroom, she claimed, had been "repaired" the previous year, probably as a result of Hilliard and the HCCO's pressure on the school board and business manager, but apparently the promised improvements were not as thorough as they needed to be. Thomas said it must have been luck that spared her and the students; if it had been a rainy day, they would have all been under the ceiling when it collapsed.[91]

Black Houstonians also lamented community violence. In my comprehensive accounting of crime reports and stories in the *Houston Informer* from 1950 through 1959 and a sampling of those same years in the *Houston Post*, I witnessed the frustration black Houstonians had with violence in their neighborhoods but also with the ways it was framed. Ironically, the *Informer* participated in framing black neighborhoods as criminal, running sensational headlines that reinforced the stigmas surrounding black people. But sensationalism sold newspapers, and violence was a material fact. State capitalism demanded the reproduction of these stories in the same ways that it produced the racialized unemployment rate, underfunded black schools, and deputized violence workers (police) who rained additional terror on black communities.[92] Thus, even the black press was captured in the process of denigrating blackness.

In March 1958, M. J., a reader of the *Informer*, expressed dismay at the circulation of the idea in Houston that black people were predisposed to commit murder. Only a few months prior, Richardson Dilworth, mayor of Philadelphia, in an effort to dissuade interracial violence in his city, "criticized 'constant reiteration about Negro crime.'" Dilworth explained, "There's no more crime—in fact, there's less crime—in low-income Negro districts than in low-income white districts. There just happens to be more low-income Negro districts." At least on its face, the statistical evidence suggested that black people were rabid criminals, but at least for Philadelphia, the mayor argued, this was misleading. For him, the problem was economic depression rather than color.[93] Historian Khalil Gibran Muhammad skillfully demonstrates this fact across the nation's expansive geography through the nineteenth and twentieth centuries.[94] M. J.'s letter to the *Informer* expressed the same sentiments about Houston:

> I keep reading from time to time that Negroes commit more murders than anybody else in Houston. Somehow, I don't believe the picture is complete, if one just takes the total number of murders committed by any race. Are our poor housing, our lack of healthy and proper recreation centers, both combining to drive our people more into beer taverns . . . ?[95]

The *Informer*'s editorialists also noted the poor living conditions of black people across the country as the nation's black population transitioned from being primarily rural to majority urban and argued that the mass expansion of "low-income Negro ghettos" was a consequence of structural inequality, including structures maintained by patterns of "the flight of segregation-minded whites." They succinctly summarized their argument this way: "Negroes are not the creators of these conditions, they are the victims of them."[96]

These more structuralist articulations of crime risked committing what Muhammad calls "writing crime into class," and they were definitely often interpreted as such.[97] As the twentieth century progressed, overt biological racism fell out of favor and class-based explanations of crime found a productive ideological partnership with cultural racism. Namely, rather than interpreting structuralist arguments for the causes of crime as critiques of the systems that produced those conditions, people often instead rearticulated them as critiques of people living in poverty and what they—the critics—identified as the "culture of poverty," which was also a poverty of culture. The escamotage of cultural racism is remarkable: rather than using the discipline of biology to distinguish the Negro as nonhuman, it relies on the grammar of common sense to accomplish the same end. Where culture is an attribute that contributes to *Homo sapiens* groups' ontological standing as humans, the culture of poverty *as* a poverty of culture necessarily indicates something subhuman.

Responding to these facile interpretations, Gordon Blaine Hancock, writing for the Associated Negro Press, informed readers that *no* scientific studies justified a belief in either a racial or cultural link to an objective standard of "morality." He doubled down on the argument that race was a consequence rather than a cause, writing, "This column has often contended that the Negro is just what the white man made him! If he had made a better Negro, he would have had one. The present Negro is a creature of the white man's creation and that the prejudiced whites would stigmatize their own creation is unbelievable." By undermining the classist explanations for crime and deconstructing "the Negro" as a production of whiteness rather than some irreducible biological reality or economic class, Hancock cleverly exposed the machinations of racecraft and demanded Americans, black and white, revisit the historical causes of black people's poor living conditions and overexposure to crime. He demanded a genealogy of blackness, and his bet was that to attempt to uncover the truth about blackness, the auditor would and could only find the white imaginary and its accompanying transatlantic violence.[98]

Yet even as black folks in Houston and around the country developed rhetorical, scholarly, and political strategies for undermining the racialization of crime, many also had to contend with real insecurity in terms of violence against their persons or their property. This is not to say that black

Houstonians lived in constant fear of violence from their neighbors. Despite the attachment of stigmas to neighborhoods where black people predominated, most crime concentrated on main drags with commercial establishments that attracted people for shopping, drinking, and dancing. Almost 54 percent of the assaults reported in the *Informer* occurred on fewer than 70 streets out of a possible 718 streets where any assaults were reported. These streets (e.g., Dowling Street, Lyons Avenue, West Dallas Avenue, Jensen Drive, and Liberty Road) were main drags, clustered with dining and nightlife establishments that served black Houstonians. While physical assaults reported in the *Post* also tended to occur on main drags with commercial establishments, the top reported streets in that newspaper were mostly downtown (e.g., Main Street, Franklin Street, Texas Avenue, and Fannin Street). A few reflected the main drags in other white-majority areas of the city (Harrisburg Boulevard in Harrisburg and Navigation Boulevard in Second Ward).[99] However, whereas black neighborhoods were defined by the quantity of crimes on a select few thoroughfares, white neighborhoods did not carry the same stigma. Warning against this myopic tendency, W. E. B. Du Bois, in his brilliantly executed and groundbreaking study *The Philadelphia Negro*, argues so-called black-on-black crime is "a phenomenon that stands not alone, but rather as a symptom of countless wrong conditions."[100]

Those "wrong conditions" preconditioned and helped perpetuate intra-community violence. Violence committed by black people against other black people was treated more leniently than interactions in which white people were victims, if the cases were treated at all. One black Houstonian noted, "A Negro can kill another Negro and if he has the right lawyer he can come clear, but if he kills a white man he'll be electrocuted. If a white man kills a Negro he usually gets out of it without any trouble." Thus, rather than focusing on protecting black people, "many white policemen typically acted as if it were their duty to keep black folks in 'their place' and make them stand in fear." This pattern of practice toward black Houstonians would help earn the city and its police department "the dishonorable distinction of leading the Nation, and perhaps the world, in police misconduct, complaints, and litigation," defined by a failure to honor "its responsibility to protect all its citizenry."[101]

To interpret the Houston Police Department's actions as a failure to fulfill its responsibilities is to turn away from the truth of racist violence. I argue Houston's history exposes that citizenship is a legal and juridical construction which functions as shorthand for a list of rights, and the infamous *Dred Scott* decision made clear that black persons had no rights that white people had to acknowledge. During his campaign against Abraham Lincoln, Stephen Douglass reiterated the decision, noting, "The Declaration of Independence only included the white people of the United States. The Constitution of the United States was framed by the white people . . . My friends, if we wish to preserve the Government we must maintain it on the basis on which it was established, to wit: the white basis."[102] Although the Constitution's Fourteenth Amendment admitted black people into the category of citizenship, even during Reconstruction federal courts and political leaders debated the meaning of this inclusion and its effects on the sovereignty of the states. To guarantee that black people would occupy the full status of citizenship would require the deconstruction of the federalist system as it existed, conferring greater powers to federal authorities to administer citizenship rights by diminishing the power of states to proscribe those rights.[103] The truth was, it turned out, the nation was unwilling to sacrifice "state sovereignty" to fulfill the ostensible intent of the Reconstruction amendments.[104] If the dubious claim that police gain honor by protecting all its citizens was indeed true, then a failure to protect black people, who in the 1950s maintained a "steeled dissatisfaction with second-class citizenship," was in no way a dereliction of duty by police.[105]

But the Houston Police Department demonstrated more than just neglect toward black residents; it was outright hostile to them. In 1940, Charles A. Shaw, of the Watchtower Life Insurance Company, wrote to Walter White, secretary of the NAACP, about "the victimization of Negroes by police thugs in Houston." White had received a letter from a white businessman in Houston about the brutality he had witnessed and had written Shaw for further enlightenment. Shaw responded, saying, "It is true that the police department of the city of Houston has been charged, and in a number of instances, proved guilty of brutal impositions on colored people." The businessman's letter noted that Houston's "tough police" appeared to "take delight in beating up colored citizens for the fun it gives them."[106] This was gratuitous, anomic violence, and it concretized black people as black.

Carter Wesley's *Informer* did not shy away from publishing testimonies of police violence, perhaps because the publisher had suffered his own unprovoked attack by police in 1940. Driving near Spring, Texas, on a trip between Dallas and Houston, Wesley was "greeted" by two highway patrol officers "with licks" after they claimed that he had waved at a passing car. Wesley denied their claim and denied their secondary claim that the waving was an attempt to "mash," or flirt, with a white woman. Nevertheless, after being beaten on the road and arrested, Wesley emerged from jail with a charge of resisting arrest. Writing to his fellow attorney and friend, Thurgood Marshall, Wesley noted, "My jaws are swollen up like somebody having the mumps and my lips are cut clear through where those babies kicked me after they got me down."[107] Wesley, then, well apprehended the lengths officers were willing to go to cover their unlawful arrests and assaults. As a black space, Wesley himself was always perceived by white supremacists as a ready site for physical, psychological, and existential violence. His body was a plaything where they could express their basest fantasies and desires—to degrade, mutilate, dominate, and kill without any consequence to their conscience or to their recognition by others as good people.

This was gratuitous violence on full display, and it terrorized black Houston daily. Through the 1950s, the *Informer* published eighty-two cases of police brutality, the majority of which occurred in Third, Fourth, and Fifth Wards, where black Houstonians were most densely compacted and closest to the central business district. There, they survived precariously on the border between their relegated spaces and the city's most important white financial institutions as "outcasts of society . . . forced to live in . . . dirty hovels."[108] The production of racialized spaces not only delivered black Houstonians into spaces of exception from the moral world of Man wherein human lives carried value, it also rendered black people, as component parts of the assemblage of black space, as an excepted "third zone between subjecthood and objecthood." White folks may have spoken about their "reasons" for violence against black people in Houston and across the nation, but reason need not be the point of the story. As in many horror stories, the terrorizing figure sometimes acted violently *because they could*.[109]

These "because they could" stories are ubiquitous in the archive. (I point to several of them in the following footnote, but I find little value in exhuming those dead black bodies for the purpose of parading their suffering.)[110] Moreover, overpolicing and underprotection coupled with employment discrimination, political disfranchisement, and residential exclusion manufactured the structural conditions under which violent crime proliferated in the form of assaults, murders, and rampant and pernicious intimate partner violence.[111] White people also saw black neighborhoods as interzones—spaces where the libidinal economy of race was on full display as white hatred of black people manifested as intense sexual desire for black bodies.[112]

The violence black communities like Third Ward endured was therefore infrastructural, libidinal, psychological, economic, environmental, and institutional. Through these forms of violence, white Houstonians—leaders and voters—constructed the built environs and translated black people's bodies as black spaces—ontological voids that rendered value to humanity itself as the property of whiteness. However, in a post-*Shelley* world, black Houstonians who could afford to do so gained the capacity to at least escape the physical barriers that created "black neighborhoods." Residential desegregation for black folks with economic means seemed inevitable. Moreover, because of the atrocities witnessed in Nazi Germany during the Second World War (and despite the simultaneous atrocities committed against Japanese, black, and Mexican-descended folks in the United States), white Americans had learned, some more readily than others, that the ultimate outcome of biological racist logic was genocide. This accentuated a sense of moral dissonance between widely held liberal individualist philosophical orientations and the persistence of Jim Crow segregation. To quell the nagging question of black people's human and civil rights, white Houstonians pointed to black criminality. Indeed, in 1938, the first words of Houston's acting chief of police, Dave G. Turner, to investigators working with Gunnar Myrdal for the project that eventually would become *An American Dilemma* were: "Well, niggers commit more crime than white people."[113] Using "race" to justify racism had always been a means through which to restrict black people from the category of human—indeed, it was this practice that produced "black people." Whether the discourse was biological or cultural made no difference. These were the many forms of violence that the Caesars endeavored to escape. But the depravity of anti-blackness followed them wherever they went, diminished the beauty of their new neighborhood, ultimately and literally razed the ground on which their home stood, and indicated the impossibility of the American Dream for the Negro.

DEATH OF THE SUBURBAN DREAM[114]

The case of Houston elucidates that anti-blackness was not predicated on the economic status of black people, their educations, or their neighborhood conditions in terms of home quality, noise, or the prevalence of crime. Acres Homes (and its economic blight) was but one example of the early suburbanization of black people in Houston. "As early as the 1920s," real estate developers planned and built "subdivisions which offered the black middle class segregated, middle-class homes."[115] And recognizing the demand for quality homes among black Houstonians, in 1941 Cortez Ewing King helped establish the Clinton Park Development Company (CPDC) as lead developer. Their goal was to build the "largest . . . development ever built exclusively" for black Americans. Unlike many of the Houston area's other all-black or majority-black projects, Clinton Park's developers aspired for the area to feel like a middle-class suburb, and by 1959, Clinton Park was a bona fide black suburb. Covering nearly 90 percent of its construction costs with funds from the Federal Housing Administration (FHA), the CPDC built 533 houses in the new Clinton Park Addition on Houston's eastern edge. The area, which included the Fidelity Addition and eventually Pleasantville, would create a tri-community of suburbs predominantly occupied by black families.[116] Home owners, on average, would live in four- or five-room houses, with plenty of green space on their lots for "individual flower and 'victory' vegetable gardens."[117]

By August 1942, more than five hundred black families had "moved from overcrowded and substandard quarters" in places like Third Ward and into Clinton Park. Purchasers made $25 down payments on homes worth $2,435. Funds also provided for police patrols, firefighters, and garbage collection.[118] The Clinton Park community quickly saw businesses crop up to serve residents' needs, including small grocery stores, washer services, barber shops, and drugstores—"all operated by Negro employees."[119] In 1945 the *Indianapolis Recorder*, remarking on the success of the FHA project, reported: "Clinton Park is now in operation as a complete, self-sufficient community with a decidedly active community spirit."[120] Residents contributed both money and time to improvements for the neighborhood, establishing their own bus company to "transport workers to war industries along the Ship Channel." They also worked with developers to establish the Clinton Park Country Club, which included a nine-hole golf course. As Clinton Park grew, it coalesced with the growing and neighboring black communities of Fidelity and the "fashionable subdivision" of Pleasantville to form a black belt around the northeast corner of Houston.[121]

Nevertheless, even Houston's black suburbs of Pleasantville, Fidelity, and Clinton Park suffered a "history of municipal neglect," despite that they had been developed with conveniences of paved roads and modern plumbing. Houston's rapid annexation of outlying suburban areas in the 1940s and 1950s had increased the city's tax base, but, generally, these suburbs endured a lack of services as municipal boundaries grew faster than the city's ability to meet residents' needs. However, residents of predominantly black subdivisions annexed by the city noted lengthier waits before they received city services. The Fidelity area of Clinton Park, for example, did not receive water service from the city until 1954. As many residents of independent black subdivisions had felt prior to annexation, Fidelity's home owners did not trust that the city had their best interests in mind when they debated their community's inclusion in the city's newly developed water plan that year. At a Fidelity Civic Club meeting the previous year, several speakers voiced concerns about water quality and "stated that about 3 children [have] taken sick from the water that is being drank from the wells." The contaminated water had given the children typhoid fever, the Civic Club learned a week later. Members complained that "the mayor" had no "concern" for the community, and neither did Houston's industrial leaders whose trucks dumped trash on the side of the railroad tracks that ran through their neighborhood. Their fears came to fruition: even though the city agreed to service the community with running water in 1954, Fidelity remained without improvements to their streets, sewage system, and drainage ditches.[122]

Annexation proved to be a point of contention for Houston's suburbanites—and especially for predominantly black communities. They noted the systemic neglect city leaders displayed toward black areas already incorporated into the city, and worried that like those black families, they too might bear the burden of "unfair tax-money distribution," as the authorities used tax revenue to improve white communities at the expense of black ones. Houston annexed Brookhaven, the northernmost portion of the southside black suburb Sunnyside, in 1949 and the remainder of Sunnyside in 1956.[123] Unfortunately for its residents, city councilwoman Ada Edwards noted in 2007, "Sunnyside has been marginalized. They were annexed in, and then they were forgotten. What was once a jewel became a dumping ground for the city." Indeed, Sunnyside, like Fourth Ward, the Clinton Park tri-community, and Acres Homes, became a literal dumping ground for Houston. In 1967 the city added an incinerator to the Holmes Road Dump, "the city's principal landfill from the 1940s through the mid-1960s." The dump was adjacent to a community park and just across from Sunnyside Elementary School on Bellfort Street and had always presented a health risk to the surrounding community. In fact, Sunnyside had been developed as a black suburb around the preexisting dump. The incinerator was "designed to burn 800 tons of garbage a day," releasing toxic byproducts into the air where Sunnyside residents lived, worked, and played. As historian Robert D. Bullard argues, the city government sited dumps and incinerators with particular attention to the racial makeup of the communities: "All five of the large city-owned garbage incinerators were located in African American and Latino neighborhoods." In 1946, Houston suffered a polio outbreak of "epidemic proportions," setting a record of "19 new cases and three deaths for any 15-day period." The city's health officer, Dr. Fred K. Laurentz, believed that the Holmes Road garbage dump and its community of flies were to blame.[124]

The Holmes Road dump marked Sunnyside, already engraved as a "black" area in Houstonians' social geography, as filthy and disease-ridden. Indeed, it seemed a universal rule in the United States that "race and class biases shaped both the disposition of environmental hazards and response to them."[125] The intentional siting of the incinerator in a black community and the intentional siting of a black community around a preexisting dump indicated the ways city and county officials, as well as private enterprise, responded to the demands of white communities and *created* black spaces as appropriate containers for filth and refuse and as voids with "no humans involved."[126] Environmental violence was only one trait black suburbs shared with the black inner city.

Despite being *bona fide* suburbs, looking and feeling differently than did the inner-city core neighborhoods of Third, Fourth, and Fifth Wards, like the residents of those black urban enclaves, Clinton Park, Fidelity, and Pleasantville suffered criminalization and police harassment. Judson Robinson Jr., son of black real estate agent and precinct judge of Pleasantville, followed in his father's footsteps and also served as precinct judge beginning in 1967. Earlier, he aided Hattie Mae White, the first black school board member, in her campaigns for office, had served as a delegate with Christia Adair at the Texas Democratic Convention where both were denied seats, and also eventually became the first black city councilman in the city since Reconstruction in 1971. But in 1958, the senior Robinson was still a precinct judge, and the junior Robinson and his wife resided in the tri-community area. One night that year, after building a new addition to their house, he and his wife, Margerette Robinson, a nurse at the Veterans Hospital, hosted several friends over for a party.[127] One of his neighbors, invited but too ill to attend, suddenly knocked on the door and warned the Robinsons that "there are policemen in your back yard." Judson looked out of the large picture window at the rear of his house, and "sure enough," he remembered, "there are 3 policemen":[128]

> And I said, "What are you doing?" And they said, "Who are you?" I said, "I live here. This is my house. What do you want?" They said, "You want to be smart don't you?" I said to myself, Uh-oh. I'm out here by myself. These guys will jump on me and say all kinds of things. I said, "Officer, if you think something is wrong, why don't you come inside." I figured if I got them in there, then I had a better of chance of them not jumping all over me. So he said, "You think you're smart. Let me let you see what this flashlight feels like." I said, "You don't have to do that. Just come in and you can see." Finally, I get them in. They're 3 spies. One of them is just out for kicks. He wasn't even a policeman. . . . Now these policemen are inside. My brother just finished law school . . . We asked them what was wrong. Well, here are these officers sitting there: "We're going to arrest you all for consuming liquor after hours." I said, "But, sir, I'm in my house." He said, "I don't care. It's against the law." My brother said, "No, it isn't. I'm a lawyer." So anyway, they called the sergeant. The sergeant comes out, he sees what's going on, he recognizes that my father is the precinct judge, and stuff like that. He tried to smooth it over. . . . So we go to council, and they suspend all the guys for five days each. My wife and I lived in fear

for six months. . . . They would call every night and say, "Nigger, I'm gonna get you tonight. I'm gonna get you." I'd be afraid to go out my house. So I know what it is. I've had the abuse and things.[129]

The suburbs were no reprieve from gratuitous violence; they could be geographies of racial terror. Terrified to *simply be alive*. For six months. One hundred eighty days where every creaking floorboard, each moving shadow, and even the whistle of the wind could shorten the breath and quicken the heart and send the mind running. Robinson's dream turned into a nightmare, and that does not sound like life, it sounds like death.

When asked how black Houstonians felt about the police, Robinson answered, ". . . if you asked the average black person what he thought of the police department, they'd always tell you the same thing. They oppress us. They're mean. They're here to keep us under control." Moments like these in the tri-community area demonstrated that even those black areas of Houston that did not look or feel like inner-city "slums" and that did not see high rates of crime remained vulnerable to abuses by white police officers who exerted racial and institutional authority over the segregated black population. Keeping black people under "control," then, had little to do with actual crime rates or any of its neighborhood or educational covariates. It had little to do with the postwar "urban crisis" at the center of much twentieth-century urban historiography. Criminality and inferiority were inherent in the social significance of blackness in this white imaginary, and thus black people were always subject to white domination.[130]

That is, "black space" retained its essential, structurally antagonistic relationship to whiteness regardless of the observable differences between black neighborhoods. Whether zoned like the Clinton Park tri-community or unzoned like Third Ward; whether rural like Acres Homes, suburban like Sunnyside, or urban like Fourth Ward; whether populated mostly by an upwardly mobile population like Pleasantville or transient like parts of Fifth Ward, black neighborhoods suffered underinvestment, underprotection and overpolicing, and economic devaluation. The anti-black structural conditions that marked a space as "black" encouraged underground economies and physical violence within black neighborhoods. It is no surprise, then, that white supremacist imaginaries made blackness (the condition of being a black person, in this case) the genealogical origin of criminality, imaginaries that came to colonize the ways many black people thought about and talked about their own neighborhoods, a topic to which I turn in the next chapter.

However, what tends to be "sorely missing" from scholarship "is recognition [that] criminalization is not the problem but rather an indication of a problem: the ongoing and indispensable deployment of blackness to suture the coherence of society's leading ethical dilemmas," including crime, democracy, security, and torture.[131] The "myth" of black criminality, indeed, was "crucial to the maintenance of the postwar liberal consensus."[132] White Americans justified the continued social, economic, and political exclusion of black Americans after claiming to have fought a war against fascism by continuing to invoke the trope of the black criminal and by asserting a liberal, individualistic right to select against living with black neighbors.

This story, which began with the history of Third Ward, demonstrates that black space was never without value to white Houstonians. It was a container for the so-called unskilled longshoremen, domestics, chauffeurs, and bellboys who were forced to subsidize Houston's economic growth by way of their low wages, use of segregated public transit, unequitably distributed school tax dollars, and so on. When the Caesars moved in, they threatened to be a vanguard that might undo the economic, affective, and psychological value of whiteness, which we have seen was defined by the achievement of binary gender differentiation and sexual purity. So terror followed, and so I argue, invited a reckoning with the argument, that theirs was an Impossible American Dream.

Still, despite the empirical evidence of their ongoing dispossession, black Houstonians gazed toward liberal idealism. Namely, leaders like Carter Wesley retained faith in black people's ability to be included into the world of Man. But *this world* was economically and politically built with the idea that the "Negro race" was "the *female race* within the human family, as the white is the *male race*." Thus, like "for a woman, the black is deprived of the intellectual aptitude for politics and science," and thus, the Negro race was to be property, void of standing within civil society.[133] To be included, the race needed to achieve "manhood," but this, too, was an impossible dream. However, it was a dream that shaped black political thought at its naissance. Surreptitiously subtending the ways capture worked at the individual, group, and institutional levels was the foundational ideology of race that fundamentally shaped the modern episteme. Here was not just the enactment *of gender roles*, which we witnessed with Christia Adair, but the *role of gender* as a crucial means by which racial difference was articulated and maintained. There could be no "manhood" for the Negro race, for the Negro race was a fiction against which manhood was defined; Wesley's project bought "the poison by way of the decoy"—to seek inclusion into a world that would always be hostile to but dependent upon bleak, black existence.

4

CAPTURED BY THE ROLE OF GENDER

Carter Wesley's "Frustrating Compromises" and the Establishment of Texas Southern University

> In my eyes, the world in all meaningful ways was governed by the racial distinction between captive and free, between slave and Man, between human and object. One hundred and fifty years after emancipation, I knew on which side of the divide I reside, the eternal alien still wasn't a citizen and perhaps no longer desired to be.
>
> Saidiya Hartman, "The Dead Book Revisited," *History of the Present*

The bombing of the Caesar residence prompted many Houstonians to articulate their visions for the future of race in Houston. Under Carter Wesley's leadership, the *Houston Informer* consistently publicized and editorialized the bombing of the Caesars' home and the subsequent criminal trial. The editorialists at the newspaper praised Houston's law enforcement and Mayor Hofheinz for quickly addressing the act of terror, believing that after the prosecution of Red Davis and George Howell, "a major chapter in Houston residential history will probably be closed." Houston's criminal legal process would be a testament "to the sanctification of the rule of law which makes our civilization possible." *Informer* editorialists also noted their pride in Houston; it had once again proved that it was not of "the South" like similarly situated cities.[1]

Additionally, Wesley himself often took aim at the broader issue of residential segregation and admonished Houstonians to obey the law and respect the rights of white and black citizens to sell and buy real estate as individual capitalists. Houston's efforts to protect a black family against white terror, however belated, encouraged the vision of a raceless future wherein individualism would one day supplant the old tribalism of race.[2] This enduring faith in the law and its ideals made it impossible to imagine that perhaps the Caesars' case merely suggested, to call on Frank Wilderson again, an "equilibrium," but that ultimately there was no arc to the story. There was no climax and resolution, but instead a sense of noneventfulness. The Caesars were ultimately displaced against their will, and black Houstonians by and large continued to suffer the depravities of residential segregation. The case did not change Houstonians' epistemologies; it hardened the very legal arguments and philosophical logics that made segregation possible: the sanctity of the property rights of Man that allowed for racial restrictions which, if not enforceable legally, were enforced nonetheless.

Wesley seemed to understand this intuitively. Following the bombing at the Caesars' residence, he took aim at "the average white citizen," who viewed the movement of black citizens into "white neighborhoods" as "encroachment."[3] He informed them that black folk were not invading white neighborhoods, nor were they forcing themselves into white communities, but rather white residents, "because of improved economic conditions," were leaving their old homes for even better ones. Moreover, he pointed out, white owners knew they could sell their homes to black citizens above market value, and so were motivated by profit to "induc[e] and invit[e] Negroes to buy" from them. Wesley argued that "contrary to the assumption that Negroes were pushing into white neighborhoods, it was the whites who were pulling Negroes into the white neighborhoods." But white Houstonians did not face moral threat for these actions; residents "wouldn't dare encroach upon the white man's right to move where he pleases, and sell his property to whom he pleases." Wesley called on city officials and "those of the men who from behind the scenes really run this town" to protect the rights and peace of black home owners.[4]

Wesley's rhetoric was structured by his belief in the American mythology of rugged individualism and democratic equality, as well as the hope Houston seemed to offer for what he called a "raceless" future.[5] Despite his awareness of the relationship between individualism, property rights, and the guarantee of racial exclusion by "choice," Wesley maintained his commitment to the former two. His work thereby indicated, as did each instance in the previous chapter, the unyielding gravitational pull of the Impossible American Dream. So far, I have invited extensive meditation on the implication of recognizing the law as a political construction that presupposes value as a fact rather than a social construction, namely that such recognition exposes the claims of the law and liberal humanism as occlusions that make it impermissible to ask the nihilistic question: what if there is no meaning for the suffering people (who are made black) are forced to endure? Avoiding this question allows the modern world and its attendant moral signs, like democracy, liberty, and freedom, to maintain their coherence and legitimacy. In other words, following Calvin Warren, I have recommended an encounter with nothingness (the impossible and the meaningless).

Consequently, I treat Carter Wesley's writing as his philosophical autobiography in order to expose the ways normative gender ideology, an equally powerful moral sign, directed and directs political attention away from nothingness, for there is little in the world of Man that obtains as much value as gender, "a foundational archetype unique to our situation as humans." But, as Sylvia Wynter explains, gender is merely a "*genre*-specific term of our *fictive modes of kind*," a technique by which we have learned to organize the social world and imbue it within meaning that appears to be naturally informed, but which conceals that gender is without objective meaning or intrinsic value. Gender functions as a technology of "(neo)Liberal-humanist secular Man's" self-replication by ways of reterritorializing the "code of symbolic life/death as that of *naturally selected/eugenic* versus *naturally dysselected/dysgenic* humanity." In many ways, a person and group's relative achievement of normative gender roles is used to interpret their place in the world and determine whether they will be valorized through a discourse of life/living or made valueless through a politics of death/killing/dying. Gender, as a method through which Man's world organizes symbolic life and death, a world in which blackness is coterminous with deathliness (or absence of presence), necessarily replicates blackness as such, and thus cannot promise to inaugurate a world absent of anti-blackness.[6] But it is precisely the insidiousness of gender ideology that suggests otherwise and that captured the political imaginations of Christia Adair in the first chapter, and of Carter Wesley here.

In one telling incident in January 1953, Carter Wesley approached Lockwood Inn, a black-owned barbecue house in Houston's Fifth Ward. He and his wife, Doris, had never patronized the restaurant before, but on that day she asked her husband to grab takeout from there for dinner. A crisis-of-manhood moment followed as Wesley faced an ironic "facet" of Jim Crow—in his own words, "segregation by Negroes of Negroes." As he walked to the entrance a white couple held the door open for him, and as he approached the counter an older white man made room for him. Things seemed quite civil that day in "Heavenly Houston." The clerk at the counter continued about his business, seemingly nonplussed at Wesley's arrival. Soon the manager, tall and rotund, approached Wesley and asked him, "Will you move over there?" Without protest, Wesley moved around the counter's corner. Perhaps he had just been in the way. Soon enough, however, another employee approached Wesley and asked that he "stand in there"—the kitchen. Now there was no mistaking the intent behind the humiliating requests; even a white family in Wesley's earshot noticed and made comment. Obviously, Negroes could be custodians of Jim Crow, too. Once in the kitchen, he was again relocated to a table out of sight from the front of the house. Somewhere in between, the manager finally took his order, but by this point the pattern of service was clear: this black-owned business sought to siphon some of the value of whiteness for itself—seating and serving white patrons before black ones, thereby appealing to and appeasing a white clientele only accustomed to the dictates of Jim Crow.[7]

Wesley spared no words for the manager, locking him in his "Ram's Horn"—the name of his editorial column in the *Houston Informer*, which he owned and published—calling him "a little, timid, cowardly man" who dishonored his children, his community, Christianity, and the Constitution because he was "afraid to be a man." Wesley left the back door of the Lockwood Inn, telling the waiter who asked if he wanted his order, in so many words, that Jim Crow barbecue was not appetizing. After Doris heard the story, she told her husband she was "glad" he left the Lockwood Inn behind with his own manhood intact. She went into the kitchen and fried him a dozen oysters.[8]

Carter Wesley could be described as a lot of things—ambitious, brash, stubborn, jovial—but never timid. His *Informer* was "the most vocal advocate of African American civil rights in Houston and possibly all of Texas," achieving a circulation of forty-five thousand.[9] Like other black newspaper editors, he shouldered much of the burden of publicizing and galvanizing support for issues that affected his community, being a bit freer to speak more loudly because he was self-employed.[10] During the 1940s and 1950s, he created a coherent civil rights project that linked rights to education, jobs, and voting with protection from physical, sexual, and state violence as interlocking needs for racial advancement. And he wrote frequently that this project could never be realized by the spineless, like the Lockwood Inn owner. Manhood was necessary, not simply for the black male, but for the black race. For instance, as 1953 turned to 1954 and Houstonians awaited the Supreme Court's final decision in *Brown v. Board of Education*, Wesley called for an end to cowardice among his readers: emancipation would never arrive for a race without manhood. Perhaps this was why the Lockwood Inn manager raised his ire: he embodied the broken, the feminine, and the slavish. Indeed, Wesley castigated the manager for his "cowardliness." He believed every man had an obligation to provide for his family and every black man was better off pursuing financial independence as he had. But he also noted that provision was not just financial. Wesley argued a man should "provide honor for his family . . . [and] live honorably and with integrity in the community." Integrity demanded "honor[ing] the principles of Christianity, the principles of the Constitution, and the general Golden Rule of good will toward ALL men." To dishonor the community was to be a failed man—to fail to corroborate the manhood of the race.[11]

As editor of the *Informer*, Wesley constructed a coherent narrative that linked, in one broad emancipatory project, school desegregation, fair employment and housing, electoral rights, access to public services, physical and sexual protection of black women, decriminalization of "the Negro," and accountability for police abuses of power. This project derided cowardice. It valorized manliness and individualism and indeed it understood manhood as the achievement of individualism. Importantly, this should not be understood as evidence of the mimetic thesis that posits black men as aspiring patriarchs, historically seeking gender advantage over black women by imitating the behaviors and values of white men.[12] Black men and women were collectively concerned with achieving and protecting the "manhood of the race," which was in some ways a statement about the recognition of black men as equal with other men, but which hearkened back to a more basic Western philosophy of gender.[13]

Gender ideology had been fundamental to the debasement of black people—that is, foundational to the construction of race itself. Civilized races were said to be those that had achieved gender differentiation; blackness was defined as having never accomplished a distinction between the masculine and feminine (as if these were facts of human existence anyway). The Negro race itself was constructed as feminine in relation to the white/masculine, namely Man as a rational subject, a subject whose libido was conquered by the rational mind.[14] Thus, the aspiration to individualism, Western pragmatism, abstract agency, and property rights as the basis of civil standing was an appeal by black people of all genders to the very paradigm of manhood that was used to degrade black people in the first instance of racialization. Therefore, the concern in this chapter is not Carter's black masculinit(ies), but rather the anti-black properties of manhood as a racial construct and the foreclosure of black revolutionary thought in relation to this discursive and material history.

This foreclosure of thought is dreadfully entangled with the history of slavery and its persisting afterlives. As Saidiya Hartman has argued, the nonevent of emancipation following the Civil War compelled freedpeople into a new political economy governed by the same old paradigm of white supremacy. Rather than merely being compelled to labor and to social subservience under the terroristic threat of the whip, rape, and dismemberment—all of which continued after slavery's ostensible end—freedpeople were also coerced to racial subjugation behind the masquerade of consent. For freedpeople, treated as civil subjects with free wills, "history receded before the individual anointed as the master of his fate." As Hartman explains, "freedom" inaugurated the economic and moral debt of the freedperson to planters and to the nation, and any resistance to recognizing or paying down those imposed burdens was criminalized. In effect, black people were disciplined to see themselves as the masters of their own fate even as they lived an antithetical experience and, complementarily, the nation abdicated any responsibility to redress their historical dispossession. Without respect for the past's purchase on their present, white Americans in the aftermath of the Civil War and Reconstruction codified race as merely a "neutral" and natural category of distinction rather than the consequence and corporeal manifestation of racism as sexual violence that produced group dishonor, political disfranchisement, economic subjugation, and premature death for black people and reputation, privilege, and power for white people.[15] At times, black people like Wesley would also invest in this deceptive conceptualization of race.

In one of the closing issues of the *Informer*'s run in 1953, Wesley explained this position as the South debated the future of public school segregation ahead of the Supreme Court's decision in *Brown v. Board of Education* the following year. At the time, governors Hugh White of Mississippi and Jimmy Byrnes of South Carolina and US senator James Eastland of Mississippi were publicly discussing (and disagreeing about) a plan of action for keeping schools segregated if the Supreme Court ruled Jim Crow educational facilities unconstitutional. Foundationally, they agreed that such a decision would be federal interposition on a states' rights issue. Wesley, a trained attorney, wrote, "I don't know what states' rights means legally. . . . The state has no right to discriminate against Negroes or to put any restriction on Negroes' privileges or ability to go where they want. . . . No state has the right, under the Constitution, to make any distinction based on color."[16] For him, Constitutional principles forbade legal recognition of race, though as political theorist Wendy Brown explains, "Liberal equality guarantees that the state will regard us all as equally abstracted from the social powers constituting our existence, equally decontextualized from the unequal conditions of our lives."[17] Thus, counterintuitive to hegemonic ideas about the Reconstruction amendments, equal protection *assured* continued discrimination against black Americans. The fact that black Houstonians still endured Jim Crow a century after the Civil War corroborates this claim. How could Wesley have missed this?

Indeed, the editorialists of Wesley's *Informer* wrote in commemoration of Thanksgiving 1953: "An era is dying and a new era is slowly coming to life for the era of repression of Negroes is on the way out and one of raceless equality is certainly being born before the eyes of all who have eyes to see."[18] The editorialists claimed that this vision of democracy was "at the core of the perennial

Negro agitation and complaint." They continued, "It is the beginning, and the end, of the Negro struggle. Once it is recognized and met without subterfuge or reservation, or unworthy and unchristian rationalization.... Then will the Negro struggle dissolve. This 'Negro goal' is essentially an American goal." (I maintain that the goal was the achievement of the same individualism that guaranteed discrimination as opposed to, say, reparation that promised revolutionary/apocalyptic upheaval.) The editorialists concluded: "It [the 'Negro goal'] is squarely in line with American political and social philosophy as outlined in the constitution of the United States" wherein "race is not a factor in citizenship" and the "rights of citizens and individuals" were stressed.[19] In other words, they could accept race as a natural fact of human geography but maintained it was neutral in its meaning. This was the deception that shrouded biological essentialism by way of social constructivist language, a disciplinary practice still common among scholars and nonscholars alike.[20] Nevertheless, for Wesley and many Americans during the Cold War, any conceptualization of society that failed to center the individual as the atom in which the rights of Man inhered was undemocratic and un-American and therefore impermissible.[21] Thus, for them, the eventual solution to social sicknesses caused by racism was the veneration of the individual and the eventual deconstruction of collectivist solidarities. This future state would, of course, be raceless—a future where race would be neutral but would not disappear as a cultural or social fact.

As a prolific editorialist, Wesley has provided an autobiography of thought, laying bare not his most private self but leaving imprints of the narratives that captured his approach to his world. Mutually reinforcing narratives about the rightfulness of Christian democracy and the honor inherent in proper gender comportment cemented his investments in liberal individualism, rationality, and pragmatism. He understood racism and its manifestation in segregation as an illness infecting the nation; there was nothing intrinsically wrong with the United States or its stated values. It needed some fixing in order to become an emblem of perfect democracy, and American society needed a little massaging to ease its racial anxieties. The goal was, as one of Wesley's readers wrote: "We want in, not out." To incorporate black people into full citizenship, the legal institutions of the nation would have to guarantee the social, political, and economic protection of individuals *as* individuals and the "Negro race" would have to mature by developing and practicing a robust and unflinching manhood.[22]

Guided by these narratives—that the Negro had to abandon cowardliness, that America would inevitably realize its promise of a raceless democracy constituted by individuals, and that the race had to achieve manhood in order to push the nation toward that promise—Wesley affirmed rather than disrupted the very ideas that had produced the racialized world in which he lived. He thereby—unwittingly, I argue, after reading every page of his *Informer* from 1946 through 1960—participated in the reproduction of anti-blackness, providing meaning to racial inequality and black suffering by justifying their persistence as a failure to achieve racial manhood. Indeed, he bought into the naturalization and hierarchization of gender, although he did so not by opposing men to women or masculinity to femininity, but by positioning his ideal of manliness (the achievement of the white race) against cowardly, "irrational" manhood (the curse of the black race).[23] There was, then, "only one destiny": the end of "the Negro" and the perpetuity of whiteness.[24] He eagerly embraced the same liberal individualism that ultimately failed Johnnie Lee Morris and the Caesar family, and which undergirded the criminalization of "the Negro." His commitment to these ideas rendered him intransigent at times, pitting him in verbal battles with other black leaders who shared his dreams but who reasoned differently about how to realize them. He was captured by what he had learned about being Man—a self-possessed individual guided by the ideal masculine traits of rationality and pragmatism. Wesley demonstrated the limited capacity of *this (racist) world*'s vocabulary and methods to service its own undoing.[25] This was true, as we have seen, in the institutions of housing and criminal courts. Crucially, it was also true for the matter of equal educational opportunities, debates around which Wesley would eventually have to admit his own failures in retrospect following the establishment of Texas State University for Negroes (TSUN).

Thus, the chapter proceeds in three sections. First, I discuss the meaning of Wesley's rationalism within the context of debates between him and other black leaders concerning whether to pursue equalization or desegregation in civil suits regarding educational opportunities for black Texans. This was a particular form of rationalism—Western, bourgeois, and liberal—and it presupposed the law as inherently valuable. Rationally, Wesley decided that equalization was exigent. He later lamented this conclusion when, following TSUN's establishment, it suffered underfunding and white supremacist governance, problems which I lay out in the second section. In the final section of the chapter, I explain why this outcome was inevitable—a word historians tend to be allergic to, but I have uncovered no evidence that it could have been different, for there was no meaning for and no reasoning with anti-blackness. Methodologically, I focus the chapter's energy on interpreting how Wesley and others understood their world and the developments therein, rather than deploy the archive to provide a play-by-play, for instance, of the state politics of TSUN's establishment. Here I am less concerned with how TSUN came to be than with what it meant for black Houstonians and what the meanings they ascribed to it reveal about liberalism's stranglehold on black people's political imaginations.

ASPIRATION TO MANHOOD AND THE TRAP OF RATIONALISM

As a self-described realist, Wesley's approach to activism in the 1940s was to "avoid an 'open attack'" on Jim Crow. He wanted to prevent white backlash and believed that black anger and impatience would spark recalcitrance among white liberals and the "white establishment."[26] After the Supreme Court decided *Brown v. Board of Education* in May of 1954, Wesley promoted the decision as proof of the inevitable dissolution of Jim Crow, but he also implored black people to understand that "easy does it" and that "it isn't necessary to pull our hair out" over "bitter, dyed-in-the-wool segregationists" who were preventing school desegregation in Houston.[27]

All black Texans did not share Wesley's approach. That June, he expressed dismay at the tactics of black San Antonians. There were no laws in that city designating swimming pools as segregated, but by custom ten of the city's pools were used by white patrons only and the remaining two were used by black residents. When six black males, two adults and four young boys, joined the crowd of white swimmers in the Woodlawn Pool—at which they remained for a mere twenty minutes—the white people jumped out, and the following day all the city's pools were closed, allegedly for "cleaning and repairs." R. L. Lester, mayor pro tempore, called the city council to a special Saturday morning meeting, where they decided after three hours in a 5–2 vote to create an ordinance that would legally designate city pools by race. The council told the public the decision was "advisable in order to prevent violence, conserve the peace, and to protect the safety and welfare of citizens."[28] In his *Dallas Express*, Wesley encouraged black Texans "to go slowly and be cautious in selecting targets for desegregation," pointing to the new San Antonio pool ordinance as an example of an uncalculated, unpragmatic stand against Jim Crow. Instead, black people should continue to fight for integration in less intimate spaces first, such as in public libraries, parks, and golf courses. Leaders "should refuse any public statement but quietly keep . . . talking with people who control the parks and golf links."[29]

Wesley's concerns about black Texans' approaches to civil rights activism diverted attention from the material implication of the San Antonio city council decision: that segregation was constitutive of peace, safety, and the welfare of citizens. The only people guaranteed peace, safety, and welfare under Jim Crow were those marked as white, and thus only those marked as white obtained citizenship. Black people were not included in the designation "citizens," for the conditions of Jim Crow rule had left them always exposed to violence. Herein lay the capture: preventing white backlash, which Wesley believed was necessary in order to achieve integration, was the same rationalization the city council used to codify segregation. Nevertheless, Wesley advocated gently chipping away at Jim Crow with calculated moves toward the goal of inclusion of the individual into the American body politic—in his case, the Negro individual stripped of the historical significance of race, or in other words, the individual remade as no longer black. (Keep in mind that by "black" I am not referring to identity, culture, or phenotype, but rather to nothing. And nothing cannot be remade into something by way of metaphysical instruments like civil rights law. Thus, Wesley's goal of incorporation was always an impossibility. The problems that burdened black existence in the 1940s persist in the twenty-first century, a testament to this impossibility.) Wesley "hammered away repeatedly and insistently on this same theme," historian John Egerton notes: an unwavering desire for "a role—in combat, in the workplace, in the national scheme of things."[30]

Throughout the 1940s, Wesley literally bought into the NAACP Legal Defense Fund's work as one of three major funders of the group's eventual and effective challenge to the white Democratic primary in Texas—*Smith v. Allwright* (1944).[31] He was also pivotal to the efforts leading to the legal showdown *Sweatt v. Painter* (1950), in which attorneys would argue for the desegregation of the University of Texas's law school for the plaintiff Heman Sweatt. Counsel argued that Texas had failed to establish even one law school that would train black attorneys, that black Texans had to leave the state in order to receive such training, that this was a violation of the Equal Protection Clause of the Fourteenth Amendment, and that the state's belated efforts to establish a law school for black Texans in 1947 was not in good faith nor did they satisfy the equalization mandate of *Plessy v. Ferguson* (1896). The NAACP's attack on Texas's higher education institutions had been a calculated one, and Heman Sweatt had been recruited by Lulu B. White to be the face of the case, a charge he took on only with the blessing of his employer, Carter Wesley. Wesley also fund-raised more than $7,000 to provide for Sweatt's legal complaint, and the aspiring attorney applied to register at the University of Texas in Austin in February 1946.[32]

Wesley's approach created affinities and caused friction between himself and other civil rights leaders both in Houston and nationally. Despite his important role in these efforts, Wesley's formal relationship with the Houston NAACP ended before *Sweatt* was decided when he quit the organization in

1947.³³ He staunchly disagreed with the approach to the desegregation suit. Charles Hamilton Houston and Thurgood Marshall had adopted Nathan Margold's strategy to attack segregated schools by forcing southern districts to equalize school funding and teacher pay, which Margold argued would ultimately make racially separate schools undesirable if only because they would be financially unfeasible. Margold reasoned that the entire system of educational segregation would collapse under the pressure of financial equalization.³⁴ To wit, throughout the history of public education in the South, black citizens had been doubly taxed. Local governments used black folks' tax dollars to subsidize the educations of white children, which meant black southerners were left to provide education for their own children by taxing themselves again—raising money to build and maintain schools, to buy books for studying, and to purchase buses for transportation. Historian James Anderson demonstrates that "double taxation of black southerners was a widespread and long-standing custom" and argues that the "traditions of double taxation and extraordinary sacrifice had distinct limits, beyond which they were both unjust and dangerous":

> One limit was the point at which "self-help" became unconscious submission to oppression. In vital respects, the regionwide process of double taxation was an accommodation to the oppressive nature of southern society. It made the regular process of excluding black children from the benefits of tax-supported public education easier and more bearable for both whites and blacks. It said much about blacks' desire for education and their willingness to sacrifice for it, but it also said much about their powerlessness, their taxation without representation, and their oppression.³⁵

That is, segregation was expensive, and black people's "accommodation to double taxation helped extend over them the power of their oppressors."³⁶ While Anderson's use of "accommodation" and "helped" here suggests a willful transaction and black people's culpability in their own oppression, I maintain that the paradox indicated capture. This was not a matter of choice, willingness, or self-sacrifice; these freed persons had already been sacrificed under the law to the benefit of white children. Margold's strategy, then, was to lay bare the costs being paid by black Americans to subsidize whiteness—to literally add economic value to it—and to undo that system by making white people bear the cost of their historical exploitation.³⁷

However, one problem was, as Sweatt's case demonstrated, black people would have to tax themselves *again* through fund-raising in order to bring their grievances before the nation's courts. Attorneys and court fees and travel costs needed to be paid. The Legal Defense Fund understood that this was unsustainable, and thus ultimately even though they brought Sweatt's case on the basis of equal protection, their endgame was not a separate but equal law school for black Texans; rather, it was the full integration of public graduate and professional education in the state. Wesley disagreed bitterly with this endgame, suggesting that the struggle for equalization remain distinct from the battle against segregation. He attacked Thurgood Marshall, who petitioned for Sweatt alongside William J. Durham (who would be one of Johnnie Lee Morris's attorneys a few years later) and Lulu B. White, the director of the NAACP's Texas branches and Christia Adair's predecessor, arguing, "We should demand our right to equality."[38]

The equalization of educational funds was, at least, an immediately realizable goal for Wesley. Since the 1940s, he had been complaining about the state of black schools in Houston, and in February 1953 the *Informer* reported that "the school administration knows about 'horrible' conditions existing in our schools." The schools were "improperly" heated, too many students were being crowded into classrooms that were too small, the desks were "worn out," and the "sanitary conditions" of the buildings were "insufficient." The *Informer* noted that Sid Hilliard, representative of the Harris County Council of Organizations (HCCO), implored the Houston Independent School District (HISD) board at its February 23 meeting to give black schools a fairer share of the recently passed $10 million bond and notified the board that lawsuits were being brought against its members for negligence toward their duty to ensure that Houston's segregated schools were equally funded.[39] An editorial in the *Informer* praised the HCCO and Hilliard for "sustained interest" in equalization as a "corrective measure." The column also admired that Hilliard made his statements in a public forum and "not behind closed doors where 'deals' can be made." Hilliard's approach was direct, but civil. It was reasonable and therefore the appropriate "American way" to force the board to address the "school needs of Negroes."[40]

The HCCO and Hilliard continued their struggle into April. They offered the board until September to show considerable progress in fixing "Houston's horrible schools." Hilliard noted, "Our protest earlier this year was a conscientious effort to make school officials take note of these conditions and do something about them." The school business manager assured the *Informer* that repairs were being made, and Hilliard promised that the HCCO would reinspect the schools for themselves to guarantee that there was proper heating, improved restrooms, better drainage, and sanitary cafeterias.[41]

When school began again in September, the director of Colored Schools,

Allen E. Norton, had received a "'new' administration office" at an old school that had been condemned ten years prior "as a hazard to life and health by the Fire Department." The *Informer* inspected the building and found "partitions" made of a "heavy type of cardboard and wood type" to divide spaces in the building. The floor remained unfinished, and "the women's toilet," the paper reported, "shows its age through a coating of paint and the flimsy doors and walls which separate the stalls."[42]

The actual schools were in shabby condition as well. "The Houston Public Schools opened this week to enroll the largest number of students in the history of the community," read an editorial. "Numbers, however, was not the really big news of the week. The big news was need." A lack of space, both in classrooms and in outside play areas—areas that were quickly disappearing to make way for temporary structures to house more classrooms—exacerbated the challenges that black residents faced in their unequal schools the previous year. Large class sizes, the editorialist explained, "reduced teacher effectiveness" and stole some "value of the school program" away from "the individual student."[43] And though the *Informer* guessed that black Houstonians would be willing to pay higher taxes in order to have their needs met, by November the paper read, "Negro voters would be more than foolish to increase the district's tax take without some assurance that the inequality presently existing between Negro and white educational opportunities, facilities in the district will be speedily corrected. A vote for the school board proposition on the part of Negroes would be an endorsement of present board policy."[44]

Particularly important from the February 23 meeting for Wesley and the *Informer* as both news and editorial fodder, though, would be the back-and-forth story concerning the board's refusal to accept superintendent William E. Moreland's recommendation to look into the Lamar Fleming Estate, land near Texas Southern University that had reportedly been offered to HISD at a cost, on which a new black high school could be built.[45] This issue would recede while the debate over equalization took precedent, but it would not disappear for long. After the roof collapsed at Crawford Elementary School in March of 1954, Hilliard was joined by fellow HCCO leader George T. Nelson at the March 22 board meeting to "remind the Board of the critical conditions that exist in Negro schools." They and black community members "demanded HISD stop 'trifling around' with Negro school children and provide them better facilities." The Monday night meeting began at 7:30 and lasted for six hours into early Tuesday morning. Hilliard resurrected the issue of the Lamar Fleming Estate, showing that despite white protestations to board members that building a black high school in that location would depreciate their home values, the proposed neighborhood, located on Wheeler and Sampson, was a

"Negro area" by any measure.⁴⁶ Additionally, he argued that even as the neighborhood became dominated by black residents, home prices had increased for some homes by nearly three times their original cost within the past thirty years. Economic facts notwithstanding, Hilliard also pointed out that the petition submitted to the board on behalf of white residents who opposed building a new high school on the Fleming tract had far too many signatures to have come from the sparse number of white residents still living in the area.⁴⁷

The board refused Hilliard's logic and instead moved forward with a plan to build a high school at the location of Dodson Elementary School, a tract of only seven acres of land a mile and a half north of the Fleming Estate. In the meantime, old schools that had formerly been used for white students would be turned over to the department for "Colored schools." Wesley pointed out what he saw as the conspiratorial hands of a racist school board, saying that there was no discernible reason for the board to avoid purchasing the land that Fleming made available except that it wanted to use those funds for white schools. He opined: "There is no mistaking the fact that the people are angry. Even the women, who are normally the ones who caution against getting angry, are aroused, meeting, talking over the telephone, and projecting plans to fight what they count as an insult as well as a threat of irreparable injury to the education of their children." He pointed forward to the five school desegregation cases pending a decision by the Supreme Court and optimistically noted that "whatever the decision," the Texas state constitution would not allow for such gross inequalities in school facilities to exist; HISD was opening itself up for legal bombardment and desegregation, for given "the architect's report that seven acres are not adequate" and a clear history that no white high schools in the city of Houston had been built on seven acres in over two decades, "Negroes will be justified in insisting upon being permitted to go to the nearest adequate high school." In short, Wesley believed the school board was shortsighted and setting itself up for backfire. Jack Yates High School had already been unaccredited for reasons related to overpopulation, and this new high school would suffer the same fate. A school built at the Dodson site would therefore "be no good and it would be wasted money."⁴⁸

An editorial column made clear that such conditions were untenable according to the *Plessy* doctrine, and explained, "If inequalities exist in the schools it is the fault of the board and of the boards that preceded the present one. . . . When Negroes begin to recognize this the foundation of progress in schools will be laid."⁴⁹ The *Informer* repeatedly encouraged black Houstonians to attend the Monday night school board meetings and demand better educational facilities and fairer distribution of tax dollars for their children.⁵⁰ Protest or not, the school board refused to reverse its decision to dismiss the Lamar

Fleming tract as a possible site for a new high school in Third Ward until several months after the Supreme Court ruled against Jim Crow schools. Only then did they consider a belated effort to provide black students with better educational facilities as a deterrent to schemes for integration.[51] However, the Fleming tract would ultimately not house a black school, demonstrating nearly seven years after the *Sweatt* case and with the *Brown* decision looming that equalization cases were not the guarantee that Wesley believed they could be. His arguments with his *Sweatt* contemporaries would ultimately prove him wrong and them correct. Wesley's practical approach to the problem of racial segregation was never equipped to inaugurate his envisioned age of a raceless democracy, for the tools he found practical (obsequiousness to case law and management of white people's fears) were necessarily the ones most readily available for replicating rather than deconstructing the social structure he resisted.

The context of black Houstonians' long struggle for due investment in their children's formal education indicates why Wesley may have remained committed to the equalization strategy. But the point here is not to assess whether Wesley was wrong or right or to speculate how his support of the desegregation strategy may have yielded some remarkably different outcome for black Texans. Rather, Wesley's words, including his disagreements with others, provide opportunities to uncover the philosophical presumptions that guided and constrained black political imaginaries. Wesley's stubborn faith in the inherent capacity of rationalism to work against racism becomes apparent, for racism had never demonstrated weakness when countenanced with a rational argument. As Du Bois lamented, "The race problem has been rationalized in every way. . . . But all this reasoning has its logical pitfalls," and so alongside the ways race was given legitimacy through theology, natural sciences, social sciences, and humanities, "there followed those unconscious acts and irrational reactions, unpierced by reason."[52] Racial beliefs were thereby inoculated against rationalism, even as liberalism convinced folks like Wesley, and even his nemeses, that in rationalism inhered irreducible political value.

Historians Merline Pitre and Amilcar Shabazz have detailed the bitter words exchanged between Carter Wesley, Lulu B. White, and Thurgood Marshall.[53] Succinctly stated, Wesley was angry at Marshall and White because, in his interpretation, they "accused him of supporting segregated schools." Marshall, for his part, compared Wesley's opinion that the NAACP should continue their equalization suits unfavorably with Booker T. Washington's infamous accommodationism. He accused Wesley of being satisfied with "Jim Crow Deluxe"—what Marshall called "the easy way out."[54] But Wesley was not alone in his dissatisfaction with Marshall's adopted strategy. Indeed, black

Americans were deeply conflicted in choosing between the two battlefronts, at once hopeful for the end of segregation but unsure they were willing to risk equalization funds should the NAACP's blatant assault on Jim Crow fail. Walter Vaught of Dallas, one of Wesley's readers, wrote to the *Informer* that he was disturbed by the NAACP's efforts: "If Southern whites are so mean, why do we try to associate with them? . . . We ought to stick together and build an empire of our own."[55] Segregation, it appeared, was its own antidote.

However, Wesley was not a separatist. His advocacy for equalization was not, in his mind, capitulation to the system of segregation. He believed that system would eventually be dismantled, but in the interim black students and professionals still needed training. In fact, their training might yield the cultural and financial capital needed to take on Jim Crow. So when Texas attempted to avoid admitting Heman Sweatt into the University of Texas School of Law by proposing the creation of Texas State University for Negroes (TSUN) and establishing a law school there in 1947, Wesley supported the proposition while Marshall and White opposed it. Wesley's fear was that a failure in the Sweatt case would not only set back desegregation efforts but also require sacrificing an opportunity for institutionalized financial support for the education of black Texans. The risk was not worth it, especially since Wesley, Marshall, and White all agreed, at least, that *Plessy* would "inevitably" be defeated. If schools and swimming pools carried the same weight of "social integration" that white people feared the most, desegregate the libraries and parks first, Wesley maintained, and do so quietly.[56]

Through these debates, the ad hominem attacks that Wesley hurled at Marshall both publicly and privately revealed his capture by gender ideology. The sign "manhood" grounded those attacks. For Wesley, manhood was a necessary achievement for the advancement of black civil rights. He accused Marshall of "undermining black schools and especially black colleges" and concluded that Marshall was a "stupid man" and a "damned ingrate."[57] Writing back to Wesley, Marshall offered a candid assessment of the newspaper editor's folly and lack of foresight: "You are not only unwilling to see other people's sides of a question, but are a little careless with the truth."[58] Indeed, at this point in his career, Wesley promoted only one rational strategy in the civil rights struggle: "gradual reform" that "encouraged blacks to work for improvement but to accept often frustrating compromises."[59]

For Wesley, living in a Jim Crow world as a black person required pragmatism/rationality. This was the essence of manhood upon which he offered his autobiography: "Men today do not possess their own souls, they let fear take over . . . to find a safe spot to stand during the storm. I believe a man ought always be in possession of his soul, and that the only way he can be is always willing to do whatever is necessary to stand for the right and never to get away from it."⁶⁰ Marshall's accusation that Wesley was taking the easy way out intimated that Wesley was being led by fear. In this way, Wesley embodied the impossibility of manhood as something that could be achieved for the Negro, for it was not rationality/pragmatism that afforded manhood its value, but rather manhood obtained value via its inverse relationship to Negro race, which became signified as the "female race" among the so-called human races.

On the one hand, Wesley had been disciplined to think of himself as self-possessed and willful. He would speak in a register as if he had an unencumbered freedom to think and to choose. Above all, he was a man demanding the recognition of his standing as Man. Despite that his demand for recognition from the white world remained unheeded, Wesley sutured together his self-image by using the qualifier "necessary": the necessary provided context for not only what was possible but what was useful. The ability to discern the necessary allowed the achievement of manhood even in the absence of recognition. He surely did not see himself as adrift in a sea of soulless men, for through reason he believed he had the power to extract meaning from the law and its attendant notion of citizenship, though as I discussed in the previous chapter, there is no inherent meaning to extract from either of these. Nevertheless, for Wesley, reason above all else had to fulfill practical and predictable goals. He could not predict whether Sweatt would win admission into the University of Texas, but he understood that white people feared the outcome, that they would do what they could to avoid it, and that this was all but a guarantee that *Sweatt* could win the establishment of a state-funded university for black Texans if properly leveraged.

On the other hand, from Marshall's point of view, Wesley merely refracted the will of white segregationists. Wesley was not operating with "free will." He certainly had not achieved recognition as Man, despite his embrace and promulgation of Man's propaganda. He was, to gesture to Frantz Fanon and David Marriott, unconsciously white: "It would appear that the self-deceived black is caught up in a tragic interplay: he can only reveal himself as a (black) subject via the oblique confirmation of an imaginary whiteness whose power and culture he wants to acquire." This is not to say that Wesley consciously thought of blackness in derogatory terms, but that he appealed to be recognized as the very thing—Man—that was constituted by way of his own degradation. Simply put, normative manhood was unachievable for Wesley and it was unachievable for the race. By "preserv[ing] the illusions of the ego," perhaps unavoidably so, Wesley compromised the potential of black revolutionary thought and sustained in writing and practice the liberalism that had guaranteed the dispossession of black people.⁶¹

The "frustrating compromise" at the heart of the *Sweatt* case was that if black Texans gave up their desegregation fight, they could finally get their own state university. However, statutorily, the state's Permanent University Fund could only outlay financial capital to the University of Texas and Texas A&M University, and state officials, including Dudley K. Woodward Jr., chair of UT's board of regents, did not intend to share that endowment with black Texans. As the *Sweatt* case stalled in state court, the governor, Coke Stevenson, called for a biracial commission to provide recommendations that would ameliorate the problem *Sweatt* had made unavoidable. The makeshift law school for black students that UT established in August, which "consisted of four rooms," no library, and three enrollees, did not appease Sweatt or his attorneys. As a member of the biracial committee, Wesley, alongside Joseph J. Rhoads, president of Dallas Baptist College, demanded a statutory black university that would be eligible for funds from the state. "Under the terms of S.B. 140," historian Neil Sapper explains, "the Houston College for Negroes . . . became the nucleus for a black analogue to the University of Texas. . . . Hugh R. Cullen, chairman of the Board of Regents of the University of Houston, matched with a personal gift of $100,000 the $93,000 raised by the black people of Houston." White Houstonians contributed an additional $90,000 for the school's building fund.[62] There it was: another small "win"—a "separate but equal" education for Negroes.

BORN IN SIN: THE DISAPPOINTMENT OF TEXAS SOUTHERN UNIVERSITY

My elaboration on Wesley's "frustrating compromise" is not merely didactic, for the equalization strategy had very real consequences for black Texans seeking higher education. Despite what was presented as generosity and largesse on the part of white Texans, according to the eventual dean of TSU's law school, Kenneth S. Tollett, the institution was one "born in sin," and its accursed status troubled it in its infancy and continues to condemn it to inferior regard by the state in terms of financial outlays and institutional governance. While Tollett was referring to the compromise Wesley and others made to ensure TSU's establishment, the history of what eventually became known as Texas Southern University was an example of the double taxation of black Houstonians and the state's neglect for the welfare of black people.

In 1925, Wiley College, a private, historically black, Methodist Episcopal-affiliated school in Marshall, Texas, established a teacher's college for black Texans. For the first academic year, students attended classes at Colored High School on San Felipe Street in Fourth Ward. In the fall of 1926, classes moved to Jack Yates High School on Elgin Street in Third Ward to accommodate increasing interest in training. The following year the Houston Public School Board provided funds to develop a segregated junior college system, providing a loan of $2,800 to help black Houstonians establish Houston Colored Junior College. By 1931 the growing institution had received accreditation from the Southern Association of Colleges, and in 1934 the Houston school board transitioned the junior college into a four-year institution, the Houston College for Negroes. In need of a larger campus to accommodate its growing undergraduate body of about fourteen hundred students and its new graduate program established in 1943, the college undertook a fund-raising campaign. Mamie Fairchild, Third Ward resident, college graduate, and the widow of Watchtower Life Insurance Company founder Thornton McNair Fairchild, contributed to the building fund, which the school honored by naming its first building after her late husband. Anna and Clarence Dupree were also among the "prime contributors" for the first permanent building for the Houston College for Negroes, giving $11,000 to the project in 1946, one year after the Houston school board ended its governing relationship with the school.[63]

In March 1947, following Heman Sweatt's legal challenge to the University of Texas for admission into its law school, Texas legislators introduced several bills "providing for the establishment, support, maintenance, and direction of a University of the first class for the instruction and training of the colored people of this State to be known as 'The Texas State University for Negroes' and to be located in Houston, Harris County." Essentially, Houston College for Negroes became a state-supported school with a new name. In 1951 the House passed representative John Bell Murphy's bill to remove "for Negroes" from the name in response to requests made by "a delegation of students who went to Austin to petition." That same legislation changed the school's name to Texas Southern University. The legislature's efforts to maintain segregation by showing good faith toward the *Plessy* separate-but-equal standard helped catapult TSU into what some accepted as "the best Black institution of higher learning west of the Mississippi." In 1947 more than two thousand students enrolled to attend the schools of Vocational and Industrial Education, Law, Arts and Sciences, or Pharmacy under the leadership of the university's first president, Dr. Raphael O'Hara Lanier.[64]

TSU's initial years of operation were mired by conflicts between Lanier and its board of regents. Like other predominantly black residential spaces in the city, TSU was designed as a "black space"—void and fungible—and suffered from similar forms of neglect and abuse. The school necessarily offered remedial courses because its pool of applicants largely consisted of students who had suffered "poor education . . . in segregated Negro public schools."

State money, despite promises, was hard to come by. "There are no counselors for the dormitories, the dean of men doubles as the dean of student life," one reporter noted. An English faculty member admitted, "Much of TSU is veneer." The library was "ill-equipped" for research, and "many of the courses listed and described in the catalogue year after year" were never actually offered. Though Carter Wesley had great hopes for the institution at its founding, by 1953 he concluded that TSU was "not . . . a Negro school, but one dominated by whites, for the interests of whites, and contrary and against the interests of Negroes."[65] Marshall and White had been prescient.

Prior to his arrival in Houston, Lanier had been the dean of faculty at Hampton Institute (now Hampton University), dean at Florida A&M University, special assistant in the United Nations Relief and Rehabilitation Administration, and US minister to Liberia under President Harry Truman in 1946. Historian Mary Beth Rogers notes that Lanier "was easily recognizable as one of [the] Talented Tenth," having completed graduate work at Stanford University and postdoctoral studies at Columbia University and Harvard University. He was also known and respected among black Houstonians, having served as dean of Houston College for Negroes during the Great Depression. Despite his remarkable educational and professional pedigree, Lanier still managed to "amaze" psychologists at the segregated University of Houston when, as the only black person submitted to their experiment, he "scor[ed] 3,000 words a minute in a remedial reading test" and "exceeded that of any person tested at the University" in 1954. Most black Houstonians who had an opinion about Lanier looked upon him as a symbol of racial pride and welcomed his leadership at the university.[66]

Throughout Lanier's tenure as president, historian Gary M. Lavergne notes that the legislature only "grudgingly appropriated funds to keep TSUN running in order to keep the University of Texas white," refusing to provide him with a budget to meet their supposed goal to establish a "first class" institution for the state's black residents.[67] Lanier also suffered repeated attacks by the university's board of regents in 1953. Board member Ralph Lee, "an avowed and bitter Dixiecrat," claimed Lanier was "incompetent, cannot stick to decisions, is negligent, insubordinate to the board, and . . . some of his actions are not in accordance with good American principles." Among other grievances, Lee opposed Lanier's failure to notify faculty of their reemployment until two weeks prior to the start of the 1953–1954 academic year. Claudius William Rice, the owner of *Negro Labor News*, based in Houston, also openly expressed his distaste for Lanier's governance. Rice and J. D. Moore, a local activist and minister, claimed that Lanier had lost control of the student body—that they had become unmanageable in the spring semester of 1953. The *Chronicle*, which had been unfriendly toward Lanier since his arrival, amplified complaints against the president, writing that the campus had exploded after the faculty committee refused to allow the school auditorium to be used for a review of Whittaker Chambers's *The Witness*.⁶⁸

Lanier responded to Rice's personal attacks by noting that he and Rice had worked well together when the former had been dean at Houston College for Negroes because as dean he had been able to use his influence to Rice's benefit. However, after Rice failed in his bid to be chosen for the board of regents at TSU, he began printing damaging op-eds about the university president. The newspaper editor, Lanier claimed, "will print anything he is paid to print." Like the *Chronicle*, Rice was "out to embarrass [Lanier] at every opportunity." Carter Wesley, Sid Hilliard, and Claude A. Barnett of the Associated Negro Press used their ink to preserve Lanier's reputation. Barnett implored Lanier to send him any updates on the politics surrounding his presidency, believing that "[p]lenty of misinformation can be spread about merely because those who know the truth do not present that side."⁶⁹

Barnett also corresponded directly with Ben Hawkins, the staff writer at the *Chronicle* who had written about the "unwholesome situation" of student protesters on campus. Sparing no words, he called the article "both misleading and wholly exaggerated" and lambasted the reporter for having no real interest in "pav[ing] the way for a greater and more progressive Texas Southern." He claimed, "The *Chronicle* and *Labor News* are deliberately creating insignificant and petty situations, so as to confuse the Citizenry, spread distrust among students and faculty, and to elevate this unfortunate situation to such a high and depressing state until the President resigns to disgust," and they had done all this without having once "proved nor attempted to prove" their "allegations." Despite Rice's and the *Chronicle*'s efforts to "destroy" the president and whispers that Lanier was a Communist in both newspapers, by Wesley's estimation, most black Houstonians remained strong supporters of Lanier. Sid Hilliard's HCCO and its forty clubs and groups "sent letter[s] of endorsement to the board of TSU, to Governor [Allan] Shivers, and to the local press" testifying that Lanier had "served [black Houstonians] faithfully and well and enjoys a rare bit of trust and confidence here and throughout the state as a leader." Indeed, Wesley argued, the legislature's tepid establishment of TSUN in 1947 would have met with greater resistance from black Houstonians if they had not hired Lanier, whose reputation and credentials commanded respect from white people and fostered admiration among black people. Wesley suggested the board "stop paying any attention to Rice's cackling, because he is just eaten up with hatred of Lanier," and that Rice was so afraid of white men that he was best described as a "slave."⁷⁰

In fact, despite protests otherwise and inadequate funding from the state, which the *Informer* believed would ultimately result in TSU's demise, Lanier boasted several accomplishments as president. Under his leadership the university was "recognized as a Class A institution by the Texas Association of Colleges and Secondary Schools," its art program was regionally ranked, and its profile had grown among higher-education professional associations. Students took ownership of the campus, taxing themselves in order to build a Student Union.[71] The football program had advanced and was winning conference and national championships. Enrollment had tripled since 1947. And in further defense of their president, in the first week of June 1953 student government leaders also testified in letters to the board of regents that "there is no unrest or dissension" on campus and indicated their "full support of the actions of the president, Dr. R. O'Hara Lanier."[72]

Nevertheless, on June 8, 1953, the *Chronicle*'s Ben Hawkins reported that Governor Shivers had ordered a probe into TSU's affairs after the local American Legion "Negro post" requested that he make an "impartial investigation of conditions" at the university. Hawkins noted that the "campus has been the center of reports of faculty unrest and fear, plotting, and inefficient management," and cited multiple instances of students picketing downtown and on campus and multiple faculty "resigning in disgust." The next day, however, the *Chronicle* reported that according to board chair Mack Hannah, a successful black entrepreneur out of Port Arthur, Shivers had not yet ordered an investigation into the school. The governor did eventually order the requested probe in July, which would turn out to be a waste of both time and money.[73]

Following the early June articles, Wesley immediately tackled the *Chronicle*'s efforts to signal TSU as a dangerous space. In an editorial he titled "Conspiracies?" he asked whether there existed "a plan or a design by somebody to kill off TSU?" "Or," he wondered, "is the plan or design to kill Lanier, with a willingness to kill the school to get Lanier?" He charged that the *Chronicle* had no evidence to back up its claims against the university president or the student body, attacks that it had been "regularly . . . hauling" at the institution "since 1949." The *Chronicle*'s efforts to keep the attention of Governor Shivers and its desire to crack down on "any grave or dangerous unrest" ignored, in Wesley's opinion, that the only threat that existed at Texas Southern was its mostly white board of regents—composed of five white and four black members. Indeed, the board had been established by the Texas legislature and individually appointed by the governor as a failsafe to maintain control of the state-funded institution. Wesley concluded that any inefficiencies on campus were the result of the board's auditor's decision to take the financial office from the president's administration and institute "dual control," making all financial decisions subject to their input and approval.[74] Wesley's frustration with the *Chronicle*'s attempts to defame TSU and the board of regents' constant rebuttals of Lanier's administrative and financial efforts led him to suggest out loud:

> I am beginning to think that it may be time for Negroes, who have been trying to go along with the establishment of TSU, to take up arms against the sea of troubles and by opposing them thus end them, or push them out in the open so we can see some heads and tails of them. Why don't we join the NAACP and others who have been against TSU from the start, and put up the means to file a series of suits to enter the undergraduate schools of the University of Texas, on the ground that TSU has been made untenable and impossible for ever serving the Negro interests?[75]

Wesley's patience had worn thin. The conflict over Lanier's administration had demonstrated for him, without any room for doubt, that as a space built in the interest of white people and despite the best efforts of Lanier, his faculty, and his staff to transform it, TSU was another manifestation of white supremacy.[76] The promise of equalization had been a trap.

After investigating the school's finances, faculty, student satisfaction, and staffing policies, the special board of investigators concluded "there is no unrest or turmoil" at TSU and wrote in their final report to the board, "We want to emphasize that we find absolutely nothing evidencing any subversive or communistic affiliation or association by the administration and find no evidence of any subversive or communistic teaching at the University." Dr. Lanier's administration, the *Informer* said in its interpretation of the report, "was above reproach."[77]

Despite this vindication, Lanier only remained at the institution for two more academic years, resigning on June 8, 1955. The announcement by the board of regents hit black Houstonians invested in TSU "like a bomb, with stunning impact." Citizens across the city speculated about "the reason behind the resignation," since there had been no public indication of any further dissatisfaction with Lanier's administration. Nevertheless, after a "secret session" meeting among board members, from which Lanier was excluded, he asked to resign and they "immediately and unanimously" approved, offering him thirty days to vacate his university residence. Rumors of a conspiracy of subterfuge among two or three faculty members, the board, and Dr. Joseph Pierce, who replaced Lanier as acting president, quickly spread. Claude Barnett sent a personal note, expressing his shock and wondering if Lanier might share an account of why he resigned, but also praising him because "[t]hat Texas mustang was a tough horse to ride but it appeared you had tamed her." By July, black Houstonians had still failed to learn why Lanier had resigned and his family had migrated from Houston to Miami, leaving leaders like Lulu B. White uncertain about whether the fight with the effectively white board and their interests had ever truly been resolved.[78]

CAPTURED IN THE LIBERAL TRAP OF INDIVIDUALISM

Wesley's support for the establishment of TSUN in the 1940s reflected his understanding of the nature of racism, an understanding shaped by the narratives that structured his identity: that true Americanism was an inevitable accomplishment, that this accomplishment was "raceless" democracy, and that racelessness required the coronation of the liberal individual subject as the most sacred object of civilization. This raceless democracy would be one where men could simply be men. This constituted much of Wesley's "body of knowledge," the container of intellectual and cultural resources available for him to draw from, and it was defined, constrained, and demonstrated by his traffic in bourgeois rationalism. This common gendered capture has been analyzed and documented by historians and sociologists alike and was in no way unique to Wesley.[79]

But as I have maintained, the liberal discourse of manhood did not treat it as an essential property or expression of maleness, but rather an accomplishment of natural selection. It was not primarily a trait of individual men, but that of a racial group. Gender organized Man's world into male and female races, where the quintessential masculine race was the white race and its feminine Other was the Negro race. The Negro race was the fantastical invention that allowed manhood to obtain coherence, for it was the murder of Afrodescendant people and their reconstitution as "the Negro race" that demonstrated the omnipotence of self-possession and rationality: the slave ledger, mortality charts, crime statistics, and philosophical musings that appeared to successfully measure and thereby give form to "the Negro race" proved the superior achievement of Western liberal thought and science. Wesley's emancipatory work, exhaustive and progressive as it was, was thus decidedly narrow and conservative. Because it was founded on the constrained terms of American manhood—admittedly, a gender symbol that is "multiple" (co-constituted by and with race, class, sexuality, and ability)—it was always hierarchical and exclusionary. It prevented Wesley from considering Marshall's and White's perspectives and rendered inaccessible any vocabulary that would expose the relationship between whiteness and rationalism: the two had always been imbricated in the arrangement of slavery, the management of the plantation, the business of housing segregation, the leasing of convict labor, and the criminalization of race and space.[80]

The individualism Wesley proffered in the pages of the *Informer* proposed a future in which the purity of the individual subject would be unencumbered by the pollutant of race. This utopian hope, expressed by his editorial staff, was "anchored deeply in our fundamental religious beliefs and in our concept of man as a creature of intelligence and will—under God the master of his ship, the arbiter of his fate." This was the place of "contingency" in popular theodicy—that black suffering had a divine purpose, that what appeared to be nothing was indeed something. To them, the United States was fundamentally a Christian democracy, temporarily plagued by race prejudice, but they were sure that "While there are still strong forces and factors seeking to stratify American life along racial lines and permanently jell the Negro group into a place of inferiority, these forces and factors are on the defensive almost everywhere. . . . Everywhere the idea of a single standard of citizenship and opportunity is on the march." Thus, to bring in the New Year in 1953, they called on "Negroes to recognize (and discharge) two obligations as Americans—the obligations of citizenship, and the obligations of Negro Americans."[81]

Their immediate duty as Texans and Americans was to pay the poll tax and vote. The editors wrote, "Literally nothing should loom larger in the mind of the individual than the necessity of qualifying as a voter and exercising the prerogatives of a voter." The polling booth was "the people's forum." For Wesley and the *Informer*, *Smith v. Allwright* had propelled the nation toward its destiny as a raceless democracy. As legal individuals, then, if they did not vote, black Texans were "disenfranchising" themselves; if the law was race-blind, then race ceased to exist at the ballot box and racial inequality in voting was not structural but the aggregation of individuals' choices.[82] Because the master narrative of American democracy as fundamentally, naturally, and theologically right guided their reasoning, the editors at the *Informer* treated race as an "anomaly that was never justifiable except on the basis of expediency . . . an expediency recognized as temporary from the court."[83] Therefore, racism was a harmful but nonfatal mutation in American history that, once surgically removed by legal or judicial decree, left behind people who were then individually responsible for practicing the citizenship they had once been denied.

Of course, Wesley and his staff lived in a world where racialization remained inescapable. His individualism did not preclude an immediate and pragmatic collectivism. He argued, for example, that black Houstonians should "'buy Negro' even at the expense of sacrifice on your part."[84] However, this was not an appeal to racial solidarity for the sake of race as an essential and perpetual category of life. The editorialists noted:

> The Negro individual owes it to himself . . . to support Negro effort whenever he can. He owes it to himself to 'buy Negro' as often as possible, and even to go out of his way to do so. . . . This is not an appeal to prejudice. It is an appeal to reason. On the basis of prejudice Negro businessmen are not entitled to preferential treatment from Negroes since prejudice itself is wrong. On the basis of reason they are entitled to such treatment, and should be given it as often as possible.[85]

Of course, this would mean supporting the *Informer* and its staff, but that aside, their logic was reminiscent of Booker T. Washington's when they wrote: "It seems doubtful that Negroes as a group can ever achieve full non-racial acceptance as long as they remain an impoverished, poverty-stricken group." Thus, what appeared to be racial chauvinism, the editorialists claimed, was actually "realistic" and temporarily necessary. Prejudice was inherently evil, but insofar as black people suffered the economic and political consequences of discrimination, they would have to work together toward the shared goal of self-possession. That is, group progress would lead to "individual progress."[86] Therefore, the tension between individualism and collectivism was resolved for Wesley through an unqualified rejection of all "prejudice" and through an appeal to the liberal masculinist construction of "reason," which allowed for collectivism insofar as legal discrimination persisted.

For Wesley, the realization of individualism required the erasure of the legal significance of color. At the *Informer*, the "American dream" was the realization of "individual worth and dignity under the law."[87] Racism and prejudice were un-American precisely because they were anti-individualist and therefore undemocratic. As reader Donna D'Ray wrote to the editors:

> Why is America so un-American to the Negro? The blame cannot be laid to the country or the Constitution, for he belongs to the country and the Constitution covers his freedom and privileges the same as anyone else's. The blame lies in the individual. The individuals who sprawl over two bus seats to prevent a Negro from sitting down is not being American. The individual who kicks about eating in the same cafeteria with the Negroes is not being Democratic. Such people have shackled the Negro to a shameful chain of limitations. Americans should not be doled limited freedom. One less than another. . . . They are traitors. . . . They live a lie. They make a mockery of the

Constitution of the United States of America. God grant the day will come when all of us will wake up to the meaning of these words and practice them diligently, for then and only then will all individuals be actually and truly American.[88]

D'Ray's letter was candid and thoroughly consonant with the views expressed in Wesley's *Informer*. American values, made legible by the Constitution, were not to blame for racism and prejudice. The Constitution itself was color-blind in D'Ray's assessment, and she demonstrated the selfsame faith that Wesley had in its ultimate triumph over the un-American impulses that attempted to degrade it.

D'Ray and Wesley, like all people raised to believe in the immutability of the written contract—because the written word was afforded inherent value as an obliging force on its own—operated in a world where "[t]he relationship between the written word . . . and the community was not one of transparent representation; rather, it was one of authority." Its authority was not merely in its lettering or its promise, but in what they understood as its relationship to the divine.[89] Indeed, the American Christianity that Wesley and his contemporaries had inherited was predicated entirely on the "fact" of the self-possessed, personally responsible agent who could sin but who could also be redeemed.[90] Thus, the Constitution was divinely lettered, and in its relationship to the divine it garnered its authority. Rather than considering that the law was based on nothing, they maintained that it was based on a greater Law. Under this greater Law, racial segregation was a "sin" and "contrary to the ideas, the aims, and the teachings of Christianity to which the nation subscribes," according to the *Informer*.[91] "Can [Americans] insist on racial segregation . . . and at the same time follow loyally the Christian way?" the editorialists asked rhetorically.[92]

Wesley himself could not divorce American democracy from individualism. On November 7, 1953, he reported that he had started rereading W. E. B. Du Bois's *Souls of Black Folk*. He praised the preeminent American sociologist and reminisced on his experiences in college when he and his peers debated over the leadership of Du Bois and Booker T. Washington. Wesley said that Du Bois's "courageous" writing and political stance "proved prescient." However, he expressed confusion, disappointment, and "disgust" at the idea that Du Bois was turning "Red." The only way he could rationalize Du Bois's apparent swing to the left was in "imagin[ing] that he dares to support some of these crazy movements because he has the courage to deliberately want to embarrass the government in its practices of discrimination." Wesley thought it impossible that Du Bois, a man of fearless democratic vision, could "ever really be a Communist."⁹³ In his inability to accept Du Bois's support of socialist tenets, Wesley exposed the limits of his "body of knowledge," in which any conceptualization of society that failed to treat individualism and capitalism as good and necessary features of civilization was to be cursed.⁹⁴

Political theorist and feminist scholar Iris Marion Young explains why and how liberal individualism is inherently subjugating. Wesley could not find a way to rationalize Du Bois's move toward socialism because, as Young notes, "According to liberal individualism, categorizing people in groups by race, gender, religion, and sexuality, and acting as though these ascriptions say something significant about the person . . . is invidious and oppressive." In its insistence that people be viewed as "variable and unique," liberalism "in fact obscures oppression." When Wesley imagined a dissipation of "the Negro" group once legal recognition of race ended, he rendered impossible any "concept [of] oppression as a systematic, structured, institutional process." For liberalists, if (dis)advantages manifested in an individualist society, they resulted from the individual's skills, talents, behaviors, actions, and choices, a remarkably antihistorical concept of inequality.⁹⁵

Moreover, even in an obviously racist society, the notion of the indivisible individual maintained. One popular discourse in which this notion facilitated the continued degradation of black folks was that of criminality. The *Informer* struggled between writing about crime as structured action and presenting it as an individual failing. It ultimately trafficked in rhetoric about "Negro crime" that contributed to the criminalization of race and space that justified segregation as a reasonable demand by white people for safety.⁹⁶ Indeed, as liberal individualists, Houston's black leaders never escaped the habit of blaming "the race" for its condition. "Though armed with physical freedom, a good education, and rights guaranteed us by the Constitution," wrote columnist Olivia A. Adams, black Americans had not achieved their "American dream" because they had not taken "individual initiative."⁹⁷

Surely, Wesley's individualism was not his own. The master narratives that shaped his understanding of racism as an anomaly, individualism as the solution, and the Constitution as a divinely inspired decree were widespread and held even by those with whom he disagreed, like Thurgood Marshall, whose speech on the rightfulness of meritocracy Wesley quoted after their feud ended.⁹⁸ Legal scholar and civil rights activist Lani Guinier notes that Marshall and the Legal Defense Fund "redefine[d] equality not as a fair and just distribution of resources, but as the absence of formal, legal barriers that separate the races."⁹⁹ Marshall's individualism, then, was constructed in much the same way as Wesley's: a focus on the law as arbiter of identities and a forward gaze toward colorlessness. Wesley and his editors made clear: "To us Americanism signifies that approach to organized society that takes into account individual merit without prejudice created by wealth, or position, or race. It is that approach that recognizes the worth of the individual; that sees all men as created equal; that jealously guards the right of each to equal opportunity without legal proscription."[100] Thus, to speak of "Wesley's individualism" is not to suggest that it is uniquely his, that he created it, or that it ended with him. However, Wesley and his *Informer* gave voice to individualism, consistently and quite coherently, as the guiding philosophy for Houston's mid-twentieth-century civil rights struggle.

For Wesley and his editors, this individualism was an all-encompassing ideology, but it was also a market mechanism. In true American capitalist fashion, Wesley's *Informer* claimed that once the legal distinctions of race were gone, all that would be left was the economic, then social, assimilation of black people into "American life."[101] Through individual advancement in technical training and engineering, the market's unquenchable demand for their highly skilled and specialized labor would cause centuries of race prejudice and discrimination to fade away.[102] In their minds, this must have been possible only if they understood it as a structural or institutional problem that could not exceed the law. (As I have argued following Calvin Warren, racism is the violence that allows the ontology of the modern genre of humanity, Man, to maintain coherence when faced with the challenge nothingness presents for that ontology, and thus law and economic rationalism, as expressions of that ontology, cannot impound racism.) "The basic question involved," the editors claim, "is really a moral one."[103] The ethical problem of race prejudice was outside of the state's ability to legislate; however, the "American economic machine" could and would reorient the sick prejudicial mind toward a healthy view of each American individual.[104] Legal historian Reva Siegel argues that this thinking actually rationalized social stratification because it suggested that the "market institutionalizes racial justice" for individuals and lends credence to "society's efforts to delegitimize status-race claims."[105]

This capture in liberal individualist philosophy helped maintain the structurally antagonistic relationship between whiteness and blackness. Surely, there had been change on the ground in the decade after *Sweatt*: black Texans had a new, if underfunded, state university and the Houston school board had a single black member elected with biracial support. However, the same liberalist understandings of the indivisibility of individuals and the self-correcting rationality of the economic market also undergirded the court-enforced "freedom of choice" plan for Houston's public schools in 1966. This plan delayed desegregation and resulted in the continued exclusion of "Negro and Mexican American students from Anglo schools."[106] It was no surprise, then, that Wesley was unable to "see other people's sides of a question," as he was epistemologically captured by these structuring narratives of individualism, racelessness, and the inherent righteousness and inevitable realization of democracy. It also meant that his rhetoric would always be susceptible to co-optation, for the very basis of his freedom dreams (self-possessed individualism) was what made *this world* possible, and hence birthed him as Man-Not via its racializing assemblages. Indeed, as black lawyers and activists pushed Jim Crow toward its grave, white people used the same language of individualism and choice to frame their resistance to integration. Political scientist Julie Novkov writes, "Any theory that starts from abstract principles rather than analysis of the history of power relations on the ground is readily open to transformation once these abstract principles have become generally accepted."[107] Wesley adopted such intangible values as emancipatory tools, undoubtedly as a product of his time and space, believing in the ideal but ignoring the historical and empirical reality that inaugurated the need for emancipation in the first place: American democracy and liberal individualism lived with, not against, slavery and Jim Crow, and these systems of domination were not anomalous—they were *all* that America had known. Contingency (theodicy) could only explain black suffering (that is, afford it meaning and value) and point toward an unknowable future by refusing the empirical. In a *Time* article lauded on the front page of the *Informer* for its exposé about life from a "Negro" perspective, black photographer Gordon Parks expressed the same hope as Wesley, saying, "You can't walk around with your race piled on your back." However, with "persistent doubt," he added, "Anyway, that's what I tell my kids. Maybe I'm just bluffing myself."[108] Persistent doubt sounds about right.

Thus, retrospectively, it seemed likely that TSUN, birthed as it was out of the logics of accommodation to *this world*'s terms, would disappoint Wesley. In 1946, when Sweatt attempted to register at the University of Texas, there had been no law school that black Texans could attend in their own state. The state's university endowment had been hoarded by its white leaders, and black taxpayers compensated by doubly taxing themselves. By the 1950s, they could at least argue that there was public investment in their higher learning that had not existed before. But the structurally antagonistic relationship between whiteness and blackness had not changed: TSUN was white-governed despite its president's racial identity; it was grossly underfunded and expected to use limited resources to build up a people who had been educated in schools where a roof might collapse and classrooms were overcrowded; and it relieved pressure on historically white institutions by providing a safety valve of "equal opportunity" in the form of a new segregated school. Moreover, at the symbolic level, TSUN did not disarticulate blackness from evil. It did, however, seem to affirm the inevitability of a raceless democracy. It stood as an emblem of what black people could accomplish by slowly, methodically, and reasonably chipping away at institutional racism. At this level of argument, the narrative itself is captured in stasis, ending where it began: all was calm in "Heavenly Houston" this day, insofar as white patrons were seated and served before black ones. Appealing to and appeasing a white clientele only quelled their racial and ontological anxieties. And fealty to the sincere fictions of liberalism still failed to achieve manhood for the Negro race.

5
CAPTURED BY BLACKNESS
Prior Tortures and Law Enforcement's Reign of Terror at Texas Southern University

> How is the chronicle of death foretold, expectant and always looming on a slave ship, dissimilar to the threat of death that hangs over the head of a population that remains the target of the state's militarized violence? The point here is not to conflate these two moments—what happened then and our now—but to think about the constellation formed by them. The intimacy with death that was first experienced in the hold continues to determine black existence . . . and yields a huge pile of corpses; the accumulation, expropriated capacity, and extracted surplus constitutive of racial capitalism and modernity; and the premature death, social precarity, and incarceration that characterize the present. Our dispossession is ongoing. The hold continues to shape how we live.
>
> Saidiya Hartman, "The Dead Book Revisited," *History of the Present*

Since the Civil War, black Houstonians fought valiantly for their incorporation into American civil society. By the 1960s, the powers against which they struggled remained stubbornly in place, even if differently manifested. Segregation, mob intimidation, and police violence persisted, exceeding and outliving the political economy of Jim Crow.[1] In neighborhoods and on the campus of Texas Southern University (TSU), black Houstonians resisted but never escaped the consequences of the white supremacist regime that exacted all forms of violence against them.

There is an event in Houston's history that encapsulates this will-to-resist bound to and by this inability-to-escape: the police attack at TSU in May 1967. But this chapter is not about the attack per se. I offer a historical revision of this event, but not merely to correct how the so-called TSU Riot is remembered. Rather, I begin the chapter with the attack to think backward in time and maintain that the attack was continuous with the "prior torture" that followed black Houstonians through the decades. Tryon P. Woods writes that the "disappearance of black torture victims from historical memory" often fails to register as a methodological problem for historians because these victims *appear* to be represented in spectacular events, like the police assault at TSU, while those black subjects in fact remain "too deracinated, too stripped of ontological presence, to register as a victim of torture or even 'to be credited a prior torture.'" Importantly, Woods explains, this torture is not simply other iterations of state or spectacular violence, but "violence located at the constitution of being itself."[2]

This is one sense in which to think of Calvin Warren's "ontological terror": the various "antiblack technologies, tactics, and practices" by which Man attempts to destroy nothing by inventing black being. That is, Man struggles to avoid the ontological terror of nothingness—that which exceeds our capacity to see, measure, and know. Man, a genre of "human" socially constructed by way of scientific instruments, insists on the omnipotence of metaphysics to ascertain objective truth concerning existence. Thus, nothing terrifies Man, for it exposes the limits of Man's ability to know. Man passes this terror onto persons marked as black. This passing on manifests as attempts to dominate nothing—to turn it into something/corporealize it so that it cannot threaten Man's sense of security in its capacity to apply meaning to everything. This compulsive avoidance continues despite that if nothing is made into something, then it is no longer the nothing that was the aim of domination. Consequently, Warren argues, anti-black violence is necessary for and unending within *this world*. Accordingly, Saidiya Hartman laments, "Our dispossession is ongoing. The hold continues to shape how we live." Given the pattern, of which the police assault at TSU is only one data point, it is also no surprise that Hartman identifies "the state's militarized violence" as integral to the hold's structural stability in the early twenty-first century.[3]

Thus, this chapter continues the theme of capture that travels through *Houston and the Permanence of Segregation*, a theme that also describes the challenge of archival lack. We have been afforded a scintilla of the work Christia Adair did day-to-day, even in her own oral history interview; very little of what Johnnie Lee Morris had to say about his case or its disposition; nothing of what the Caesars felt after the land on which their new home was built was seized for highway construction; and mere hints of the fullness, complexity, and internal consistencies and contradictions of Carter Wesley's political vision. Given the archival dearth, those chapters should be read and remembered as interpretations and the subjects as *representational* rather than positivist reproductions of full, interior lives.

In those chapters, I do not run away from the methodological limits inherent in the writing of history, but rather embrace them. The archival silences provide an aperture through which to see and analyze how revolutionary (or apocalyptic, nihilistic, and/or pessimistic) thoughts were made impermissible. Wesley would not countenance certain ideas in his newspaper: even as he supported social safety nets toward the elimination of poor housing, poverty, and unemployment, he decried "socialism." Despite the mobs, the Caesars never issued an outright condemnation of their new white neighbors, and instead spoke of the racial civility of Houston and their rights under the law. Morris was literally forced to speak a confession while his own story and voice remained inadmissible. Meanwhile, his supporters were compelled to acquiesce to the verdict, believing simultaneously in his innocence and the injustice of his life sentence, but also celebrating the "fairness" of his trial.

This chapter departs from those. It can do so in part because of the archival repository that grounds it. Through disruptive protests during the early 1960s, Houston's college students compelled the city to desegregate its spaces of public accommodation and its downtown businesses. As the decade grew longer and segregation and other forms of discrimination persisted, so too did black activism in the city increase, as did police efforts to suppress that activism. After the police attack on the men's dormitories at TSU, interviews of more than one hundred students who had been direct victims of the attack were recorded and preserved in the records of the NAACP. Historians have rarely consulted these.[4] While there are certainly opportunities to use these sources to do work similar to this book's prior chapters, the testimonies of 135 students offer a remarkable rejoinder to the ambiguousness that characterizes the ways most historians have addressed the police attack and its causes as well as the meanings scholars have ascribed to it in the history of Houston's desegregation period.

For example, comparing the "TSU incident" to the "open warfare in Watts, Detroit, and Newark," historian William Clayson notes that it "was minor." Hundreds of rounds of gunfire into dormitories and $30,000 in property damage notwithstanding, it seemed that TSU's night of terror could only register as a major event if the black students had engaged in more violence and if more blood had been spilt.[5] In an endnote in his work, Wesley Phelps remarked, "Disagreement remains over who was responsible for firing the first shot of the 'TSU Riot.'"[6] The passive voice makes it unclear who is disagreeing and why; it elides that there may be no merit to the disagreement and suggests that the competing accounts have equivalent amounts and quality of evidence. This interpretation does not appear to me an innocuous practice of restraint by historians, but an indication of methodological decay. This is in part due to the major source for Phelps's remarks about the violence at TSU, which was historian Dwight Watson's monograph, *Race and the Houston Police Department*. Watson relied heavily on interviews with fired professor Mack Jones (who was not present at the event) and Bill Lawson (who had been in jail until the late night) and accounts published in the *Houston Post* and *Houston Chronicle*.[7] Missing from this bibliography were the student testimonies that convincingly corroborated each other and that were unambiguous when identifying the police as firing the first shots before storming the dorm.

Likewise, psychologist Sidney E. Cleveland explains that "there are many versions of what took place at TSU," and there were two "extreme" accounts, one that castigated the ill-trained Houston Police Department for rioting and the other that claimed it was a student riot appropriately quelled by a professional police force. He says, "Obviously what happened at TSU has been extremely difficult to reconstruct," and concludes, "reality lies somewhere between these extremes."[8] However, there is no compelling reason to buy Cleveland's claim about the methodological difficulty of telling this story; there are, in fact, sources aplenty. The fact that these sources disagree should neither surprise nor stump the historian because contextualizing sources to aid interpretation, including adjudication of their trustworthiness, is the historians' task. Searching for the "reality" between two "extremes" (defined as such by Cleveland) when given the long history of brutal police violence against black people and the well-documented police assaults on college students all around the United States in the 1960s requires a doubt toward black students' and black communities' version of events that appears to me uncalled for. Given the remarkably consistent accounts provided by students from different dormitories, most of whom had no relation to each other, I firmly maintain that the violence at TSU was a police riot and an act of anti-black terror. Additionally, I argue that it was only one act in a continuum, and it is this continuum that provides the context in which I assess the veracity of the students' claims.

There was no ambiguity in the student testimonies, and I commit to believing them. Not only are their independent testimonies consistent in terms of the timing and sequence of events, but the students also rendered the same emotional and affective responses: fear, anxiety, hatred, depression, and helplessness. So, whereas in previous chapters I skeptically investigated what the subjects therein *concealed* and what kinds of thinking were impermissible, here I emphasize what is *revealed* in the archive by way of empathy. I ask what does this archive of student testimony reveal about black resistance, black politics, and their bleak im/possibilities even as Jim Crow weakened?

To get at this question, I de-center the spectacular event of the police riot. Rather than functioning as the climax of the chapter, the assault at TSU begins the chapter in its first section. This revised account relies heavily on student testimonies to provide the timeline. I privilege their firsthand accounts over other sources, though not exclusively, given that they were the only parties present prior to, during, and after the entire attack, and the only parties who relived the trauma, thus folding the past into the present. Their collective story of the police attack points to a persistent theme articulated by Saidiya Hartman: that living a black existence is to have "the threat of death" always hanging if not already killing.[9] Black folks living in the hold could not help but to be perennially confronted with mortality, and this anxiety cannot be analytically stripped from the dispositions, politics, actions, and inactions of black people—in this case, TSU student activists and black residents.

Importantly, the hold could never limit all movement; black Houstonians did push against the dictates of white supremacy. I argue that the movement of people as well as movements of thought were/are endemic features of black existence. However, whereas many scholars tend to valorize resistance, I avoid applying any great moral meaning to it. I count it no surprise that black people fought against their own deprivation; these black folks remained captured precisely because their existence was considered unruly—resistant to the genocidal prerogatives of white supremacist capitalism that sought to order the modern world. Still, even if not inherently meaningful, even if not consequential enough to rescue black people from the capture of anti-blackness, I count these movements as important.

To understand the nature and implications of these movements, I borrow historian Alex Byrd's conceptual framework in *Captives and Voyagers* to consider how "the nature of white power and white decision making significantly affected how captives adjusted" to changing exigencies. Though the "captives" herein are the TSU students whose encounters with mortality in an anti-black world provide the substance of this chapter, like the enslaved people in the British Atlantic in Byrd's text, they "navigated a particular ecological and ideological environment that threw up incredible limits concerning the worlds they would build and join, but at the same time offered remarkable opportunities." For black Houstonians, those opportunities included a collectivism—a kind of ad hoc adoption and incorporation of nonbiological kin in order to stave off the threat of death, remarkable perhaps because in efforts to avert social and physical death these folks drew themselves closer to mortal danger. Namely, when white terrorists threatened black families in Houston's northside, TSU students volunteered their time and their safety to join these families—to sup with them, sleep with them, and guard their homes with arms. As had been true in the Caesar case, the nuclear family proved an insufficient social construction for the protection of black property and sanity.

As was true for the captives Byrd writes about in the eighteenth-century British Atlantic, this creative development was made possible in twentieth-century Houston because of the varied movements/migrations of captive people. But these movements were "fundamentally shaped and defined" by "coercion, not choice." Like Byrd, I emphasize "violence and coercion" not merely as "part of the experience" of captives, but to get at the "ways they shaped the process" of movement. Analytically, then, I assert my own heuristic value to the "subsequent formation" of communities they manufactured.[10]

Telling this "twin story of desperation—of people desperately choosing or being forced to move"—requires something more than the positivist methodology that is meant to ground history as a testable, replicable social science. (Hence why I admit I am imputing heuristic value rather than, say, uncovering ontological value or restoring voice to the voiceless.) Therefore, in the second section of the chapter I continue to employ some elements of Saidiya Hartman's method of critical fabulation. This method provides a way of writing about the unrecoverable, to say out loud what might have been. The tools include, but are not limited to, negotiating the archive's limits by way of advancing speculative arguments and exploiting the subjunctive tense. Narratively, it does not resist the unverifiable because it fully concedes that the archive is replete with "fictions"—"the rumors, scandals, lies, invented evidence, fabricated confessions, volatile facts, impossible metaphors, chance events, and fantasies that constitute the archive and determine what can be said about the past." Additionally, Hartman advises restraint against the compulsive drive to "fill in the gaps and provide closure" or to "give voice" to the captive.[11]

David Kazanjian suggests an extension of Hartman's work by treating the archives of the captives as scenes of speculation. His proposed method is "overreading," whereby "quotidiana" is excavated, though not to determine questions of "who did what, where, and when," nor to recover "imputed subjectivities" to the subjects whereby, as historians, we supposedly determine the "willful, desirous interiority" we already presuppose is the engine of human action. Rather, he suggests reading archives "to unfix our presumptions about political agency" and shift focus to the "other kinds of political thought and action [that] animated freedom struggles on a quotidian scale."[12]

Houston and the Permanence of Segregation sustains an argument against the presumption of agency throughout. Taking for granted that such a notion of agency is incommensurate with the experiences of people who have been made black, this chapter studies "the lives" black people "made in motion" and by doing so necessarily refers to the conditions that initiated the need to move, namely the "violence and disaster," the "duress and catastrophe" that were "central . . . to the formation and articulation" of *blackened* people and their methods of survival.[13] Thus, restated, in the second section I push the limits of historical disciplinary methods with Saidiya Hartman's critical fabulation, raising questions that compel me to overread like David Kazanjian while thinking about the creativity of black political thought and means of survival. However, I do not overstate creativity's capacity or promise, but rather, like Alex Byrd, am drawn in a circle to accentuate the context that degraded black living/being to the extent that black living might be better described as survival/existence without being, as Calvin Warren might say.

Concern with death, and perhaps the anxiety that comes with the inability to know *nothing* beyond death, was unavoidable for those TSU students and so too for me as a historian digging through the records they left behind. But some scholars have reproached what they view as the fetishization of death in some black studies frameworks. "Afropessimism (2.0)," as dubbed by Greg Thomas, has been critiqued as a "death cult" that reproduces and rebrands colonial attitudes of "Afropessimism (1.0)," a school of thought that predicted the inevitable demise of sub-Saharan Africa and its varied peoples, arguing that there is no hope for Africa.[14] Though, according to Tryon P. Woods, significant work should be done to think about these two Afropessimisms' historical and epistemological relation to each other, both he and I maintain that "Afropessimism (2.0)" does not request worship of/through death.[15] Rather, "the whole point of the enterprise" of Afropessimism "at some level" is "that black life is not social, or rather that black life is *lived* in social *death*." As Jared Sexton writes, "Black life is not lived in the world that the world lives in, but it is lived underground, in outer space."[16]

Thus, I accept that black people have been rendered socially dead in *this world* without conceding that this amounts to the dead end of black existence. Rather, what appears to be a dead end, or the abyss/nothing, can be a site of creativity—of thought in motion. *This world* was/is held together and simultaneously thrown into chaos by a persistent "contradiction . . . between a profitable method of production and notions of human dignity," black contemporaries to the assault at TSU argued. Theirs was not an "exclusive class analysis" (or what academics might call class reductionist), but one that refused to turn away from the foundational fact of racial slavery and its afterlives. As they wrote, "Emancipation did not bring freedom, but only a change of one master for another." Thus, in full pessimist tenor, they proclaimed, "it is

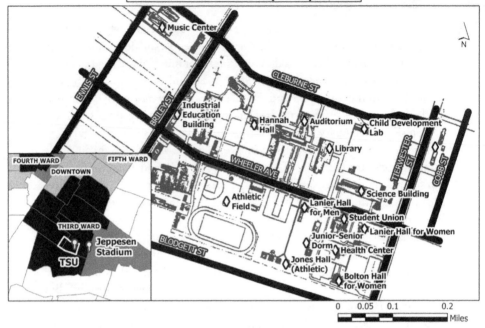

Map 9 *Texas Southern University with extent map indicating the relative location of Jeppesen Stadium to the campus.*

not possible under the present system of private property" for black people to live a life unencumbered by the death-dealing violence that established them as black in the first place. Within that pessimist proclamation, however, was creative vision—an optimism that did not promise utopia but that envisioned apocalypse.[17]

Therefore, a final way to approach this chapter is to consider it as a meditation on life. Black life in Jim Crow Houston, which was called into being as *black* life by the violence that produced social death, exceeded what registered as properly social. What appears to be dead in the episteme of *this world* was always teeming with creative possibilities—the revolutionary epistemes that ordinary black people developed with each other in response to the coercions of anti-blackness. Those possibilities appear grim to some. Where the preceding chapters have argued that liberal humanism and its attendant values and presuppositions captured black people's political imaginaries in ways that facilitated the reproduction of anti-blackness, and while this chapter maintains that this is all that is possible in *this world* (hence, the "decades of capture" identified in the introductory chapter's title are not bookended in the 1960s), it simultaneously argues that *this world* is not all that is possible. I have hereto sustained contemplation on the meaninglessness of black suffering when historical narrative is voided of presumptions like agency, resistance, and free will as facts of existence, in part to suggest that if *this world* and all its trappings have no inherent value, then there need be no fear in imagining and calling for their dissolution. As "scenes of speculation," the archives left behind by TSU's students demonstrate that meaning and value are created, and that they are not sacred but always political and moral contests. I see in these archives that because black people have been made to survive in the zone of indistinction—the void between the theoretical and inherent dignity of all homo sapiens and the empirical reality of unabating anti-black terror—they necessarily and regularly faced their own mortality. This encounter with death-for-no-reason helped them produce the optimism of black nihilism: that if *this world* is void of inherent meaning, then they could create meaning, that they could conjure a vision of life lived differently. They did not do this naively. Ahead of the police assault at TSU, the Student Nonviolent Coordinating Committee (SNCC) spoke of a strong student movement, literally conceptualizing politics as movement: "You don't sit still."[18] Theirs was both physical and epistemological movement *toward* apocalypse.

THE 1967 POLICE RIOT AT TEXAS SOUTHERN UNIVERSITY

Every historical account of the "TSU Riot" announces three immediate precipitating events that led to that night. First, resident protests at the Holmes Road Dump in the city's Sunnyside Addition reflected the community's concern with the habitual siting of environmental hazards around black neighborhoods (and the siting of black neighborhoods around environmental hazards). Demands to close the dump grew louder after young and black Victor George drowned there on May 8, 1967. "[W]hat is happening to Negroes in Sunnyside can happen to Negroes anywhere," activists warned.[19]

Second, on the north side of town, residents protested at Northwood Junior High School. Like many schools and districts around the country, those in the Houston area had resisted the desegregation orders of the courts since the 1955 *Brown II* Supreme Court decision and were still, in 1967, trying to stall integration through such tactics as the expulsion of black students for minor offenses.[20] At Northwood, black students literally fought back against white students' bullying and teachers' harassment of them. Administrators expelled black students from school for the duration of the year while only punishing the white students with minor suspensions. Black students reported regular abuses by faculty and staff at the school, including one Mr. Bill who "likes to put his hands on the girls' chest[s]"—specifically and only those girls who were "Colored!"[21] (This harassment is an example of "prior torture" that has not been attended to in any other academic discussion of Northwood. The point is not that historians failed to get "all the facts," but rather that the ordinariness of white terrorism has been occluded by the habit of narrating the spectacular in making compelling causal claims.)

Similar protests were happening in metropolitan areas all across the United States at the same time in what has been called "the long, hot summer" of 1967.[22] Students from Texas Southern University and others from the University of Houston (UH), many of whom were involved with anti-poverty organizations around the city, with the Friends of SNCC at TSU, and with the Committee on Better Race Relations (COBRR) at UH had been variously and regularly traveling to Sunnyside and Northwood to support the residents there. Thus, an interracial student movement supplemented wider community activism.

Third and contemporaneously, a black campus movement at TSU guided by the Friends of SNCC and their supporters protested the university with a list of grievances that mirrored demonstrations on historically black campuses elsewhere.[23] Particularly, they wanted Professor Mack Jones rehired. They believed that the university administration had fired the Friends of SNCC's faculty adviser for his support of the student group. They also wanted a guarantee of academic freedom for their professors, a curriculum that would privilege black scholars and scholarship, and increased pay for all faculty and staff on campus. Concurrently, they demanded social improvements, including an end to the sexist curfew for female students, improved cafeteria food, and a student council to judge student disciplinary cases.

Students grew impatient with TSU's nonresponsiveness to their demands and over the course of the spring 1967 semester increasingly targeted their protests on the most visible sign of the academic and social neglect they suffered: Wheeler Avenue. The east-west thoroughfare bifurcated their campus between academic and residential buildings. Car traffic not only made crossing the street precarious, but also exposed students to verbal and physical harassment by white passers-through. Students complained of KKK sightings, of drivers and passengers "throwing cocktails out of the windows and driving with a [Confederate] flag," of "individuals" who rode "up and down our campus yelling insulting remarks at us," and of white men prowling around the windows of the women's dormitories. After repeated refusals by the city and the police department to close the street to vehicular traffic, students decided that spring that they would close the street themselves, variously dragging construction materials onto the roadway to block traffic and throwing projectiles at white passers-by. What started as a protest became a nightly ritual of student revelry. Female students also used the opportunity to disobey their curfew, risking "automatic expulsion" as they attended the nightly "street dance" where a record player, sandwiches, and soft drinks turned a site of terror into a scene of aliveness.[24] Wheeler Avenue thus became contested geography. The students challenged the city's ownership of the space and the police department's monopoly on ethical violence. They also felt justified in their reclamation of the campus as a black space through violence in a city that had managed to avoid earning a bad reputation for its so-called race relations.[25]

Finally, on the night of May 16, the Houston Police Department reasserted its authority after white officer Robert G. Blaylock—dispatched to campus with his partner James Norris and their guns to watch and intimidate student protesters—suffered a gunshot wound, allegedly from a student sniper. As the story has been told, riotous students compelled the frustrated police chief Herman Short to order his officers: "Goddamn it, clean this place up!" Hundreds of officers fired "thousands of rounds of rifle, pistol, submachine-gun, and riot-gun fire into the dormitories" in the early hours of the morning after many students had put away their final exam study materials and gone to sleep. Officer Louis Kuba was killed during the assault. Over four hundred male students were ripped from their dormitories, many of them near naked and confused, forced to lie on damp pest-infested grass, and were eventually arrested and jailed without any charges.[26]

This fairly neat sequence of events relies on the *spectacle* of injustice to devise a narrative of cause and effect. In what might be called an anti-racist summation, we see simply that Houston police reacted to black protest which was a reaction to white racism, all of which compelled more black protest and more police repression until "the TSU Disturbance marked the demise of the civil rights movement in Houston."[27] Editorialization aside, the "facts" are mostly evidenced in the archives, but their canonization as *the* precipitating events may only reflect that they are fantastical displays of racism. They become convincing explanations of the terror at TSU because they appear to be "in excess of permissible behaviors."[28] In a swift sleight of hand, this narrative about the excesses of racist violence manages to occlude that this "excess" was normal—that it did not indicate a state of exception. Rather, the historiography inadvertently affirms the sovereign state's moral right to stop and molest, to chain bodies and extract labor, to kill in the name of humanity and of civilization—to keep "us" all safe from the savage, even if the state sometimes exceeds moral norms to do so.[29] The historiography conforms to the "existing cultural preference in America for political narratives emphasizing personal responsibility and will over social context and structural constraints on freedom" because such narratives demand no "fundamental changes in the status quo of wealth and power."[30]

In other words, the preponderance of the historical narratives concerning the attack at TSU replicate the ambiguity of the archives they rely on and approach what happened with positivist methods—usually sourced from popular newspapers, police department and city administration statements, and university administrators' responses. Occasionally, historians have also consulted the congressional investigation transcripts that followed the urban rebellions of 1966 and 1967, hearings which were always hostile to the victims and conciliatory toward the police. Here, I begin revising this account through student testimonies about the sequence of events on the night of May 16. They made clear that the police were not responding to a student riot and depicted officers as antagonists who deployed psychological, physical, and sexual violence in the name of public safety.

A Revision: The Police Riot at Texas Southern University

Around nine o'clock that night, students Douglas Waller and Floyd Nichols split ways. They had been part of a larger group of TSU students who had been moving all around Houston that day, protesting on the north and south sides of town, galvanizing local communities to join in the agitation against the discriminations they suffered, and drinking alcohol as the evening grew darker. Back on campus, Waller entered the student coffeehouse on TSU's campus and Nichols joined a growing crowd of students outside of the Student Union, where students had been gathering nightly to shut down traffic on Wheeler Avenue, discuss politics, and dance to the music. That night, many students were spreading rumors about and reporting on the conditions from the Northwood area and Sunnyside. Two HPD vehicles were parked across the street near the Science Building, stationed there by Chief Short. Trazawell Franklin was also among the crowd, discussing with campus police his "experience in jail" and the treatment of black families by Northwood's school administration. As the crowd grew, Nichols spoke with Sergeant William D. Butler, head of campus police, telling him that the students wanted HPD "to move out of the way and go on because we were tired of people treating us wrong." Rather than seeing police officers as protectors—even the black security forces hired by the university—Nichols saw them as a threat. He was quite prescient that night.[31]

Concurrently in the coffeehouse, around 9:30, an intoxicated Waller forced an altercation with an athlete named Maurice Hopson. Hopson and several other students were playing cards, and Waller expressed his disgust, demanding that they join him and other activists to plan another demonstration at

Northwood. Like most students, Hopson did not see his interests as tied to those of black Houstonians' struggles elsewhere in the city. Hopson told Waller "he did not have to fool with him and went on playing cards," and that "the north side had nothing to do with him," at which point Waller "slapped him." Hopson stood to retaliate, but Waller may have brandished one of three guns he had in his possession—guns he had carried with him from a family residence on the north side for reasons I will discuss in the chapter's second section—prompting Hopson's friends to take him away from the coffeehouse and back to Jones Hall, the athletic dormitory. Waller left the building and joined the growing crowds of students outside the Student Union.[32]

Outside, students grew more agitated at the continued presence of the HPD vehicles. But other students were there in "The Pit," a sunken patio in front of the Student Union, as typical undergraduates spending a fun evening with each other as their semester neared its end. Professor Leon Hardy, who witnessed the events of the night from the beginning, testified "that many, in fact most were there just for the excitement." He continued, "Crowds like that are *usual* in front of the Union Building." Charles Freeman estimated that nearly two hundred students were "in the area at the time." Nearby, an intoxicated Nichols was passing a gun to another student when he released a shot into the ground, perhaps the first gunshot of the night. A student named Larry Johnson yelled, "Preacher, you almost shot my foot off." Within the hour, friends escorted the intoxicated Nichols to a family residence on the north side of town. Nichols would later be among five students charged with the murder of Officer Kuba despite not being on campus when Kuba was killed.[33]

Sergeant Butler had started his night shift at ten o'clock and joined the crowd in front of the Student Union. Around this time, Hopson and several other athletes arrived—perhaps thirty of them—from the athletic dormitory to the front of the Student Union where Waller was, ready to retaliate for Waller's earlier attack. Waller "fired one shot and . . . dispersed the crowd," though most students did not go very far and many quickly came back to the scene. Campus security guards and black HPD officers Albert Blair and Charles Howard speedily intervened and took Waller's gun. Blaylock and Norris remained in their car for ten minutes while campus security argued with Waller. Some students in the crowd became frustrated with the rising tension, and Butler reported that some "started throwing bottles and bricks into the street at cars." Blair and Howard attempted to quell the students but failed. Waller, annoyed by the police presence, demanded that the cops tell him why they had parked on Wheeler. Blair and Howard "immediately ordered him to move on." Waller refused.[34]

Trazawell Franklin caught sight of Blaylock "jump out" of his police vehicle and "cock his . . . gun." The show of aggression angered observing students. The black officers stopped arguing with Waller and arrested him. He told them about his two additional firearms and turned them over. He later told officers that he had intended to distribute the guns to other students for self-protection, given the recent spate of violence against black people around Houston. Prosecutors would later charge him with a robbery committed with one of the weapons, despite that he had only come into possession of the firearms that day. Shortly thereafter, Blaylock and Norris left campus with the prisoner and drove about three blocks east, where a police wagon picked up Waller and drove him downtown.[35]

Around 10:30, the white officers returned to their parking spot in front of the Science Building, across from the Student Union. Students responded by tossing rocks and bottles at the police vehicles. About this same time, students reported hearing the first round of gunfire. These shots, undergraduate Chester Logan guessed, had come from police officers, since some bullets were hitting the men's dormitories closest to Wheeler—Lanier Hall and the Junior-Senior dorm. Undergraduate Willie Robinson witnessed the shootings firsthand, saying that at this time only the police had been shooting, playing target practice with the bottles and construction material students had been throwing in the street to prevent vehicular traffic down the avenue. Further provoked, students threw projectiles at the officers. The officers ducked behind their cars and called in reinforcements.[36]

At least one student threw a firecracker onto Wheeler Avenue, according to Officer Williams, who, along with Sergeant Butler, had begun turning vehicular traffic away. Throughout the early part of the night, many students assumed the intermittent gunshots they had heard were firecrackers, "because there are a lot of pranks going around—always shooting fireworks." For this reason, sophomore V. J. Hollins said he did not pay the noisy events of the night "too much attention." About that time, Hollins remembered that "the street was just filled with . . . people just throwing bottles and bricks at passing cars," and after another firecracker landed in the street, "one of the officers . . . started shooting." Some students fired guns, though witnesses noted repeatedly that they were targeting streetlamps and "shooting out the lights of the police car," which had been pointed toward the dorms.[37]

Shortly after eleven o'clock, a bullet struck Blaylock, which one student found ironic: "Oddly enough, the first police officer wounded in the melee was the same officer who was instrumental in provoking the entire incident" by aggressively brandishing his carbine rifle at Waller, which Blaylock admitted was in his hand when he left the police car during his deposition. Not only had Blaylock been involved in Waller's arrest, but he, his partner, and the black officers on the scene also chased students between the dormitories in their police vehicles after the students threw objects at the black officers' car. The students interpreted this as a dangerous and unnecessary escalation. Blaylock had called in reinforcements, and four additional police parked their vehicles in the construction lot near the Student Union. However, even Blaylock only mentioned that there was "a disturbance and rock chunking and so forth here into the street" when he asked for help, calling into doubt suggestions in other accounts that student snipers had raised the stakes that night. Indeed, the sum of Blaylock's deposition indicated that the vast majority of students were not outside and were not involved in throwing projectiles. Additionally, his testimony corroborates the claim that students who were shooting guns were not aiming at the officers but rather at their vehicles. They seemed to be following the same tactic that had worked for shutting Wheeler Avenue to traffic, namely, if authorities would not heed the students' verbal requests, then those students would make the environment so inhospitable that the officers would abandon their posts. Blaylock was admitted to Ben Taub Hospital for observation due to a gunshot wound to the left thigh just below the buttocks. He was not in pain nor bleeding when examined by the doctor and was scheduled for surgery to remove the bullet. The medical report claims that he was shot "while controlling rioters at TSU." Thus, even before the alleged riot, the narrative that TSU students were rioting in Third Ward was already being propagated and treated as fact in what would become archival documents.[38]

Blaylock's wound likely came from a .22 caliber weapon in the possession of a student, though this was never determined. However, given Blaylock's own testimony and the students' accounts, it appears that by eleven o'clock there were five police cars with headlights pointed at the Student Union as an intimidation tactic. Additionally, though denied by Blaylock, officers had discharged their firearms throughout the evening. Under the cover of night, students threw objects and some fired guns at the streetlights overhead and at the headlights on the patrol vehicles in an attempt to elude further surveillance. But traffic on Wheeler had only been shut down for a few minutes prior to Blaylock's wounding. And most students remained unaware and uninterested in what was happening outside, some even walking undisturbed across campus from academic buildings to the dorms. James Young, an undergraduate resident in the Junior-Senior dorm, left the campus library around eleven o'clock that night. As he crossed Wheeler Avenue, he noticed some youths gathered in front of the Student Union. An officer was standing in front of them. Young thought nothing of it, "because 60 kids on the front is a usual occurrence these days." He went to his second-floor dorm room, occasionally hearing a few rocks crash or bottles burst as he prepared for bed. However, "as the night grew longer," the residents of the Junior-Senior dorm continued hearing gunshots, and by eleven thirty, the gunfire was coming so rapidly and so often that Thomas Turner and his roommate moved to the bathroom. They stayed there for about ten minutes but had to vacate their beds again around midnight when the gunshots intensified again. Finally, around thirty minutes after midnight, or perhaps closer to one o'clock, many students reported similarly that "we finally went to sleep."[39] That is, despite accounts in Houston's press and by historians in subsequent decades, the campus was not in turmoil and the police were not confronting a riot, as one lieutenant later unwittingly admitted.[40] There had been no student riot.

The chaos began around two o'clock in the morning. Students living closest to Wheeler Avenue awakened to a campus that sounded like a war zone. The quiet in the previous hour had been due to efforts at negotiation between the students who continued to protest and the police officers, facilitated by Bill Lawson, who had been released from jail around one o'clock, and three other black ministers: Frederick Douglass Kirkpatrick, Earl Allen, and Robert J. Moody. They had been called in under the advice of Blair Justice, adviser to the mayor, Louie Welch, and the Harris County Community Action Association, an anti-poverty initiative funded by the Office of Economic Opportunity.[41] While Lawson had been in jail, Kirkpatrick and Allen (and a drunken Floyd Nichols) had been with the Thompson family. The Thompsons' children had been dismissed from school and were at the heart of the protest at Northwood Junior High. The ministers received two frantic calls from campus reporting that there was trouble afoot at TSU. The second call was more anxious than the first, with a young woman on the other end of the phone saying "that the cops was over there shooting at the students in the dormitory." Believing the woman was pranking them, the folks at Mrs. Thompson's turned on the radio, "and we heard they was really shooting over there." Allen and Kirkpatrick left, making their way back to campus, as Mrs. Thompson and her guests listened to radio announcers attempt to relate the details from the scene.[42]

Allen and Kirkpatrick arrived on the eastern edge of the campus, at Ennis Street and Wheeler Avenue, but "could not get on the campus proper because the street was barricaded by police officers." The ministers tried to convince police officers to let them through the barricades so they could try to speak with the students, but the officers refused the request unless they could "get word from a higher official." The ministers made their way around to the western side of campus, where Justice and Lawson had abandoned the squad car that brought them to campus because it could not get through the "scores of squad cars and hundreds of riot-helmeted policemen."[43]

There, at Justice's request, the ministers convinced the chief to de-escalate the situation by removing his officers from Wheeler Avenue. Short responded indignantly, saying, "You don't tell me what to do. I know what to do." Kirkpatrick replied, "Man, you don't know what to do with Negroes. I been living with them all my life. I know what they want." Short eventually agreed, moving his officers off Wheeler Avenue and back to Tierwester Street. As they approached the dorms, Lawson recalled:

> Girls inside the dormitory yelled affably at Rev. Kirkpatrick. Boys in the driveway between the Student Union Building and the Men's Dormitory shouted at us terms of brotherly acceptance. Several of the more vocal students, obviously in hopes that the police had gone, came to the front walk where the three of us stood. One of us began to report to them that the Chief seemed to be moving the officers and the cars.[44]

Things calmed significantly enough that campus police officer W. T. Adams, who was scheduled to be on duty again a few hours later, left the scene with the apparent blessings of his colleagues—Sergeant Butler and officer Milton Laberier. Lawson assured the students that the conflict "was all over" and convinced many of them to turn in for the night. Kirkpatrick and Moody then attempted to talk to some of the students, among them probably Franklin Alexander, who remained agitated. Despite the calm the ministers brought with them, "it was obvious to them and to us," Lawson stated, "that they [the officers] were not leaving the vicinity, only the front of the dormitory." The students' simple demand for the night was that Short close off Wheeler Avenue to traffic, which he said was not in his power to do. The chief refused to call the mayor for permission to close the street as well. The students, frustrated, decided to close the street themselves, yelling, "Let's light up the street," throwing construction material in the street and rolling a barrel of tar into the thoroughfare, setting it on fire with gunshots.[45]

Triggered, Chief Short ordered his officers to storm the dormitories, but he did so without a direction or a plan. What ensued was a bloodbath avoided only by the incompetence of the police officers on the ground and the construction of the dorms. Some students jerked out of their sleep and stumbled out of their beds when they heard the gunfire. Bullets crashed into their windows and found residence in their walls as well as some bed posts and mattresses. They admitted that they "started to get scared," unaware that Chief Short had dispensed with de-escalation. In the process, officers killed one of their own, rookie Louis Kuba, a murder for which they accused John Parker, Trazawell Franklin, Floyd Nichols, Douglas Waller, and Charles Freeman, despite three of them not even being on campus during the siege. The TSU Five were eventually indicted under Texas Penal Code, Title 9, Chapter Two, Article 468, which allows a jury to find defendants guilty of any crime committed during a riot in which they took part. They were specifically indicted for the murder of Kuba and two charges of assault with intent to murder for gunshot wounds to Blaylock and another officer, Dale Duggar.[46] Houston's media helped promote the narrative that students had targeted officers and killed Kuba. Kuba's inquest later revealed that he had been killed by a .30-caliber bullet, one of the standard bullet types used by the Houston Police Department. Kuba had been killed by his own, but Chief Short was never held responsible.[47] Short had given the order to "erratic and undisciplined" officers; one rookie cop lost his sanity and fired his gun aimlessly as he shrieked. Officers fired at their own snipers who had made their way to the roof of Lanier Hall. And officers who had stormed the dormitories "were afraid to go outside for fear of being shot by police." They would grab a student and force him out of the buildings first "to see if he would be shot." At least two officers wondered on the scene "whether the search, siege, etc. was worth an officer being shot and killed." The "TSU Riot" was now underway, but it was a riot by policemen.[48]

A crucial vehicle by which the verbal and physical violence traveled was sexuality. Sexuality had been critical to the project of race-making since the advent of racial slavery. Simultaneous revulsion and desire for the consumption of black bodies had always been characteristic of white people's sadism as they constructed the Negro as a biological fact. They argued, in scientific texts, travel pamphlets, and theological treatises, that the black race was accursed and that it was defined by overdeveloped sex organs and underdeveloped mental capacity. Not only were Negroes incapable of controlling their own libidinal desires, white thinkers maintained, but they could also compel white people into sex by way of some hypnotic emanation. Historian Winthrop Jordan presents voluminous evidence of the ways "white men projected their own desires onto Negroes" and speculates that in addition to their uncontrolled desires for sex with black women, white men also feared "the Negro better performed his nocturnal offices than the white man." Indeed, much ink has been used, and rightfully so, to expose the severe sexual violence that black women endured at the hands of white men under slavery and Jim Crow. Likewise, it is an impossible project to write about anti-black-male violence without attending to sexuality, given that oftentimes, especially in situations of open black rebellion, "the white man's sexual anxiety focused on the Negro male."[49]

Importantly, sexuality and sexual violation should not be limited to the legal definition of forcible rape, which has historically configured white women as vulnerable to rape to the exclusion of other women and black men.⁵⁰ Sociologist Nick J. Fox and sexuality scholar Pam Alldred argue that sexuality is an "impersonal affective flow" that can augment, diminish, interrupt, or otherwise transform the capacities of "bodies, things, ideas and social institutions." It is a mechanism of procreation by which bodies are changed, producing "specific desires, attractions and identities." The performance of sexuality, and sexual violence, may have everything or nothing to do with the meeting of genital organs, for essential to sexual violence are the dynamics of "domination or submission" and "exhibition or concealment," for instance. The violence against the young men at TSU, which "might not seem sexual at all" in popular conceptions of sex, was indeed reterritorializing by way of such dynamics, reducing the capacities of the victims to maintain their own bodily integrity and destabilizing their sense of identity and security.⁵¹

The students' affidavits comprise the most significant archival evidence of what transpired next and were consistent despite which dorms the students lived in, which jail cells they ended up in, or whether they had been aware of the police's mobilization on campus. They reported being frightened out of their sleep, sometimes with guns in their faces. Dogs nipped at and were sometimes ordered to bite them. Some suffered deep wounds. Recounting the ordeal, Robert Lewis Jr. stated, "[T]he police invaded our room and shooting . . . came in and got us out, they were shooting to kill." Police forced them out of their dorm rooms and threatened them with lethal force if they tried to put on shirts or pants. Students frequently emphasized this sexualized exposure in their accounts. Their half-naked bodies were sexually targeted as well, as officers hit them on their butts and in their groins with sticks while yelling "niggers," "motherfuckers," and "sons of bitches."⁵²

As other scholars have argued, throughout history black men have faced specific physical and sexual vulnerability, though they have not been appreciated as victims of sexual abuse. Thomas Foster argues that the history of black men in fact demands expansion of the definition of sexual assault beyond the gender essentialism that posits "female bodies" as uniquely susceptible to rape. The "terror of the mundane and the quotidian," wrapped as it is in white patriarchal sexualized discourses of manhood and accompanied, in this case, by the genital assault and bodily exposure of black men lying nearly bare on a damp campus lawn, "might be as influential as a single physical penetrative assault."⁵³

Naked and exposed, students were powerless to avoid the gaze of police photographer Don Benskin's and *Houston Chronicle* staffer Blair Pittman's cameras. Their lenses captured the young men, often clad in white underwear, forced to lie face-down on the ground as officers towered over them with long rifles. Many were detained for more than eighteen hours in jail cells and remained in their underwear for the duration. One photograph published in the *Forward Times* freezes in time a moment in which about a dozen officers surrounded a group of students lying prostrate on the ground. One student appears to have just been brought over and is halfway to the ground with a rifle-wielding cop leaning over him threateningly. In the foreground, another officer bends over a student who is already lying down. His nightstick is extended as if he is about to hit the student on the back, despite there being no indication of any physical resistance on the part of the student.[54] Student Cleve McDowell swore before Congress that he indeed witnessed policemen who "periodically struck these confused students for no reason what-so-ever."[55]

It is not difficult to imagine that these students would have felt vulnerable and embarrassed, feelings exacerbated by the cameras that locked them in time as objects of the officers' frustrations, hatred, and capriciousness. What did they think as they lay on the cold grass? Were they concerned with the immediate physical pains? Did the cold, the insect stings, the bleeding wounds on their heads and legs, and the undressed dog bites beg for attention? Were they so frightened, so lost that they dared not move to massage their own bruises or offer aid to a friend beaten so badly that they lay unconscious on the concrete? Or did they think about home and family, wondering if they would make it through the night? Did they thirst for water, mouths dry with anxiety? Did they hope for a breath of fresh air, chests heavy with fear? Did some run away from reality and find refuge in a fantasy—a world of interracial peace or perhaps one where only black people resided?

It is impossible to know, but it is our duty to imagine. And the purpose of this duty is not to impute subjectivity to those victims of violence or to expose their internal lives. Rather, its purpose is to force empathy into the method of reading the photography/archive, to get a sense of the moral gravity of the suffering in ways that mere positivist description does not facilitate. This is crucial, given that these photographs were not mere documentation, but tools of propaganda. They were published in Houston's dailies to promote an image of the police department's white power and its ability to control black dissent. They were used in the black press to indicate what black editors viewed as actions in excess of police duty. In both cases, they were necessary to feed Americans' "devouring scopophilia," which allowed onlookers to take the spectacle in so that they could "control," "torment," and "spit" the subject out. Like so many exploitative photos of black men, "these pictures bear witness to a demand to make black men absent from the scene of the human while lining the eye with deep, libidinal satisfaction." David Marriott presses scholars to see the ways this technology of white supremacist gazing "disfigures" black men, making them "gaping wounds in their own imaginations." What did these black undergraduates see when they finally caught sight of these photos? Could they see themselves as anything more than the unclothed, unwashed savage, made to lie and breathe in the dirt, controlled and protected from their own baser instincts by the superior technology of the white guard? For Marriott, following Frantz Fanon, even if they could see something more than that, they would also necessarily see themselves in this way. The *imago* of the Negro was always and already pressing against their self-consciousness, and it was always interfering with their ability to see themselves without reference to the ways they understood that white people viewed them.[56]

I am alluding to Tryon P. Wood's argument that anti-black violence is not just the spectacular, that which can be captured, for instance, by photography, but also and primarily violence "at the constitution of being itself." The photograph stands as evidence of the psychological and ontological terror the students were made to endure even before we take account of their words. How must they have understood their humanity or the concept of shared humanity when they were ripped from their beds, humiliated, beaten, cursed at, and reminded through words and actions that they were "niggers"? What implications would this have for their mental health for the remaining years of their lives? Would they come to hate white people generally? Perhaps. But they would certainly be "aware that one is not black without problems." They would live a life of double consciousness—not torn between being Negro (a racial identity) and being American (a national identity), but forced into an internal war "between who the young black man is and who he imagines himself to be."[57]

However, this internal war is not necessarily between two equally opposed visions of the self and the racial group. Because blackness is the product of racialization and not merely phenotype, it is not an individual characteristic or status, but rather a group status. Oliver Cromwell Cox would call "black" a political class, defined by conflict, as opposed to a social class, which lacks organization. As such, within *this world* blackness was/is always a group political status (even if it is phenomenologically, morphologically, and phenotypically heterogeneous). Regardless of class ascension or capitalist accumulation, this status was defined within a system in which every member of society carries a "sense of group position," "a sense of where racial groups *belong*," according to Herbert Blumer.[58] Thus, even if the black person vociferously disagreed with the sociopolitical positioning of blackness at the bottom of the American racial hierarchy, the black person was nevertheless aware that all Americans shared a hegemonic sense that "black" was the least-desired, least-valued racial category. Thus, Marriott laments, "Indeed, one of the ongoing problems . . . is how those fantasies that entered our lives so early, so unwanted, so irresistibly, so much in conflict with our pleasures and our freedoms—so relentless in our lived experience—may already be part of that dreaming and its future provenance."[59]

In this way, photography itself became a technology of anti-black violence, and as it becomes a part of the archive, the archive itself becomes an extension of that technology. History, too, extends this violence. Even here, I am incapable of rendering a different image of the young black men at TSU. I could offer a narrative of resistance at odds with the photographs and with the weight of student testimonies, pointing to their survival, their protest, their support of the TSU Five, but to conceptualize it in terms of resistance I would diminish the violence inflicted on them at the level of ontology and consciousness. In one sense, all the students survived the night, which is not insignificant, but the biological notion of survival should not occlude that death was also dealt to the students.

Robert Lewis had fallen to sleep in his bed after the noise had quieted down around that one o'clock hour. But no sooner had he fully drifted off than he began hearing "shotgun shots, machine guns, and people hollering, girls screaming, and about that time I heard somebody kick on the door and say, 'All you black mother-fuckers come out here or I'll blow your damn head off.'" The roommates remembered the officers calling them "niggers," "sons-of-bitches," "mother-fuckers," and "damn niggers." Lewis, disoriented, recalled kicking at the door before six police officers stormed into the room and ordered the students to stay still or be shot dead. Lewis gestured to put on his pants and an officer aimed at him with a gun. After searching the closet for any hiding residents, the officers ordered the nearly naked men out of their room, "beating us all on the butts" with their nightsticks. "It's fortunate I didn't get hit on the head," Lewis seemed to sigh. Looking for a reason to shed more blood, the officers attempted to goad Lewis into "provoking" them to fire: "And they kept saying run nigger run but I never did run." Like other students, Lewis was marched out of the door and forced to lie prostrate on the dewy ground in front of Lanier Hall, while officers continued to break down doors with axes. Officers warned him that the sentence for talking was "they would blow your damn head off."[60]

James Young had been forced to lie down in the middle of the growing carpet of student bodies in front of Lanier Hall for Men, and was thereby insulated from the snarling police dogs, flying nightsticks, and thrusting shotgun butts. The slightest infraction provoked the police to attack the prostrate students. An officer told John Booker, "Eat dirt nigger," when he saw the student's head raised off the ground. The cop "came by and hit me on the head with the nightstick," Booker recalled. "So, I just ate dirt." Clarence Hall remembered how often he and the other students moved their hands in order to scratch themselves, saying, "You couldn't help but scratch because different stuff was crawling on you, with bugs and things you couldn't help but scratch." The officers responded by addressing them as "niggers," commanding them to keep their hands on their heads and reinforcing their orders with kicks. Once outside, Oscar McNair, also an undergraduate, saw dogs biting "a number of people" before he was forced to the ground. When an investigator asked Lewis if the officers came to the dorms "peacefully," Lewis responded: "Well, it's according to how you define peacefully; if there's peace in hell, well I would say so." V. J. Hollins expressed the same sentiment, saying, "They acted like savages."[61]

The discursive violence of the racist slurs and curses affirmed the students' status as less-than-humans and homogenized them as a unit, all dangerous, all guilty, all punishable, all capable of being slaughtered with impunity. Placed outside the dynamic of human relations, the students viewed the world as a place of torment. *This world* was hell. Thus, the notion of "peace," propaganda promoted by the police department and the city administration, lost all coherence as a concept unless it was synonymous with terrible violence. If, as was commonly understood among American Protestants, hell represented an end of life, a total separation from grace, and an eternal status as the subject of evil, then Lewis's metaphor of deathliness appears as analog to Orlando Patterson's "social death" and Saidiya Hartman's "hold."

Student James Young swore that he went to sleep around 11:30 that night and was awakened by the chaotic police force. He remembered, "Most of the students were sleepy, most of the students that I saw came out in their underwear and didn't know too much about what was going on, and so they couldn't offer any resistance. You are standing directly in the face of a double barrel shotgun, rifle, or man with a billy club or gun butt ready to hit you upside the head, you don't offer too much resistance." This was accompanied by constant taunts.[62] The students certainly experienced degradation and a diminished capacity to act, move, think, or fight back; the hold was not just a metaphor. Othello Sullivan seemed to weep, "My character was damaged, and I suffered undue humiliation and verbal abuse."[63] The students' helplessness is palpable in their testimonies, and their encounter with their own mortality is a persistent refrain.

The Houston Police Department worked collaboratively to avoid any publicity of improper conduct, making false claims about their behavior to the local and national media and before Congress. They claimed, for instance, that dogs were not used on the students, though students and the dorm matron, Mattie Harbert, repeatedly testified that they witnessed police dogs attacking students, and several students had bite marks on them when they completed affidavits in early June. Officers also denied causing any damage to the dorms, but when students returned from jail the following evening, they found their clothing doused with bleach, their musical instruments destroyed, their money missing, their windows shattered, their doors broken down by axes, and their rooms unlivable.[64] The Houston Police Department provided a series of affidavits to Congress swearing that no officers allowed dogs to attack students, that all dogs were held on short leashes, and that when dogs did nip at running students they merely sank their teeth into pants and not into flesh.[65] Given that most students were in their night shorts and underwear, this seems fabricated.

Through their actions, officers secured authority, dominance, and control, but they could have very well acquired these without the use of racial slurs, parading the students around half naked, and declaring "white power."[66] These served an additional purpose. To push beyond what the police code of silence produced as archival concealment, we can approach the archive through the subjunctive. What was the physiological reaction among the officers when they were finally let off their leash under the authority of Chief Short? Did they find the excitement intoxicating? Were they caught up in the rapture of unbound violence? Why did they react so wildly, so indiscriminately that they killed one of their own? Did they see only the Negro beast, vulnerable to the hunter with his superior weaponry, organization, and superior mind? Why did they make Mattie Harbert lie on her stomach before they walked across her back if not to derive some pleasure from her degradation? What incensed them so much when students walked too slowly or asked for a chance to put on their clothes that they beat them with nightsticks and tossed them down stairways, leaving some of them bloody and unconscious on the concrete? Why did one white officer barge into John Parker's room and upon seeing the young student jump out of bed with shorts on, tell him to "take [his] underwear off" before carting him outside?[67]

English scholar Vincent Woodward provides some context by which these speculative questions can be considered. His posthumous work, *The Delectable Negro*, provides a history of practices of human consumption by way of homoeroticism in the United States during the eighteenth and nineteenth centuries. Consumption might refer to literal forms of cannibalism or to other means of consumption that involved "incremental feeding upon the human host," but that in any case involved "masters" hiding "their appetites and hunger in stereotypes and ideologies that attributed these characteristics to the slaves." Thus, the officers' lies about the students reveal much about their own actions. Officers claimed students destroyed their own possessions in order to conceal the joy of their own wanton violence. Despite finding no stockpile of firearms, they said students were shooting at them, justifying their own wild behaviors as they stormed the dorms. They refused the possibility of modesty among the students, allowing none the chance to robe, leaving them vulnerable to a gaze that at once was repulsed by contact with the "Negro form" but unable to look away. Long-standing "racial assumptions, political aspirations, gender codes, philosophical frameworks, and cosmologies . . . dictated the feelings of arousal on the part of European and white Americans toward black males and hunger for black male flesh." This hunger was "less about literal consumption and more about the cultivated taste the white person developed for the African" that was "satiated . . . through acts of violence, sexual exploitation . . . or through staged rituals designed to incrementally harvest black spirit and soul." When Sullivan said, "My character was damaged, and I suffered undue humiliation and verbal abuse," he described both the outcome (damaged character) and the process by which he was made into something less than he had known himself to be (humiliation). This act of general dishonor, a key component of Orlando Patterson's concept of social death, was consumptive, leaving behind the waste of shame.[68]

For Woodward, homoerotic violence did not always refer to homosexuality as an identity or a practice, but rather the arrangement of the homosocial. Still, sometimes explicit acts of same-sex sexual violence and sexual discourse rose to the surface of these interactions. James Burroughs was a white swimmer and an exchange student from Detroit. He was "kneed in the groin and hit in the side" by police. While in jail, officers asked Burroughs "was he a half-breed or something . . . because he was with us Negroes." Though the officers interrogated all the students with disgust, according to student Shelton Dotson, they seemed to find Burroughs especially repugnant. TSU's investigative committee noted that Burroughs "was beaten extensively by the police because he is a 'white' student." After all, white allies had long been targeted by vigilantes and police officers. That is, as a violent process of dysselection, blackness could reconfigure out-of-place white persons as vulnerable to premature death. This was the case with Viola Liuzzo, killed by white men in Alabama for her efforts to help black voters register and explicitly called a "white nigger" in formal court proceedings following her death.[69] Officers told Burroughs he was a "homosexual prostitute for 'Nigger Athletes,'" and threatened him and other "scum of the earth," "white trash" visiting students, "[I]f we see you on that TSU campus again, I'm going to kill you."[70]

The officers seemed unable to imagine that white and black men might live as equals. It upended their sense of manhood and whiteness, both of which were crucially defined by the dominance of black male objects. Insofar as the nonrelation between white and black men would always be defined by anti-black subordination, the officers could only conceive of Burroughs as a prostitute, most likely a receptive sexual partner for black men. So disgusted by the possible inversion of the imagined sexual dynamic by which white men fashioned their superiority over black men, they issued one of the most brutal beatings of the night on Burroughs's body. He testified, "They beat me to a state of shock and fear so that I, after it was over, lost over 15 pounds in 3 to 4 days and was very ill for a period of not less than two to three weeks." Another visiting white student named Ponteneau, from the University of Wisconsin, described similar abuses. Two officers barged into his bathroom where he was hiding with his roommate. With "raised shotguns" they appeared "shocked (at the fact that we were white) and stated, 'Well, what have we got here?'" Ponteneau noted, "Their demeanor suggested they were obviously having fun." After officers "walloped" him to the point where he probably suffered a concussion, Ponteneau was taken to jail, interrogated about his sexuality, and "lectured" about the "error" of his association with black students. Officers warned Ponteneau and other non-black students not to return to campus or "they would kill us."[71]

The attacks on Burroughs and other white-identified students, including William Fontenot, a black student who could but did not choose to "pass" into whiteness, indicated that manhood was an animating concern of the police. Between their snarled "white power" chants, police officers reminded students that "this is [the] white man's world." They barked, "Since you want to act like men, we're going to treat you like men." Indeed, women's voices were mostly absent from this archive not because they were uninvolved in the protest; despite being locked in by a female-specific curfew, they participated by throwing firecrackers from their windows. Though the police did threaten female students hanging out the windows earlier that evening, shot into some of the windows, aimed their guns at the second floor of the women's dorms, and took some of their possessions, the officers did not focus on the young women.[72] They specifically targeted the men for attack and arrest. However, this was not a contest of manhood/a relation between black and white men. Rather, as the students' statements intimate in their silence concerning manhood, it was a contest between white men and "everything that the wishful, shameless fantasies culture wants [black men] to be, an enigma of inversion and of hate."[73]

The attacks also revealed that so-called race relations in Houston were "heavenly" only insofar as white and black people fulfilled their spatial obligations, residing solely in their proscribed boundaries. And finally, they demonstrated that blackness, rather than being a matter of identity, yielded a structural position to which even white-identified people out of their racially appropriate place could be relegated. The capture of Christine Morris in 1951 and Jimmy Burroughs in 1967 were parallel experiences.

I maintain that there was no reason for this violence, even if police offered rationalizations for it. This was mere anti-blackness, and, as Calvin Warren asserts, anti-blackness was anti-nothing—the avoidance of a reckoning with the meaninglessness of (black) suffering. Black Houstonians had long been pressing for an encounter with this meaninglessness. They proclaimed at the Holmes Road Dump that nothing could justify the systemic siting of environmental hazards in black communities. They protested at Northwood Junior High that the unfair distribution of punishment toward black kids revealed the vacuity of rules, procedures, and school authority. They exposed the arbitrariness of the law, the excessiveness of the power it imparted to police, and the police power that exceeded the law's boundaries and thereby made it inconsequential in police officers' street conduct. (Indeed, black Houstonians repeatedly rated Houston police as abusive and inept at fulfilling their supposed duties.)[74] The officers denied the claims that they were the rioters, putting the blame on students, many of whom were asleep in their beds and some of whom were not on campus during those late hours, all to occlude the meaninglessness of the police action and the innumerable prior tortures that had animated black protest in the first place as black Houstonians constantly expressed the precariousness and cheapness of black life. Even as life in the hold remained desperate, it was also, by virtue of existing in the hold, always in motion.

VOYAGERS AND CAPTIVES: PRIOR TORTURES AND DESPERATE MOVEMENTS

Significant developments in the early 1960s provide context for understanding why (desperation) and how (by moving their feet) black Houstonians made "lives in motion." In August 1959, police attacked TSU law student Eldreway Stearns during a traffic stop after finding a photo of a white female friend in his wallet. The beating inspired Stearns and TSU students to become activists, and both the campus movement and the student movement grew in consequence, manifesting in the form of protest marches and sit-ins at local businesses.[75] In efforts to intimidate the movements out of existence, white terrorists threatened and attacked black residents, including twenty-seven-year-old Felton Turner. Four white men abducted Turner while he walked near TSU's campus and in a neighboring wooded area, tied his hands and knees, hung him from a tree by his feet, beat him, and carved two rows of the letters

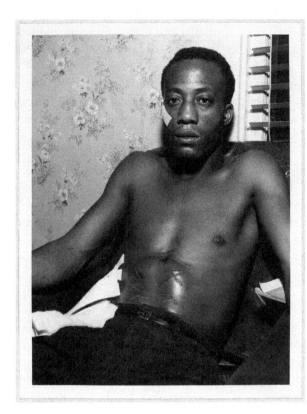

Figure 5.1 *In response to the Texas Southern University (TSU) student movement to desegregate businesses in Houston, white terrorists frequented the Third Ward and other black neighborhoods in efforts to intimidate black Houstonians. In 1960, a group attacked Felton Turner near TSU's campus, carving three rows of "KKK" into his torso. The Houston Police Department claims to have never found the assailants. Photograph by Benny Joseph, 1960. Permission for reproduction authorized by the Museum of Fine Arts, Houston http://mfah.org.*

"KKK" in his torso before telling him to warn the NAACP to stop agitating in Houston. The story further galvanized students. They threatened more protests and dared Houston's leaders to shame the city on a national stage.[76] Disagreement between mayor Lewis Cutrer and police chief Carl Shuptrine about how to deal with the protestors hinged on whether suppressing their freedom of speech would yield embarrassment, as similar suppressive efforts had elsewhere.[77] The student movement successfully desegregated downtown businesses, local eateries, and theaters.[78] However, as the police riot at TSU demonstrated, despite these accomplishments, desegregation was, in Foucauldian terms, a "non-event." That is, time changed, but epistemology did not. Blackness was still abjection, and the quieted desegregation of downtown Houston affirmed this abjection as evident in city leadership's refusal to announce a new relationship between whiteness and blackness.[79]

In those early days, the student movement focused on the areas immediately surrounding TSU's campus, Third Ward, and downtown. Most often, they voyaged on their feet, pushing the invisible boundaries of racial geography as they did so. This was movement compelled by captivity, a rebellion against inertia.[80] Once in motion, the student movement spread, but it faced new challenges as the decade continued. TSU president Samuel Nabrit resigned in 1966 and was replaced by acting president Dr. Joseph Pierce, who was much more beholden to white benefactors and less tolerant of what he saw as disruptive behavior on the part of the students.[81] Simultaneously, the old guard of middle-class-dominated civil rights and civic organizations like the NAACP and the Harris County Council of Organizations were losing prominence, in part due to the Texas courts' censure of the NAACP in 1957 and the loss of Christia Adair's leadership.[82] In this vacuum rose the profiles of SNCC, the Deacons for Defense, and the Black Power Freedom Army. These direct-action and defensive organizations would meet an intransigent set of new city leaders, especially as the old business class that had run Houston's political affairs began to lose cohesion. Louie Welch was elected as mayor in 1964 and appointed Herman Short as chief of police. Short was more outwardly hostile to black people. Indeed, he maintained "surveillance files" on "prominent" black leaders, and when his officers were accused of being KKK members, he replied: "I am not a Klansman, and I know of no police officer who is a Klansman. You can't fault a man, however, for praising God, country, and obedience to law and order. That's what we all stand for."[83] Meanwhile, the federal War on Poverty breathed financial life into anti-poverty organizations like the Harris County Community Action Association, which represented black community interests that were sometimes at odds with the priorities of the student and campus movements.[84] With a blatant racist at the head of the police department, a neglectful mayor, fractured civil rights leadership, and an unfriendly TSU administration, the late 1960s certainly represented different terrain—a return to disequilibrium—for any black Houstonians engaging in civil disobedience. Additionally, Houston's varied black freedom efforts faced the challenges of the city's great geographical expanse and different intraracial priorities.

Subsidized by federal funds for the War on Crime, law enforcement agencies began targeting "low-income neighborhoods as a means to control unruly teens." Following the student sit-in movement and the appointment of Herman Short as police chief, TSU figured as one such place in need of police "control." Indeed, police lieutenant Mallie L. Singleton testified that he had placed two officers on surveillance duty at the campus in 1967, and the Criminal Intelligence Division watched Friends of SNCC members. One black man, a Vietnam veteran and enrolled student at TSU, worked as a spy for the police department "infiltrat[ing] Negro organizations." The man worked with the department to silence "black power" because "Negro extremists are 'becoming increasingly active and a threat to tranquility.'"[85]

Empirically, tranquility must have meant the continued subjugation of black Houstonians absent of their protests against it, rather than the cessation of anti-black terror. The aforementioned bomb threat, the mutilation of Felton Turner, and the constant surveillance by police notwithstanding, historians and others continue to repeat and publish in textbooks the claim that "public facilities in Houston and most other Texas cities had been peacefully desegregated."[86] In order for this refrain to maintain coherence, the word "peaceful" must obscure significant violence. Historians would have to dismiss as irrelevant the kind of daily terror experienced by black folks like Giles Barrs, who, after moving into his new home on the city's north side, "found a crude wooden cross in flames on his front yard," and this was after an earlier incident when "a shot was fired through his front window." Likewise, Walter Daymon's yard in Houston Heights turned bright when local white supremacists lit an eleven-foot cross there. A Confederate flag removed any ambiguity as to the message of the cross.[87] These moments of "prior torture" have never been treated as important for contextualizing the police assault at TSU.

Discussing an array of discriminatory practices against black Houstonians, John Reuben Sheeler, historian and professor at TSU, noted, "Negroes are frustrated with laws which make promises, but cannot deliver while prejudice, apathy, and deprivation continue. The failure of local, state, and federal government to listen to moderate Negro leaders is causing many of them to despair of moderate approaches and give into those proposing two separate American societies that are not going to be equal nor are they going to be peaceful." He wrote of the ways black Americans were beginning to see legal doctrines such as due process as chimera.[88] The racial violence endured by black Houstonians compounded over the decades, burdening them with an existence that always felt on the brink of extinguishment. In 1966, Lucille Davis, a resident in the MacGregor area, reported constant harassment at the hands of her white neighbors: "These include gasoline, which she said was poured on her lawn on several occasions, firecrackers exploded on her porch, air being let out of her tires, and abusive language directed at her." Davis filed numerous police reports alleging vandalism and mischief, including incidents of "cars . . . coming by her residence and tossing bricks and other objects at her house." Mayor Welch and the Houston Police Department responded to her complaints by increasing patrols in the area and discussing the possible consequences of the mischief with her neighbors. They made clear that their interest was not Davis's sanity or safety, but rather the reputation of the city: "It was explained . . . that with all the racial unrest all over the country, this type of harassment could set off uncontrolled violence such as has been experienced in other parts of the country."[89]

More enshrouded than these spectacular incidences of racial violence, however, are the ways these tortures only hinted at the "violence at the constitution of being itself."[90] Speaking before the Texas NAACP branches gathered in San Antonio in 1962, Clarence Laws, the Southwest regional secretary for the organization, recognized the "outstanding contributions to American life and history" by black folks, including in the military and "in education, in religion, in arts and sciences, on the screen and stage," and "in songs and sports." "Still," he lamented, "The fact is that in much of the South, as elsewhere, Negroes after 100 years of 'freedom' are still perpetual aliens in their own country. We are unequals except for the purposes of tax and military service."[91] Like the term "peace," the experiences of black Americans exposed the emptiness of "freedom," and in turn, that emptiness provided space for the production of anti-black terror. And terror it was. Lucille Davis did not just complain about the harassment and threats; she bore it in her body: "she said she was going to be forced to use a gun that she now says she sits up with every night." Her fiancé, who lived in Kashmere Gardens on the north side of town, had "started spending part of the evening at her home with a gun to assist in protection."[92]

Ms. Davis must have been distressed. Where in *this world* could she feel safe? Her home was not a refuge from the terror outside. Who could she turn to for relief? The police department was only built to attend to her needs when they intersected with the interests of the state, and here the interest was not her relief but Houston's reputation. What did she feel in her body? Did her heart race, did her shoulders tense, did her throat become thickened by anxiety? Did she keep her gun near her side as she sat in a dimly lit room, or did she clutch it in her hands, eyes trained on the door and peeking between the curtains that lined her windows as she watched every car drive down her street with steady suspicion? Did she lose focus at the V.A. Hospital where she worked as a medical research technician? Did she worry she might return to a burned-down home after every shift, or did her time away from home press the terror waiting there to the back of her mind for a few hours? How did her fears affect her relationship with her daughter? Did she restrict her child's freedom after a car "swerved towards her" as she played in the front yard one evening?[93] Did her daughter understand the stakes, however old she may have been? Did she know about the bombing at Sixteenth Street Baptist Church in Alabama three years prior? Did she imagine herself as one of the four girls assassinated in that attack? Did it keep her up at night, depress her performance at school, fix her in an angry disposition toward white people, or leave her paralyzed when she tried to imagine a future in which she could realize her wildest dreams? Could she even dream if she could not sleep? Was her mother at her wit's end, deciding to have her fiancé stay late into the evening for a sense of security while she also risked damage to her reputation as a woman in good moral standing? Was it worth that risk if it afforded her a night's rest? And how did her fiancé manage his feelings? Should not a man be able to protect his betrothed? If he could not, what did that make him? Could he sustain a life where he traveled miles between his home and hers while he still had to attend to his own work obligations? Did the couple hold each other through the evening? Or perhaps did they bicker, stressed beyond reason and with no other place to vent their frustrations?

The answers to these questions are unknowable, of course, but empirically determining the answers is not the intent of critical fabulation. Where the archive fails, the subjunctive cannot fill the void. We may never know for sure what happened in Davis's home and much less what happened in and to her body, but we can be sure that the terror she endured was not inconsequential. It infringed on her identity and any sense of security she had in her home, her person, and the law. In the world of human *beings*, Davis did not register as such, for, as Frantz Fanon would write, "Ontology—once it is admitted as leaving existence by the wayside—does not permit us to understand the being of the Black [person]."[94] Within the philosophy of *this world*, "being" had been reduced to a set of "facts via metaphysics," and the facts were that the principle of equal protection under the law easily coexisted with anti-black discrimination, that anti-black terror did not announce as terror under the law or in politics, that "freedom" was not a property right of black Houstonians, and that "peace" indicated the maintenance of the structural relationship between whiteness and blackness, which was maintained by way of anti-black violence.[95]

Rendered a nonbeing within *this world*, Davis still had to manage surviving in it. What did her actions express about how she speculated on the meaning of "freedom in the pores of the quotidian?"[96] Her words arrive in the archive filtered by the Houston Police Department and by Blair Justice, the white Rice Institute sociologist who worked under the mayor as an investigator of racial tensions in the city in order to prevent any damage to Houston's reputation. Those documents noted that Davis repeatedly refused to press charges against her neighbors but that she was told she could and should. It is impossible to know whether this advice was ever given to her. If she was offered the opportunity but refused to press charges, why? Was she afraid that it would spark further retaliation? That the proceedings would be all for show but its publicization might make her a more visible target? Or did she have no faith that a stern talking-to by the police would compel her neighbors to stop tormenting her? If she had been discouraged from pressing charges, did she understand this as mandatory? Could she have felt encouraged when the people to whom she expressed her ire were all white men in positions of authority? Did she agree with other black Houstonians that the police "are white and serve us no useful purpose," that "they are not public servants and act only when bugged enough"?[97] In either case, what did it mean when she sighed in desperation and fought off sleep so she could guard her home with her gun "every night"? Did she understand freedom, not as a guarantee of being nor a product of the law, but as something that could only be grasped by black people who were willing to do the anti-ethical—who were willing to point the barrel of a gun toward the white threat and rain fire? Did she even dream of freedom anymore, or did she just hope with scarce optimism for an end to her torment with no sure vision of what that end would look like? Would the arrival of freedom for black people necessitate the street executions of white terrorists? Could black Houstonians survive such a war when their political orientations to the problem of white supremacy, how to wrestle against it, or whether to wrestle against it all were sometimes at odds?

In the year following Davis's complaints and a few months after the police attack at TSU, black Houstonians attacked and burned several white-owned businesses in the Sunnyside area. On August 16, a white service station operator, Rule Scott, shot a black man, Leon Perry Jr., in the leg. Scott claimed Perry had tried to rob him. Perry maintained that he was just trying to use the restroom. Still, after his wounds were dressed, he was turned over to police custody and charged with attempted robbery by assault. Black Houstonians lit at least eight buildings ablaze in the three nights that followed the shooting. Meanwhile, the *Houston Chronicle* splashed its front page with stories about how well Mayor Welch and assistant chief of police George Seber helped maintain "cool." Rather than publicizing the grievances of Sunnyside residents, the newspaper promoted the views of black leaders who spoke poorly of CORE, SNCC, and participants in the rebellion. The message was clear: that most Houstonians had good sense, and that these rabble-rousers were not representative of any legitimate segment of the black population.

However, in October, Blair Justice released the results of a community survey to Mayor Welch. The survey results perhaps reveal less than they boast, laden as it was with leading questions and closed responses. Justice asked, "Do you think the people who did this were protesting against bad living conditions in the city, or about lack of job opportunities, or about broken promises by the city, or about 'police brutality,' or were they just vandals who were trying to stir up trouble and start a riot?" Respondents could only choose one answer, and all were compelled to select one from the list provided. Accordingly, about 29 percent answered "stir up trouble." Thus, while it is not clear exactly what black Houstonians believed about the causes of the disturbance, the overwhelming majority answered there was some precipitating trigger. Like Davis, did they hold anxiety and fear as tension in the body until, punctured by the rumor of another unjustified shooting of a black man, it exceeded the boundaries of flesh and manifested as firebombs and looting? Whereas in this survey item less than 10 percent of respondents believed "broken promises" precipitated the outrage, in a later item nearly 63 percent of respondents were sure that the tensions were related to the "lack of progress in giving Negroes equality with white people."[98] In the previous year, 86 percent of the 164 black Houstonian respondents to a different, open-ended (rather than multiple choice) survey administered by Justice answered that "racial tensions in Houston" were caused by some array of employment and wage discrimination, school segregation and a lack of educational opportunities, poverty and poor housing, mistreatment by police, and "general discrimination."[99] What registered as mere, even if poor, conditions of life in a survey would be more accurately apprehended as the tortures black people had been made to endure for as long as and beyond what each person could remember. Houston's story of a peaceful era of desegregation is thereby exposed as a powerful and sincere fiction, except if peace is understood as a condition in which anti-black violence is unending, nonexceptional, unworthy of note.

For black Houstonians, torture was quotidian, for even if the cross burnings and KKK threats could be described as rare—a characterization I would reject—each act of spectacular violence reflected the terror at the core of what it meant to be made black. Anti-black terror instantiated any existence that could be defined as black. Situated "at the constitution of being itself," anti-black terror inhered in the experience of blackness and induced the conditions for alternative worldmaking. Worldmaking, or as Alex Byrd put it, the "lives" captives and voyagers "made in motion," were simply the "adjustments" black people made under the constraints of "white power." Still, as Saidiya Hartman asks, "If the matrix of death and dispossession constitute the black ordinary, even if not solely or exclusively, then how are we to think of practices in the hold?"[100]

Lucille Davis's adjustment to white power was not a protracted plan against the structure of white supremacy, but an effort to survive each night and a plea to be recognized as a person inherently worthy of dignity. And she was not an anomaly. As former SNCC field secretary and Africana studies scholar Charles E. Cobb Jr. elucidates, by the start of the modern civil rights efforts of the mid-twentieth century, black southerners had long developed and sustained a culture of armed self-defense. While some historians view this as an attempt by black men to shore up their manhood, Cobb maintains that "something more complicated but absolutely normal was at play": the desire to keep loved ones safe. Thus, as Cobb and others demonstrate, though black women "have generally been ignored," the culture of armed self-defense among black southerners was as much the effort of black women as it was of black men.[101] This culture did not guarantee safety or tranquility for black people, but rather was a manifestation of the absence of conditions of peace. Thus, "the matrix of death and dispossession" did not disappear, even as black folks laid the ground for practices that could threaten the integrity of the hold or lessen the severity of its conditions.

The weeks leading up to the police assault at TSU were replete with instances of anti-black terror across Houston's expansive cityscape, the self-same cityscape that consumed black neighborhoods but also facilitated the movement of black activists across the city. The highways that completely erased vibrant parts of Third Ward, Fourth Ward, and Fifth Ward were partly constitutive of the hold, especially apparent in Fifth Ward where the East Freeway (I-10), running east to west, was constructed perpendicular to the Eastex Freeway (U.S. 59). Bounded on the south by Buffalo Bayou, Fifth Ward's "Bottom," which had formerly been "choice real estate," now housed "the biggest rats, meanest dogs, worst stench, and deepest mud in Fifth Ward, all this in a shroud of constant steam and smoke from burning rice-hull piles stacked by the nearby Comet Rice Company." Complete negligence toward the economic, environmental, and social effects of I-10 turned the Bottom into a "literal . . . dump." The two noisy freeways and the smog they brought with them hugged Kelly Courts, which had been opened in 1940 as black public housing, and physically separated those residents from the rest of the community. The environmental and commercial impact on Fifth Ward was undeniable. Historian Joe R. Feagin argues, "These two freeway systems literally crucified the area by creating large freeways in a cross pattern through its heart. This massive cross disrupted community life during its construction and permanently destroyed many black homes and businesses." Businesses "all but abandoned" the people in Fifth Ward, and once the highways were completed, the city returned to its habit of disinterest in the area.[102]

Those highways also provided the fastest route from TSU to the far north side. Following the expulsion of the Northwood Junior High students, Mrs. Wendell Thompson, a parent of one of the suspended students, invited the

TSU students to her house, where they talked to her and some of the Northwood students to learn about the problems they faced and their plan for further protest. "They told us that K.K.K. had been shooting out there," Trazawell Franklin recalled, "and burned a cross in [front of] Mr. Batese's house and he was frightened because he didn't have no kind of protection." That night, May 15, four male TSU students, including Franklin and Floyd Nichols, stayed at the Batese residence, their time and energy torn between preparing for final exams and standing guard for their ad hoc family.[103] After an uneventful night, the TSU students helped the Batese family get their children to school safely while keeping watch over one middle school-aged son who had been suspended. Then they reconvened at the Thompson residence, learning that organizers had arranged for more TSU students to arrive for a protest at the junior high school. The plan was that Northwood students would lead and TSU students would "stand on the sideline and watch." Expecting trouble, some students suggested taking guns with them to the protest.[104]

However "masculinist" the discourse of armed resistance is often framed by historians, the students did not express interest in keeping guns at hand for the sake of asserting, proving, or preserving their manhood. Indeed, black people of all genders engaged a long tradition of armed self-defense across the South that predated the black nationalism of the 1960s.[105] Certainly, black men had publicly articulated manhood with family defense since at least the nineteenth century.[106] However, as Jasmin Young points out, black women have an equally long tradition of armed self-defense, sometimes captured in discourses of womanhood, oftentimes motivated by exigencies.[107] Rather than indicating a masculinist posture, the evidence points toward the students' daily encounters with their mortality. It indicated their relegation to the structural position of blackness: "a realm of experience which is situated between two zones of death—social and corporeal death."[108] Student leaders Douglass Wayne "Wayno" Waller and Floyd Nichols had gotten into the habit of carrying guns with them, not to protect their manhood, but to preserve their lives.[109] Nichols explained:

> On the north side there was a brick-throwing incident wherein a white man pulled a gun on me and this started me to getting ready to carry mine, but I didn't report it to the police. Another one of my friends had a gun pulled on him on Wheeler where I witnessed it. Also, on the north side, another man poked his gun [out of his truck] window. I later sawed off my shotgun and started carrying it. All this was after these guns were pulled on us.[110]

This was something more fundamental than men trying to prove their manhood—something prior to the excesses of gender performativity. TSU students had frequently been compelled to confront their very mortality, whether they were active in protests or not. Since the sit-in protests in the early 1960s, the students and their campus had been targeted by white supremacist gangs. This terror did not just happen to folks like Felton Turner; the physical scars on his body indelibly marked the souls of all black folks who heard of his fate. The lynching, though it did not result in Turner's physical death, served its fatal function—to make the body black, to void it of value and of ontology, an inert nothingness to be disfigured and dismembered, to make way for the humans and their right to own, possess, consume, and discard.[111] Within the terms of *this world*, and witnessing Turner's scars, each student experienced their "black body" as "just an encasing for a primordial death," "a breathing tomb."[112]

After some debate the students decided not to carry guns with them to the Northwood protest on May 16. When Trazawell Franklin and the others arrived at the scene around 11 a.m., police had already begun charging across Homestead Road toward the middle-schoolers. With "riot guns and dogs" they "advanced on the peaceful picket line, billy clubs and rifle butts swinging." The officers arrested the entire crowd, landing blows on the young children in the process. From the back of one police wagon, TSU student O. C. Brown observed nearby cops "beating some of the juveniles." One suffered a blow to his genitals from a police officer's blackjack. He could also hear the officers degrade the students: "You damn niggers." Attempting to avoid the confrontation, the TSU students with Franklin began driving away from the scene but were stopped and detained until the county sheriff's department arrived to cart the men, but not the women, off to the county jail. It is not immediately evident why the female students were allowed to leave, though Black Male Studies scholars offer a compelling elaboration of such phenomena as gendercide.[113]

Waller had not been present at Northwood that day. He was a twenty-one-year-old Vietnam War veteran who had enrolled at TSU and then became active with the Friends of SNCC. By the time he arrived on campus from his sister and brother-in-law's home, it was already 1:00 in the afternoon. He found Lee Otis Johnson and other students in the coffee shop discussing the arrests at Northwood and learned that his roommate Bobby had been among the arrestees. Waller agreed to travel north to see if he could help bail Bobby out. They found the Thompson residence packed with parents of arrested youths, student leaders, and "a few of the girls from the campus." Many of the guests stayed at the Thompson residence until they learned of the protesters' releases. Several students, including Nichols and Waller, left the Thompson residence around 6:00 that evening when they heard rumors that a young child had been shot nearby. The young men decided to patrol the neighborhood themselves to look for the perpetrators.[114]

Perhaps thirty minutes later, the group made its way back toward campus, with Nichols and Waller taking a pit stop to purchase a gallon of wine. While they sat in a car in the TSU parking lot drinking, Paula, a University of Houston student, came by and told them about another set of arrests that had happened in Sunnyside and plans for a meeting at Riverbrook Missionary Baptist Church in that neighborhood. The group got back into their vehicle to travel southward, stopping at Worthing High School to speak to a crowd there before heading to the church.[115] Earlier that day, Sunnyside residents, TSU and UH students, and community leader Bill Lawson had been arrested and charged with "loitering" for blockading the Holmes Road Dump.[116] Nichols made an impassioned speech at the church, admonishing gatherers "to protect themselves with arms because they don't know who might be shooting at them next." Afterward, the group, now joined by Trazawell Franklin, headed back toward the north side with a pitstop at campus. Nichols remained agitated throughout the trip. He kept his sawed-off shotgun nearby and "he was saying that he was going to kill a honkey tonight." Franklin asked him to put the gun away, warning him that the police already had a target trained on his back.[117]

Probably around 7:30 in the evening, a separate group of students arrived at Mrs. Thompson's for food and protest planning. Nichols, Waller, Kirkpatrick, Johnson, and several other TSU students were already there. While eating, the students heard gunshots. They went outside and student O. C. Brown saw "these little kids, they were running, and some Klans were shooting on the other side of this park and so myself and a few more of the guys, I forget their names, I know them when I see them, we went out there so they fired a shot at us at the same time." One man with Brown's group pulled his own firearm and shot back at the Klansmen, who ducked between bushes. Meanwhile, Mrs. Thompson had called the police to the scene, but when they arrived, they only took unsigned statements from Thompson and her guests. A prisoner in her own home, Mrs. Thompson requested that several of the TSU students stay with her through the night in order to protect her home against any "night riders" who might come by to terrorize her family. Other families of suspended students, including a Mrs. Virgie Eaton, also had TSU students stay with them for overnight protection.[118]

This was the "twin story of desperation" of mid-twentieth-century black America presaged by that told by Alex Byrd concerning enslaved and non-enslaved black people in the eighteenth and nineteenth centuries. In those prior centuries, they were crowded into the hold of the slave ship or precariously contained on vessels headed to the western African coast. In either case, they moved because they were coerced, and in the process, they developed strategies of survival: "The more that material hardship and white violence threatened their very existence," Byrd writes, "the more they banded together for survival." Their practices varied, from the development of mutual aid societies that held within them a promise of social democracy to the marauding societies that dispensed with notions of white property-holding as sacred.[119]

Likewise, black Houstonians in the twentieth century were forced to move out of desperation even as they strategized about how, when, and where to move. In doing so, they too showed signs of what other modes of living could look like. There, in the Batese, Thompson, and Eaton residences, among others whose names are not revealed in the archives, the families of the Northwood area and TSU students fashioned an alternative to the nuclear family. Their animating concern was the protection of children, for which all parties took responsibility. Their bond was not blood, but their shared anxiety—the ongoing encounters with mortality brought about by racial terror. They ate collectively. They slept in the same home, albeit probably in shifts. The TSU students acted as guardians for the younger children, escorting them to school and watching over them as they played outdoors in the afternoon.[120] Eaton, unmarried and caring for three children—the oldest a nine-year-old boy by the name of Garlin who had been suspended from Northwood—noted that she had "high regard for the 'guys'" of SNCC as they "lifted" her during a difficult time.[121]

While other scholars have written in further detail about the civil rights and anti-poverty organizations in Houston during the same time period, I highlight these instances of less-spectacular worldmaking.[122] There was nothing on a grand scale happening in the north-side family residences. Indeed, the practices of mutual care and protection in those homes were ordinary. However, their ordinariness reflected the normality of anti-black terror. Thus, to offer one answer to Hartman's question concerning how we are to apprehend practices in the hold, we are to always consider the coercions that precipitated them. Anti-blackness was ongoing and therefore so too was the political construction of blackness, which was not a fixed ontological fact but rather a constantly reconstituted condition.

Additionally, it is fruitful to follow David Kazanjian and analyze the practices in the hold not merely for what they describe—the anxiety, the fear, the fatigue, the gun-in-hand, the food-on-table, the chasing-the-Klans. Rather, the practices reflect thought, or better yet, they were thought in motion. If blackness was a constantly reconstituted condition, then it certainly "cast doubt on the capaciousness of transgression," at once capturing black people in material conditions of dispossession while providing such an enduring sense of ontological insecurity that it laid bare, in many instances, the emptiness of the ethics of *this world*.[123] Thus, this ad hoc familial arrangement may be thought of as anti-ethical and antithetical practices, dispensing with the nuclear family as the divinely ordained unit of social organization. They broke bread as a community, sharing perhaps beyond their capacity to provide more than mere sustenance, but recognizing that communal care was necessary for communal survival. They carried firearms, and though they did not hope to face death, at times they yearned to rid white terrorists of their breath and the world of white terrorists, uniformed or not. They dared to try alternative ways of living, even adopting illegal practices and frightening rhetoric (for white folks and some advocates of nonviolence). And yes, they did this alongside making police reports, paying cash bails, and making formal protest to the city and school board. That is, although black Houstonians responded creatively to the ongoing torture, they also made more predictable moves in their attempts to be recognized by the formal powers that structurally organized their lives as less valuable than their white counterparts.

Meditation on Anti-ethical Worldmaking
There is no climax here, no sudden break that justifies my focus on some fleeting practices in a few families in one city. But that's precisely the point. The freedom movement has been punctuated in historiography by major events—notable assassinations, mass protests, and high court decisions. But the ordinary was perhaps always a better reflection of the exigent and the structural, for the creative practices black folk developed in the quotidian were the evidence that the terror supposedly undone by desegregation orders, Supreme Court decisions, professionalized policing, and color blindness had never abated. The anti-ethical thoughts of black Houstonians who had no qualms with the idea of shooting a Klansman dead on sight or who wished more police officers had died from friendly fire during the attack at TSU reject the ethics of *this world*—an ethics that yielded a world where black people had no guaranteed right of self-defense against white terrorists and where police were called peace officers despite their empirical practice as "violence workers."[124]

We can speculate about the moral principles that gave shape to black anti-ethics. They appeared to include a commitment to the idea of linked fate for black people that held black life as sacred and black collective survival as a first priority in all decision-making. Specific practices seemed to align with this commitment, at times making gun-wielding pragmatic and at other times recognizing it as a threat to communal well-being. Despite appearances of impropriety, Lucille Davis's fiancé spent late evenings at her place to ensure her protection. And TSU students, although they valued their education, were willing to sacrifice their time and even shut down academic buildings in order to ensure that their education would be amenable to their well-being and ultimately serve the communal rather than individualistic interests of black Houstonians.

Even absent a climax, there remains something valuable in recognizing creative worldmaking in the "black ordinary." It makes more apparent that while the ethics of *this world* appear to be universal and universally valued, they are not. Juxtaposed with the material conditions of the hold, creative black worldmaking provides a rare glimpse into "the order as it really *is*" rather than in ways it "*needs to be known*."[125] Where the institutionalized civil rights movement is often narratively co-opted as an example of the promise of American democracy, even if not yet fully realized, the black ordinary cannot help but to reflect the empirical that rejects this propaganda. The circumstances under which the TSU students and the families they joined had to labor revealed that rebellion and revolt were not necessarily cultural or reflective of some systematized ideology against white supremacy, but rather, to borrow the words of Frantz Fanon, "It is because quite simply it was, in more than one way, becoming impossible for [them] to breathe."[126] It was out of desperation that *black* worldmaking occurred, for blackness was not, at its base, a culture or a race or a phenotype or an ancestry, but the consequence of violence that gave rise to the Negro as a biological essence within the human imaginary. Black worldmaking does not just describe black people's survival tactics, but the ways those tactics help us see the senselessness of black people's suffering and that clarify that anti-racism must be anti-ethical—that "There will be no peace in America until whites begin to hate their whiteness, asking from the depths of their being: 'How can we become black?'" This is not to say that white people must learn to hate their skin color, but rather that racism is sustained by white Americans' refusals to relinquish the accoutrement that affords white people more social, economic, and political value than others.[127]

Thus, finally, in adopting even fleeting anti-ethical poses and practices against *this world*, the black ordinary also revealed "against the raceless credo" that "racism cannot be rejected without a dialectic in which humanity experiences the blackened world."[128] The blackened world lacked (and lacks) temporal distinction, being nowhere and nothing within the ontology of *this world* while simultaneously materially everywhere and too apparent for comfort.[129] Within this "zone of nonbeing," Fanon asserts, "authentic upheaval can be born," and the practices in the hold suggest as much. What would it mean for humanity to experience this blackened world? Based on the words and actions of black Houstonians, it does not appear that it would mean revenge from black people toward white people or the mere inverse of racial supremacy born of spite. Rather, if black people could not be secure in their own homes, then the sacredness of private property was an open question, and white people, too, would have to live under conditions where it was a question rather than a presumed fact. If police threatened rather than protected black lives, then their existence was not necessary for societal security, and thus white people would have to endure a world absent of such officers of the law. This might look like a world wherein black people policed, prosecuted, and executed sentencing against white terrorists, not necessarily in accordance with some written law, but always on their own terms. If racial capitalism had reinforced segregation even as Jim Crow waned, made concrete by way of highways, underbounding, dump and incinerator siting, underfunded schools, and governance by a racially hostile majority, then white people would have to burden the financial costs necessary for redressing centuries of dispossession. In sum, they would have to live in a world that exposed the meaninglessness of black suffering and the arbitrariness of white power, and be compelled to repay the debt they owed, with its exponential appreciation and interest, to the people whose progeny they continued to fleece and flog.

CODA
Why Not Dream Impossible Dreams?

Throughout the last half of the twentieth century, black Houstonians would applaud themselves for several small "wins." They had brought attention to environmental racism and finally secured the closing of the Holmes Road Dump in 1974. However, a park now sits adjacent to the former site of the dump, and under the leadership of a black mayor, Sylvester Turner, the city endeavored to build a social services center on the former landfill, despite a report by the Texas Commission on Environmental Quality that indicates the site remains toxic, replete with volatile and semi-volatile organic compounds, metals, solvents, and pesticides that still contaminate groundwater in the community. Scholars have demonstrated that communities exposed to these toxins in their air, water, and soil have suffered higher mortality rates, due to disruptions in the endocrine system, and development of cancers. Still, Sunnyside residents fight in the twenty-first century to avoid having another waste facility sited next to their homes. Likewise, in 2019, reports revealed leukemia, throat, and lung cancer clusters in Fifth Ward related to contamination of soil, air, and water.[1]

Mayor Turner, a product of Acres Homes and a graduate of the University of Houston and Harvard Law School, has not challenged the structure of race and class in Houston. In many ways, he has supported it. In the early days of January 2017, the US Department of Housing and Urban Development (HUD) delivered a scathing critique of Turner, exposing how he "refused" to allow the city council to consider the development of a private low-income housing project in a wealthy Uptown neighborhood. Wealthy white residents complained that the project would lower property values, increase traffic, and overcrowd their allegedly packed schools. The Houston Housing Authority rebutted them, noting that the construction of a new elementary school in the neighborhood would be completed prior to the housing project's completion and the Houston Independent School District confirmed that no estimates could corroborate the claim that the new residents would increase crowding in neighborhood schools. Economists, meanwhile, have repeatedly demonstrated that low-income housing does not lower property values in wealthy neighborhoods or produce declines in school performance measures. The resistance to the project, HUD found, was "unsupported by the facts," and the department concluded that the city's pattern of refusal to allow low-income housing projects to move forward in high-opportunity neighborhoods was "racially motivated" and served to "perpetuate segregation." Underneath the rhetoric about schools and property values, HUD discovered the same kind of criminalizing rhetoric that surfaced in desegregation debates throughout the 1950s and 1960s. Residents complained, "Crime in the area will go up. Do you remember how bad the crime was after Katrina? Regardless of how charitable we would like to be, the reality is that in the lower income areas of Houston the crime is higher." HUD concluded that this was a racist dog-whistle.[2]

Turner, for his part, seemed well-attuned to the dog-whistle and capable of sending out his own thinly veiled reassurances to white Houstonians that he would protect them and the property/value of whiteness.[3] When he shut down the project, he claimed that it would cost too much money. Instead, he preferred that low-income housing be built in low-income neighborhoods.[4] Turner responded to HUD's charges of racism by writing:

> [T]here should be no misunderstanding about my commitment to providing options for low income families. I do not believe that only wealthy areas can provide what our children need. I have chosen to stay in the neighborhood where I grew up and I will not tell children in similar communities they must live somewhere else. Our underprivileged families should have the right to choose where they want to live, and that choice should include the right to stay in the neighborhoods where they have grown up. I categorically reject any position to the contrary.[5]

Turner avoided discussing race and segregation, attuned as he is to the color-blind, economic-class-first rhetoric preferred by his wealthy white constituents. Nevertheless, the codes are there. High-opportunity neighborhoods have proved to reduce educational, career, and income gaps for impoverished people who have had the opportunity to move into them. Yet Turner argues that his underserved, predominantly black, disproportionately low-income neighborhood represents a "choice" for entire groups of people seeking to escape poverty. Indeed, by framing this as a matter of choice while denying low-income Houstonians the very opportunities that would give them real options to choose from, Turner pretends as if the city's so-called race relations are characterized by "complementarity, reciprocity, and shared values." As mayor, Turner constricted the residential choices available for low-income Houstonians and provided cover for the racial meaning of this constriction, using "the stipulation of abstract equality" to reproduce "white entitlements and black subjugation" by way of the "promulgation of formal equality."[6]

As a black mayor in a southern city, Turner does not necessarily turn away from talking about race and racism all the time. He lauds a $7.5 million grant provided in 2022 to Houston by Wells Fargo's Wealth Opportunities Restored Through Homeownership program, noting, "Sadly, home ownership opportunities have not been made equally, especially to people of color."[7] But without a hint of irony, Turner has also requested and approved the city's 2023 budget of $5.71 billion, almost 60 percent of which will be provided for "public safety"—40 percent of which will go to fire safety, municipal courts, and the Houston Emergency Center and the remaining 60 percent for police.[8]

At least some of these funds are provided by way of the city's Asset Forfeiture Fund. Asset forfeiture allows law enforcement agencies across the country to steal money from American citizens based on mere suspicion of the assets' involvement in or relation to criminal activity. As Michelle Alexander exposed, "The overwhelming majority of forfeiture cases do not involve any criminal charges," and the cost of recouping assets stolen by law enforcement agencies is often more prohibitive than the value of the assets taken.[9] In 2021, the Houston Police Department seized $3 million in assets. That number is expected to be $17 million in 2022, and the city has a target to confiscate an additional $17 million in assets in 2023.[10] Additionally, HPD receives money from the "Child Safety Fund," revenue of which comes in part from "municipal court fees on non-criminal municipal violations." This helps pay for crossing guards at public, religious, and private schools, reminiscent of the ways tax dollars were siphoned from struggling black communities in the early days of Reconstruction to subsidize all-white schools.[11]

The racial distribution of the city's resources continues in the present as it has in the past, with the police department serving as an important institution for white middle-class employment. In 2022, the department's civilian workforce was 21 percent white, which is about commensurate with the city's white, non-Latinx population proportion. However, the classified workforce, which is almost 40 percent white and about 30 percent Latinx, is paid significantly more than the civilian workforce, with employees in the former averaging $150,607 and those in the latter averaging $65,728. The classified workforce is about 21 percent black, commensurate with the city's population, but the civilian workforce is 45 percent black. That is, relative to their size of the city's population, black workers are most likely to be working the lowest-paid jobs in the Houston Police Department.[12] This kind of racial occupational segmentation, which masks inequities in ways outright exclusion could not, is common across the United States.[13] That is, white Houstonians enjoy greater financial benefits of tax dollars than do their black counterparts, an indication of a stubborn racial structure.

In his address to the city, Turner indicated the fiscal challenges the city faces in the age of COVID-19, noting that the budget uses $160 million provided by the federal government's American Rescue Plan Act. Almost $11 million of that federal aid had initially been allotted for overtime pay for police officers, most of whom—about 80 percent—do not reside in the city. Lauding the success of his "One Safe Houston" initiative, Turner increased the allotment to $13.2 million.[14] The police department's short-term goals include "reduc[ing] the number of external complaints below that of FY2022," which is not necessarily the same as a goal of reducing officer misconduct or reducing crime.[15] Indeed, insofar as HPD's budget relies in part on revenue streams like asset forfeiture, police officers are incentivized to exploit the most vulnerable populations in the city to pad their coffers. Meanwhile, "One Safe Houston" provides no direct funding to address Houston's housing and homelessness crises. While the police will receive 20 percent of the city's public improvement programs money, only about 1 percent of those funds are allotted to address homelessness and housing.[16] The paltry $400,000 budget of the city's Housing and Community Development Department, which among other things is tasked with addressing the issues of housing insecurity in the city, is dwarfed by the police department's $1 billion allotment, demonstrating that for Turner and his city council "safety" means more policing, not social and economic security.[17] The mayor's office and the Houston Police Department celebrated a 1 percent decrease in the city's murder rate the first three quarters of 2022 following a 70 percent increase in the previous year, using this data to promote the success of the One Safe Houston initiative. However, they offered no compelling data that the funding had anything to do with what amounts to, in absolute value, only four fewer murders in eight months.[18]

Although this book has not been primarily about city governance, I present this information about the Turner administration to indicate how the priorities of governance have not changed despite the election of a black mayor. Segregation has always been about structuring the occupation and use of space and the distribution of resources.

In 1966, Blair Justice wrote to Mayor Welch about his research among black Houstonians regarding their attitudes toward the city, their living conditions, and white people. He asked, "What are the causes of racial tension in Houston?" Black residents responded unanimously that "low wages," "underemployment," and "housing" shaped and perpetuated racial distance and animosity.[19] "Heavenly Houston," for all its bluster as a city of progress, has failed to ameliorate these issues. Its earliest attempts at desegregation, despite being seemingly calm, did result in violence: fights between white and black students at Cullen Junior High School affecting Sunnyside children, at McArthur Elementary School affecting Acres Homes children, and at McReynolds Junior High School affecting Pleasantville children were among the many underreported instances of white terror exacted upon black Houstonians in the 1960s. As a result of this violence, the Harris County Council of Organizations urged black families to "register their children at the closest school to them," even if that school would not be the best for them.[20] This was another indication of a "must choose" situation rather than an actual opportunity to make choices. Segregation within the Houston Independent School District, both at the district level and within schools, remains a challenge.[21] This, unfortunately, is a national story. Residential segregation, police brutality, unfair sentencing practices, and educational inequality continue to form a web of constraint around black people in America.

Toward the close of the twentieth century, black Houstonians counted other "wins." The stretch of Wheeler Avenue on TSU's campus was closed to traffic and transformed into a promenade in 1984, increasing pedestrian and biking activity on and around the campus. Coincidentally, that same year marked a settlement between the NAACP and Mexican-American Legal Defense and Education Fund with the Houston Independent School District, which finally ended the policy of segregation in Houston schools. This settlement did not, however, integrate Houston's schools; structurally, Houston's public schools remain "just as segregated today" as they had been when *Brown v. Board of Education* was decided. And Wheeler Avenue remained contested ground into the twenty-first century as Houston METRO plotted to reopen the campus to traffic so that it could install a light-rail line through it.[22]

At the state level, TSU's financial appropriations continued to mirror the treatment it had received at the time of its birth as a state-funded institution. In 1999, TSU students, faculty, and staff filed suit against Governor George Bush Jr. over proposed legislation to use $955 million of the state's tobacco settlement fund to convey money to every state-funded higher education institution in the state *except* for TSU and Prairie View A&M, both historically black colleges. The plaintiffs argued for a long historical view of the state's treatment of TSU, writing, "The proposed distribution of the tobacco settlement money is only the latest in a series of continuing state actions which have had the purpose and/or effect of segregating, isolating, discriminating against, and disrupting Texas Southern University." Moreover, acutely aware of the interwovenness of educational and residential segregation, they maintained that "these state actions have resulted in extreme residential segregation throughout the greater Third Ward Community," thereby ensuring the "unequal delegation" of "opportunities for advancement" between black and white Houstonians. Moreover, the plaintiffs expressed disgust at the idea that the state's tobacco settlement would service white Texans and their institutions—a settlement that was won against tobacco companies ostensibly as a remedy for the effects of their predatory marketing on the health of Texans, which disproportionately affected black residents. Asked about the unequal distribution of funds, "a prominent white attorney who litigated the settlement for the state replied, 'We take care of family, and frankly, Texas Southern is not in any of our families.'" The case was dismissed without prejudice.[23]

Time has passed and times have changed. On the ground, black Houstonians meaningfully adjusted the quotidian, most notably by desegregating public spaces. However, the city's institutions were not integrated. Neither were its neighborhoods. Black communities still suffer a deprivation of resources. The Houston Police Department and its leadership never paid for the material, psychological, and emotional damage they caused at TSU, either in funds or in kind. Black neighborhoods continue to carry the stigma of being criminal spaces, and the economic devastation they suffered as a result of highway construction was never remediated. In some ways, then, deprivation increased rather than abated with desegregation. The conceit of legal desegregation was that, by decree, a judge or a group of legislators could transform a group of nonhumans into individuated human subjects.

In 1954, TSU sociologist Henry Allen Bullock argued that the Supreme Court's *Brown* presented an opportunity to inaugurate a new relationship between whiteness and blackness. He also warned if black Americans failed to rise to the occasion and improve themselves that "segregation will be replaced by one of a milder form, separating people and depriving them nonetheless."[24] Bullock was prescient in at least one way: in the wake of Jim Crow's death, segregation remained. This was not due, however, to the "personal qualities" of black Americans. As the plaintiffs had pointed out in *Benjamin v. Bush*, the structural circumstances in which black Texans lived were created and maintained by the state even before the Civil War. Moreover, as legal scholars and historians have since demonstrated, the antidiscrimination jurisprudence of *Brown* was decided on the basis of abstract equality rather than on principles of justice and equity, and thus while it supports "color-blindness," or anticlassification, under the guise of individual freedom, it mandates no remedy to group subordination.[25] Indeed, despite all the "wins" tallied for the civil rights movement, scholars still bear witness to ongoing racial subordination, tracing back to the state's sugar plantation industry and through its manifestation of late twentieth-century mass incarceration, its racially disparate use of the death penalty, and its voter disfranchisement practices (including Senate Bill 1, which was passed by a Republican majority and signed by Governor Greg Abbott at the time of this writing, and which blatantly aims to suppress Texas's black, Latinx, and poor voters)—and this list could continue indefinitely.[26]

The Friends of SNCC and other black nationalist organizations at TSU challenged Bullock's perspective—literally standing in his way to prevent him from teaching during their boycott of classes in the 1960s. They refused the terms of nonviolence and respectability that promised but failed to produce change in the fundamental anti-black structural organization of society. As black activists sought to escape the capture of the politics that preceded them, law enforcement officials rained hell on them and their skinfolk in the form of six thousand rounds of ammunition. Captured once again, in their dorm rooms, in their blackened bodies, the students at TSU argued, indeed, that they occupied a structural position in relation to whiteness that did not change with linear time: "This proves that no matter what we fight for, especially when we are right, we will go to prison. . . . A black brother of ours once stated that he was once in prison and we should become shocked to hear that because, 'We as black people in America are still in prison.'"[27]

Black Americans have long been realists in this regard, and while their diagnoses of America's intransigent racism may read pessimistically, these Americans have always been dreamers. Likewise, Afropessimism is a call to dream, but with attention to the very real constraints on our capacity to dream freely. For instance, if racism is indeed a permanent feature of American society and the degree, extent, and consequences of racial segregation are metrics by which we can empirically verify this claim, then even the dream of integration as the solution to the problem indicates a capture of the imagination. But if this simply diagnoses the state of things, what now?

Now, we have some space to imagine other worlds. This requires descent into the void of uncertainty, where everything of value, including the social construction of value itself, must be evacuated of meaning in order to wrest as much imagination as is possible from the constraints of our present epistemology. Importantly, this does not mean that there can be no meaning at all, but rather that we can allow ourselves the grace to decide how and on what bases meaning gets constructed. In the search "for a normative source" for a foundation for ethical world-making, legal scholar Mari Matsuda recommends "looking to the bottom—adopting the perspective of those who have seen and felt the falsity of the liberal promise." We must also, then, eschew abstractions (like formal equality) and hypotheticals, and instead attend to the actual experiences of the racially dysselected and socioeconomically dispossessed. This is not a retreat to absolute relativism, Matsuda notes: "When notions of right and wrong, justice and injustice, are examined not from an abstract position but from the positions of groups who have suffered through history, moral relativism recedes and identifiable normative priorities emerge."[28] Reimagining the very foundations upon which worlds are made is not a call to invert existing relations where the oppressed become superior members on the same hierarchal structure, but rather is an opportunity to invent or inaugurate new ways of relation—to each other, to property (or better yet, to the idea of property), to environment, to space, and to power.

What might a world look like where the health of the planet is prioritized over the accumulation of property? Might we have massive projects of "sprawl clearance" and "environmental renewal" that, while decimating suburbs and exurbs, revitalize higher-density living, that necessitate investments in public transit and basic infrastructure, that integrate neighborhoods, that concentrate rather than disperse the distribution of public resources, and that conserve environmental resources like water while encouraging cleaner sources of energy production? If, as many historians have demonstrated, suburbanization has been a pivotal component of the decimation of the environment and natural habitats as well as a mechanism for racial subordination, would ameliorating these problems be worth a departure from the status quo?

Of course, this would exact a painful price on those tethered to value as it is defined in this world. But such pain is not unimaginable, given that "slum clearance" and "urban renewal" have been justified, legally and morally, to destroy thriving black communities, while actual renewal remained an empty promise in the wake of that devastation.[29] This is not a question of feasibility, then, but rather one of will. It is not a question of capacity, for the wealthiest nation in known history has the economic capacity and the labor force to re-create its political geography. Rather, it is a question of the will to undo existing relations—the property investment in whiteness, the "natural" economic appreciation of land, the exorbitant accumulation and concentration of wealth of an aristocratic class, and the protection of industries "too big to fail" among them.

I should caution at this point that I am not providing a solution or even a road map to a solution, but rather am experimenting out loud with an idea. If, looking from the bottom, I understand the health of the planet to be of immanent importance to the multigenerational longevity of populations most vulnerable to climate change and environmental degeneration, then what else must we imagine for a world where their well-being becomes the premier basis for social, economic, and political projects? And while there is no guarantee that these projects would eliminate racism, especially if they are executed in color-blind ways, the kind of reordering of society they would require also makes it impossible to know for sure what the outcome would be. This is what it means to descend into the void of uncertainty, however. And looking to, from, and for the bottom of society, what we do know is that the existing order's anti-black violence will be unending without some significant break, without producing some new "shatter zone" out of which a new culture of politics and politics of culture can emerge.[30]

So, let us imagine more. What might a world look like where everyone is guaranteed a truly livable wage, where the necessities of life are guaranteed, and the consumption of luxuries is a matter of personal taste and appreciation? (This assumes a world where wages still exist, though there is no reason we cannot or should not imagine a world where wages are unnecessary.) This, too, is not unimaginable, given the many projects the American government has implemented to "initiate long-range economic reform and to implement a social welfare safety net that would restructure the future relationship between U.S. citizens and their government," despite desperate opposition by capitalists and despite that these projects intentionally excluded black Americans.[31]

What might a world look like where a society's first priority was eradicating homelessness and providing free access to higher education and technical training? Certainly, the costs would be great, but they would not be prohibitive. A 2012 analysis by the Vera Institute of Justice calculated that in forty states for which data was available, $39 billion of taxpayer money was spent on the prison system annually. This is dwarfed by the $81 billion the federal government spends to operate its carceral system and the additional $100 billion spent by families on associated fees and other costs. That is, a modest estimate of the *annual* cost of mass incarceration is over $200 billion.[32] In comparison, a 2013 study found that "the first-year cost of moving one chronically homeless person into permanent supportive housing is $55,600." Even considering inflation in the years of the ongoing COVID-19 pandemic, the sum of those first-year costs would only be in the low tens of millions, less than 0.01 percent of the amount spent on the nation's prison systems.[33] Likewise, while the eleven-year cost of a tuition-free public higher education system is estimated to cost $800 billion, a recent report indicates that cost-benefit analysis of free higher education, looking out fifty years into the future but based on existing data from Illinois's tuition subsidy program, predicts that it "will yield benefits far beyond the costs."[34] And in Texas, free access to community college increased enrollment, did not result in lower graduation rates, and made four-year degrees more affordable, especially for black students, who were likely to "divert attendance from universities to community college" for the first two years.[35] For a free college program to work, it would have to avoid pitfalls we have witnessed elsewhere, including failures to fully fund our public universities, which might mean a reduction in aid to private institutions and more institutional freedom from partisan legislatures.[36]

Again, while these costs are high, the promise of economic benefits appears to outweigh those costs in terms of mere dollar amounts, let alone the social benefits of a society in which people are given the freedom to explore intellectual and creative passions without the burden of exorbitant debt. Moreover, the nation's leaders have demonstrated their will to allot astronomical figures, without significant oversight, to military programs. The Department of Defense's F-35 Lightning II Program *alone* is estimated to cost $1.7 trillion over the next six and a half decades, or about $26 billion per year on average.[37]

Still, this cannot be the limit of our imagination on this topic—merely increasing financial outlays to cover tuition costs or justifying costs on the basis of their future economic benefits. Would this new world we imagine not demand two- or four-year degrees? Might the outcome of higher education be something more than or less than a diploma? Would the value of education be measured as something other than what it can afford a person in the job market? Could higher education be an ongoing gift? Would that require some kind of system where full-time work is reduced or paid sabbaticals are granted for personal enrichment through service learning, study abroad, or creative projects? If such fundamental changes are necessary in order to provide a fulfilling educational experience for all Americans and noncitizen residents, that would require reimagining labor, child care and child rearing, citizenship, and even international relations and global security. Might we be compelled to find better ways of relating to the varied peoples with whom we share this planet so that we can invest our resources in enriching the lives of everyone rather than losing resources and lives to the Department of Defense, which will receive $847.3 billion in the fiscal year of 2023 alone under President Joe Biden?[38]

In "The Education of a Storyteller," the grandmother (or any elder) of a young Toni Cade Bambara (or any "colored girl") asks, "What are you pretending not to know today, Sweetheart?" Grandma Dorothy believes that, as black women, they "know everything there is to know."[39] What we pretend not to know in *this world* is that a great deal of the suffering we endure is not merely "the human condition." High rates of gun violence, homelessness of queer youth, racialized wealth inequities, and the mass migration of displaced refugees and dispossessed workers are not what it means to *be* human. Rather, these are consequences of contests over power, including the power to command resources and discipline populations. This should be a liberating admission, even if a terrifying one, for it means that we need not take anything for granted in our practices of imagining a new world.

But we face considerable constraints in inaugurating something new, which US history attests to: lynching, house and church bombings, internment camps, political assassinations, and mass incarceration are some of the more blatantly violent mechanisms. And we also see the consequences of contests over power that have benefited the wealthy while creating precarious living conditions for the majority of us: cycles of economic boom and bust, expansions of corporate welfare, decreases in support for needy families, closures of rural hospitals, increases in public surveillance technologies, and losses of land, homes, and businesses to the consequences of climate change.

In *this world*, we value near-absolute religious freedom, but in a new world might we value the lives and mental well-being of lesbian, gay, bisexual, and transgender youths over beliefs that compel them to view themselves as less than worthy of all the joy life can bring?[40] In *this world*, we value a near-absolute right to bear arms—for white people, at least—but in a new world might we abandon that value for the sake of reducing preventable deaths, something we at least know is possible given empirical evidence of the effects of restrictive gun laws in parts of the United States but especially in other nations? (It is, after all, not hard to imagine a devaluation of the Second Amendment, since it was done without complaint by white Americans with regard to the Black Panther Party in California.)[41] In *this world*, we value democracy without question. It is the greatest symbol of the progress of humanity, we are taught. But in a new world, might democracy look different from the system of republicanism by which power is not held by the *demos* but by representatives who are elected, in large part, by the mighty dollar and partisan gerrymanders? In a new world, might we inaugurate something other than democracy and also other than the other systems of exploitative, subordinating government that have been documented in recorded history?

These are not questions that seek answers, but rather questions that provoke wondering and wandering. The point is not to arrive at a foretold destination—to write or think toward utopia—for what we can imagine is still captured, in ways big and small, by the epistemology of the world from which we think. That is, I have not abandoned the thesis of this book: segregation is a permanent feature in *this world*. However, imagining other worlds can help us see the absurdities in our own, including the suffering that we accept as inevitable and the dishonest stories we tell ourselves to justify it. This book has been an inquiry into thinking about how we think, about what constrains the forging of new ideas and ways of being, and about what role history as a discipline plays in concealing those constraints and what it can do better to expose them. It has been an effort to compel us to come together to look at a meaningless world, abandon it and the selves we are tethered to in it, and then, left with nothing, reimagine who we might decide to be accountable to as scholars, as citizens, and as neighbors on a small blue dot in a vast universe.

Students and audiences often ask me, "How do we end segregation?" The actual answer is quite simple: we end segregation. Of course, the mechanisms will be varied and complex, but this answer, to me, is clear. *This world* was manufactured, and black Americans have paid and continue to pay the price to sustain it. Manufacturing worlds, then, seems well within our collective capacity. However, if you cannot see how it might be possible to end segregation in *this world*, for whatever reasons, then you too might engage Afropessimism and experiment with your wildest ideas, for therein might lie the fruit of something new.

NOTES

Introduction
Derrick Bell, *Faces at the Bottom of the Well: The Permanence of Racism* (New York: Basic Books, 1992), 12.
1. Kevin M. Kruse, *White Flight: Atlanta and the Making of Modern Conservatism* (Princeton, NJ: Princeton University Press, 2013); Joe W. Trotter and Jared N. Day, *Race and Renaissance: African Americans in Pittsburgh since World War II* (Pittsburgh: University of Pittsburgh Press, 2010); Thomas J. Sugrue, *The Origins of the Urban Crisis: Race and Inequality in Postwar Detroit* (Princeton, NJ: Princeton University Press, 1996).
2. Kruse, *White Flight*.
3. Matthew D. Lassiter, *The Silent Majority: Suburban Politics in the Sunbelt South* (Princeton, NJ: Princeton University Press, 2006); Robert O. Self, *American Babylon: Race and the Struggle for Postwar Oakland* (Princeton, NJ: Princeton University Press, 2005).
4. Andrew Wiese, *Places of Their Own: African American Suburbanization in the Twentieth Century* (Chicago: University of Chicago Press, 2009); Emily E. Straus, *Death of a Suburban Dream: Race and Schools in Compton, California* (Philadelphia: University of Pennsylvania Press, 2014); N. D. B. Connolly, *A World More Concrete: Real Estate and the Remaking of Jim Crow South Florida* (Chicago: University of Chicago Press, 2014).
5. Michael K. Brown et al., *Whitewashing Race: The Myth of a Color-Blind Society* (Berkeley: University of California Press, 2003), 30–31.
6. Destin Jenkins and Justin Leroy, "The Old History of Capitalism," in *Histories of Racial Capitalism*, ed. Destin Jenkins and Justin Leroy (New York: Columbia University Press, 2021), 10–12.
7. Kenneth L. Kusmer and Joe W. Trotter, *African American Urban History since World War II* (Chicago: University of Chicago Press, 2009), 4, 15.
8. Lassiter, *The Silent Majority*; Wiese, *Places of Their Own*; Harold X. Connolly, "Black Movement into the Suburbs: Suburbs Doubling Their Black Populations during the 1960s," *Urban Affairs Quarterly* 9, no. 1 (September 1973): 91–111.
9. Tyina Steptoe, *Houston Bound: Culture and Color in a Jim Crow City* (Berkeley: University of California Press, 2015); Brian D. Behnken, *Fighting Their Own Battles: Mexican Americans, African Americans, and the Struggle for Civil Rights in Texas* (Chapel Hill: University of North Carolina Press, 2011); Wesley G. Phelps, *A People's War on Poverty: Urban Politics and Grassroots Activists in Houston* (Athens: University of Georgia Press, 2014); Howard Beeth and Cary D. Wintz, *Black Dixie: Afro-Texan History and Culture in Houston* (College Station: Texas A&M University Press, 2000); Kyle Shelton, *Power Moves: Transportation, Politics, and Development in Houston* (Austin: University of Texas Press, 2018).
10. Oscar Newman, "Creating Defensible Space" (Washington, DC: US Department

of Housing and Urban Development—Office of Policy Development and Research, April 1996); Rashad Shabazz, *Spatializing Blackness: Architectures of Confinement and Black Masculinity in Chicago* (Urbana: University of Illinois Press, 2015); Elizabeth Hinton, "'A War within Our Own Boundaries': Lyndon Johnson's Great Society and the Rise of the Carceral State," *Journal of American History* 102, no. 1 (June 1, 2015): 100–112, https://doi.org/10.1093/jahist/jav328.

11. Arnold R. Hirsch, *Making the Second Ghetto: Race and Housing in Chicago, 1940–1960* (New York: Cambridge University Press, 1983), 27.

12. "Setback for Communist Propaganda," *Houston Informer*, May 22, 1954, 12.

13. Jared Sexton, "Ante-Anti-Blackness: Afterthoughts," *Lateral*, no. 1 (2012), https://csalateral.org/issue/1/ante-anti-blackness-afterthoughts-sexton/.

14. "World" does not refer to the planet, but rather to historically specific existence. *This world* began with the advent of the transatlantic slave trade and the establishment of racialized chattel slavery. *This world* is defined by its epistemology, "where anti-blackness is . . . a foundational structure." Anti-blackness functions to preserve liberal humanism's conceit that we are all "human" because of evolutionary biology despite that law and politics organize us into categories of "human" and "less-than-human." Anti-blackness allows the world's many dilemmas (e.g., inequalities within democratic societies that make equal political participation impossible) to appear as aberrations or otherwise as results of the moral failings of subordinated populations. *This world* is not the only world that has existed in history, nor does it foreclose the possibility of other worlds, or even the simultaneous existence of alternative worlds, albeit those worlds are constrained by the violence and reach of the predominating one. Rinaldo Walcott, "Fanon's Heirs," *Amerikastudien / American Studies* 59, no. 3 (2014): 436; David Livingstone Smith, *Less Than Human: Why We Demean, Enslave, and Exterminate Others*, 1st ed. (New York: St. Martin's Griffin, 2012); Derrick Bell, "The Permanence of Racism," *Southwestern University Law Review* 22 (1993): 1103–1113.

15. David Marriott, *Whither Fanon? Studies in the Blackness of Being*, Cultural Memory in the Present Series (Stanford, CA: Stanford University Press, 2018), 278–281.

16. Trevon D. Logan and John M. Parman, "The National Rise in Residential Segregation," *Journal of Economic History* 77, no. 1 (March 2017): 129–130, https://doi.org/10.1017/S0022050717000079.

17. Connolly, "Black Movement Into the Suburbs"; John F. Kain, "Housing Segregation, Negro Employment, and Metropolitan Decentralization," *Quarterly Journal of Economics* 82, no. 2 (May 1968): 175, https://doi.org/10.2307/1885893; Joe Darden, Ron Malega, and Rebecca Stallings, "Social and Economic Consequences of Black Residential Segregation by Neighbourhood Socioeconomic Characteristics: The Case of Metropolitan Detroit," *Urban Studies* (Sage Publications, Ltd.) 56, no. 1 (January 2019): 115; Joe T. Darden, "Black Residential Segregation since the 1948 *Shelley v. Kraemer* Decision," *Journal of Black Studies* 25, no. 6 (July 1995): 680–692; Lassiter, *The Silent Majority*. Others warned against overextending conclusions from these kinds of cities to the rest of the nation: Thomas L. Van Valey, Wade Clark Roof, and Jerome E. Wilcox, "Trends in Residential Segregation: 1960–1970," *American Journal of Sociology* 82, no. 4 (1977): 826–844.

18. I came to these conclusions through a geostatistical analysis of US Census data for the year 1960 using SAS and ArcGIS. US Bureau of the Census, *1960 Censuses of Population and Housing: Procedural History* (Washington, DC: Government Printing Office, 1966), http://www2.census.gov/prod2/decennial/documents/1960/proceduralHistory/1960proceduralhistory.zip.

19. US Bureau of the Census.

20. Joe T. Darden and Sameh M. Kamel, "Black Residential Segregation in the City and Suburbs of Detroit: Does Socioeconomic Status Matter?" *Journal of Urban Affairs* 22, no. 1 (March 1, 2000): 1–13, https://doi.org/10.1111/0735-2166.00036; Ronald H. Bayor, *Race and the Shaping of Twentieth-Century Atlanta* (Chapel Hill: University of North Carolina Press, 1996).

21. Kenneth T. Jackson, *Crabgrass Frontier: The Suburbanization of the United States* (New York: Oxford University Press, 1985), 283.

22. See the Census of Population and Housing reports of the US Census Bureau for 1950, 1960, and 1970. Also helpful are the SMSA Selected Population and Housing Characteristic reports at http://www.census.gov and http://www.archive.org.

23. Peggy Pascoe, "Miscegenation Law, Court Cases, and Ideologies of 'Race' in Twentieth-Century America," *Journal of American History* 83, no. 1 (1996): 44–69, https://doi.org/10.2307/2945474; Peggy Pascoe, *What Comes Naturally: Miscegenation Law and the Making of Race in America* (New York: Oxford University Press, 2009).

24. Valerie A. Lewis, Michael O. Emerson, and Stephen L. Klineberg, "Who We'll Live With: Neighborhood Racial Composition Preferences of Whites, Blacks and Latinos," *Social Forces* 89, no. 4 (June 1, 2011): 1385–1407; Nora E. Taplin-Kaguru, *Grasping for the American Dream: Racial Segregation, Social Mobility, and Homeownership* (New York: Routledge, 2021), 8; Elizabeth Korver-Glenn, *Race Brokers: Housing Markets and Racial Segregation in 21st Century Urban America* (New York: Oxford University Press, 2021); Michael O. Emerson et al., "Houston Region Grows More Racially/Ethnically Diverse, with Small Declines in Segregation: A Joint Report Analyzing Census Data from 1990, 2000, and 2010" (Houston: Kinder Institute for Urban Research & the Hobby Center for the Study of Texas, 2012), http://kinder.rice.edu.

25. Nathan Glazer and Davis McEntire, "Minority Group Housing in Two Texas Cities," in *Studies in Housing & Minority Groups*, ed. Jack E. Dodson and Davis McEntire (Berkeley: University of California Press, 1960), 84–109.

26. Guadalupe San Miguel Jr., *Brown, Not White: School Integration and the Chicano Movement in Houston* (College Station: Texas A&M University Press, 2001); G. Reginald Daniel, "From Multiracial to Monoracial: The Formation of Mexican American Identities in the U.S. Southwest," *Genealogy* 6, no. 2 (June 2022): 28, https://doi.org/10.3390/genealogy6020028.

27. Steptoe, *Houston Bound*, 143.

28. Saidiya Hartman, "The Hold of Slavery," *New York Review of Books*, October 24, 2022, https://www.nybooks.com/online/2022/10/24/the-hold-of-slavery-hartman.

29. Sylvia Wynter, "The Re-Enchantment of Humanism: An Interview with Sylvia Wynter," *Small Axe: A Caribbean Journal of Criticism* 4, no. 2 (September 2000): 197.

30. Marriott, *Whither Fanon?* 280.

31. Wynter, "The Re-Enchantment of Humanism," 198.

32. Michel-Rolph Trouillot, *Silencing the Past: Power and the Production of History* (Boston: Beacon Press, 2015), xxiii, 27.

33. Steptoe, *Houston Bound*; Shelton, *Power Moves*; Behnken, *Fighting Their Own Battles*; Phelps, *A People's War on Poverty*; William Henry Kellar, *Make Haste Slowly: Moderates, Conservatives, and School Desegregation in Houston* (College Station: Texas A&M University Press, 1999).

34. Ansley T. Erickson, *Making the Unequal Metropolis: School Desegregation and Its Limits*, Historical Studies of Urban America (Chicago: University of Chicago Press, 2016), 151–152, 304, 316.

35. Lewis Ricardo Gordon, *Her Majesty's Other Children: Sketches of Racism from a Neocolonial Age* (Lanham, MD: Rowman & Littlefield, 1997), 67.

36. Lani Guinier, "From Racial Liberalism to Racial Literacy: *Brown v. Board of Education* and the Interest-Divergence Dilemma," *Journal of American History* 91, no. 1 (June 1, 2004): 92–118, https://doi.org/10.2307/3659616; Justin Hollander, *A Research Agenda for Shrinking Cities* (Northampton, MA: Edward Elgar Publishing, 2018).

37. Allan Megill, "History's Unresolving Tensions: Reality and Implications," *Rethinking History* 23, no. 3 (September 2019): 279–303, https://doi.org/10.1080/13642529.2019.1625544; Alun Munslow, "History, Skepticism and the Past," *Rethinking History* 21, no. 4 (October 2, 2017): 474–488, https://doi.org/10.1080/13642529.2017.1333287; Frank B. Wilderson III, "The Vengeance of Vertigo: Aphasia and Abjection in the Political Trials of Black Insurgents," *InTensions*, no. 5 (Fall/Winter 2011), http://www.yorku.ca/intent/issue5/articles/frankbwildersoniii.php.

38. Liane Carlson, *Contingency and the Limits of History: How Touch Shapes Experience and Meaning* (New York: Columbia University Press, 2019), e-book, emphasis added.

39. Alun Munslow, "Genre and History/Historying," *Rethinking History* 19, no. 2 (April 3, 2015): 158–176, https://doi.org/10.1080/13642529.2014.973711.

40. Capture indicates the limitation of mobility outside of a system, even if there is movement inside of it. I contend that in *this world* anti/blackness, as a form of capture, traverses time and defies change over time. This means that at times throughout the book I dispense with linear chronology altogether, evident even in the ways past and present tenses collide in this introduction. The temporal collisions in my syntax are in part a consequence of my commitment to thinking of history as the present as well as my attempts to confront the gravitational pull of the discipline to write in terms of contingency and agency.

41. Bell, *Faces at the Bottom of the Well.*

42. Sylvia Wynter, "No Humans Involved: An Open Letter to My Colleagues," *Knowledge on Trial* 1, no. 1 (1994): 49–50; Alexander G. Weheliye, *Habeas Viscus: Racializing Assemblages, Biopolitics, and Black Feminist Theories of the Human* (Durham, NC: Duke University Press, 2014).

43. Tryon P. Woods, *Blackhood against the Police Power: Punishment and Disavowal in the "Post-Racial" Era* (East Lansing: Michigan State University Press, 2019), 56.

44. Jared Sexton, "The Social Life of Social Death: On Afro-Pessimism and Black Optimism," *InTensions*, no. 5 (Fall/Winter 2011): 1–47.

45. Calvin L. Warren, *Ontological Terror: Blackness, Nihilism, and Emancipation* (Durham, NC: Duke University Press, 2018), 39, 182n27; Frantz Fanon, *Black Skin, White Masks* (New York: Grove Press, 2008), 149.

46. Warren, *Ontological Terror*, 182n27; Fanon, *Black Skin, White Masks*, 149; Saidiya Hartman, "The Dead Book Revisited," *History of the Present* 6, no. 2 (2016): 210.

47. Martin Woessner, "Reconsidering the Slaughter Bench of History: Genocide, Theodicy, and the Philosophy of History," *Journal of Genocide Research* 13, no. 1–2 (June 1, 2011): 91.

48. Frank Wilderson III, *Afropessimism* (New York: Liveright, 2020), 102.

49. Walter Johnson, *Soul by Soul: Life inside the Antebellum Slave Market* (Cambridge, MA: Harvard University Press, 1999), 15; Walter Johnson, "Inconsistency, Contradiction, and Complete Confusion: The Everyday Life of the Law of Slavery," *Law and Social Inquiry* 22, no. 2 (Spring 1997): 430.

50. Stephanie E. Smallwood, *Saltwater Slavery: A Middle Passage from Africa to American Diaspora* (Cambridge, MA: Harvard University Press, 2008), 201–202.

51. Frank B. Wilderson III, "Social Death and Narrative Aporia in *12 Years a Slave*," *Black Camera* 7, no. 1 (2015): 135, https://doi.org/10.2979/blackcamera.7.1.134.

52. Corey J. Miles, "Sociology of Vibe: Blackness, Felt Criminality, and Emotional Epistemology," *Humanity & Society*, December 16, 2022, https://doi.org/10.1177/01605976221146733.

53. David Eltis, *The Rise of African Slavery in the Americas* (New York: Cambridge University Press, 2000); Herman L. Bennett, *Colonial Blackness: A History of Afro-Mexico* (Bloomington: Indiana University Press, 2011); Frank T. Proctor, *Damned Notions of Liberty: Slavery, Culture, and Power in Colonial Mexico, 1640–1769* (Albuquerque: University of New Mexico Press, 2010).

54. P. Khalil Saucier and Tryon P. Woods, "Racial Optimism and the Drag of Thymotics," in *Conceptual Aphasia in Black: Displacing Racial Formation*, ed. P. Khalil Saucier and Tryon P. Woods (Lanham, MD: Lexington Books, 2016), 15.

55. Wilderson, "The Vengeance of Vertigo," 19.

56. Marriott, *Whither Fanon?* 278–310.

57. Frank B. Wilderson III, "Blacks and the Master/Slave Relation 2015," in *Afro-Pessimism: An Introduction*, 2017, 15–30, https://libcom.org/files/Afro-Pessimism2.pdf; Warren, *Ontological Terror*.

58. Megill, "History's Unresolving Tensions," 299n13.

59. Tyler Stovall, *White Freedom: The Racial History of an Idea* (Princeton, NJ: Princeton University Press, 2021), 102; Nell Irvin Painter, *The History of White People* (New York: W. W. Norton & Company, 2011), 94.

60. Louise Seamster and Victor Ray argue "that agency itself is deeply racialized, as social structures essentially foreclose certain paths to future action": "Against Teleology in the Study of Race," 332; Walter Johnson, "On Agency," *Journal of Social History* 37, no. 1 (2003): 114, 117–118.

61. W. E. B. Du Bois, *The Souls of Black Folk* (Chicago: A. C. McClurg and Co., 1907); Fanon, *Black Skin, White Masks*; Wynter, "No Humans Involved."

62. Weheliye, *Habeas Viscus*, 20–21.

63. Woods, *Blackhood against the Police Power*; Woessner, "Reconsidering the Slaughter Bench of History."

64. Marriott, *Whither Fanon?* 279.

65. Edward Hallett Carr, *What Is History?* (New York: Knopf, 1961), 86; Tosh, *Pursuit of History: Aims, Methods, and New Directions in the Study of History*, 2nd ed. (New York: Longman, 1991), 66.

66. Saidiya Hartman, "Venus in Two Acts," *Small Axe* 12, no. 2 (July 17, 2008): 1–14.

67. Saidiya V. Hartman and Frank B. Wilderson, "'The Position of the Unthought': An Interview with Saidiya V. Hartman," *Qui Parle* 13, no. 2 (2003): 185–186.

68. Michael Hawkins, "Our Present Concern: Historicism, Teleology, and Contingent Histories of a More Democratic Global Past," *Rethinking History* 15, no. 3 (September 2011): 375–376.

69. Hannu Salmi, "Cultural History, the Possible, and the Principle of Plenitude," *History and Theory* 50, no. 2 (2011): 173.

70. Frank B. Wilderson III, *Red, White & Black: Cinema and the Structure of U.S. Antagonisms* (Durham, NC: Duke University Press, 2010).

71. Hawkins, "Our Present Concern," 389.

72. Woods, *Blackhood against the Police Power*, 83.

73. Zakiyyah Iman Jackson, *Becoming Human: Matter and Meaning in an Antiblack World* (New York: NYU Press, 2020), 1, 46.

74. Hartman and Wilderson, "The Position of the Unthought," 183–201; Miles, "Sociology of Vibe."

75. This is not to suggest that I am any freer to think critically than the subjects I study, many of whom were invested in the terms of "the human."

76. Woods, *Blackhood against the Police Power*.

77. Donna L. Franklin, *Ensuring Inequality: The Structural Transformation of the African American Family* (New York: Oxford University Press, 2015), 3–26.

78. Some outstanding examples include Proctor, *Damned Notions of Liberty*; Alexander X. Byrd, *Captives and Voyagers: Black Migrants across the Eighteenth-Century British Atlantic World* (Baton Rouge: Louisiana State University Press, 2008); Jill Lepore, *New York Burning: Liberty, Slavery, and Conspiracy in Eighteenth-Century Manhattan* (New York: Alfred A. Knopf, 2005); C. L. R. James and James Walvin, *The Black Jacobins: Toussaint L'Ouverture and the San Domingo Revolution*, 2nd ed. (New York: Vintage Books, 1963).

79. Johnson, "On Agency," 117–118.

80. Hartman, "Venus in Two Acts," 1–14.

81. Wilderson, "The Vengeance of Vertigo," 11; Andrew Santana Kaplan, "Notes Toward (Inhabiting) the Black Messianic in Afro-Pessimism's Apocalyptic Thought," *The Comparatist* 43, no. 1 (2019): 70, https://doi.org/10.1353/com.2019.0004.

82. George Weddington, "Political Ontology and Race Research: A Response to 'Critical Race Theory, Afro-Pessimism, and Racial Progress Narratives,'" *Sociology of Race and Ethnicity* 5, no. 2 (April 1, 2019): 278–288, https://doi.org/10.1177/2332649218785921.

83. Somers suggests a dichotomy between the kind of representational form of narrative that I describe in the previous paragraph and argues instead for narrative as ontological. For her, the latter acknowledges that narratives are not just stories that we tell, but how we constitute who we are and what we *be*. Succinctly, narrativity is constitutive of subjectivity. I, however, do not see a distinction between representational forms and ontological narrativity, perhaps because while Somers sees "agents" at work in narrative production, I see actors captured by narrative, even as they produce it. Margaret R. Somers, "The Narrative Constitution of Identity: A Relational and Network Approach," *Theory and Society* 23, no. 5 (1994): 605–649.

84. Somers, "The Narrative Constitution of Identity," 617–620.

85. Hartman, "Venus in Two Acts"; David Kazanjian, "Scenes of Speculation," *Social Text* 33, no. 4 (125) (December 1, 2015): 77–84, https://doi.org/10.1215/01642472-3315778; Wilderson, "Blacks and the Master/Slave Relation 2015."

86. Woods, *Blackhood against the Police Power*, 61–63; W. E. B. Du Bois, *Black Reconstruction in America: Toward a History of the Part Which Black Folk Played in the Attempt to Reconstruct Democracy in America, 1860–1880* (New Brunswick, NJ: Transaction Publishers, 2013).

87. Nahum D. Chandler, "Of Exorbitance: The Problem of the Negro as a Problem for Thought," *Criticism* 50, no. 3 (2008): 348, 387.

88. Michelle Alexander, *The New Jim Crow: Mass Incarceration in the Age of Colorblindness* (New York: New Press, 2012); Lani Guinier and Gerald Torres, *The Miner's Canary: Enlisting Race, Resisting Power, Transforming Democracy* (Cambridge, MA: Harvard University Press, 2009), 225.

89. Hartman, "The Dead Book Revisited," 209.

90. Emerson et al., "Houston Region," 24; Elizabeth Korver-Glenn, "Compounding

Inequalities: How Racial Stereotypes and Discrimination Accumulate across the Stages of Housing Exchange," *American Sociological Review* 83, no. 4 (August 1, 2018): 627–656, https://doi.org/10.1177/0003122418781774; Lewis, Emerson, and Klineberg, "Who We'll Live With"; Lawrence Bobo and Camille L. Zubrinsky, "Attitudes on Residential Integration: Perceived Status Differences, Mere In-Group Preference, or Racial Prejudice?" *Social Forces* 74, no. 3 (1996): 883–909, https://doi.org/10.2307/2580385; William A. V. Clark, "Residential Preferences and Residential Choices in a Multiethnic Context," *Demography* 29, no. 3 (August 1, 1992): 451–466, https://doi.org/10.2307/2061828.

Chapter 1: Captured by Gender Roles
Hartman, "The Dead Book Revisited," 213–214.

1. James H. Sweet, *Recreating Africa: Culture, Kinship, and Religion in the African-Portuguese World, 1441–1770* (Chapel Hill: University of North Carolina Press, 2003); Winthrop D. Jordan, *White over Black: American Attitudes toward the Negro, 1550–1812* (Chapel Hill: University of North Carolina Press, 1968); Vincent Woodard, *The Delectable Negro: Human Consumption and Homoeroticism within US Slave Culture* (New York: NYU Press, 2014).

2. Hartman, "The Dead Book Revisited," 213.

3. Marcus Rediker, *The Slave Ship: A Human History* (New York: Viking, 2007), 60.

4. Sylviane A. Diouf, *Slavery's Exiles: The Story of the American Maroons* (New York: NYU Press, 2014), 11.

5. W. E. B. Du Bois, *The Souls of Black Folk* (Chicago: A. C. McClurg & Co., 1907); Warren, *Ontological Terror*, 146–150.

6. Philippa Levine, "States of Undress: Nakedness and the Colonial Imagination," *Victorian Studies* 50, no. 2 (2008): 207; George M. Fredrickson, *The Black Image in the White Mind: The Debate on Afro-American Character and Destiny, 1817–1914* (Middletown, CT: Wesleyan University Press, 1987), 115.

7. Mia Bay, *To Tell the Truth Freely: The Life of Ida B. Wells* (New York: Macmillan, 2010); Paula J. Giddings, *When and Where I Enter: The Impact of Black Women on Race and Sex in America* (New York: William Morrow, 1984).

8. Linda L. Black, "Female Community Leaders in Houston, Texas: A Study of the Education of Ima Hogg and Christia Daniels Adair" (Ph.D. diss., Texas A&M University, 2008), 157.

9. Christia Adair and Dorothy R. Robinson, Black Women Oral History Project, September 1977, box 4, folder 1, Christia V. Adair Collection MSS 109, Houston Metropolitan Research Center, Houston Public Library, hereafter HMRC, HPL.

10. Adair and Robinson, Black Women Oral History Project.

11. Theodore Rosengarten, *All God's Dangers: The Life of Nate Shaw* (New York: Knopf Doubleday Publishing Group, 1974); Guy Lancaster, *Racial Cleansing in Arkansas, 1883–1924: Politics, Land, Labor, and Criminality* (Lanham, MD: Lexington Books, 2014).

12. Adair and Robinson, Black Women Oral History Project.

13. Evelyn Brooks Higginbotham, "African-American Women's History and the Metalanguage of Race," *Signs* 17, no. 2 (January 1, 1992): 16; Anne M. Valk and Leslie Brown, *Living with Jim Crow: African American Women and Memories of the Segregated South*, Palgrave Studies in Oral History (New York: Palgrave Macmillan, 2010), 8.

14. C. Riley Snorton, *Black on Both Sides: A Racial History of Trans Identity* (Minneapolis: University of Minnesota Press, 2017), 12; Gregory D. Smithers, "The 'Pursuits of the Civilized Man': Race and the Meaning of Civilization in the United States and Australia,

1790s-1850s," *Journal of World History* 20, no. 2 (2009): 245–272; Jackson, *Becoming Human*; Sarah Haley, "'Like I Was a Man': Chain Gangs, Gender, and the Domestic Carceral Sphere in Jim Crow Georgia," *Signs* 39, no. 1 (2013): 53–77, https://doi.org/10.1086/670769.

15. Danielle L. McGuire, "'It Was Like All of Us Had Been Raped': Sexual Violence, Community Mobilization, and the African American Freedom Struggle," *Journal of American History* 91, no. 3 (December 1, 2004): 910, https://doi.org/10.2307/3662860; Kimberlé Crenshaw, "Mapping the Margins: Intersectionality, Identity Politics, and Violence against Women of Color," *Stanford Law Review* 43, no. 6 (July 1, 1991): 1285, https://doi.org/10.2307/1229039; Thomas A. Foster, "The Sexual Abuse of Black Men under American Slavery," *Journal of the History of Sexuality* 20, no. 3 (2011): 445–464, https://doi.org/10.1353/sex.2011.0059.

16. Judith Butler, *Gender Trouble: Feminism and the Subversion of Identity* (New York: Routledge, 1999), 9; Barbara J. Risman, "Gender as a Social Structure: Theory Wrestling with Activism," *Gender and Society* 18, no. 4 (August 1, 2004): 429–450.

17. Bay, *To Tell the Truth Freely*, 230, 321; W. E. B. Du Bois, *Dusk of Dawn*, ed. Henry Louis Gates Jr. (New York: Oxford University Press, 2007), 58–59.

18. Reuben Shannon Lovinggood, "The Negro Seer: His Preparation and Mission," Commencement Address given at Prairie View State Normal and Industrial College, Prairie View, Texas, June 4, 1907, http://hdl.handle.net/2027/nnc2.ark:/13960/t6b31t631.

19. James D. Anderson, *The Education of Blacks in the South, 1860–1935* (Chapel Hill: University of North Carolina Press, 1988).

20. Adair and Robinson, Black Women Oral History Project.

21. Adair and Robinson, Black Women Oral History Project.

22. Adair and Robinson, Black Women Oral History Project.

23. Adair and Robinson, Black Women Oral History Project.

24. Adair and Robinson, Black Women Oral History Project.

25. Adair and Robinson, Black Women Oral History Project.

26. Houston National Association for the Advancement of Colored People, "Your Help Is Needed [Ad]," *Houston Informer*, June 7, 1919; Darlene Clark Hine, *Black Victory: The Rise and Fall of the White Primary in Texas* (Columbia: University of Missouri Press, 2003).

27. Adair and Robinson, Black Women Oral History Project.

28. "Texas Political Calendar for 1920–1921," *Fairfield Recorder*, January 30, 1920, 3.

29. Adair and Robinson, Black Women Oral History Project.

30. "Equal Rights League Urges Suffragists to Stand against Color Line," *Dallas Express*, September 18, 1920, 1.

31. Adair and Robinson, Black Women Oral History Project.

32. Courtney Q. Shah, "'Against Their Own Weakness': Policing Sexuality and Women in San Antonio, Texas, during World War I," *Journal of the History of Sexuality* 19, no. 3 (2010): 470; Courtney Q. Shah, *Sex Ed, Segregated: The Quest for Sexual Knowledge in Progressive-Era America* (Rochester, NY: University of Rochester Press, 2015), 118; William S. Bush, *Who Gets a Childhood? Race and Juvenile Justice in Twentieth-Century Texas* (Athens: University of Georgia Press, 2010), 74–76; Margaret Reeves, *Training Schools for Delinquent Girls* (New York: Russell Sage Foundation, 1929).

33. "Historical Marker Detail for Acres Homes Community," Harris County Historical Commission, n.d..

34. Keeanga-Yamahtta Taylor, *Race for Profit: How Banks and the Real Estate Industry*

Undermined Black Homeownership, electronic resource, Justice, Power, and Politics Series (Chapel Hill: University of North Carolina Press, 2019).

35. "Growth of Acres Homes Area Depends on Alertness of Citizens to Its Needs," *Houston Informer*, May 26, 1951, 1; "Acreas [sic] Homes: Profile of a Negro Suburban Area," *Houston Informer*, February 25, 1950, 19.

36. Marvin D. Cloud, "Acres Homes: Largest U.S. 'Negro' Community Receives Official Texas Historical Marker," *African American News & Issues*, November 4, 2009, 1, box 1, folder 3, Linda Austin Collection MSS.0024, African American Library at the Gregory School, Houston Public Library; Debra Blackflock-Sloan, "The Harris County Historical Commission Welcomes You to the Dedication of an Official Texas Historical Marker for Acres Homes Community," November 7, 2009, box 1, folder 4, Linda Austin Collection MSS.0024, AAL at the Gregory School, HPL; "Acreas Homes: Profile of a Negro Suburban Area," 19.

37. Cloud, "Acres Homes: Largest U.S. 'Negro' Community Receives Official Texas Historical Marker," 1, 13; Doris Elaine Childress, "Bus Ride to Liberation: A Historical Video Documentary of the Acres Homes Transit Company in Houston, Texas" (master's thesis, University of North Texas, 1994), 6, UNT Digital Library, http://digital.library.unt.edu/ark:/67531/metadc279071/; "Acreas Homes: Profile of a Negro Suburban Area," 19.

38. *Census of Population, 1960: The Eighteenth Decennial Census of the United States* (Washington, DC: Government Printing Office, 1963).

39. "Some Call Acres Homes Houston's Dumping Ground," *Forward Times*, October 7, 1967, 10.

40. Childress, "Bus Ride to Liberation"; Roger Townsend Ward, "Acres Homes Transit Company," The Handbook of Texas Online, Texas State Historical Association (TSHA), December 17, 2015, https://tshaonline.org/handbook/online/articles/dgama; "Acres Homes Citizens Retain Attorney in Transportation Case," *Houston Informer*, July 26, 1952, 10; "Two Bus Lines in Acres Homes Cause Tension," *Houston Informer*, August 15, 1959, sec. 1, 1; "Acres Home Citizens Boycott Yale Transportation," *Houston Informer*, July 19, 1952, sec. 1, 1; Ninian McGowan, "Residents of Acres Homes May Soon Have Bus Service: Community Leaders Apply for Franchise," *Houston Informer*, March 7, 1959, 1, 10.

41. "Will Acres Homes Become All-Negro Town? Incorporation Pleas to Be Heard Monday," *Houston Informer*, August 17, 1957, 1, 10; "Acres Homes Voters Rebuke Proposed All-Negro Town," *Houston Informer*, October 19, 1957, 3.

42. Advisory Committee on Intergovernmental Relations, *Fiscal Balance in the American Federal System*, vol. 2: *Metropolitan Fiscal Disparities* (Washington, DC: US Department of Housing and Urban Development, 1967), 31, 328; "Independent Offices and Department of Housing and Urban Development Appropriations for 1970. Part 4: Department of Housing and Urban Development; Testimony of Members of Congress and Other Individuals and Organizations," Cong. Rec. 91st Cong., 1st sess., 1969, 707; Kevin L. Glasper, "The Political, Economic & Social Implications of Mayor Lee P. Brown," in *Perspectives in Black Politics and Black Leadership*, ed. John Davis (Lanham, MD: University Press of America, 2007), 338.

43. Charles S. Aiken, "Race as a Factor in Municipal Underbounding," *Annals of the Association of American Geographers* 77, no. 4 (1987): 564–579.

44. R. T. Tatum, "Ellie Walls Montgomery," *Texas Standard*, September 1935, 39, University of North Texas Libraries, Portal to Texas History, https://texashistory.unt.edu, crediting Prairie View A&M University; Patricia S Prather, "Henderson, Nathaniel Q.," The

Handbook of Texas Online, Texas State Historical Association (TSHA), March 7, 2017, https://tshaonline.org/handbook/online/articles/fhe96.

45. "Dorcas Home's Future at Stake; Will Race Fall Down on the Job?" *Houston Informer*, March 19, 1921, 7.

46. Adair and Robinson, Black Women Oral History Project.

47. Haley, "'Like I Was a Man'"; Tanya Amith Bryce, "The Treatment of African American Girls in Progressive Era North Carolina's Juvenile Justice System (1890–1930)" (Ph.D. diss., University of North Carolina at Chapel Hill, 2003), 8.

48. Mary Macey Dietzler, *Detention Houses and Reformatories as Protective Social Agencies in the Campaign of the United States Government against Venereal Disease* (Washington, DC: Government Printing Office, 1922), 215; Sarah Haley, *No Mercy Here: Gender, Punishment, and the Making of Jim Crow Modernity* (Chapel Hill: University of North Carolina Press, 2016).

49. "Botkin Indicted on Murder Count," *Galveston Daily News*, May 3, 1930, 4; Adair and Robinson, Black Women Oral History Project.

50. Adair and Robinson, Black Women Oral History Project.

51. Randy J. Sparks, "'Heavenly Houston' or 'Hellish Houston'? Black Unemployment and Relief Efforts, 1929–1936," *Southern Studies: An Interdisciplinary Journal of the South* 25, no. 4 (October 1986): 353–366; David Ponton III, "Disentangling Desire in 1950s Houston: On Assemblages and Racial Disparity in American Criminal Justice" (December 10, 2013), Rice University Digital Scholarship Archive, https://scholarship.rice.edu/handle/1911/75930; Adair and Robinson, Black Women Oral History Project; "Adair, Christia V.," n.d., Houston Oral History Project MSS0109, Houston Area Digital Archives, Houston Public Library.

52. Adair and Robinson, Black Women Oral History Project; Merline Pitre, *In Struggle against Jim Crow: Lulu B. White and the NAACP, 1900–1957* (College Station: Texas A&M University Press, 2010).

53. Mark Michael Smith, *How Race Is Made: Slavery, Segregation, and the Senses* (Chapel Hill: University of North Carolina Press, 2006), 126; Fanon, *Black Skin, White Masks*, 121–184; Jordan, *White over Black*, 468–470; Tera W. Hunter, *To 'joy My Freedom: Southern Black Women's Lives and Labors after the Civil War* (Cambridge, MA: Harvard University Press, 1997), 197, 203; Tommy J. Curry, *The Man-Not: Race, Class, Genre, and the Dilemmas of Black Manhood* (Philadelphia: Temple University Press, 2017); David Marriott, *On Black Men* (New York: Columbia University Press, 2000).

54. Fredrickson, *The Black Image in the White Mind*, 275–282.

55. William Lee Howard, "The Negro as a Distinct Ethnic Factor in Civilization," *Medicine* 10 (1903): 426.

56. Warren, *Ontological Terror*, 5–8; Fanon, *Black Skin, White Masks*, 117–120.

57. Rebecca Anne Goetz, "Rethinking the 'Unthinking Decision': Old Questions and New Problems in the History of Slavery and Race in the Colonial South," *Journal of Southern History* 75, no. 3 (2009): 599–612; Jordan, *White over Black*, 44–45.

58. E. Franklin Frazier, "The Pathology of Race Prejudice," *The Forum*, June 1927.

59. Claudia Tate, "Freud and His 'Negro': Psychoanalysis as Ally and Enemy of African Americans," *Journal for the Psychoanalysis of Culture & Society* 1, no. 1 (1996): 53–62.

60. David Theo Goldberg, "Racism and Rationality: The Need for a New Critique," *Philosophy of the Social Sciences* 20, no. 3 (September 1, 1990): 342, https://doi.org/10.1177/004839319002000303.

61. P. Khalil Saucier and Tryon P. Woods, eds., *Conceptual Aphasia in Black: Displacing Racial Formation* (Lanham, MD: Lexington Books, 2016), 2.

62. Fanon, *Black Skin, White Masks*, 120.

63. Notably, W. E. B. Du Bois thought this in his early life, but over time learned to conceive of ignorance not as a lack of education but as a domain of education. Ignorance is not a lack of knowledge, but a practice of education that makes certain claims impermissible for consideration. W. E. B. Du Bois, *Darkwater: Voices from within the Veil* (New York: Harcourt, Brace and Howe, 1920), 40.

64. Adair and Robinson, Black Women Oral History Project.

65. Adair and Robinson, Black Women Oral History Project.

66. Adair and Robinson, Black Women Oral History Project; C. V. Adair to Sound Off, *Houston Post*, March 24, 1959; C. V. Adair to A. McFarland, April 1959; C. V. Adair to Sound Off, *Houston Post*, June 21, 1961; A. McFarland to C. V. Adair, March 31, 1959; all in box 4, folder 9, Christia V. Adair Collection MSS 109, HMRC, HPL.

67. C. V. Adair to Sound Off, *Houston Post*, March 24, 1959; Adair to McFarland, April 1959; C. V. Adair to Sound Off, *Houston Post*, June 21, 1961; McFarland to Adair, March 31, 1959; all in box 4, folder 9, Christia V. Adair Collection MSS 109, HMRC, HPL.

68. Adair to McFarland, April 1959, box 4, folder 9, Christia V. Adair Collection MSS 109, HMRC, HPL.

69. Du Bois, *The Souls of Black Folk*, 1.

70. "Dual Airport Facilities Condemned by CAA," *Houston Informer*, December 8, 1951, sec. 1, 1, 6; "Citizens Expose Bias at Airport: City Blamed," *Houston Informer*, October 6, 1951, sec. 1, 1, 10; Kellar, *Make Haste Slowly*, 45; Mrs. C. V. Adair, "Annual Report of Branch Activities," January 15, 1954, 16, Papers of the NAACP Part 26: Selected Branch Files, 1940–1955, Series A: The South, Group II, Series C, folder Houston, Texas, 1954, ProQuest History Vault; "Interview of Fred Hofheinz, May 21, 1987 Former Mayor of Houston" (May 21, 1987), box 2, folder 14, Margeurite Johnston Papers, Woodson Research Center, Fondren Library, Rice University.

71. Barbara Karkabi, "'Fire in Her Belly': Hundreds Honor Lifelong Civil-Rights Fight," *Houston Chronicle*, June 8, 1990, box 4, folder 1, Christia V. Adair Collection MSS 109, HMRC, HPL; Fred Hofheinz and Ronnie Dugger, "Houston Has Desegregation Model," August 5, 1955, box 4Jc62, folder "Research Files: Housing, 1955, 1964, 1969, 1970," Texas Observer Records, Dolph Briscoe Center for American History, University of Texas at Austin; "Interview of Fred Hofheinz, May 21, 1987, Former Mayor of Houston"; Adair and Robinson, Black Women Oral History Project.

72. Bell, "The Permanence of Racism."

73. Gunnar Myrdal, *An American Dilemma*, vol. 2: *The Negro Problem and Modern Democracy* (New York: McGraw-Hill Book Company, 1964), 587.

74. Ida B. Wells-Barnett, *On Lynchings* (Mineola, NY: Dover Publications, Inc., 2014); Bay, *To Tell the Truth Freely*; Danielle L. McGuire, *At the Dark End of the Street: Black Women, Rape, and Resistance—A New History of the Civil Rights Movement from Rosa Parks to the Rise of Black Power* (New York: Alfred A. Knopf, 2010).

75. "Vote Plot Blamed for Texas Riot," *Baltimore Afro-American*, June 26, 1943, 24; "Negro's Attack on Woman Starts Violence in Which White Man Is Killed and Work at Shipyard Halted," *New York Times*, June 17, 1943, 42; "Mob Destruction Sweeping Nation," *New York Amsterdam News*, June 26, 1943, 1; "23 Dead, 650 Hurt as Violence Grows," *Chicago Defender*, June 26, 1943, 1; "Beaumont Negro Section in Ruins after

Riot," *Chicago Defender*, June 26, 1943, 1; Ralph Matthews, "Nazi Pogroms Tame to Texas Rioters," *Baltimore Afro-American*, June 26, 1943, 1, 7.

76. Adair and Robinson, Black Women Oral History Project; *White v. State*, 139 Tex. Crim. 660 (Court of Criminal Appeals of Texas 1940); Randolph Boehm, "Papers of the NAACP, Part 08: Discrimination in the Criminal Justice System, 1910–1955, Series A & B: Legal Department and Central Office Records" (University Publications of America, 1982), Kelley Center for Government Information, Data, and Geospatial Services, Fondren Library, Rice University.

77. Jackson, *Becoming Human*, 5.

78. Stephen Valocchi, "Not Yet Queer Enough: The Lessons of Queer Theory for the Sociology of Gender and Sexuality," *Gender and Society* 19, no. 6 (December 1, 2005): 755–756.

Chapter 2: Captured by the Rule of Law
Hartman, "The Dead Book Revisited," 210.

1. Blair Murphy Kelley, *Right to Ride: Streetcar Boycotts and African American Citizenship in the Era of* Plessy v. Ferguson (Chapel Hill: University of North Carolina Press, 2010).

2. Bessie Pavlicek, "Re: Stabbing of F. A. Nowak," October 11, 1951, Inquest Records (1889–1956), vol. 51, Harris County Archives. Several documents spell Morris's first name "Johnny." When directly quoting or citing from them, I will use that spelling. However, outside of direct citations I will spell his first name as "Johnnie" because that is how he signed all the official court documents.

3. "TV Plea Brings Bus Killer Clue," *Houston Post*, October 12, 1951, 1.

4. "Davis to Seek Quick Morris Indictment," *Houston Post*, October 17, 1951, sec. 1, 7.

5. "State Asks for More Time in J. K. Morris's Case: Charge Veniremen Dismissed without Being Questioned," *Houston Informer*, December 15, 1951, sec. 1, 1, 10.

6. Shelton, *Power Moves*; Tom Watson McKinney, "Superhighway Deluxe: Houston's Gulf Freeway" (Ph.D. diss., University of Houston, 2006).

7. Charles F. Robinson II, "Legislated Love in the Lone Star State: Texas and Miscegenation," *Southwestern Historical Quarterly* 108, no. 1 (July 1, 2004): 65–87.

8. Lisa Lindquist Dorr, *White Women, Rape, and the Power of Race in Virginia, 1900–1960* (Chapel Hill: University of North Carolina Press, 2004); Tracey Owens Patton and Julie Snyder-Yuly, "Any Four Black Men Will Do: Rape, Race, and the Ultimate Scapegoat," *Journal of Black Studies* 37, no. 6 (July 1, 2007): 859–895.

9. McGuire, *At the Dark End of the Street*; Diane Miller Sommerville, *Rape and Race in the Nineteenth-Century South* (Chapel Hill: University of North Carolina Press, 2004); Kevin J. Mumford, *Interzones: Black/White Sex Districts in Chicago and New York in the Early Twentieth Century* (New York: Columbia University Press, 1997).

10. Monte Akers, *Flames after Midnight: Murder, Vengeance, and the Desolation of a Texas Community*, rev. ed. (Austin: University of Texas Press, 2011), 146–147; James Martin SoRelle, "The Darker Side of 'Heaven': The Black Community in Houston, Texas, 1917–1945" (Ph.D. diss., Kent State University, 1980). Jennifer Lynn Ritterhouse discusses racial etiquette as "the power-relations process" through which Jim Crow was maintained through racial performativity in *Growing Up Jim Crow: How Black and White Southern Children Learned Race* (Chapel Hill: University of North Carolina Press, 2006), 6. The quotes attributed to Adair appear in Adair and Robinson, Black Women Oral History Project. The quote about Morris's case attracting widespread attention appears in Sonny Wells,

"Johnnie Lee Morris Takes a Bride," *Houston Forward Times*, November 4, 1967, 3. The case did eventually lead to an appeal, which Adair was happy to note was one of the major successes of the Houston NAACP in 1951. Mrs. C. V. Adair, "Annual Report of Branch Activities," February 21, 1952, Papers of the NAACP, Part 25: Branch Department Files, Series A: Regional Files and Special Reports, 1941–1955, Group II, Series C, ProQuest History Vault.

11. Jenkins and Leroy, "The Old History of Capitalism," 2–6.

12. Kathryn Yusoff, *A Billion Black Anthropocenes or None* (Minneapolis: University of Minnesota Press, 2018).

13. Nirej Sekhon, "Police and the Limit of Law," *Columbia Law Review* 119, no. 6 (2019): 1719.

14. W. E. B. Du Bois, *The Philadelphia Negro: A Social Study* (New York: Schocken Books, 1967), 386.

15. Woods, *Blackhood against the Police Power*.

16. *Harris County Sheriff's Department, 1837–2005* (Nashville: Turner Publishing Company, 2005), 14.

17. Dwight Watson, *Race and the Houston Police Department, 1930–1990: A Change Did Come* (College Station: Texas A&M University Press, 2005), 59.

18. "The State of Texas vs. Johnny Lee Morris: Motion to Suppress Evidence and Purported Confession," December 10, 1951, Harris County District Clerk's Office; "Deputy Outraged over Fellow Officers' Conduct," *Houston Informer*, April 26, 1952, 1; Center for Research in Social Change and Economic Development at Rice University, "[Confidential Report]," July 13, 1967, box 1, folder 3, Louie Welch Papers, MSS 0051, HMRC, HPL.

19. "Indicted in Bus Killing," *Houston Informer*, October 20, 1951, sec. 1, 1, 12; "The State of Texas vs. Johnny Lee Morris: Indictment," October 17, 1951, Harris County District Clerk's Office; Adair and Robinson, Black Women Oral History Project.

20. "Indicted in Bus Killing," 1, 12.

21. "TV Plea Brings Bus Killer Clue," 1; "Witnesses Said Threatened in Fatal Stabbing," *Big Spring Daily Herald*, November 18, 1951, 4. Also see Milton Gabel and Hortense Gabel, "Texas Newspaper Opinion: II," *Public Opinion Quarterly* 10, no. 2 (1946): 201; Gabel and Gabel, "Texas Newspaper Opinion"; E. Bun Lee, *TSU Meets the Press: White Newspaper Coverage of a Black University in Houston, Texas, 1947–1987* (Houston: D. Armstrong Co. Inc., 1989); Steven M. Chermak, *Searching for a Demon: The Media Construction of the Militia Movement* (Boston: Northeastern University Press, 2002); Robert M. Entman and Kimberly A. Gross, "Race to Judgment: Stereotyping Media and Criminal Defendants," *Law and Contemporary Problems* 71, no. 4 (2008): 93–133.

22. See cultivation theory in Mary Beth Oliver, "African American Men as 'Criminal and Dangerous': Implications of Media Portrayals of Crime on the 'Criminalization' of African American Men," *Journal of African American Studies* 7, no. 2 (2003): 3–18.

23. "J. L. Morris' Trial Is Postponed: Wife Freed of 'Vag' Charge," *Houston Informer*, November 10, 1951, sec. 1, 1, 10; "Bond Hearing for J. L. Morris Is Set for November First: Grants Writ after D. A. Denies Bail," *Houston Informer*, November 3, 1951, sec. 1, 1, 12.

24. Ariela Julie Gross, *What Blood Won't Tell: A History of Race on Trial in America* (Cambridge, MA: Harvard University Press, 2008).

25. Keven McAlester, "The Icebox Revisited," *Dallas Observer*, March 11, 2004, https://www.dallasobserver.com/news/the-icebox-revisited-6386139.

26. Ben Hartman, "My Grandfather Was a Death Row Doctor. He Tested Psychedelic Drugs on Texas Inmates," *Houston Chronicle*, July 7, 2017, https://www.chron.com/news/health/article/My-grandfather-was-a-death-row-doctor-He-tested-11271396.php.

27. Estelle B. Freedman, *Redefining Rape* (Cambridge, MA: Harvard University Press, 2013), 263; Earl Smith and Angela J. Hattery, "Race, Wrongful Conviction & Exoneration," *Journal of African American Studies* 15, no. 1 (2011): 88–89.

28. *Johnson v. State*, 169 Tex. Crim. 612 (Court of Criminal Appeals of Texas 1960); *Johnson v. Ellis*, 194 F. Supp. 258 (United States District Court, S.D. Texas, Houston Division 1961); Hartman, "My Grandfather Was a Death Row Doctor"; McAlester, "The Icebox Revisited."

29. Alex D. Pokorny, "A Comparison of Homicides in Two Cities," *Journal of Criminal Law and Criminology* 56, no. 4 (December 1965): 484.

30. "We're Innocent! Murder Suspects Weep; Refute Initial Statements," *Houston Informer*, July 25, 1959, 1, 10.

31. McAlester, "The Icebox Revisited"; "Pleads Innocence, Texas Boy, 17, Gets Death," *Jet*, October 15, 1959, 46.

32. "We're Innocent! Murder Suspects Weep; Refute Initial Statements," 10.

33. "Murder Victim's Mother Points Out a Vital Truth," *Houston Informer*, August 8, 1959, 10; "White Mother Asks Tolerance in Son's Brutal Sex Slaying," *Jet*, August 20, 1959, 46–48.

34. Gilbert King, *Devil in the Grove: Thurgood Marshall, the Groveland Boys, and the Dawn of a New America* (New York: Harper, 2013); Eric W. Rise, *The Martinsville Seven: Race, Rape, and Capital Punishment* (Charlottesville: University of Virginia Press, 1998); Haywood Patterson and Earl Conrad, *Scottsboro Boy* (Garden City, NY: Doubleday, 1950).

35. Kazanjian, "Scenes of Speculation," 80–83; David Kazanjian, "Freedom's Surprise: Two Paths through Slavery's Archives," *History of the Present* 6, no. 2 (2016): 140, https://doi.org/10.5406/historypresent.6.2.0133.

36. Hartman, "Venus in Two Acts."

37. Marriott, *On Black Men*, x.

38. Sekhon, "Police and the Limit of Law"; David Ponton, "Clothed in Blue Flesh: Police Brutality and the Disciplining of Race, Gender, and the 'Human,'" *Theory & Event* 19, no. 3 (2016), http://muse.jhu.edu/article/623994.

39. Alan Hunt, "The Theory of Critical Legal Studies," *Oxford Journal of Legal Studies* 6, no. 1 (1986): 4.

40. Austin Sarat and Conor Clarke, "Beyond Discretion: Prosecution, the Logic of Sovereignty, and the Limits of Law," *Law & Social Inquiry* 33, no. 2 (2008): 390.

41. Derrick A. Bell, "Brown v. Board of Education and the Interest-Convergence Dilemma," *Harvard Law Review* 93, no. 3 (January 1980): 518–533; Howell S. Baum, *Brown in Baltimore: School Desegregation and the Limits of Liberalism* (Ithaca, NY: Cornell University Press, 2010); Douglas S. Massey and Jonathan Tannen, "Suburbanization and Segregation in the United States: 1970–2010," *Ethnic and Racial Studies* 41, no. 9 (July 15, 2018): 1594–1611, https://doi.org/10.1080/01419870.2017.1312010; "Blacks Most Segregated Minority," *New York Times*, November 28, 2002, sec. A, 33.

42. Charles W. Collier, "The New Logic of Affirmative Action," *Duke Law Journal* 45, no. 3 (1995): 559–578, https://doi.org/10.2307/1372891.

43. John V. Kane and David C. Wilson, "Controversy and Costs: Investigating the Consensus on American Voter ID Laws," *Political Behavior* 43, no. 1 (March 1, 2021): 397–421, https://doi.org/10.1007/s11109-020-09643-0; David C. Wilson and Paul R.

Brewer, "The Foundations of Public Opinion on Voter ID Laws: Political Predispositions, Racial Resentment, and Information Effects," *Public Opinion Quarterly* 77, no. 4 (December 1, 2013): 962–984.

44. Michael Serota and Ethan J. Leib, "The Political Morality of Voting in Direct Democracy," *Minnesota Law Review* 97, no. 5 (2012): 1610.

45. "Motion to Suppress Evidence and Purported Confession"; "Deputy Outraged over Fellow Officers' Conduct," 1; *Harris County Sheriff's Department, 1837–2005*, 14.

46. "Indicted in Bus Killing," 1, 12; "TV Plea Brings Bus Killer Clue," 1, 8.

47. Robin D. G. Kelley, "'We Are Not What We Seem': Rethinking Black Working-Class Opposition in the Jim Crow South," *Journal of American History* 80, no. 1 (June 1, 1993): 78, https://doi.org/10.2307/2079698.

48. Kelley, "We Are Not What We Seem," 103–104; Kelley, *Right to Ride*; Bay, *To Tell the Truth Freely*; Edward L. Ayers, *The Promise of the New South: Life after Reconstruction*, 15th Anniversary ed. (New York: Oxford University Press, 2007).

49. Jennifer L. Morgan, *Laboring Women: Reproduction and Gender in New World Slavery* (Philadelphia: University of Pennsylvania Press, 2011), 79–89.

50. Darlene Clark Hine, *Hine Sight: Black Women and the Re-Construction of American History* (Brooklyn, NY: Carlson Pub., 1994), 37–41.

51. "Editorially Speaking: Trouble on the Bus," *Houston Informer*, October 27, 1951, sec. 2, 2.

52. Kelley, "We Are Not What We Seem," 78, 110.

53. Wilderson, *Red, White & Black*, 31.

54. Saucier and Woods, "Racial Optimism and the Drag of Thymotics," 14–15.

55. "Inquest Proceedings: Florian Antone Nowak, H2H North Arlington Street, Houston, Texas," October 11, 1951, Inquest Records (1889–1956), vol. 51, Harris County Archives; "The State of Texas vs. Johnny Lee Morris: Defendant's Amended Motion to Set Aside the Verdict of the Jury and to Grant a New Trial," January 30, 1952, Harris County District Clerk's Office; *Johnny Lee Morris v. State*, 251 S.W.2d 731 (Court of Criminal Appeals of Texas 1952).

56. Fanon, *Black Skin, White Masks*, 113.

57. Fanon, *Black Skin, White Masks*, 83.

58. Warren, *Ontological Terror*, 140–150.

59. Nick Bromell, "Democratic Indignation: Black American Thought and the Politics of Dignity," *Political Theory* 41, no. 2 (2013): 296.

60. "Johnnie Lee Morris Defense Fund Interest Increases: For Morris a Fair Trial Is Goal," *Houston Informer*, October 27, 1951, 10.

61. "Negro Admits Crime Spree, Shooting Officer," *Houston Chronicle*, October 13, 1951, 1; "Bounty Posted for Gunman," *Houston Post*, October 12, 1951, 1, 8; "Johnnie Lee Morris Defense Fund Interest Increases," 10.

62. "Witnesses Describe Broussard Shooting by Police: Says J. Broussaurd Was Beaten after Officer Shot Him," *Houston Informer*, October 27, 1951, sec. 1, 1, 10.

63. "Sheriff Slays Handcuffed Man, Telegram Charges," *Houston Informer*, November 10, 1951, 1; King, *Devil in the Grove*; Carter Wesley, "Ram's Horn: Police Brutality," *Houston Informer*, July 25, 1953, sec. 2, 3.

64. "It Is to Laugh," *Houston Informer*, November 21, 1951, sec. 2, 2.

65. "Indicted in Bus Killing," 12.

66. P. G. F., "Notes on Recent Developments in the South," *Political Affairs* 31 (May 5, 1952): 49–50.

67. Dora Apel, "Scottsboro, the Communist Party, and the NAACP: Conflicts and Desires," in Apel, *Imagery of Lynching: Black Men, White Women, and the Mob* (New Brunswick, NJ: Rutgers University Press, 2004), 47–82.

68. "Americanism in the Schools," *Houston Informer*, April 17, 1954, 14.

69. Hortense Spillers et al., "'Whatcha Gonna Do?': Revisiting 'Mama's Baby, Papa's Maybe: An American Grammar Book': A Conversation with Hortense Spillers, Saidiya Hartman, Farah Jasmine Griffin, Shelly Eversley, & Jennifer L. Morgan," *Women's Studies Quarterly* 35, no. 1/2 (2007): 306.

70. *Dennis v. United States*, 341 U.S. 494 (1951); William M. Wiecek, "The Legal Foundations of Domestic Anticommunism: The Background of Dennis v United States," *Supreme Court Review* 2001 (January 1, 2001): 375–434; John A. Gorfinkel and Julian W. Mack II, "Dennis v. United States and the Clear and Present Danger Rule," *California Law Review* 39, no. 4 (December 1, 1951): 475–501, https://doi.org/10.2307/3477951; Joy Gleason Carew, *Blacks, Reds, and Russians: Sojourners in Search of the Soviet Promise* (New Brunswick, NJ: Rutgers University Press, 2010).

71. Cedric Dover, "Focus on Dr. Du Bois Indictment," *Houston Informer*, November 3, 1951, sec. 2, 2; "Smith Act Ruling Danger to Negro People, Labor," *Houston Post*, October 30, 1951, sec. 2, 2; Louis Lautier, "Government Rests in Trial of Du Bois: Action in Case Sudden," *Houston Informer*, November 24, 1951, sec. 1, 1, 10; Louis Lautier, "Defense in Dubois Case Shows Sign of Weakening," *Houston Informer*, November 24, 1951, sec. 1, 2; George Streator, "Du Bois Declares Socialism a Haven," *New York Times*, 1947, 11; David Levering Lewis, *W. E. B. Du Bois, 1919–1963: The Fight for Equality and the American Century* (New York: Henry Holt and Company, 2000), 546–549.

72. Gregory P. Adams, "Our Readers Write," *Houston Informer*, October 17, 1953, sec. 1, 12.

73. "Editorially Speaking: Trouble on the Bus," 2; "It Is to Laugh," 2; "Johnnie Lee Morris Defense Fund Interest Increases," 1.

74. "NAACP to Bar Reds from Morris Defense Fund: Group Seek Dent and Foreman as Defense Lawyers," *Houston Informer*, October 20, 1951, 1, 12.

75. Mary Ellen Curtin, "Strong People and Strong Leaders: African American Women and the Modern Black Freedom Struggle," in *The Practice of U.S. Women's History Narratives, Intersections, and Dialogues*, ed. S. J. Kleinberg, Eileen Boris, and Vicki Ruíz (New Brunswick, NJ: Rutgers University Press, 2007), 316; "Houston Negroes to Back Accused," *Corpus Christi Caller-Times*, October 21, 1951, 11; "Johnnie Lee Morris Defense Fund Interest Increases," 1.

76. *Herman Lee Ross v. State*, 156 Tex. Crim. 164 (Court of Criminal Appeals of Texas 1950); "Appeals Court Rejects Request of Herman Ross," *Galveston Daily News*, March 13, 1952, 13; "Galveston, Texas, Bar Group Admits Negro," *Jet*, February 21, 1952, 17; Robert H. Johnson Jr., "Texas Editor Has Witnessed 129 Executions," *Orange Leader*, October 24, 1954, 2, University of North Texas Libraries, Portal to Texas History, texashistory.unt.edu, crediting Lamar State College-Orange.

77. "Friends Honor Associate Justice Henry E. Doyle First Court of Appeals with a Retirement Celebration (Retirement Celebration Program)," n.d., copy in author's possession; Thomas D. Russell, "'Keep Negroes Out of Most Classes Where There Are a Large Number of Girls': The Unseen Power of the Ku Klux Klan and Standardized Testing at the University of Texas, 1899–1999," in *Law, Society, and History: Themes in the Legal Sociology and Legal History of Lawrence M. Friedman*, ed. Robert W. Gordon and Morton J. Horwitz (New York: Cambridge University Press, 2011), 315; Richard Kluger, *Simple Justice: The*

History of Brown v. Board of Education and Black America's Struggle for Equality (New York: Vintage Books, 2004); Kellar, *Make Haste Slowly*; Virgie Lemond Mouton, "And So He Rose Alone: The Legacy of Judge Henry Eman Doyle, the First Graduate of Texas Southern University School of Law, Presently Known as Texas Southern University Thurgood Marshall School of Law," Texas State Historical Association 112th Annual Meeting, Corpus Christi, Texas, March 7, 2008; DeCarlous Spearman, "Henry Elman Doyle," in *African American National Biography*, ed. Henry Louis Gates Jr. and Evelyn Brooks Higginbotham (New York: Oxford University Press, 2008); "Bond Hearing for J. L. Morris Is Set for November First: Grants Writ after D. A. Denies Bail," 1; "Defend Slayer of Bus Driver," *Jet*, November 22, 1951, 24.

78. James A. Miller, *Remembering Scottsboro: The Legacy of an Infamous Trial* (Princeton, NJ: Princeton University Press, 2009).

79. "Johnny Lee Morris vs. C. V. Kern: Writ of Habeas Corpus," October 31, 1951, Harris County District Clerk's Office; "Morris Bond Try Is Failure," *Houston Informer*, December 1, 1951, sec. 1, 1, 10.

80. Hans Peter Mareus Neilsen Gammel, *The Laws of Texas, 1822–1897*, vol. 3 (Austin: Gammel Book Company, 1898), 65–66.

81. Ex parte Morris, 243 S.W.2d 852 (Court of Criminal Appeals of Texas 1951); "The State of Texas vs. Johnny Lee Morris: Motion to Hear Motion to Suppress Evidence and Purported Confession," December 10, 1951, Harris County District Clerk's Office; "Motion to Suppress Evidence and Purported Confession."

82. "The State of Texas vs. Johnny Lee Morris: Motion to Quash Indictment #1," December 10, 1951, Harris County District Clerk's Office; *Norris v. Alabama*, 294 U.S. 587 (Supreme Court of the United States 1935); *Carter v. Texas*, 177 U.S. 442 (1900).

83. "The State of Texas vs. Johnny Lee Morris: The State's Answer to the Defendants Motion to Quash Indictment," December 10, 1951, Harris County District Clerk's Office.

84. *Johnny Lee Morris v. State*, 158 Tex. Crim. 516 (Court of Criminal Appeals of Texas 1952); Henry E. Doyle, Johnnie Lee Morris, *Petitioner, v. State of Texas*: Petitioner's Brief, 345 U.S. 951 (n.d.); John Ben Shepherd, Brief in Opposition, 345 U.S. 951 (n.d.); *Morris v. State*, 39 Tex.Cr. R. 371, No. 46 S.W. 253 (Court of Criminal Appeals of Texas June 27, 1953); "He Was Exempted," *Daily News (Perth, Washington)*, June 15, 1938, City Final edition, 3; Allan Shivers to John J. Herrera, March 23, 1954, University of North Texas Libraries, Portal to Texas History, crediting HMRC, HPL, http://texashistory.unt.edu; Larry Karson, "Choosing Justice: The Implications of a Key-Man System for Selecting a Grand Jury," Southwestern Association of Criminal Justice Conference, Houston, Texas, October 8, 2004.

85. "Houston Murder Trial Jury Being Selected," [*Corpus Christi*] *Times*, December 12, 1951, 18.

86. Howard A. Carney, "Relating to Providing That in Capital Cases the State and the Defendant Shall Be Entitled to Fifteen Peremptory Challenges; Providing That When Two or More Defendants Are Tried Together the State Shall Be Entitled to Eight Peremptory Challenges; Providing That in Capital Cases Where the Death Penalty Has Been Waived by the State's Attorney by Filing His Written Waiver Which Has Been Approved by the Court, the State and the Defendant Shall Be Entitled to the Number of Peremptory Challenges as Is Now Provided by Law in the Trial of Noncapital Felony Cases," 140 SB § (1951).

87. "The State of Texas vs. Johnny Lee Morris: Writ to Serve Copy of Special Venire," December 6, 1951, Harris County District Clerk's Office; "Special Venire in Capital Cases," *Texas Code of Criminal Procedure* Title 1, Chapter 34 (December 1, 1966); "The

State of Texas vs. Johnny Lee Morris: Motion to Quash Trial Jury," December 13, 1951, Harris County District Clerk's Office.

88. "The State of Texas vs. Johnny Lee Morris: Motion to Quash Trial Jury"; "Negro Attys. Ably Defend Morris Here for 2 Courts," *Houston Informer*, December 15, 1951, sec. 1, 1, 10.

89. *Smith v. Texas*, 311 U.S. 128 (Supreme Court of the United States 1940); "The State of Texas vs. Johnny Lee Morris: Motion to Quash Trial Jury."

90. "Def. Exhibit A," December 13, 1951, Harris County District Clerk's Office.

91. "The State of Texas vs. Johnny Lee Morris: State's Answer to Dents Motion to Quash the Trial Jury," December 13, 1951, Harris County District Clerk's Office; "The State of Texas vs. Johnny Lee Morris: Motion to Quash Trial Jury."

92. "The State of Texas vs. Johnny Lee Morris: Charge of the Court," December 14, 1951, Harris County District Clerk's Office.

93. "The State of Texas vs. Johnny Lee Morris: Charge of the Court."

94. "The State of Texas vs. Johnny Lee Morris: Charge of the Court"; "The State of Texas vs. Johnny Lee Morris: Defendant's Objection to the Courts Special Charge," December 14, 1951, Harris County District Clerk's Office.

95. Howard Jones, *The Red Diary: A Chronological History of Black Americans in Houston and Some Neighboring Harris County Communities—122 Years Later* (Austin: Nortex Press, 1991), 172; "Luther Collins Case," *The Crisis* 29, no. 2 (December 1924): 71; James Weldon Johnson, "The Luther Collins Case," in *In Search of Democracy: The NAACP Writings of James Weldon Johnson, Walter White, and Roy Wilkins (1920–1977)*, ed. Sondra Kathryn Wilson (New York: Oxford University Press, 1999), 64; Tyina Leaneice Steptoe, "Dixie West: Race, Migration, and the Color Lines in Jim Crow Houston" (Ph.D. diss., University of Wisconsin–Madison, 2008), 96–100.

96. Dorr, *White Women, Rape, and the Power of Race in Virginia*, 9–10.

97. Dorr, *White Women, Rape, and the Power of Race in Virginia*, 229.

98. Phillip Samuels, "Making Mandingo: Racial Archetypes, Pornography, and Black Male Subjectivity" (Ph.D. diss., University of Kansas), 72.

99. Tommy J. Curry, "Expendables for Whom: Terry Crews and the Erasure of Black Male Victims of Sexual Assault and Rape," *Women's Studies in Communication* 42, no. 3 (July 3, 2019): 287–307, https://doi.org/10.1080/07491409.2019.1641874; Woodard, *The Delectable Negro*, 266n31; Thomas A. Foster, *Rethinking Rufus: Sexual Violations of Enslaved Men* (Athens: University of Georgia Press, 2019); McGuire, *At the Dark End of the Street*.

100. Ponton, "Clothed in Blue Flesh."

101. Genna Rae McNeil, *Groundwork: Charles Hamilton Houston and the Struggle for Civil Rights* (Philadelphia: University of Pennsylvania Press, 2011), 93; "Thurgood Marshall," *Baltimore Afro-American*, February 20, 1999, sec. B, 2; Thurgood Marshall and Mark V. Tushnet, *Thurgood Marshall: His Speeches, Writings, Arguments, Opinions, and Reminiscences* (Chicago: Lawrence Hill Books, 2001), xix; José Felipé Anderson, "Freedom of Association, the Communist Party, and the Hollywood Ten: The Forgotten First Amendment Legacy of Charles Hamilton Houston," *McGeorge Law Review* 40, no. 25 (2009): E-Journal; Arthur Weinberg and Lila Shaffer Weinberg, *Clarence Darrow, a Sentimental Rebel* (New York: Atheneum, 1987), 270; Sherrilyn A. Ifill, *On the Courthouse Lawn: Confronting the Legacy of Lynching in the Twenty-First Century* (Boston: Beacon Press, 2007), e-book, chapter 3.

102. "Negro Bus Slayer Gets Life Sentence," *Houston Chronicle*, December 15, 1951, 5.

103. Susan N. Herman, "Why the Court Loves Batson: Representation-Reinforcement, Colorblindness, and the Jury," *Tulane Law Review* 67 (1993): 1807; Michael J. Klarman, "The Racial Origins of Modern Criminal Procedure," *Michigan Law Review* 99, no. 7 (2000): (electronic); Pamela S. Karlan, "Race, Rights, and Remedies in Criminal Adjudication," *Michigan Law Review* 96, no. 7 (1998): 2001–2030; Dan T. Carter, *Scottsboro: A Tragedy of the American South* (Baton Rouge: Louisiana State University Press, 1969).

104. Carter, *Scottsboro*, 163.

105. "A New Chicago In The Making," n.d., box 2, folder 12, Houston Subdivision Collection MSS.0118, HMRC, HPL; Carter Wesley, "Houston's Better Relations," *Houston Informer*, February 28, 1959, sec. 2, 1; Carter Wesley, "We'll Support Mrs. White," *Houston Informer*, October 11, 1958, sec. 1, 2; Carter Wesley, "Whites, Negroes Unite to Elect Mrs. C E White," *Houston Informer*, November 8, 1958, sec. 1, 1, 10.

106. Hannu Salmi, "Cultural History, the Possible, and the Principle of Plenitude," *History and Theory* 50, no. 2 (2011): 173; Frances Fox Piven and Richard A. Cloward, *Poor People's Movements: Why They Succeed, How They Fail* (New York: Vintage Books, 1979), xiii; Jennifer Frost, *An Interracial Movement of the Poor: Community Organizing and the New Left in the 1960s*, electronic resource (New York: NYU Press, 2001), 173; Ross Webb, "'I Am Voting for Myself, My Children and My Race This Time': Black Labour, Community Mobilisation and Civil Rights Unionism: The Brotherhood Of Sleeping Car Porters In The 1920s," *Australasian Journal of American Studies* 31, no. 1 (2012): 49.

107. Martha Broom, "Constructing an Identity of 'Relation' in Régine Robin's 'L'immense Fatigue Des Pierres,'" *Romance Notes* 48, no. 3 (2008): 342.

108. Hayden White, "The Historical Text as Literary Artefact," in *The Writing of History: Literary Form and Historical Understanding*, ed. Robert H. Canary and Henry Kozicki (Madison: University of Wisconsin Press, 1978), 53.

109. Jared Sexton, "Afro-Pessimism: The Unclear Word," *Rhizomes: Cultural Studies in Emerging Knowledge* no. 29 (2016), https://doi.org/10.20415/rhiz/029.e02.

110. Woods, *Blackhood against the Police Power*, 55.

111. I remain captured, too, you see.

112. I think about this in relation to critical history, but I am less convinced of the possibility of fugitivity suggested by Saidiya Hartman than I am compelled by the emphasis on constraint expressed by Fred Moten. Brian Connolly and Marisa Fuentes, "Introduction: From Archives of Slavery to Liberated Futures?" *History of the Present* 6, no. 2 (2016): 105–116; Hartman, "The Dead Book Revisited"; Fred Moten, "Blackness," in *Keywords for African American Studies*, ed. Erica R. Edwards, Roderick A. Ferguson, and Jeffrey O. G. Ogbar, vol. 8 (New York: NYU Press, 2018), 27–29, https://www.jstor.org/stable/j.ctvwrm5v9.8.

Chapter 3: Captured in the Impossible American Dream

Hartman, "The Dead Book Revisited," 210.

1. "Pair Charged in House Bombing," *Houston Post*, April 18, 1953, sec. 1, 1, 5; "Two Held in Home Bombing," *Houston Chronicle*, April 18, 1953, sec. 1, 1; "To Hold Bomb Hearing," *Houston Informer*, May 2, 1953, sec. 1, 1.

2. Adair and Robinson, Black Women Oral History Project.

3. Micol Seigel, *Violence Work: State Power and the Limits of Police* (Durham, NC: Duke University Press, 2018), 120; Weheliye, *Habeas Viscus*.

4. Mary Pattillo, *Black on the Block: The Politics of Race and Class in the City* (Chicago: University of Chicago Press, 2010), 32; Edward González-Tennant, *The Rosewood Massacre:*

An Archaeology and History of Intersectional Violence (Gainesville: University Press of Florida, 2019); Robin Wagner-Pacifici, *Discourse and Destruction: The City of Philadelphia Versus MOVE* (Chicago: University of Chicago Press, 1994).

5. David T. Ballantyne, "Remembering the Colfax Massacre: Race, Sex, and the Meanings of Reconstruction Violence," *Journal of Southern History* 87, no. 3 (2021): 427–466, https://doi.org/10.1353/soh.2021.0086; Alexander, *The New Jim Crow*.

6. Wilderson, *Afropessimism*, 216.

7. Robin Blackburn, *The Making of New World Slavery: From the Baroque to the Modern, 1492–1800*, electronic resource (New York: Verso, 2010), 585.

8. Kevin Boyle, *Arc of Justice: A Saga of Race, Civil Rights, and Murder in the Jazz Age* (New York: Henry Holt and Co., 2005); Cynthia M. Blair, *I've Got to Make My Livin': Black Women's Sex Work in Turn-of-the-Century Chicago* (Chicago: University of Chicago Press, 2010); Connolly, *A World More Concrete*.

9. "A New Chicago in the Making"; Wesley, "Houston's Better Relations," 1; Wesley, "We'll Support Mrs. White," 2.

10. Carter Wesley, "Segregation's Double Standard," *Houston Informer*, June 6, 1959, sec. 1, 2; "Thanksgiving: An American Holiday," *Houston Informer*, November 28, 1953, sec. 1, 12.

11. Lewis R. Gordon, "Race, Biraciality, and Mixed Race," in *"Mixed Race" Studies: A Reader*, ed. Jayne O. Ifekwunigwe (New York: Routledge, 2015), 164.

12. Nancy Fraser, "Recognition or Redistribution? A Critical Reading of Iris Young's Justice and the Politics of Difference," *Journal of Political Philosophy* 3, no. 2 (June 1, 1995): 166–180, https://doi.org/10.1111/j.1467-9760.1995.tb00033.x; Warren, *Ontological Terror*.

13. I say "black inner-city living" to signal that Houston's inner-city core also had very well-off white-only neighborhoods that did not suffer these forms of violence. Jackson, *Crabgrass Frontier*.

14. Wiese, *Places of Their Own*; Straus, *Death of a Suburban Dream*; Connolly, "Black Movement into the Suburbs."

15. Du Bois, *The Philadelphia Negro: A Social Study*; Sugrue, *The Origins of the Urban Crisis*; June Manning Thomas, *Redevelopment and Race: Planning a Finer City in Postwar Detroit* (Detroit: Wayne State University Press, 2013); Jeffrey Mirel, *The Rise and Fall of an Urban School System: Detroit, 1907–81* (Ann Arbor: University of Michigan Press, 1993); Self, *American Babylon*; Phelps, *A People's War on Poverty*; William S. Clayson, *Freedom Is Not Enough: The War on Poverty and the Civil Rights Movement in Texas* (Austin: University of Texas Press, 2011); St. Clair Drake and Horace R. Cayton, *Black Metropolis: A Study of Negro Life in a Northern City* (Chicago: University Of Chicago Press, 1993); Dan T. Carter, "More than Race: Conservatism in the White South since V.O. Key Jr.," in *Unlocking V. O. Key Jr.: "Southern Politics" for the Twenty-First Century*, ed. Angie Maxwell and Todd G. Shields (Fayetteville: University of Arkansas Press, 2011), 129–160; Lassiter, *The Silent Majority*; Kruse, *White Flight*; Lisa McGirr, *Suburban Warriors: The Origins of the New American Right* (Princeton, NJ: Princeton University Press, 2002).

16. Woods, *Blackhood against the Police Power*, 64–65.

17. Woods, *Blackhood against the Police Power*, 64–65.

18. Jerold J. Savory, "The Rending of the Veil in W. E. B. Du Bois's 'The Souls of Black Folk,'" *CLA Journal* 15, no. 3 (1972): 337; Frantz Fanon, *The Wretched of the Earth*, trans. Richard Philcox (New York: Grove Press, 2005).

19. Joe R. Feagin and Vera Hernán, *White Racism: The Basics* (New York: Routledge, 2000), 31; *The Strange Demise of Jim Crow*, directed by David Berman and created by Thomas R. Cole (San Francisco: California Newsreel, 1998); Kellar, *Make Haste Slowly*; Zan Dubin, "Chronicling the Quiet Desegregation of Houston," *Los Angeles Times*, February 11, 1998, https://www.latimes.com/archives/la-xpm-1998-feb-11-ca-17755-story.html; Melissa Torres, "In Houston, a Silent and Sudden Integration," *Houston Chronicle*, March 8, 2017, sec. Gray Matters, https://www.houstonchronicle.com/local/gray-matters/article/The-silent-sudden-integration-of-University-of-10983415.php.

20. Herman L. Bennett, *Colonial Blackness: A History of Afro-Mexico* (Bloomington: Indiana University Press, 2009); Jared Sexton, *Amalgamation Schemes: Antiblackness and the Critique of Multiracialism* (Minneapolis: University of Minnesota Press, 2008); Silvio Torres-Saillant, "The Tribulations of Blackness: Stages in Dominican Racial Identity," *Latin American Perspectives* 25, no. 3 (1998): 126–146; David Hollinger, "Amalgamation and Hypodescent: The Question of Ethnoracial Mixture in the History of the United States," *American Historical Review* 5, no. 108 (December 2003): 1363–1390, https://doi.org/10.1086/529971.

21. Many white southerners viewed Jim Crow as a way to maintain "separate togetherness," wherein they could "create a . . . world of masters and servants." Several of Houston's wealthy suburbs developed in the early 1900s were intentionally sited near small black neighborhoods that could be exploited for domestic labor. Stephen A. Berrey, *The Jim Crow Routine: Everyday Performances of Race, Civil Rights, and Segregation in Mississippi* (Chapel Hill: University of North Carolina Press, 2015), 46–48; Rebecca Sharpless, *Cooking in Other Women's Kitchens: Domestic Workers in the South, 1865–1960* (Chapel Hill: University of North Carolina Press, 2010).

22. Yusoff, *A Billion Black Anthropocenes or None*.

23. "Caesars Link Hoggatt in Home Deal," *Houston Informer*, June 28, 1952, sec. 1, 10.

24. "Caesars Link Hoggatt in Home Deal," 10.

25. The property no longer exists at this address. As Riverside Terrace transitioned into a mostly black community, several blocks of homes were bulldozed to make way for Highway 288 in 1959. Chris Lane, "The Changing Face of Houston—Riverside Terrace," *Houston Press*, October 13, 2014, http://www.houstonpress.com/arts/the-changing-face-of-houston-riverside-terrace-6394303. For more on patterns of racial discrimination against Riverside residents once the neighborhood racially transitioned, see Lawrence Wright, "Easy Street," *Texas Monthly*, November 1982, 174–181.

26. *This Is Our Home It Is Not for Sale*, documentary film by Jon Schwartz (Houston, Texas: Riverside Productions, 2007).

27. *This Is Our Home It Is Not for Sale*.

28. Warren, *Ontological Terror*, 26; Elizabeth Maddock Dillon, "Zombie Biopolitics," *American Quarterly* 71, no. 3 (2019): 626, https://doi.org/10.1353/aq.2019.0047.

29. Nancy Leong, "Racial Capitalism," *Harvard Law Review* 126, no. 8 (2013): 2151–2226.

30. Quoted in Clement E. Vose, *Caucasians Only: The Supreme Court, The NAACP, and the Restrictive Covenant Cases* (Berkeley: University of California Press, 1968), 83–84; *Hurd v. Hodge*, 24 U.S. 334 (1948).

31. Vose, *Caucasians Only*, 222; Earl Wright II, "The Tradition of Sociology at Fisk University," *Journal of African American Studies* 14, no. 1 (2010): 57–58.

32. *This Is Our Home It Is Not for Sale*.

33. "Houston Comes Through," *Houston Informer*, May 24, 1952, sec. 2, 2. The

editorial column did not identify the exact location of this attack, and the white press did not cover the story. The *Informer* likely reported on the story in detail in its Tuesday edition, but only the Saturday papers were available in the archive.

34. I'm borrowing language from Spillers et al., "Whatcha Gonna Do?" 306.

35. Yusoff, *A Billion Black Anthropocenes or None*; David Tisel, "Unfree Labor and American Capitalism from Slavery to the Neoliberal-Penal State," 2013, http://rave.ohiolink.edu/etdc/view?acc_num=oberlin1368618418.

36. Nahum Dimitri Chandler, "Originary Displacement," *Boundary 2* 27, no. 3 (Fall 2000): 249, 261, https://doi.org/10.1215/01903659-27-3-249.

37. Fanon, *Black Skin, White Masks*, 107.

38. Connolly and Fuentes, "Introduction."

39. Carter Wesley, "Negroes Harassed," *Houston Informer*, May 21, 1952, sec. 2, 2.

40. See, for example, "Third Explosion Occurs While Couple Sleeps," *Houston Informer*, July 13, 1950, sec. 1, 1; "Governor Refuses to Intervene in Bombing of Negro Houses in Dallas: 25 Homes Bombed; No Arrests," *Houston Informer*, July 15, 1950, sec. 1, 1; "Bombings in Negro Addition Terrorize Residents: Citizens Cry: How Long Will Our Civil Rights Be Ignored?" *Houston Informer*, June 30, 1951, sec. 1, 1; "Negro Citizens Refuse to Move in Spite of Bombs and Buyers," *Houston Informer*, February 3, 1951, sec. 1, 1. On Ossian Sweet's story, see Boyle, *Arc of Justice*.

41. "Mrs. Mattye Hilliard Buys Wichita St. Home," *Houston Informer*, July 12, 1952, sec. 1, 1.

42. Jack Ginsburg, "Atty. Ginsburg Writes to Atty. Percy Foreman on the Jack Caesar Case," *Houston Informer*, August 16, 1952, sec. 1, 1, 10.

43. "Caesars Link Hoggatt in Home Deal," 1, 10.

44. "Caesars Link Hoggatt in Home Deal," 1, 10. Inflation calculations reflect purchasing power and are provided by the Bureau of Labor Statistics' Consumer Price Index calculator.

45. Ginsburg, "Atty. Ginsburg Writes to Atty. Percy Foreman on the Jack Caesar Case," 1, 10.

46. Carter Wesley, "'Ain't That Sump'n?'" *Houston Informer*, July 12, 1952, sec. 1, 2; Carter Wesley, "Back to Reason," *Houston Informer*, July 19, 1952, sec. 1, 2.

47. "Mrs. Mattye Hilliard Buys Wichita St. Home," 1, 10. Black Americans certainly resented the kinds of sentiments Smiley expressed. Roy Wilkins to John F. Kennedy, "Re: Racial Discrimination in Federally Assisted Housing in Cocoa, Florida," November 20, 1962, Papers of the NAACP, Part 24: Group III, Series A, Administrative File, General Office File, Discrimination, Housing, 1954–62.

48. The reporter wrote, "On questioning, [Smiley] explained that the reason white people do not want to live next door to Negroes is an issue of 'biological phenomena,' intimating that he and the persons whose sentiments he expressed believed that Negroes want an opportunity to cohabit with whites rather than opportunities for better housing when they move into white neighborhoods." "Mrs. Mattye Hilliard Buys Wichita St. Home," 1, 10; Warren, *Ontological Terror*, 49–50.

49. Carter Wesley, "[Asking] for Trouble," *Houston Informer*, December 19, 1953, sec. 1, 2.

50. The unnamed woman recalled her family's feelings in *This Is Our Home It Is Not for Sale*. Jack Caesar reported on the family's activities immediately after the bombing: "Pair Charged in House Bombing," 5.

51. Stephen Meyer, *As Long as They Don't Move Next Door: Segregation and Racial Conflict in American Neighborhoods* (Lanham, MD: Rowman & Littlefield, 1999); Barbara Celarent, "Caste, Class, and Race by Oliver Cromwell Cox," *American Journal of Sociology* 115, no. 5 (2010): 1664–1669; W. Lloyd Warner, "American Class and Caste," *American Journal of Sociology* 42, no. 2 (1936): 234–237. See 1960 US Housing data for these correlations.

52. "Pair Charged in House Bombing," 5.

53. "Law Enforcement Is Always the Answer," *Houston Informer*, April 25, 1953, sec. 2, 2.

54. *This Is Our Home It Is Not for Sale*.

55. *This Is Our Home It Is Not for Sale*.

56. "Pair Charged in House Bombing," 5; Jim Whisenant, "Explosion Rocks Home in Riverside," *Houston Chronicle*, April 17, 1953, sec. 1, 1.

57. Boyle, *Arc of Justice*, 344–345. Details about the days following the bombing are in Donald Caesar's testimony in *This Is Our Home It Is Not for Sale*.

58. *This Is Our Home It Is Not for Sale*.

59. "Howell Denies Bomb Charge," *Houston Post*, April 19, 1953, sec. 1, 1, 12.

60. "Two Held in Home Bombing," 2.

61. "Two Charged in Bombing of Home," *Houston Chronicle*, April 19, 1953, sec. B, 5.

62. "Davis Gets 2 Years in Bombing," *Houston Informer*, June 25, 1953, sec. 1, 1, 10; Carter Wesley, "Bombing Trial," *Houston Informer*, June 25, 1953, sec. 1, 2.

63. *This Is Our Home It Is Not for Sale*.

64. Clarissa Rile Hayward, *How Americans Make Race: Stories, Institutions, Spaces* (New York: Cambridge University Press, 2013), 45.

65. Saidiya V. Hartman, *Scenes of Subjection: Terror, Slavery, and Self-Making in Nineteenth-Century America* (New York: Oxford University Press, 1997), 118.

66. Carter Wesley, "Restrictive Covenants," *Houston Informer*, April 25, 1953, sec. 1, 3. Wesley made additional comments in a later column, too: Carter Wesley, "They Mean It," *Houston Informer*, June 20, 1953, sec. 1, 3.

67. Richard R. W. Brooks and Carol M. Rose, *Saving the Neighborhood: Racially Restrictive Covenants, Law, and Social Norms* (Cambridge, MA: Harvard University Press, 2013), 62.

68. Robert Fisher, "'Be on the Lookout': Neighborhood Civic Clubs," *Houston Review* 6, no. 3 (1984): 112.

69. Erik Slotboom, *Houston Freeways: A Historical and Visual Journey* (O. F. Slotboom, 2003), 189.

70. Shelton, *Power Moves*, 219–220.

71. Unless otherwise indicated, the figures in this paragraph come from the 1950, 1960, and 1970 US Census tract-level data. Shelton, *Power Moves*, 77.

72. *This Is Our Home It Is Not for Sale*; Barry J. Kaplan, "Race, Income, and Ethnicity: Residential Change in a Houston Community, 1920–1970," *Houston History Magazine* (Winter 1981): 191.

73. Kaplan, "Race, Income, and Ethnicity"; Alan Ehrenhalt, *The Great Inversion and the Future of the American City* (New York: Vintage Books, 2013), 165; David G. McComb, *The City in Texas: A History* (Austin: University of Texas Press, 2015), 240; and, on Ward population data, see Beeth and Wintz, *Black Dixie*, 23.

74. C. F. Richardson, "Houston's Colored Citizens: Activities and Conditions among the Negro Population," in *Civics for Houston*, vol. 1, 1929, 14; Tommy Stringer, "Joseph

Stephen Cullinan: Pioneer in Texas Oil," *East Texas Historical Journal* 19, no. 2 (1981): 43–59; Ezell Wilson, "Third Ward, Steeped in Tradition of Self-Reliance and Achievement," *Houston History Magazine* 8, no. 2 (Spring 2011): 31–35; Demond Fernandez, "City Leaders Announce Plans to Renovate Historic Emancipation Park," ABC13 Houston, June 19, 2012, http://abc13.com/archive/8707001/; Benjamin van Loon, "On the Boards: Emancipation Park," *Green Building and Design*, June 2014, http://gbdmagazine.com/2014/27-freelon-group/; "$33 Million Emancipation Park Renovation Project Will Celebrate the History of Oldest Park in the City of Houston [Press Release]," October 25, 2013, http://www.houstongovnewsroom.org/go/doc/2155/1938841/-33-Million-Emancipation-Park-Renovation-Project-Will-Celebrate-the-History-of-Oldest-Park-in-the-City-of-Houston; Allan Turner, "Houston's Antioch Church Celebrates 150th Anniversary," *Houston Chronicle*, January 24, 2016, http://www.houstonchronicle.com/news/houston-texas/houston/article/Houston-s-Antioch-Church-celebrates-150th-6781202.php; Bernadette Pruitt, *The Other Great Migration: The Movement of Rural African Americans to Houston, 1900–1941* (College Station: Texas A&M University Press, 2013), 100; Beeth and Wintz, *Black Dixie*, 25.

75. William Broyles, "The Making of Barbara Jordan," *Texas Monthly*, October 1976, 129; Steptoe, *Houston Bound*, 162; Donald P. Lee, interview by Beatrice Mitchell, May 15, 2008, Houston Arts and Media Oral Histories, MS 524, Woodson Research Center, Fondren Library, Rice University.

76. "St. John [sic] Enters New Home," *Houston Informer*, June 4, 1921, 4; *The Red Book of Houston: A Compendium of Social, Professional, Religious, Educational and Industrial Interests of Houston's Colored Population* (Houston: Sotex Publishing Company, 1915), http://archive.org/details/redbookofhouston00sote; Lee, interview.

77. Lee, interview.

78. Lee, interview; Annabelle McMillon, interview by Beatrice Mitchell, May 28, 2008, Houston Arts and Media Oral Histories, MS 524, Woodson Research Center, Fondren Library, Rice University.

79. John Minton, "Houston Creoles and Zydeco: The Emergence of an African American Urban Popular Style," in *Ramblin' on My Mind: New Perspectives on the Blues*, ed. David Evans (Urbana: University of Illinois Press, 2008), 365; Alan B. Govenar, *Lightnin' Hopkins: His Life and Blues* (Chicago: Chicago Review Press, 2010), 34; Roger Wood and James Fraher, *Down in Houston: Bayou City Blues* (Austin: University of Texas Press, 2003), 75.

80. "Howling on Dowling," *Cite: The Architecture + Design Review of Houston*, Winter 2005, 15.

81. Kevin Quashie, *Black Aliveness, or A Poetics of Being* (Durham, NC: Duke University Press, 2021).

82. Adam Riggio, *Ecology, Ethics, and the Future of Humanity* (New York: Palgrave MacMillan, 2015), 91.

83. Calvin L. Warren, "Black Nihilism and the Politics of Hope," *CR: The New Centennial Review* 15, no. 1 (2015): 215–248, https://doi.org/10.14321/crnewcentrevi.15.1.0215.

84. Antoinette Errante, "But Sometimes You're Not Part of the Story: Oral Histories and Ways of Remembering and Telling," *Educational Researcher* 29, no. 2 (2000): 24, https://doi.org/10.2307/1177053; Nancy Grey Osterud and Lu Ann Jones, "'If I Must Say So Myself': Oral Histories of Rural Women," *Oral History Review* 17, no. 2 (1989): 4; Linda Sandino, "Introduction to Oral Histories and Design: Objects and Subjects," *Journal of Design History* 19, no. 4 (2006): 275–282.

85. Elizabeth A. Wheeler, *Uncontained: Urban Fiction in Postwar America* (New Brunswick, NJ: Rutgers University Press, 2001), 107; Thomas J. Sugrue, *Sweet Land of Liberty: The Forgotten Struggle for Civil Rights in the North* (New York: Random House, 2009), 142; Valk and Brown, *Living with Jim Crow*, 104; Ritterhouse, *Growing Up Jim Crow*.

86. Tendayi Sithole, "The Concept of the Black Subject in Fanon," *Journal of Black Studies* 47, no. 1 (January 1, 2016): 24–40, https://doi.org/10.1177/0021934715609913.

87. Christina Elizabeth Sharpe, *In the Wake: On Blackness and Being* (Durham, NC: Duke University Press, 2016), 14.

88. Warren, *Ontological Terror*.

89. Sithole, "The Concept of the Black Subject in Fanon."

90. *Census of Housing: 1950 (Taken as a Part of the Seventeenth Decennial Census of the United States)*, vol. V: Block Statistics, Pt. 4. Houston—Los Angeles (Washington, DC: Government Printing Office, 1953); Charles Farley, *Soul of the Man: Bobby "Blue" Bland* (Jackson: University Press of Mississippi, 2011), 65.

91. "37 Escape Classroom Cave-In: Ceiling Falls after Pupils Go to Lunch," *Houston Informer*, March 13, 1954, sec. 1, 1.

92. Seigel, *Violence Work*.

93. "Philadelphia Race Tension Climbing," *Lubbock Evening Journal*, October 17, 1957, 8.

94. Khalil Gibran Muhammad, *The Condemnation of Blackness: Race, Crime, and the Making of Modern Urban America* (Cambridge, MA: Harvard University Press, 2010).

95. M. J., "Negro Delinquency," *Houston Informer*, March 29, 1958, 12.

96. "Segregation Puts Blight on Most Cities," *Houston Informer*, March 1, 1958, 10.

97. Muhammad, *The Condemnation of Blackness*, 229.

98. Michele Lamont and Mario Luis Small, "How Culture Matters: Enriching Our Understanding of Poverty," in *The Colors of Poverty: Why Racial and Ethnic Disparities Persist*, ed. Ann Chih Lin and David R. Harris (New York: Russell Sage Foundation, 2008); Gordon B. Hancock, "Illegitimacy a Nat'l Problem," *Houston Informer*, June 20, 1959, 12. Hancock maintained a thoroughgoing critique of alternative explanations of the levels of crime, nonmarital births, and unemployment that black communities faced, both calling out the "callousness of the Negro middle class" and calling the nation to task for its failure to fold black Americans into its so-called democratic processes. On Hancock's work, see Raymond Gavins, *The Perils and Prospects of Southern Black Leadership* (Durham, NC: Duke University Press, 1977), 87 (quote). On racecraft, see Karen E. Fields and Barbara J. Fields, *Racecraft: The Soul of Inequality in American Life* (London: Verso, 2012), 17; Jason Farbman, "How Race Is Conjured: An Interview with Barbara J. Fields/Karen E. Fields," *Jacobin* (blog), June 29, 2015, https://www.jacobinmag.com/2015/06/karen-barbara-fields-racecraft-dolezal-racism.

99. Patricia Pando, "In the Nickel, Houston's Fifth Ward," *Houston History Magazine* 8, no. 3 (2011): 33; Blair Justice, *Violence in the City* (Fort Worth: Leo Potishman Fund, Texas Christian University Press, 1969), 76. Henry Allen Bullock's data of homicide in Houston produced similar findings in "Urban Homicide in Theory and Fact," *Journal of Criminal Law and Criminology* 45, no. 5 (1955): 565–575.

100. Du Bois, *The Philadelphia Negro: A Social Study*.

101. James Q. Wilson and Richard J. Herrnstein, *Crime and Human Nature: The Definitive Study of the Causes of Crime* (New York: Simon and Schuster, 1998), 476; Mitchel P. Roth and Tom Kennedy, *Houston Blue: The Story of the Houston Police Department* (Denton: University of North Texas Press, 2012), 113–114; B. T. Brooks, Source Material for

Patterns of Negro Segregation: Houston Texas, interview by H. J. Walker, August 10, 1939, 6; Pitre, *In Struggle against Jim Crow*, 51; *Police Brutality: Subcommittee on Civil and Constitutional Rights, Committee on the Judiciary, House of Representatives* (Washington, DC: Government Printing Office, 1991), 21, 161.

102. *Political Debates between Hon. Abraham Lincoln and Hon. Stephen A. Douglas, in the Celebrated Campaign of 1858 in Illinois; Including the Preceding Speeches of Each, at Chicago, Springfield, Etc.; Also the Two Great Speeches of Mr. Lincoln in Ohio, in 1859, as Carefully Prepared by the Reporter of Each Party and Published at the Times of Their Delivery* (Columbus, OH: Follett, Foster and Company, 1860), 50–53.

103. Kirt H. Wilson, *The Reconstruction Desegregation Debate: The Politics of Equality and the Rhetoric of Place, 1870–1875*, electronic resource (East Lansing: Michigan State University Press, 2002).

104. Anna Dickinson, *A Tour of Reconstruction: Travel Letters of 1875*, ed. J. Matthew Gallman (Lexington: University Press of Kentucky, 2011), 45.

105. "What Are the Branches Doing?" *The Crisis*, May 1950, 316.

106. Chas A. Shaw to Walter F. White, April 10, 1940, and A Houston Citizen to Walter F. White, March 25, 1940, both in Papers of the NAACP Part 18, Special Subjects, 1940–1955, Series A, Legal Department Files, folder Wesley, Carter *Houston Informer* 1940–41, ProQuest History Vault.

107. Carter W. Wesley to Thurgood Marshall, May 7, 1940, Papers of the NAACP Part 18, Special Subjects, 1940–1955, Series A, Legal Department Files, folder Wesley, Carter *Houston Informer* 1940–41, ProQuest History Vault.

108. "Slums Are Barrier to City's Growth," *Houston Informer*, July 8, 1950.

109. Achille Mbembé, "Necropolitics," trans. Libby Meintjes, *Public Culture* 15, no. 1 (March 25, 2003): 14, 26–28.

110. "Await Action in Charge of Police Beating," *Houston Informer*, June 24, 1950, 1; "Two Teenagers, Adult Charge Police Brutality," *Houston Informer*, June 24, 1950, 1; "Says Beaten on Own Step and Then Jailed," *Houston Informer*, June 24, 1950, 1; "Police Brutality Protested," *Houston Informer*, May 24, 1952, 1; "Grand Jury Probe Asked in Drowning," *Houston Informer*, April 26, 1952, 1; "Brakeman's Abuse Charge Is Being Probed," *Houston Informer*, April 26, 1952, 1, 10; "Angry Man, 22, Charges Three Cops with Brutality," *Houston Informer*, March 26, 1955, 1, 12; "Man Brutally Beaten after Alleged Arrest by Police," *Houston Informer*, September 17, 1955, 1, 12; "Cop Abused Him, Told Him to Run, Man Says," *Houston Informer*, June 6, 1959, 10; "Cripple's Mother Calls His Killing 'Murder,'" *Houston Informer*, May 24, 1952, 1, 10; "Cop Charged with Murder," *Houston Informer*, June 19, 1959, 1; "Insurance Woman Charges Police Brutality," *Houston Informer*, December 23, 1950, 1, 10; "Committee Says Chief 'Was Cool,'" *Houston Informer*, June 21, 1952, sec. 1, 1, 10; "Says Officer Wrong on 'Shut Up' Demand of Insurance Woman," *Houston Informer*, January 4, 1951, 1; "Waf Charges Police Brutality," *Houston Informer*, April 4, 1953, 1; "Expectant Mother Charges Police with Brutality," *Houston Informer*, May 24, 1952, 1; "Citizens Feel 'Robbed' as Grand Jury 'Clears' Cops," *Houston Informer*, November 28, 1953, sec. 1, 1; "Citizens Express Anger," *Houston Informer*, December 5, 1953, sec. 1, 1; "Mother Blames Officers," *Houston Informer*, June 28, 1952, 1; "Woman Asserts Police Broke Her Arm," *Houston Informer*, January 26, 1952, 10; "Police Brutality Again," *Houston Informer*, December 30, 1950, 13; "The Case against Policeman," *Houston Informer*, March 8, 1952, sec. 2, 2; C. R. Johnson, "Rape—Law—Women," *Houston Informer*, December 5, 1953, sec. 1, 12; "Comments by Subjects Recorded by Interviewers," April 18, 1967, box 33, Louie Welch Papers, MSS 0051, HMRC, HPL.

111. David Ponton III, "Private Matters in Public Spaces: Intimate Partner Violence against Black Women in Jim Crow Houston," *Frontiers* 39, no. 2 (2018): 58–96.

112. Mumford, *Interzones*; "Vice Squad Tip Nets Arrests in 'Sugar Hill Love Nest' Nabbing," *Houston Informer*, August 16, 1958, 1; "Upper Sugarhill Residents Fight to Keep Area Exclusively Residential," *Houston Informer*, April 19, 1958, 1; "Business Told to 'Quit' Sugarhill Site," *Houston Informer*, June 7, 1958, 1; "Narcotic Officers 'Cleaning House' In Sugar Hill Area," *Houston Informer*, n.d., 1, 10; "Woman Molested by White Man," *Houston Informer*, February 6, 1954, 1; "White Men Molest Women," *Houston Informer*, September 26, 1953, 1; "White Man Molests 8-Year-Old Girl," *Houston Informer*, November 28, 1953, 1; "GooGoo Eyes," *Houston Informer*, December 27, 1952, 1; "White Man's Immoral Acts in Front of Tots Rile Parents," *Houston Informer*, March 26, 1955, 1; George A. McElroy, "Female Impersonator Charged in Third Ward 'Mystery Death,'" *Houston Informer*, July 20, 1957, sec. 1, 1; "Impersonator Was a Quiet Neighbor, Says Female Tenant," *Houston Informer*, October 24, 1959, 1; "'Johnnie Mae' to Go on Trial Mon for Killing," *Houston Informer*, November 30, 1957, sec. 1, 1; Martin Van Dyke, "Masquerade," *Official Detective Stories*, April 1960, 44–46; "Dying Stab Victim's Car Hops Curb, Hits Truck," *Houston Post*, October 18, 1959, Harris County Archives; "Dress Wearer Admits Stabbing," *Houston Press*, October 20, 1959, Harris County Archives; "Stabbing Admitted by Porter," *Houston Post*, October 20, 1959, Harris County Archives; "Woman Admits Scuffle, Denies Stabbing Driver," *Houston Chronicle*, October 19, 1959, Harris County Archives; "Man Admits Slaying during Knife Struggle," *Houston Chronicle*, October 20, 1959, Harris County Archives; *Mahaffey v. Official Detective Stories, Inc.*, 210 F. Supp. 251 (U.S. District Court for the Western District of Louisiana 1962); J. E. Clarke and Joseph A. Jachimczyk, "Autopsy Report Case 59-1310 Pathological Diagnosis on the Body of Billy Celton Mahaffey," October 18, 1959, Harris County Archives.

113. Charles Spurgeon Johnson, *Patterns of Negro Segregation* (New York: Harper & Brothers, 1943), 33.

114. I borrow this phrase from Emily Straus's *Death of a Suburban Dream*.

115. Clyde O. McDaniel Jr., "Housing Segregation of Blacks in the South," in *Urban Housing Segregation of Minorities in Western Europe and the United States*, ed. Elizabeth D. Huttman (Durham, NC: Duke University Press, 1991), 279.

116. Paul Alejandro Levengood, "For the Duration and Beyond: World War II and the Creation of Modern Houston, Texas" (Ph.D. diss., Rice University, 1999), 377; "History 75 Years in the Making . . .," *Clinton Park* (blog), n.d., http://clintonpark.org/index.php/history; Jim Mousner, "Negro Suburbia: The Most Compelling Reason Is Clear: 'I Want a Home of My Own,'" *Houston Post*, February 22, 1959, sec. Suburbia, part 2, 9; "Tex. City FHA Builds 'Homes Project,'" *Indianapolis Record*, July 7, 1945, 2nd ed., 27, Hoosier State Chronicles: Indiana's Digital Historic Newspaper Program. C. E. King resided at 2012 Rice Boulevard. *Study and Investigation of Housing: Hearings before the Joint Committee on Housing Eightieth Congress, First Session* (Washington, DC: Government Printing Office, 1948), 1571.

117. Levengood, "For the Duration and Beyond," 377; "History 75 Years in the Making . . ."; "Tex. City FHA Builds 'Homes Project,'" 27; *Clinton Park Development Company v. Commissioner*, 11 T.C.M. 768 (United States Tax Court 1952); Mousner, "Negro Suburbia," 9; Wiese, *Places of Their Own*.

118. "Tex. City FHA Builds 'Homes Project,'" 27; *Clinton Park Development Company v. Commissioner*, 11 T.C.M.; "Houston Trains 12 as Firemen," *Baltimore Afro-American*, November 1, 1958, 39; Mousner, "Negro Suburbia," 9. Although "the Negro smoke-eaters"

would work at "all-Negro station[s]," they would nevertheless "answer fire alarms and calls in any community in the immediate area" including the "three white areas and scores of industrial establishments nearby." "Houston to Hire Negro Firefighters," *San Antonio Register*, August 12, 1955, 1.

119. "Tex. City FHA Builds 'Homes Project,'" 27.

120. "Tex. City FHA Builds 'Homes Project,'" 27.

121. Pruitt, *The Other Great Migration*, 169; Watson, *Race and the Houston Police Department, 1930–1990*, 165n103; Mousner, "Negro Suburbia," 9. Pleasantville was one of the oldest majority-black suburbs of Houston, managed and maintained by its residents rather than the city. However, in the 1940s, during an explosive period of annexation, Pleasantville became a part of the city limits of Houston, and Clinton Park followed in 1950. "Street Light Installation Underway in Pleasantville," *Houston Informer*, April 5, 1958, 1, 8; City of Houston Planning & Development Department, "Annexations in Houston or How We Grew to 667 Square Miles in 175 Years"; "Housing for Negroes Needed, Speakers Say at Ceremony," *Houston Post*, October 19, 1952, sec. 4, 4.

122. Robert D. Bullard, *Invisible Houston: The Black Experience in Boom and Bust* (College Station: Texas A&M University Press, 1987), 36; "Fidelity Addition to Get City Water," *Houston Informer*, September 25, 1954, 20; "[Minutes Notebook]," November 23, 1953, November 30, 1953, March 26, 1956, May 25, 1959, box 1, folder 2, Helen G. Perry Family Collection, MSS.0276, HMRC, HPL; "Cloverland Residents Complain to Mayor, City Fathers about Water Rates, Sts," *Houston Informer*, July 11, 1959, 10; "Contract for Trinity Gdns Sewers Let," *Houston Informer*, August 11, 1959, 10; "Negro Neighborhood Neglect," *Houston Informer*, November 8, 1958, 10.

123. "Dear Sunnyside Community Residents [Houston Hope Newsletter]," March 11, 2008, http://www.houstontx.gov/citizensnet/hope-sunnyside9.html.

124. Salatheia Bryant, "Group Revels in Sunnyside's Past," *Houston Chronicle*, August 18, 2004, http://www.chron.com/news/houston-texas/article/Group-revels-in-Sunnyside-s-past-1975407.php; "Incinerator Still Not Opening," *Corpus Christi Times*, January 13, 1971, 15–C; John Suval, "Mixing It Up," *Houston Press*, May 10, 2001, http://www.houstonpress.com/news/mixing-it-up-6562324; Robert D. Bullard, "The Legacy of American Apartheid and Environmental Racism," *Journal of Civil Rights and Economic Development* 9, no. 2 (1994): 458; "The Flooded Fifth Warders Angry," *Houston Informer*, January 22, 1955, 1. Bullard's very important and critical argument is that the siting of environmental hazards in Houston's historical development has paid little attention to environmental science or social equity, and instead has depended on how space has been defined racially and economically. Robert D. Bullard, *Dumping in Dixie: Race, Class, and Environmental Quality*, 3rd ed. (Boulder, CO: Westview Press, 2000), 208–209.

125. Ellen Griffith Spears, *Baptized in PCBs: Race, Pollution, and Justice in an All-American Town* (Chapel Hill: University of North Carolina Press, 2016), 10.

126. "New Polio Epidemic Flares in Houston," *The American* [Odessa, Texas], November 15, 1946, 1; "Bellaire Residents Enraged by Newspaper Blast," *Southwestern Times (Official Publication for the Cities of West University Place, Bellaire, and Southside Place)*, July 17, 1952, 1, 8; "Holmes Road Lounge," *Rice Thresher*, October 19, 1956, 4; Suval, "Mixing It Up" (Williams quote); Wynter, "No Humans Involved: An Open Letter to My Colleagues."

127. Shawna D. Williams, "Robinson Judson Wilbur, Sr.," The Handbook of Texas Online, Texas State Historical Association (TSHA), June 17, 2013, https://tshaonline.org/handbook/online/articles/froco; Shawna D. Williams, "Robinson Judson Wilbur,

Jr.," The Handbook of Texas Online, Texas State Historical Association (TSHA), May 24, 2013, https://tshaonline.org/handbook/online/articles/frobu; Bernadette Pruitt, "For the Advancement of the Race: African-American Migration and Community Building in Houston, 1914–1945" (Ph.D. diss., University of Houston, 2001), 337; "[Finding Aid]," n.d., box 1, folder 1, Judson Robinson, Sr., Family Collection, MSS.0316, HMRC, HPL; Linda L. Black, "Female Community Leaders in Houston, Texas: A Study of the Education of Ima Hogg and Christia Daniels Adair" (Ph.D. diss., Texas A&M University, 2008), 176.

128. Judson Robinson, Jr., interview by Florence Coleman, September 3, 1974, Houston Oral History Project, Houston Public Library, http://digital.houstonlibrary.org/cdm/ref/collection/Interviews/id/249.

129. Robinson Jr., interview.

130. Robinson Jr., interview.

131. Tryon P. Woods, "'Something of the Fever and the Fret': Antiblackness in the Critical Prison Studies Fold," in *Conceptual Aphasia in Black: Displacing Racial Formation*, ed. P. Khalil Saucier and Tryon P. Woods (Lanham, MD: Lexington Books, 2016), 136–138.

132. Robin Marie Averbeck, *Liberalism Is Not Enough: Race and Poverty in Postwar Political Thought* (Chapel Hill: University of North Carolina Press, 2018), 42.

133. Rozanne McGrew Stringer, "Hybrid Zones: Representations of Race in Late Nineteenth-Century French Visual Culture" (Ph.D. diss., University of Kansas, 2011), 59.

Chapter 4: Captured by the Role of Gender
Hartman, "The Dead Book Revisited," 210.
1. "Law Enforcement Is Always the Answer," 2.
2. *This Is Our Home It Is Not for Sale.*
3. Carter Wesley, "The Real Responsibility," *Houston Informer*, May 21, 1952, sec. 2, 2; on "encroachment," see *This Is Our Home It Is Not for Sale.*
4. Wesley, "The Real Responsibility," 2. Historian Nathan Connolly points out that black property owners in Miami also benefited from price-gouging black renters. The artificial constraints of a racist housing market on black residential choice created opportunities for white and black real estate agents to form unholy alliances that capitalized on black poverty, overcharging black people for homes and failing to deliver repairs and services. This was likely the case in Houston as well, where a study on housing in 1948 revealed that since 1940, "16,000 new dwelling units" had been built in the city, with only "1,791 for nonwhites." Forty-five percent of all black homes in the city were assessed as "substandard." At 1420 Mason Street in Fourth Ward, Rufus Baldwin testified that the lot had "one house with four rooms and the landlord has cut that house in half in two and getting $22 a week for four rooms." Sid Hilliard testified that similar situations existed in black areas throughout the city, noting: "I can give you an instance where some of my people have rented houses from some of the builders at $5 a week. They are three-room apartments. Recently those people they rented the house from instead of renting it for $5 a week they would either have to share their three rooms or their rent would be raised to $12.50." One woman, he noted, "had to move out of her house and make room for two other families to move in because she wasn't able to pay that kind of rent" as her job only paid $20 per week. *Study and Investigation of Housing: Hearings before the Joint Committee on Housing*, 80th Cong., 1st sess., 1616, 1648–1649. Also see Connolly, *A World More Concrete.*
5. The *Informer* insisted that Jim Crow was inconsistent with "the teachings of Christianity to which the nation subscribes." Also see "Leadership from San Antonio," *Houston Informer*, April 17, 1954, sec. 1, 14. For a discussion on bourgeois individualism, see James

D. Young, *Socialism since 1889: A Biographical History* (London: Pinter, 1988). For more on black people and liberal individualism, see bell hooks, *Killing Rage: Ending Racism* (New York: H. Holt and Co, 1995); James Todd Uhlman, "Geographies of Desire: Bayard Taylor and the Romance of Travel in Bourgeois American Culture 1820–1880" (Ph.D. diss., Rutgers University, 2007).

6. Wynter, "The Re-Enchantment of Humanism," 186; Sylvia Wynter, "The Ceremony Found: Towards the Autopoetic Turn/Overturn, Its Autonomy of Human Agency and Extraterritoriality of (Self-) Cognition," in *Black Knowledges/Black Struggles: Essays in Critical Epistemology*, ed. Jason R. Ambroise and Sabine Broeck (Liverpool, UK: Liverpool University Press, 2015), 243, http://www.jstor.org/stable/j.ctt1gn6bfp.12.

7. Carter Wesley, "Negroes Not Wanted," *Houston Informer*, January 10, 1953, sec. 1, 3.

8. Wesley, "Negroes Not Wanted," 3.

9. Charles O. Cook, "Houston Informer," in *Encyclopedia of African American History, 1896 to the Present: From the Age of Segregation to the Twenty-First Century*, ed. Paul Finkelman (New York: Oxford University Press, 2009), 462–463.

10. Cary D. Wintz, "'The Struggle for Dignity': African Americans in Twentieth-Century Texas," in *Twentieth-Century Texas: A Social and Cultural History*, ed. John W. Storey and Mary L. Scheer (Denton: University of North Texas Press, 2008), 87.

11. Wesley, "Negroes Not Wanted," 3.

12. Curry, *The Man-Not*.

13. Tiffany M. Gill, "Civic Beauty: Beauty Culturists and the Politics of African American Female Entrepreneurship, 1900–1965," *Enterprise & Society* 5, no. 4 (2004): 583–593; William F. Pinar, "Black Protest and the Emergence of Ida B. Wells," *Counterpoints* 163 (2001): 419–486.

14. Michele Mitchell, "'The Black Man's Burdens': African Americans, Imperialism and Notions of Racial Manhood 1890–1910," in *Complicating Categories: Gender, Class, Race and Ethnicity*, ed. Eileen Boris and Angélique Janssens (New York: Cambridge University Press, 1999), 77–100.

15. Hartman, *Scenes of Subjection*, 152, 168–173.

16. "Gov. White Says Private Schools Won't Solve School Issue," *Houston Informer*, December 12, 1953, sec. 1, 1; Carter Wesley, "State's Rights," *Houston Informer*, December 12, 1953, sec. 1, 10.

17. Wendy Brown, *States of Injury: Power and Freedom in Late Modernity* (Princeton, NJ: Princeton University Press, 1995), 110.

18. "Thanksgiving: An American Holiday," 12.

19. "Negroes Are Americans First," *Houston Informer*, October 23, 1954, sec. 1, 12.

20. Ann Morning, "'Everyone Knows It's a Social Construct': Contemporary Science and the Nature of Race," *Sociological Focus* 40, no. 4 (2007): 436–454; Michael O. Hardimon, *Rethinking Race: The Case for Deflationary Realism* (Cambridge, MA: Harvard University Press, 2017).

21. "Freedom of Choice," *Houston Informer*, May 1, 1954, sec. 1, 12. On "Man" as a Western, liberal individualist construct, see Weheliye, *Habeas Viscus*.

22. Adams, "Our Readers Write," 12; Amilcar Shabazz, "Carter Wesley and the Making of Houston's Civic Culture before the Second Reconstruction," *Houston History Review* 1, no. 2 (2004): 8–13.

23. While historians and other scholars of gender have demonstrated the development of the gender symbols of masculinity and femininity and have found that the traits associated with them are oppositional and inescapable, including rationality and irrationality,

respectively, I would caution that these symbols have been deployed differently when inflected by the condition of racialization. Indeed, because the black experience is in part defined by gender fungibility, these symbols can maintain their stability in some contexts while being disrupted and rearranged in others. Patricia Hill Collins, "A Telling Difference: Dominance, Strength, and Black Masculinities," in *Progressive Black Masculinities*, ed. Athena D. Mutua (New York: Routledge, 2006), 73–98; R. W. Connell, "The Social Organization of Masculinity," in *The Masculinities Reader*, ed. Stephen M. Whitehead and Frank Barrett (Malden, MA: Polity, 2001), 30–50; Mimi Schippers, "Recovering the Feminine Other: Masculinity, Femininity, and Gender Hegemony," *Theory and Society* 36, no. 1 (February 1, 2007): 85–102; Bart Landry, *Black Working Wives: Pioneers of the American Family Revolution* (Berkeley: University of California Press, 2002); Sally Kitch, *The Specter of Sex: Gendered Foundations of Racial Formation in the United States* (Albany: State University of New York Press, 2009).

24. Fanon, *Black Skin, White Masks*, 178.

25. After all, as historian Joan Landes has demonstrated, "reason was counterposed to femininity" as foundational to modern European society. See Landes, *Women and the Public Sphere in the Age of the French Revolution* (Ithaca, NY: Cornell University Press, 1988), 46.

26. John Egerton, *Speak Now against the Day: The Generation before the Civil Rights Movement in the South* (New York: Knopf, 2013), 314.

27. Carter Wesley, "Segregated Schools," *Houston Informer*, February 24, 1962, sec. 1, 8.

28. Robert J. Robertson, *Fair Ways: How Six Black Golfers Won Civil Rights in Beaumont, Texas* (College Station: Texas A&M University Press, 2015); "Negroes Swim in City Pool; Pool Closed," *Houston Informer*, July 3, 1953, sec. 1, 1; "Texas City Closes 12 Pools after Negroes Use One," *Jet*, July 1, 1954, 4; "Old Race Policy Break-up Begins," *California Eagle*, June 24, 1954, 3; Jon Ford, "Pools Closed to Negroes, Council Approves Race Segregation," *San Antonio Express*, June 20, 1954, sec. 1, 8.

29. Quoted in Robertson, *Fair Ways*, 87.

30. Egerton, *Speak Now against the Day*, 252–253.

31. W. Marvin Dulaney, "Whatever Happened to the Civil Rights Movement in Dallas, Texas?" in *Essays on the American Civil Rights Movement*, ed. John Dittmer et al. (College Station: Published for University of Texas at Arlington by Texas A&M University Press, 1993), 73.

32. Michael L. Gillette, *Heman Marion Sweatt: Civil Rights Plaintiff*, ed. Alwyn Barr and Robert A. Calvert (Austin: Texas State Historical Association, 1981), 175–177; Amilcar Shabazz, "The Opening of the Southern Mind: The Desegregation of Higher Education in Texas, 1865–1965" (Ph.D. diss., University of Houston, 1996), 92; Pitre, *In Struggle against Jim Crow*, 93.

33. Philip F. Rubio, *There's Always Work at the Post Office: African American Postal Workers and the Fight for Jobs, Justice, and Equality* (Chapel Hill: University of North Carolina Press, 2010), 141.

34. Kluger, *Simple Justice*.

35. Anderson, *The Education of Blacks in the South*, 184–185.

36. Anderson, *The Education of Blacks in the South*, 179.

37. Gary M. Lavergne, *Before Brown: Heman Marion Sweatt, Thurgood Marshall, and the Long Road to Justice* (Austin: University of Texas Press, 2010).

38. Pitre, *In Struggle against Jim Crow*; Lavergne, *Before Brown*, 115.

39. "Supervisors Know about Conditions in Schools," *Houston Informer*, February 28, 1953, sec. 1, 1, 10.

40. "School Business Is Your Business," *Houston Informer*, March 7, 1953, sec. 1, 8.

41. "Group Presses for School Improvement," *Houston Informer*, April 11, 1953, sec. 1, 1, 10.

42. "Negro Schools Head Moves to 'New' Office," *Houston Informer*, September 5, 1953, sec. 1, 1.

43. "School Problems to the Fore," *Houston Informer*, September 19, 1953, 1; "HISD School Board Minutes," May 6, 1957.

44. "School Election: November 14," *Houston Informer*, November 7, 1953, sec. 1, 12.

45. Lamar Fleming Jr. was a wealthy and influential business owner in Houston. See James A. Tinsley, "Fleming, Lamar Jr.," The Handbook of Texas Online, Texas State Historical Association (TSHA), June 12, 2010, https://www.tshaonline.org/handbook/online/articles/ffl09.

46. "Room for School Expansion," *Houston Informer*, April 10, 1954, sec. 1, 12; "HISD School Board Minutes," March 22, 1953.

47. "Citizens Demand New Schools: 'Stop Trifling Around' Leaders Tell Officials," *Houston Informer*, March 27, 1954, 1, 10.

48. Carter Wesley, "Hot School Issue Arouses Citizens," *Houston Informer*, April 3, 1954, 1, 10.

49. "Spotlight on Negro Schools," *Houston Informer*, April 3, 1954, 12.

50. "Public School Neglect," *Houston Informer*, April 10, 1954, 12.

51. "School Board in Reverse on Negro High School Site," *Houston Informer*, October 2, 1954, 1, 20.

52. Du Bois, *Dusk of Dawn*, 2, 70.

53. Merline Pitre, "Black Houstonians and the 'Separate but Equal' Doctrine: Carter Wesley versus Lulu B. White," in *The African American Experience in Texas: An Anthology*, ed. Bruce A. Glasrud and James Smallwood (Lubbock: Texas Tech University Press, 2007), 302–317; Shabazz, "The Opening of the Southern Mind."

54. Rubio, *There's Always Work at the Post Office*, 141.

55. Walter Vaught, "Our Readers Write," *Houston Informer*, August 29, 1953, sec. 1, 12.

56. Lavergne, *Before Brown*, 116; Lisa Aldred and Thurgood Marshall, *Thurgood Marshall: Supreme Court Justice*, ed. Heather Lehr Wagner and Nathan Irvin Huggins (Philadelphia: Chelsea House, 2004), 59.

57. Juan Williams, *Thurgood Marshall: American Revolutionary* (New York: Three Rivers Press, 2011), 181; Lavergne, *Before Brown*, 112.

58. Letter reprinted in Michael G. Long, *Marshalling Justice: The Early Civil Rights Letters of Thurgood Marshall* (New York: Amistad, 2011), 186–187.

59. Pitre, *In Struggle against Jim Crow*, 104.

60. Carter Wesley, "How They Fish," *Houston Informer*, June 27, 1953, sec. 1, 3.

61. Marriott, *Whither Fanon?*

62. Neil Gary Sapper, "A Survey of the History of the Black People of Texas, 1930–1954" (Ph.D. diss., Texas Tech University, 1972), 437; Pitre, *In Struggle against Jim Crow*, 93–95.

63. In 1873 the Freedman's Aid Society of the Methodist Episcopal Church established Wiley College in Marshall, Texas, continuing the church's tradition of providing educational opportunities to recently emancipated and enfranchised black Americans. James Douglass and Jamal Hasan, "History of Texas Southern University" [Brochure], April 1, 2010, Texas Southern University Digital Collection, HBCU Library Alliance, http://contentdm

.auctr.edu/cdm/ref/collection/TXDC/id/38. Also see Morrison & Fourmy Directory Co., *Houston City Directory 1919* (Houston: R. L. Polk & Co., n.d.), 69, 428; "New Fraternal Insurance Company Granted a Permit," *Houston Informer*, March 13, 1920, 5; Elneita W. Stewart, "Houston Omegas Host 15th Annual District Meet," *Pittsburgh Courier*, April 26, 1952, 10; Michael R. Heintze, "Black Colleges," The Handbook of Texas Online, Texas State Historical Association (TSHA), June 12, 2010, https://tshaonline.org/handbook/online/articles/khb01; "1940 US Federal Population Census (Enumeration District: 258–144, Sheet 8A)" (n.d.), Heritage Quest Online, http://heritagequestonline.com. The Fairchild building was plotted on fifty-three acres that had been donated by oil magnate Hugh Roy Cullen. Benjamin Wermund, "Histories of TSU and UH Marked by Segregation," *Houston Chronicle*, August 21, 2016, http://www.chron.com/local/history/major-stories-events/article/Houston-s-public-higher-education-history-a-9175498.php.

64. See the Legislative Reference Library of Texas (http://www.lrl.texas.gov) for House Bill 437, House Bill 780, House Joint Resolution 48, and Senate Bill 140 in the 50th Regular Session (1947). House Bill 82 (1951) dropped "for Negroes" from the school name and replaced "State" with "Southern." Douglass and Hasan state that House Bill 788 provided for $2 million for the establishment of a law school at TSUN and this has often been repeated. However, H. B. 788 is an act clarifying the powers of governing bodies of independent school districts. Douglass and Hasan, "History of Texas Southern University" [Brochure]. It was S.B. 140 that provided the financial appropriations for the new school, "$2,000,000 for land, buildings and equipment, and $500,000 per annum for maintenance for the biennium ending August 31, 1949." For a quote about TSU's attractiveness as a black university, see John S. Lash, "Texas Southern University: From Separation to Special Designation," June 1975, iv, TSU Riot Collection, Department of Special Collections, Robert J. Terry Library, Texas Southern University. On the name-change student delegation, see Roshanda Gibbs, "Texas Southern University: A Frontier in Education for Blacks in Houston," *Texas Historian* 62, no. 3 (February 2002): 2.

65. Bill Helmer, "Nightmare in Houston," *Texas Observer*, June 23, 1967, Record Group 453, Records of the US Commission on Civil Rights, National Archives, College Park, Maryland; Carter Wesley, "Conspiracies?" *Houston Informer*, June 13, 1953, sec. 1, 3.

66. Mary Beth Rogers, *Barbara Jordan: American Hero* (New York: Bantam, 2000), 51; "Dr. O'Hara Lanier's Brain Amazes Psychologists," *Jet*, September 23, 1954, 14.

67. Lavergne, *Before Brown*, 238.

68. Ben Hawkins, "T.S.U. Directors Ignored Evidence on Lanier, Charge Claims," *Houston Chronicle*, August 23, 1953, 1, Mary McLeod Bethune Papers: The Bethune Foundation Collection, Part 2: Correspondence Files, 1914–1955, folder 001390-006-0231, ProQuest History Vault; Ernest Obadele-Starks, "Black Labor, the Black Middle Class, and Organized Protest along the Upper Texas Gulf Coast, 1883–1945," *Southwestern Historical Quarterly* 103, no. 1 (1999): 61; Carter Wesley, "Rice's Revenge," *Houston Informer*, May 3, 1953, sec. 1, 2; Carter Wesley, "Ram's Horn," *Houston Informer*, April 25, 1953, sec. 1, 3; Carter Wesley, "Ram's Horn," *Houston Informer*, September 5, 1953; sec. 1, 3 (quote about Ralph Lee).

69. "C. W. Rice Target of Angry Charge," *Houston Informer*, April 11, 1953, sec. 1, 1; "Send Letters to Governor," *Houston Informer*, April 18, 1953, sec. 1, 1; Wesley, "Rice's Revenge," 2; "Protest Book Review Ban at Texas Southern U.," *Jet*, April 23, 1953, 14.

70. Claude A. Barnett to Dr. R. O'Hara Lanier, June 3, 1953, and Claude A. Barnett to Ben Hawkins, June 3, 1953, both in Claude A. Barnett Papers, 1918–1967, Series 2: Africa and Other Foreign Interests, 1925–1966, folder 252247-187-0006, ProQuest

History Vault; Carter Wesley, "Rice Sees a Book," *Houston Informer*, May 16, 1953, sec. 1, 3. Wesley spared no words for Rice, writing that unlike him, "I am not afraid of the bankers and other men of leadership. To me they are just men, and they are no better than they act. He [Rice] makes his living off of them, and he makes his living by trying to please them in every way; I make my living by trying to do what is right every day for the masses of people, and I am not afraid of anybody who wants to call me a Communist. I don't imagine Lanier is afraid of people who want to call him a Communist." He also referred to Rice as "a slave . . . of the forced inferiority that we have suffered at the hands of the racial supremacists" for the *Negro Labor News* editor's suggestion that desegregation would be harmful because it would take jobs away from black educators. Wesley, "How They Fish," 3; Carter Wesley, "Queer Notions," *Houston Informer*, September 12, 1953, sec. 1, 3.

71. Carter Wesley took issue with black students being double-taxed. Carter Wesley, "Something Special," *Houston Informer*, May 23, 1953, sec. 1, 3.

72. "Send Letters to Governor," 1; Wesley, "Ram's Horn," April 25, 1953, 3; "Can TSU Survive?" *Houston Informer*, June 6, 1953, sec. 1, 14. Wesley also reported that a friend told him someone had said, "Wesley always backs up Lanier." He admitted that this was generally the case, and also noted, speaking in the third person, "[I]n every instance where Wesley has backed up Lanier, it has turned out that Wesley was right in the end." Carter Wesley, "Investigation of TSU," *Houston Informer*, July 11, 1953, sec. 1, 3.

73. Ben Hawkins, "Legion Asks Probe of T.S.U.," *Houston Chronicle*, June 8, 1953, 1, 14.

74. Wesley, "Conspiracies?" 3. Mack Hannah replaced Craig Cullinan as chair after Cullinan resigned from the position. The other eight members of the board in 1951 included Spurgeon Bell (white lawyer and soon-to-be civil court judge), Dr. H. D. Bruce (white educator at East Texas Baptist College), Dr. M. L. Edwards (black physician at Jarvis Christian College for Negroes), Dr. W. R. Banks (black educator at Prairie View University), Tom Miller (white Austin politician), Dr. M. E. Sadler (white president of Texas Christian University), I. B. Loud (black minister and district superintendent of the San Antonio district of the Methodist Church), and S. M. "Moss" Adams (white up-and-coming attorney). Prior to Hannah's appointment in 1951, the fourth black board member was Benjamin Morgan, a businessperson out of Corsicana, Texas. Bill McCoy, "Judge Bell—from Country Lawyer to Chief Justice," *South College Texas of Law, Annotations*, August 1983, 5, University of North Texas Libraries, Portal to Texas History, texashistory.unt.edu, crediting South Texas College of Law; "[Dr. H. D. Bruce, Educator and Library Supporter], Photograph," n.d., University of North Texas Libraries, Portal to Texas History, texashistory.unt.edu, crediting Marshall Public Library; "Wood County Man Is Appointed to Bi-Racial Body," *Wood County Record*, July 22, 1946, 1, University of North Texas Libraries, Portal to Texas History, texashistory.unt.edu, crediting Mineola Memorial Library; "Journal of the Senate of the State of Texas, Regular Session of the Fifty-Second Legislature," 1951, University of North Texas Libraries, Portal to Texas History, texashistory.unt.edu, crediting UNT Libraries Government Documents Department; Neal Douglass, "Mayor Tom Miller—Citizen of the Year Presentation, Photograph," January 10, 1950, University of North Texas Libraries, Portal to Texas History, texashistory.unt.edu, crediting Austin History Center, Austin Public Library; "Church Additions in Eight Revivals Numbered 24," *Breckenridge American* (Breckenridge, Texas), March 23, 1948, 1, University of North Texas Libraries, Portal to Texas History, texashistory.unt.edu, crediting Breckenridge Public Library; "Serve on State University's Board of Directors," *San Antonio Register*, May 30,

1947, 1, University of North Texas Libraries, Portal to Texas History, texashistory.unt.edu, crediting University of Texas at San Antonio.

75. Wesley, "Conspiracies?" 3.

76. Wesley, "Investigation of TSU," 3.

77. "As Investigation Nears End State Auditor Testifies: 'TSU Records in Good Shape,'" *Houston Informer*, August 8, 1953, sec. 1, 1, 10; "TSU Board Clears Dr. Lanier, School," *Houston Informer*, August 22, 1953, sec. 1, 1, 10. Lanier's opposition continued to lambaste him in Houston's press after the investigation concluded. Wesley put them on notice: "Somebody should tell Messrs. C. W. Rice, Ralph Lee, and Ben Hawkins that the issue over TSU has been fought out and the decision has been taken, and that they lost. They are like some southerners whose grandparents forgot to come back and tell them that they lost the Civil War." Carter Wesley, "Over and Done With," *Houston Informer*, September 5, 1953, sec. 1, 3.

78. "Dr Lanier Quits as TSU Prexy," *Houston Informer*, June 11, 1955, sec. 1, 1, 12; Carter Wesley, "TSU Fuses," *Houston Informer*, June 18, 1955, sec. 1, 3; Claude A. Barnett to Dr. R. O'Hara Lanier, June 22, 1955, and Lulu B. White to Claude A. Barnett, July 15, 1955, Claude A. Barnett Papers, 1918–1967, Series 2: Africa and Other Foreign Interests, 1925–1966, folder 252247-187-0006, ProQuest History Vault; "Dr. Nabrit Succeeds Lanier as Texas Southern Head," *Jet*, July 28, 1955, 21.

79. Colin Koopman, *Genealogy as Critique: Foucault and the Problems of Modernity* (Bloomington: Indiana University Press, 2013), 37–43; Michel Foucault and Alan Sheridan, *The Archaeology of Knowledge* (New York: Pantheon Books, 1972); Michael S. Drake, *Political Sociology for a Globalizing World* (Cambridge, UK: Polity, 2010), 47–49.

80. Lorena Seebach Walsh, *Motives of Honor, Pleasure, and Profit: Plantation Management in the Colonial Chesapeake, 1607–1763* (Chapel Hill: University of North Carolina Press, 2010); Jordan, *White over Black*; Talitha L. LeFlouria, *Chained in Silence: Black Women and Convict Labor in the New South*, Justice, Power, and Politics Series (Chapel Hill: University of North Carolina Press, 2015).

81. "A New Year Dawns," *Houston Informer*, July 3, 1953, sec. 1, 12.

82. "Citizenship's First Duty," *Houston Informer*, January 3, 1953, sec. 1, 12.

83. "Leadership from San Antonio," 14.

84. "Buy Negro," *Houston Informer*, June 13, 1953, 12.

85. "Everybody's Business," *Houston Informer*, November 28, 1953.

86. "Buy Negro," 12.

87. "Editorially Speaking: Who Are the Enemies?" *Houston Informer*, May 23, 1953, 12.

88. Donna D'Ray, "On Traitors," *Houston Informer*, September 19, 1953, sec. 1, 12.

89. Raúl Coronado, *A World Not to Come: A History of Latino Writing and Print Culture* (Cambridge, MA: Harvard University Press, 2013), 273–274.

90. Michael O. Emerson, Christian Smith, and David Sikkink, "Equal in Christ, but Not in the World: White Conservative Protestants and Explanations of Black-White Inequality," *Social Problems* 46, no. 3 (August 1, 1999): 398–417, https://doi.org/10.2307/3097107; Eric Tranby and Douglas Hartmann, "Critical Whiteness Theories and the Evangelical 'Race Problem': Extending Emerson and Smith's 'Divided by Faith,'" *Journal for the Scientific Study of Religion* 47, no. 3 (2008): 341–359.

91. "Leadership from San Antonio," 14.

92. "Segregation Opposes Christian Principles," *Houston Informer*, September 4, 1954, 12.

93. Carter Wesley, "Ram's Horn," *Houston Informer*, November 7, 1953, sec. 1, 3.
94. "Freedom of Choice," 12.
95. Iris Marion Young, *Intersecting Voices: Dilemmas of Gender, Political Philosophy, and Policy* (Princeton, NJ: Princeton University Press, 1997), 17.
96. "Negro Crime," *Houston Informer*, January 17, 1953, sec. 2, 2.
97. Olivia Adams, "[Letter]," *Houston Informer*, February 13, 1954, 12.
98. "Racial Segregation Unlawful, Costly, and Immoral," *Houston Informer*, June 19, 1954, sec. 1, 14.
99. Guinier, "From Racial Liberalism to Racial Literacy," 95.
100. "Americanism in the Schools," 14.
101. "The Student's Role in Racial Progress," *Houston Informer*, September 4, 1954, 12.
102. "Opportunity Knocks," *Houston Informer*, August 15, 1953, sec. 1, 12.
103. "Leadership from San Antonio," 14.
104. "Is Negro Education Failing?" *Houston Informer*, April 18, 1953, sec. 2, 2.
105. Reva B. Siegel, "Discrimination in the Eyes of the Law: How 'Color Blindness' Discourse Disrupts and Rationalizes Social Stratification," *California Law Review* 88, no. 1 (January 1, 2000): 90–93, https://doi.org/10.2307/3481275.
106. See chapters 6 and 7 in Kellar, *Make Haste Slowly*; San Miguel, *Brown, Not White*, 128.
107. Julie Novkov, "Mobilizing Liberalism in Defense of Racism," *Good Society* 16, no. 1 (2007): 31, https://doi.org/10.1353/gso.0.0003.
108. "The U.S. Negro, 1953," *Time*, May 11, 1953; "Negro Life in U.S. Feature in Time," *Houston Informer*, May 9, 1953, sec. 1, 1.

Chapter 5: Captured by Blackness
Hartman, "The Dead Book Revisited," 208.
1. Elizabeth Hinton, *From the War on Poverty to the War on Crime: The Making of Mass Incarceration in America* (Cambridge, MA: Harvard University Press, 2016); Jonathan Simon, *Governing through Crime: How the War on Crime Transformed American Democracy and Created a Culture of Fear*, 1st ed. (Oxford, UK: Oxford University Press, 2009).
2. Woods, *Blackhood against the Police Power*, 231.
3. Warren, *Ontological Terror*, 60, 72; Emily Anne Parker, "The Human as Double Bind: Sylvia Wynter and the Genre of 'Man,'" *Journal of Speculative Philosophy* 32, no. 3 (2018): 439–449, https://doi.org/10.5325/jspecphil.32.3.0439; Hartman, "The Dead Book Revisited," 208.
4. The only historian I know of who has made substantive use of these archives is Malcolm McLaughlin in *The Long, Hot Summer of 1967: Urban Rebellion in America* (New York: Palgrave Macmillan, 2014).
5. Clayson, *Freedom Is Not Enough*, 139.
6. Phelps, *A People's War on Poverty*, e-book, chapter 4, note 22.
7. Watson, *Race and the Houston Police Department, 1930–1990*.
8. Sidney E. Cleveland, "Psychological Intervention in a Community Crisis," in *Advances in Experimental Clinical Psychology*, ed. Henry E. Adams and William K. Boardman (New York: Pergamon Press, 2013), 167–168.
9. Hartman, "The Dead Book Revisited," 208.
10. Byrd, *Captives and Voyagers*, 8, 9–11.
11. Hartman, "Venus in Two Acts," 9, 12.
12. Kazanjian, "Scenes of Speculation," 81–83; Kazanjian, "Freedom's Surprise."

13. Byrd, *Captives and Voyagers*, 10. I mean "blackened" in the sense carried by Calvin Warren and articulated through much of this book, though perhaps Christina Sharpe offers a clear and straightforward take: "We are Black people in the wake with no state or nation to protect us, with no citizenship bound to be respected" who must "think and be and act" from "the modalities of Black life lived in, as, under, despite Black death." Sharpe, *In the Wake*, 22.

14. Greg Thomas, "Afro-Blue Notes: The Death of Afro-Pessimism (2.0)?" *Theory & Event* 21, no. 1 (2018): 303.

15. Woods, *Blackhood against the Police Power*, 40–48.

16. Sexton, "Ante-Anti-Blackness."

17. "The Black Man's Role in America" (Spartacist League, n.d.), folder Black Power! Vol. I No. II, TSU Riot Collection, Department of Special Collections, Robert J. Terry Library, Texas Southern University.

18. "Black Students on the Move," *The Movement* 3, no. 5 (May 1967): 1.

19. Salinas, "UH COBRRs Arrested, Freed in Dump Protest"; "Dump Pickets Are Held"; Gene Locke, interview by David Goldstein, July 31, 2008, Houston Oral History Project, Houston Area Digital Archives, Houston Public Library; Bullard, "The Mountains of Houston: Environmental Justice and the Politics of Garbage," *Cite: The Architecture + Design Review of Houston* 93 (2014): 28–33; "Facts about the T.S.U. Five and Their Indictment for Murder and Two Assaults to 'MURDER,'" n.d., folder T.S.U. Five & Their Indictment for Murder and Two Assaults to "MURDER," Department of Special Collections, Robert J. Terry Library, Texas Southern University.

20. Kellar, *Make Haste Slowly*; San Miguel, *Brown, Not White*.

21. Rebecca B. Armstrong to NAACP General Office, March 20, 1968, Papers of the NAACP Part 28, Special Subject Files, 1966–1970, Series B: "Powell, Adam Clayton, Jr." through "White Supremacy"; General Office File, Group IV, box A-71, Schools—Texas, 1966–1968, Kelley Center for Government Information, Data & Geospatial Services, Fondren Library, Rice University, Houston, Texas; Bill Lawson, "A Second Look at the 'TSU Riots,'" *Forward Times*, May 27, 1967.

22. McLaughlin, *The Long, Hot Summer of 1967*; Daryl B. Harris, "The Logic of Black Urban Rebellions," *Journal of Black Studies* 28, no. 3 (January 1, 1998): 368–385.

23. For the differences between black campus movements and student activism and urban rebellions, see Ibram H. Rogers, "The Black Campus Movement: The Case for a New Historiography," *The Sixties: A Journal of History, Politics and Culture* 4, no. 2 (December 1, 2011): 171–186, https://doi.org/10.1080/17541328.2011.625195; Martha Biondi, *The Black Revolution on Campus* (Berkeley: University of California Press, 2014).

24. J. A. Pierce to All Students of Texas Southern University, "Organization of a Student Advisory Committee to the President," April 10, 1967, folder Misc., Department of Special Collections, Robert J. Terry Library, Texas Southern University; F. D. Kirkpatrick, "The Police Attack at Texas Southern," *Militant*, June 26, 1967, 8; "Black Power Revolt at Texas Southern," *The Movement [SNCC]* 3, no. 5 (May 1967): 1–10; Trazawell Franklin, "[Statement of Trazawell Franklin]," June 23, 1967, 1–3, Papers of the NAACP, Series A, Supplement to Part 23: Legal Department Case Files, 1960–1972, Reel 14, Group V, box 2353; Phil Maclin, "Indictments in TSU Probe Likely Today," *Houston Post*, June 2, 1967, 1, 7.

25. Berman, *The Strange Demise of Jim Crow*; Hofheinz and Dugger, "Houston Has Desegregation Model," August 5, 1955; Malone, "Unannounced and Unexpected," both in box 4Jc62, folder "Research Files: Housing, 1955, 1964, 1969, 1970," Texas Observer

Records, Dolph Briscoe Center for American History, University of Texas at Austin; Kellar, *Make Haste Slowly.*

26. "[Statement XIV]"; Lawson, "[Statement of Reverend Bill Lawson]," n.d., both in Papers of the NAACP, Series A, Supplement to Part 23: Legal Department Case Files, 1960–1972, Reel 14, Group V, box 2353, 2–3.

27. Behnken, "Count on Me," 76.

28. Woods, *Blackhood against the Police Power*, 222.

29. Mbembé, "Necropolitics"; Weheliye, *Habeas Viscus.*

30. Simon, *Governing through Crime*, 25.

31. Floyd Nichols, "[Statement of Floyd Nichols]," June 23, 1967, and Douglas Wayne Waller, "[Statement of Douglas Wayne Waller]," June 22, 1967, both in Papers of the NAACP, Series A, Supplement to Part 23: Legal Department Case Files, 1960–1972, Reel 14, Group V, box 2353.

32. Chester Logan, interview by John Biggers, July 27, 1967, 1, Papers of the NAACP, Series A, Supplement to Part 23: Legal Department Case Files, 1960–1972, Reel 14, Group V, box 2353; Waller, "[Statement of Douglas Wayne Waller]," 3–4; "Statement of Clarence Harper," n.d., 1, box 30, folder 127-30-1, George & Latane Lambert Papers, University of Texas Arlington Libraries Special Collections; Franklin, "[Statement of Trazawell Franklin]," 6; "Statement of John Booker," n.d., 3, box 30, folder 127-30-1, George & Latane Lambert Papers, University of Texas Arlington Libraries Special Collections; "[Statement of Charles Freeman]," June 23, 1967, 2, Papers of the NAACP, Series A, Supplement to Part 23: Legal Department Case Files, 1960–1972, Reel 14, Group V, box 2353; "[Handwritten Statement, Possibly of David Minor]," n.d., Papers of the NAACP, Series A, Supplement to Part 23: Legal Department Case Files, 1960–1972, Reel 14, Group V, box 2353; Maurice Hopson and Cleve McDowell, July 6, 1967, Papers of the NAACP, Series A, Supplement to Part 23: Legal Department Case Files, 1960–1972, Reel 14, Group V, box 2353.

33. "Statement of Chester Logan," n.d., 1, box 30, folder 127-30-1, Lambert Papers, University of Texas Arlington Libraries Special Collections; "[Statement of Charles Freeman]," 3; Douglas Wayne Waller, "[2nd Statement of Douglas Wayne Waller]," June 22, 1967, 1, Papers of the NAACP, Series A, Supplement to Part 23: Legal Department Case Files, 1960–1972, Reel 14, Group V, box 2353; Leon Hardy to Thomas R. Ashley, November 19, 1967, Papers of the NAACP, Series A, Supplement to Part 23: Legal Department Case Files, 1960–1972, Reel 15, Group V, box 2354.

34. "Statement of William D. Butler," n.d., box 30, folder 127-30-1, George & Latane Lambert Papers, University of Texas Arlington Libraries Special Collections.

35. Franklin, "[Statement of Trazawell Franklin]"; Waller, "[2nd Statement of Douglas Wayne Waller]."

36. Franklin, "[Statement of Trazawell Franklin]," 7; Rayford Whittingham Logan, *The Negro in American Life and Thought: The Nadir, 1877–1901* (New York: Dial Press, 1954), 1; "[Statement of Willie Robinson]," n.d., Papers of the NAACP, Series A, Supplement to Part 23: Legal Department Case Files, 1960–1972, Reel 14, Group V, box 2353.

37. "Statement of V. J. Hollins" n.d., and "Statement of Thomas Turner," n.d., both in box 30, folder 127-30-1, George & Latane Lambert Papers, University of Texas Arlington Libraries Special Collections; Logan, interview, 1.

38. "What Inspired It: (Larry Jackson—National Merit Scholar) Person on the Scene," n.d., Papers of the NAACP, Series A, Supplement to Part 23: Legal Department Case Files, 1960–1972, Reel 14, Group V, box 2353; "[Statement of Willie Robinson]"; Franklin, "[Statement of Trazawell Franklin]"; Ben Taub General Hospital, "Discharge Summary

[Robert Blaylock]," May 17, 1967, Papers of the NAACP, Series A, Supplement to Part 23: Legal Department Case Files, 1960–1972, Reel 13, Group V, box 2352 cont.-2355; "In the United States District Court for the Southern District of Texas, Houston Division. Trazawell Franklin, Jr. vs Herman Short. No. 67-H-450. Deposition of R. G. Blaylock," July 6, 1967, Papers of the NAACP, Series A, Supplement to Part 23: Legal Department Case Files, 1960–1972, Reel 16, Group V, box 2352 cont.-2355; Franklin, "[Statement of Trazawell Franklin]"; "Statement of Richard Hurndon," n.d., box 30, folder 127-30-1, George & Latane Lambert Papers, University of Texas Arlington Libraries Special Collections; "Statement of Clarence Harper."

39. "Statement of William Glaze," n.d., box 30, folder 127-30-1, George & Latane Lambert Papers, University of Texas Arlington Libraries Special Collections; "Statement of Thomas Turner"; Franklin, "[Statement of Trazawell Franklin]," 7; "Statement of James Young," n.d., box 30, folder 127-30-1, George & Latane Lambert Papers, University of Texas Arlington Libraries Special Collections.

40. Charles Culhane, "TSU Students Wrecked Dorm, Police Testify," *Houston Post*, November 7, 1967, 2.

41. *Riots, Civil and Criminal Disorders: Hearings before the Permanent Subcommittee on Investigations of the Committee on Government Operations United States Senate Ninetieth Congress, First Session (Part 3)* (Washington, DC: Government Printing Office, 1967), 875–876; *Riots, Civil and Criminal Disorders: Hearings before the Permanent Subcommittee on Investigations of the Committee on Government Operations United States Senate Ninetieth Congress, First Session (Part 1)* (Washington, DC: Government Printing Office, 1967), 61, 228; Bill Lawson, "[Statement of Reverend Bill Lawson]"; Kirkpatrick, "The Police Attack at Texas Southern," 8.

42. "Statement of Thomas Turner"; Kirkpatrick, "The Police Attack at Texas Southern," 8.

43. *Riots, Civil and Criminal Disorders: Hearings before the Permanent Subcommittee on Investigations of the Committee on Government Operations United States Senate Ninetieth Congress, First Session (Part 3)*, 875–876; *Riots, Civil and Criminal Disorders: Hearings before the Permanent Subcommittee on Investigations of the Committee on Government Operations United States Senate Ninetieth Congress, First Session (Part 1)*, 61, 228; Lawson, "[Statement of Reverend Bill Lawson]"; Kirkpatrick, "The Police Attack at Texas Southern," 8.

44. Lawson, "[Statement of Reverend Bill Lawson]," 2.

45. Lawson, "[Statement of Reverend Bill Lawson]," 2.

46. Carol S. Vance to Ronnie Dugger, January 11, 1971, Charles Freeman District Court Record 7553-C, Victoria County District Clerk's Office; *Riots, Civil and Criminal Disorders: Hearings before the Permanent Subcommittee on Investigations of the Committee on Government Operations United States Senate Ninetieth Congress, First Session (Part 1)*, 377–378.

47. James L. Turner, "Medical Examiner's Investigation Case No. 67-1219," May 17, 1967, Inquest Records, Harris County Archives; "Fund for Kuba Widow Started," *Houston Post*, May 18, 1967, sec. 1; Alex LaRotta, "The TSU Riot, 50 Years Later; Collective Memory of Incident Is Foggy, but Art Forms Present Different Views," *Houston Chronicle*, May 19, 2017, A002.

48. "Statement of Carlyn Robbin," n.d., "Statement of Howard Williams," n.d., and "Statement of W. T. Adams," n.d., all in box 30, folder 127-30-1, George & Latane Lambert Papers, University of Texas Arlington Libraries Special Collections; Franklin, "[Statement of Trazawell Franklin]," 8; *Riots, Civil and Criminal Disorders: Hearings before the Permanent Subcommittee on Investigations of the Committee on Government Operations*

United States Senate Ninetieth Congress, First Session (Part 1), 164, 369; Kirkpatrick, "The Police Attack at Texas Southern," 8; Turner, "Medical Examiner's Investigation Case No. 67-1219"; Lawson, "[Statement of Reverend Bill Lawson]"; "Statement of V. J. Hollins"; "Statement of Chester Logan." One officer said to a student, "If you want a riot, we'll give you a riot." "Statement of Anthony Fisher," n.d., box 30, folder 127-30-1, George & Latane Lambert Papers, University of Texas Arlington Libraries Special Collections.

49. Jordan, *White over Black*, 151–153; Charles White, *An Account of the Regular Gradation in Man, and in Different Animals and Vegetables . . .* (London : Printed for C. Dilly, 1799), http://archive.org/details/b24924507; Jerome Branche, *Colonialism and Race in Luso-Hispanic Literature* (Columbia: University of Missouri Press, 2006), 16–18; Foster, *Rethinking Rufus*.

50. Curry, "Expendables for Whom"; Tommy J. Curry, "He's a Rapist, Even When He's Not: Richard Wright's Account of Black Male Vulnerability in the Raping Case of Willie McGee," in *The Politics of Richard Wright: Perspectives on Resistance*, ed. Jane Anna Gordon and Cyrus Ernesto Zirakzadeh (Lexington: University Press of Kentucky, 2019), e-book; Tommy J. Curry and Ebony A. Utley, "She's Just a Friend (with Benefits): Examining the Significance of Black American Boys' Partner Choice for Initial Sexual Intercourse," in *Reimagining Black Masculinities: Race, Gender, and Public Space*, ed. Mark C. Hopson and Mika'il Petin (Lanham, MD: Lexington Books, 2020), 33–52.

51. Nick J. Fox and Pam Alldred, "The Sexuality-Assemblage: Desire, Affect, Anti-Humanism," *Sociological Review* 61, no. 4 (2013): 770, 774, 774n57, 777, https://doi.org/10.1111/1467-954X.12075; Maurice Merleau-Ponty, *Phenomenology of Perception*, trans. Colin Smith (London: Routledge Classics, 2002), 183n57, 196; Weheliye, *Habeas Viscus*, 97; Ponton, "Clothed in Blue Flesh."

52. "Statement of Henry Durley," n.d., "Statement of Madison Tyler," n.d., and "Statement of Gerald Barnes," n.d., all in box 30, folder 127-30-1, George & Latane Lambert Papers, University of Texas Arlington Libraries Special Collections.

53. Curry, *The Man-Not*, 210; Foster, *Rethinking Rufus*, 5; Foster, "The Sexual Abuse of Black Men under American Slavery"; Judith Butler, "Endangered/Endangering: Schematic Racism and White Paranoia," in *Reading Rodney King, Reading Urban Uprising*, ed. Robert Gooding-Williams (New York: Routledge, 1993), 15–22.

54. "Officer Slain, 2 Others Wounded," *Houston Chronicle*, June 17, 1967, 1; Charley Schneider, "Death Stood Next to Him: Post Reporter at TSU Rioting," *Houston Post*, May 18, 1967, sec. 1, 12; "Photo Editorial: Diagram for Disaster," *Forward Times*, May 27, 1967, 24–25; Cecilia Rucker, "Students in Jail," *Forward Times*, May 27, 1967.

55. "[Cleve McDowell Statement]," n.d., Papers of the NAACP, Series A, Supplement to Part 23: Legal Department Case Files, 1960–1972, Reel 14, Group V, box 2353.

56. Marriott, *On Black Men*, 40–41.

57. Woods, *Blackhood against the Police Power*; Marriott, *On Black Men*, 40; Fanon, *Black Skin, White Masks*, 118n15.

58. Oliver Cromwell Cox, *Caste, Class, & Race; a Study in Social Dynamics* (New York: Monthly Review Press, 1959), http://archive.org/details/casteclassracest00coxo; Herbert Blumer, "Race Prejudice as a Sense of Group Position," *Pacific Sociological Review* 1, no. 1 (April 1958): 5, https://doi.org/10.2307/1388607.

59. Marriott, *On Black Men*, viii.

60. "Statement of Robert Allison Leroy Lewis, Jr.," n.d., 2–4, box 30, folder 127-30-1, George & Latane Lambert Papers, University of Texas Arlington Libraries Special Collections.

61. "Statement of Clarence Harper," 2–3; "Statement of James Young," 2; "Statement of Gerald Barnes," 4; "Statement of John Booker," 2; "Statement of Howard Williams," 5–7; "Statement of V. J. Hollins," 3–4.

62. "Statement of James Young."

63. "TSU Students' Statement of Personal Injury or Intimidation," n.d., Record Group 453, Records of the U.S. Commission on Civil Rights, National Archives, College Park, Maryland.

64. "Statement of Mrs. Mattie Harbor," n.d., Papers of the NAACP, Series A, Supplement to Part 23: Legal Department Case Files, 1960–1972, Reel 14, Group V, box 2353; "Summary: The Students' Statement of Personal Injury or Intimidation," n.d., box 30, folder 127-30-1, George & Latane Lambert Papers, University of Texas Arlington Libraries Special Collections.

65. *Riots, Civil and Criminal Disorders: Hearings before the Permanent Subcommittee on Investigations of the Committee on Government Operations United States Senate Ninetieth Congress, First Session (Part 3A)* (Washington, DC: Government Printing Office, 1967).

66. "Statement of Theodore Washington," n.d., Papers of the NAACP, Series A, Supplement to Part 23: Legal Department Case Files, 1960–1972, Reel 14, Group V, box 2353.

67. "Statement of John Parker," n.d., Papers of the NAACP, Series A, Supplement to Part 23: Legal Department Case Files, 1960–1972, Reel 14, Group V, box 2353; "Statement of Mrs. Mattie Harbor."

68. Woodard, *The Delectable Negro*, 7, 14, 18; Orlando Patterson, *Slavery and Social Death: A Comparative Study* (Cambridge, MA: Harvard University Press, 1982).

69. McGuire, *At the Dark End of the Street*, 226.

70. "Statement of James Burroughs," n.d., Papers of the NAACP, Series A, Supplement to Part 23: Legal Department Case Files, 1960–1972, Reel 14, Group V, box 2353; "Statement of Anon #5," n.d., box 30, folder 127-30-1, George & Latane Lambert Papers, University of Texas Arlington Libraries Special Collections.

71. "Statement of James Burroughs"; "Statement of Shelton Dotson," n.d., box 30, folder 127-30-1, George & Latane Lambert Papers, University of Texas Arlington Libraries Special Collections; "[Statement VII]," n.d., Papers of the NAACP, Series A, Supplement to Part 23: Legal Department Case Files, 1960–1972, Reel 14, Group V, box 2353.

72. "[Statement Beginning 'Several Girls . . .']," n.d., Papers of the NAACP, Series A, Supplement to Part 23: Legal Department Case Files, 1960–1972, Reel 14, Group V, box 2353; "Statement of William Fontenot," n.d., box 30, folder 127-30-1, George & Latane Lambert Papers, University of Texas Arlington Libraries Special Collections.

73. Marriott, *On Black Men*, x.

74. Blair Justice, "Follow-up (After TSU Gunbattle May 16–17) on Second Questionnaire Done on Police," August 12, 1966, box 33, folder 1, Louie Welch Papers, MSS 0051, HMRC, HPL.

75. Thomas R. Cole, "Eldrewey Stearns: A Forgotten Man," *Galveston Daily News*, March 4, 1990, 6; Michael Berryhill, "Lost in the Cause," *Houston Press*, May 29, 1997, http://www.houstonpress.com/news/lost-in-the-cause-6570813; Berman, *The Strange Demise of Jim Crow*; Behnken, *Fighting Their Own Battles*.

76. Berman, *The Strange Demise of Jim Crow*; Blumer, "Race Prejudice as a Sense of Group Position."

77. "Newest Student Sitdown Move Ended Peacefully," *Houston Post*, March 8, 1960, 1, 6; "Sit-Down Spreads to Fourth Store," *Houston Chronicle*, March 8, 1960, 1, 4; Kellar, *Make Haste Slowly* (e-book); Behnken, *Fighting Their Own Battles*, 76; Michael Anderson,

"Eldreway Stearns and Houston's Student Civil Rights Movement," *Houston History* 14, no. 2 (May 2017): 25; Allison E. Schottenstein, *Changing Perspectives: Black-Jewish Relations in Houston during the Civil Rights Era* (Denton: University of North Texas Press, 2021), 178; Franklin Chandler Davidson, "Negro Politics and the Rise of the Civil Rights Movement in Houston, Texas" (Ph.D. diss., Princeton University, 1969); Berman, *The Strange Demise of Jim Crow*.

78. "Latest News—Flashes," *Baytown Sun*, March 28, 1960, 1, University of North Texas Libraries, Portal to Texas History, texashistory.unt.edu, crediting Sterling Municipal Library; "Ike Ends Triumphant South American Tour," *Taylor Daily Press*, March 3, 1960, 1, 6, University of North Texas Libraries, Portal to Texas History, texashistory.unt.edu, crediting Taylor Public Library; Anderson, "Eldreway Stearns and Houston's Student Civil Rights Movement."

79. David Carroll, "The Subject of Archeology or the Sovereignty of the Episteme," in *Michel Foucault*, ed. Barry Smart (London: Taylor & Francis, 1994), 166.

80. Berman, *The Strange Demise of Jim Crow*; Thomas R. Cole, *No Color Is My Kind: The Life of Eldreway Stearns and the Integration of Houston* (Austin: University of Texas Press, 1997); Carolina Gonzales, "54 Years Ago: Freedom Riders Jailed after Sit-in at Houston's Union Station," *Houston Chronicle*, August 12, 2015, http://www.chron.com/chrontv/this-forgotten-day-in-houston/article/54-years-ago-Freedom-Riders-jailed-after-sit-in-6440082.php; "Rice, TSU Students Fined in 'Stand-Ins,'" *Houston Press*, November 30, 1961, and "[Affidavit of Loretta M. Thompson and Dorothy M. Henry, in Connection with Their Complaint of Prejudicial and Discriminatory Practices to Which They Were Subjected at the Union Station Coffee Shop in the Union Terminal Building at Houston, Texas on May 7, 1961]," May 11, 1961, both in Civil Rights Movement and the Federal Government, Records of the Interstate Commerce Commission on Discrimination in Transportation, 1961–1970, Federal Government Records: Record Group 134, Records of the Interstate Commerce Commission, National Archives, College Park, Maryland.

81. Joseph Pratt, "8F and Many More: Business and Civic Leadership in Modern Houston," *Houston History Review* 1, no. 2 (2004): 2–7, 31–39; H. V. Savitch and John Clayton Thomas, eds., *Big City Politics in Transition* (Thousand Oaks, CA: Sage Publications, 1991), 175.

82. Bullard, *Invisible Houston*, 123; Adair and Robinson, Black Women Oral History Project.

83. Herman Short, interview by Louis J. Marchiafava, June 22, 1976, Houston Oral History Project, Houston Area Digital Archives, Houston Public Library; Mimi Swartz, "The Louie File," *Texas Monthly*, October 1985, 247.

84. Hinton, *From the War on Poverty to the War on Crime*, 100–123; *Riots, Civil and Criminal Disorders: Hearings before the Permanent Subcommittee on Investigations of the Committee on Government Operations United States Senate Ninetieth Congress, First Session (Part 1)*, 110–111; "SCLC Handbook for Freedom Army Recruits" (Civil Rights Movement Veterans, 1964), http://www.crmvet.org/docs/64_sclc_freedomarmy.pdf; Nathan Hare, "Behind the Student Black College Revolt," *Ebony*, August 1967; McLaughlin, *The Long, Hot Summer of 1967*, 61–79; Clayborne Carson, *In Struggle: SNCC and the Black Awakening of the 1960s* (Cambridge, MA: Harvard University Press, 1981); Behnken, *Fighting Their Own Battles*, 156; Lance Hill, *Deacons for Defense: Armed Resistance and the Civil Rights Movement* (Chapel Hill: University of North Carolina Press, 2006); Raymond

Arsenault, *Freedom Riders: 1961 and the Struggle for Racial Justice* (New York: Oxford University Press, 2006); Thomas L. Bynum, *NAACP Youth and the Fight for Black Freedom, 1936–1965* (Knoxville: University of Tennessee Press, 2013).

85. Hinton, *From the War on Poverty to the War on Crime*, 33, 80, 90; *Riots, Civil and Criminal Disorders: Hearings before the Permanent Subcommittee on Investigations of the Committee on Government Operations United States Senate Ninetieth Congress, First Session (Part 3)*, 822; David Brand, "Undercover Cops," *Wall Street Journal*, September 10, 1968, 1.

86. Angela Boswell, *Women in Texas History* (College Station: Texas A&M University Press, 2018), 219; Keith J. Volanto, "Strange Brew: Recent Texas Political, Economic, and Military History," in *Beyond Texas through Time: Breaking Away from Past Interpretations*, ed. Walter Louis Buenger and Arnoldo De León (College Station: Texas A&M University Press, 2011), 95; C. Vann Woodward, "The Strange Career of Jim Crow," in *When Did Southern Segregation Begin: Selections*, ed. John David Smith (New York: Bedford/St. Martin's, 2001), 172; Betty T. Chapman, "Houston Went through Peaceful Segregation Movement in Secret," *Houston Business Journal*, January 22, 2007, https://www.bizjournals.com/houston/stories/2007/01/22/newscolumn1.html; Rupert N. Richardson et al., *Texas: The Lone Star State*, 11th ed. (New York: Routledge, 2021), e-book.

87. "Sit-Down Spreads to Fifth Store," *Houston Chronicle*, March 9, 1960, 1, 16; "Negro Reports Cross Burning in Yard," *Houston Chronicle*, March 15, 1960, 2.

88. J. Rueben Sheeler, "Personalities," n.d., box 2, folder 8, "Published and unpublished works," Dr. John Rueben Sheeler Collection MSS 268, HMRC, HPL.

89. Blair Justice to Louie Welch, August 18, 1966, and Houston Police Department, "Supplementary Offense, Report U-12269, 5023 Arvilla," August 18, 1966, both in box 33, folder 1, Louie Welch Papers, MSS 0051, HMRC, HPL.

90. Woods, *Blackhood against the Police Power*, 231.

91. Clarence A. Laws, "Facing Challenges of the Second Century of Freedom," address delivered before the 26th Annual Convention of the Texas State Conference of the NAACP Branches, Mt. Zion First Baptist Church, San Antonio, Texas, November 9, 1962, box 2.325/A133 [SRH1230000250], Charlsie E. Berly Papers, Dolph Briscoe Center for American History, University of Texas at Austin.

92. Justice to Welch, August 18, 1966.

93. Houston Police Department, "Supplementary Offense, Report U-12269, 5023 Arvilla."

94. Fanon, *Black Skin, White Masks*, 109.

95. Warren, *Ontological Terror*, 64.

96. Kazanjian, "Scenes of Speculation," 79.

97. Blair Justice to Louie Welch, "[Questionnaires at Black Muslim Headquarters, 3400 Polk - Memo]," August 15, 1966, box 33, folder 1, Louie Welch Papers, MSS 0051, HMRC, HPL.

98. Blair Justice to Louie Welch, "Sunnyside Episode and Subsequent Fire-Bombings," October 14, 1967, box 33, folder 1, Louie Welch Papers, MSS 0051, HMRC, HPL.

99. Blair Justice to Louie Welch, "[Street Level Survey]," August 12, 1966, box 33, folder 1, Louie Welch Papers, MSS 0051, HMRC, HPL.

100. Byrd, *Captives and Voyagers*, 10; Hartman, "The Dead Book Revisited," 214.

101. Charles E. Cobb Jr., *This Nonviolent Stuff'll Get You Killed: How Guns Made the Civil Rights Movement Possible* (New York: Basic Books, 2014), 7; Robert F. Williams, *Negroes with Guns* (Detroit: Wayne State University Press, 1998); Jasmin A. Young,

"Strapped: A Historical Analysis of Black Women and Armed Resistance, 1959–1979" (Ph.D. diss., Rutgers University, 2018).

102. Jones, *The Red Diary*, 138; Jan Lin, *The Power of Urban Ethnic Places: Cultural Heritage and Community Life* (New York: Routledge, 2010); Joe R. Feagin, *Free Enterprise City: Houston in Political-Economic Perspective* (New Brunswick, NJ: Rutgers University Press, 1988), 248; Richard West, "Only the Strong Survive," *Texas Monthly*, February 1979, 175.

103. Franklin, "[Statement of Trazawell Franklin]," 4.

104. Kirkpatrick, "The Police Attack at Texas Southern," 8; Behnken, *Fighting Their Own Battles*, 157; "The Truth about Texas Southern University & S.N.C.C.," September 24, 1967, folder TSU (5) Five Defense Fund, TSU Riot Collection, and "News Release: Support the T.S.U. Five," n.d., folder T.S.U. Five & Their Indictment for Murder and Two Assaults to "MURDER," both in Department of Special Collections, Robert J. Terry Library, Texas Southern University; Franklin, "[Statement of Trazawell Franklin]," 5.

105. Historian Nicholas Johnson argues that the "black tradition of arms" never faded in American history—that prevailing narratives about black people's commitment to nonviolence has unjustifiably misrepresented the prevalence of armed self-defense, especially among rural black southerners. Nicholas Johnson, *Negroes and the Gun: The Black Tradition of Arms* (Amherst, NY: Prometheus Books, 2014); Timothy B. Tyson, *Radio Free Dixie: Robert F. Williams and the Roots of Black Power* (Chapel Hill: University of North Carolina Press, 1999), 149; Joshua Bloom and Waldo E. Martin Jr., *Black against Empire: The History and Politics of the Black Panther Party* (Berkeley: University of California Press, 2016).

106. Angela Frye Keaton, "Unholstered and Unquestioned: The Rise of Post-World War II American Gun Cultures" (Ph.D. diss., University of Tennessee, Knoxville, 2006), 60; Christopher Barry Strain, "Civil Rights and Self-Defense: The Fiction of Nonviolence, 1955–1968" (Ph.D. diss., University of California, Berkeley, 2000); Simon Wendt, "Protection or Path toward Revolution? Black Power and Self-Defense," *Souls: A Critical Journal of Black Politics, Culture, and Society* 9, no. 4 (2007): 320–332; Simon Wendt, "'They Finally Found Out That We Really Are Men': Violence, Non-Violence and Black Manhood in the Civil Rights Era," *Gender and History* 19, no. 3 (November 2007): 543–564; Nikol G. Alexander-Floyd, "'We Shall Have Our Manhood:' Black Macho, Black Nationalism, and the Million Man March," *Meridians* 3, no. 2 (2003): 171–203.

107. Young, "Strapped."

108. Hartman, "Venus in Two Acts," 12.

109. Waller, "[Statement of Douglas Wayne Waller]"; Nichols, "[Statement of Floyd Nichols]."

110. Nichols, "[Statement of Floyd Nichols]," 2.

111. Marriott, *On Black Men*; Marriott, *Whither Fanon?* 213; Sexton, "Afro-Pessimism"; Hartman and Wilderson, "The Position of the Unthought."

112. Warren, *Ontological Terror*, e-book.

113. "Statement of O. C. Brown," n.d., box 30, folder 127-30-1, George & Latane Lambert Papers, University of Texas Arlington Libraries Special Collections; Kirkpatrick, "The Police Attack at Texas Southern," 8; Behnken, *Fighting Their Own Battles*, 157; "The Truth about Texas Southern University & S.N.C.C."; "News Release: Support the T.S.U. Five"; Franklin, "[Statement of Trazawell Franklin]," 5; Miron J. Clay-Gilmore, "'This Is the Nature of the Threat!': Black Male Gendercide, Social Dominance Theory, and the Evolutionary Origins of Inter-Group Conflict," *Journal of Black Sexuality and Relationships* 8, no. 4 (2022): 25–53.

114. McLaughlin, *The Long, Hot Summer of 1967*, lxxii; Waller, "[Statement of Douglas Wayne Waller]," 1–2; Nichols, "[Statement of Floyd Nichols]," 2.

115. Waller, "[Statement of Douglas Wayne Waller]," 1–2; Nichols, "[Statement of Floyd Nichols]," 2; Franklin, "[Statement of Trazawell Franklin]"; "[Statement of Charles Freeman]"; "[Handwritten Statement, Possibly of David Minor]."

116. Irene Salinas, "UH COBRRs Arrested, Freed in Dump Protest," *Daily Cougar*, May 18, 1967, 1, University of Houston Special Collections; Gene Locke, interview by David Goldstein; McLaughlin, *The Long, Hot Summer of 1967*; Robert D. Bullard, "The Mountains of Houston: Environmental Justice and the Politics of Garbage," *Cite: The Architecture + Design Review of Houston* 93 (2014): 30. COBRR was founded at UH "for the purpose of bettering race relations in Academic, Social, and Political areas on this, the University of Houston campus." "University of Houston Committee on Better Race Relations Constitution," n.d., folder T.S.U. Five & Their Indictment for Murder and Two Assaults to "MURDER," Department of Special Collections, Robert J. Terry Library, Texas Southern University.

117. Franklin, "[Statement of Trazawell Franklin]," 6; Nichols, "[Statement of Floyd Nichols]," 3.

118. "Statement of O. C. Brown," 2; Wendell Thompson and Cleve McDowell, July 8, 1967, and Virgie Eaton and Cleve McDowell, July 8, 1967, both in Papers of the NAACP, Series A, Supplement to Part 23: Legal Department Case Files, 1960–1972, Reel 14, Group V, box 2353.

119. Byrd, *Captives and Voyagers*, 104, 175.

120. Waller, "[Statement of Douglas Wayne Waller]," 1–2; Nichols, "[Statement of Floyd Nichols]," 2; Franklin, "[Statement of Trazawell Franklin]"; "[Statement of Charles Freeman]," 2; "[Handwritten Statement, Possibly of David Minor]."

121. "Statement of O. C. Brown," 2; Thompson and McDowell, interview; Eaton and McDowell, interview.

122. Phelps, *A People's War on Poverty*; Pitre, *In Struggle against Jim Crow*.

123. Hartman, *Scenes of Subjection*, 55.

124. Seigel, *Violence Work*.

125. Wynter, "The Re-Enchantment of Humanism," 169.

126. Fanon, *Black Skin, White Masks*, 176.

127. James H. Cone, *A Black Theology of Liberation* (Maryknoll, NY: Orbis Books, 2010), ix; Lewis Gordon, ed., *Existence in Black: An Anthology of Black Existential Philosophy*, 2nd ed. (New York: Routledge, 1986), 67.

128. Gordon, "Race, Biraciality, and Mixed Race," 164.

129. Warren, *Ontological Terror*, 98.

Coda

1. Texas Commission on Environmental Quality, "Joint Groundwater Monitoring and Contamination Report—2015," June 2016, https://static.texastribune.org/media/documents/056-15.pdf; John D. Harden, "Houston Officials Back Off Placing New Sunnyside Center near Former Landfill," *Houston Chronicle*, February 9, 2018, https://www.chron.com/news/houston-texas/article/City-Hall-considers-new-location-for-Sunnyside-12566052.php; Steve Jansen, "Is the Sunnyside Multi-Service Center About to Move to the Old Dump? [UPDATED]," *Houston Press*, December 14, 2016, https://www.houstonpress.com/news/is-the-sunnyside-multi-service-center-about-to-move-to

-the-old-dump-updated-9022040; Dave Fehling, "Will a New Waste Facility Help or Hurt a Houston Neighborhood?" *Houston Public Media*, February 16, 2015, https://www.houstonpublicmedia.org/articles/news/2015/02/16/58038/will-a-new-waste-facility-help-or-hurt-a-houston-neighborhood/; Spears, *Baptized in PCBs*; Bullard, *Dumping in Dixie*; Dorceta Taylor, *Toxic Communities: Environmental Racism, Industrial Pollution, and Residential Mobility* (New York: NYU Press, 2014); Hannah Dellinger, "'It's Very Scary': Childhood Leukemia Cluster Frightens Neighborhood in Houston's Fifth Ward," *Houston Chronicle*, January 22, 2021, https://www.houstonchronicle.com/news/houston-texas/environment/article/cancer-cluster-fifth-ward-houston-15885717.php; Benjamin Wermund, "'They Are Being Exposed': Experts Fear Lead Poisoning Makes Fifth Ward One of 'Hundreds of Flints,'" *Houston Chronicle*, October 11, 2021, https://www.houstonchronicle.com/politics/texas/article/They-are-being-exposed-Experts-fear-lead-16519913.php.

2. U.S. Department of Housing and Urban Development to Sylvester Turner, "Letter Finding Noncompliance with Title VI of the Civil Rights Act of 1964 Case Number: 06-16-R001-6," January 11, 2017, https://www.scribd.com/document/336506979/HUD-letter-to-Mayor-Sylvester-Turner-find-civil-rights-violations.

3. Cheryl Harris, "Whiteness as Property," in *Black on White: Black Writers on What It Means to Be White*, ed. David R. Roediger (New York: Schocken, 1999), 103–118; David R. Harris, "'Property Values Drop When Blacks Move In, Because . . .': Racial and Socioeconomic Determinants of Neighborhood Desirability," *American Sociological Review* 64, no. 3 (1999): 461–479, https://doi.org/10.2307/2657496.

4. "BREAKING: HUD Says Houston Broke Law Nixing Affordable Housing Complex," Houston Public Media, January 13, 2017, https://www.houstonpublicmedia.org/articles/news/2017/01/13/183650/breaking-hud-says-houston-broke-law-nixing-affordable-housing-complex/.

5. "BREAKING: HUD Says Houston Broke Law Nixing Affordable Housing Complex."

6. Hartman, *Scenes of Subjection*, 116.

7. Courtney Carpenter and Jeff Ehling, "$7.5 Million Grant to Help Underserved Achieve Home Ownership in Houston Area," ABC13 Houston, September 6, 2022, https://abc13.com/home-ownership-houston-texas-harris-county-housing-house-sales-wealth-opportunities-restored-through-homeownership-grant/12204485/.

8. "Public Safety Leads Expenditures on Proposed City of Houston Budget," ABC13 Houston, May 10, 2022, https://abc13.com/houston-budget-public-safety-crime-fiscal-year/11835212/; "City of Houston Proposed Operating Budget for the Period July 1, 2022 to June 30, 2023," 2022, copy in author's possession.

9. Alexander, *The New Jim Crow*, 82.

10. "City of Houston Adopted Operating Budget for the Period July 1, 2022 to June 30, 2023," 2022, X–134, https://www.houstontx.gov/budget/23budadopt/FY2023_Adopted_Budget.pdf.

11. Anderson, *The Education of Blacks in the South*.

12. In 2022, classified personnel (5,300 employees) received 91 percent of the personnel budget, about $798 million, while civilian personnel (1,200 support staff) received only 9 percent of the same budget, or about $79 million. "U.S. Census Bureau QuickFacts: Houston City, Texas," accessed December 6, 2022, https://www.census.gov/quickfacts/fact/table/houstoncitytexas/RHI725221; Troy Finner and Rhonda Smith, "Houston Police Department FY 2022 Budget Workshop Presentation," May 18, 2021, https://www

.houstontx.gov/council/committees/fy22workshops/police.pdf; Troy Finner and Rhonda Smith, "Houston Police Department FY 2023 Budget Workshop Presentation," May 17, 2022, https://www.houstontx.gov/council/committees/fy23workshops/police.pd; "Chief Troy Finner's Page," accessed December 6, 2022, https://www.houstontx.gov/police/chief/.

13. Thomas D. Boston, "Segmented Labor Markets: New Evidence from a Study of Four Race-Gender Groups," *Industrial and Labor Relations Review* 44, no. 1 (1990): 99–115, https://doi.org/10.2307/2523432; André Ndobo et al., "The Ethno-Racial Segmentation Jobs: The Impacts of the Occupational Stereotypes on Hiring Decisions," *Journal of Social Psychology* 158, no. 6 (November 2018): 663–679, https://doi.org/10.1080/00224545.2017.1389685.

14. City of Houston, "One Safe Houston Funding Breakdown," November 2022, https://www.houstontx.gov/onesafehouston/public/documents/OSH-Funding-Breakdown-2022-november.pdf.

15. "City of Houston Adopted Operating Budget for the Period July 1, 2022 to June 30, 2023," III–16.

16. "City of Houston Adopted Operating Budget for the Period July 1, 2022 to June 30, 2023," XIII–3.

17. "City of Houston Adopted Operating Budget for the Period July 1, 2022 to June 30, 2023."

18. City of Houston, "One Safe Houston: Violent and Overall Crime Decreasing in Houston," October 2022, https://www.houstontx.gov/onesafehouston/public/documents/successes/overall-decrease-in-violent-crime.pdf.

19. Blair Justice to Louie Welch, "Chamber Leaders," November 7, 1966, Blair Justice to Louie Welch, "Aldine Race Trouble," September 19, 1966, and Blair Justice to Louie Welch, August 24, 1966, all in box 33, folder 1, Louie Welch Papers, MSS 0051, HMRC, HPL.

20. Blair Justice to Herman Short, "Chamber Leaders," September 21, 1966, box 33, folder 1, Louie Welch Papers, MSS 0051, HMRC, HPL.

21. Edwin C. Breeden, "Educational Politics and the Making of School Desegregation Policy in Houston, Texas" (Ph.D. diss., Rice University, 2017); Kellar, *Make Haste Slowly*; Laura Isensee, "Why Houston's Gifted and Talented Classes Are Considered 'Segregated,'" Houston Public Media, September 8, 2015, https://www.houstonpublicmedia.org/articles/news/2015/09/08/120620/why-houstons-gifted-and-talented-classes-are-considered-segregated/; Annegret Staiger, "Whiteness as Giftedness: Racial Formation at an Urban High School," *Social Problems* 51, no. 2 (May 1, 2004): 161–181, https://doi.org/10.1525/sp.2004.51.2.161.

22. Ruiz Rosanna, "Rail Plan for TSU Draws Concern—Some Fear Using Wheeler for the Line Would Be Disruptive," *Houston Chronicle*, July 25, 2006, sec. B, 3; "School Segregation Still Exists, Report Says," FOX 26 Houston, January 10, 2018, https://www.fox26houston.com/news/school-segregation-still-exists-report-says.

23. "United States Court Order, Western District of Texas, Austin Division in Patrick Benjamin, et al. vs. George W. Bush, Jr., et al.," May 26, 1999, General Counsel Litigation Files: *Benjamin v. Bush*, May–June 1999, Archives and Information Services Division, Texas State Library and Archives Commission, Records of Governor George W. Bush; "Original Complaint [United States District Court, Western District of Texas, Austin Division in Patrick Benjamin, et al. vs. George W. Bush, Jr., et al.]," May 26, 1999, General Counsel Litigation Files: *Benjamin v. Bush*, May–June 1999 2 of 3, Archives and

Information Services Division, Texas State Library and Archives Commission, Records of Governor George W. Bush; "Texas Southern University: The Stepchild of the Texas Higher Education System," *Journal of Blacks in Higher Education* no. 25 (1999): 65, https://doi.org/10.2307/2999387.

24. H. A. Bullock, "Tomorrow's Challenge: High Court Gives Us Gap to Bridge," *Houston Informer*, May 29, 1954, 12.

25. Alan David Freeman, "Legitimizing Racial Discrimination through Antidiscrimination Law: A Critical Review of Supreme Court Doctrine," in *Critical Race Theory: The Key Writings That Formed the Movement*, ed. Kimberlé Crenshaw et al. (New York: New Press, 1995), 29–45; Bruce A. Ackerman, *What Brown v. Board of Education Should Have Said: The Nation's Top Legal Experts Rewrite America's Landmark Civil Rights Decision* (New York: NYU Press, 2001); Baum, *Brown in Baltimore*; Charles T. Clotfelter, *After Brown: The Rise and Retreat of School Desegregation* (Princeton, NJ: Princeton University Press, 2004).

26. Robert T. Chase, "Civil Rights on the Cell Block: Race, Reform, and Violence in Texas Prisons and the Nation, 1945–1990" (Ph.D. diss., University of Maryland, College Park, 2009); Douglas A. Blackmon, *Slavery by Another Name: The Re-Enslavement of Black Americans from the Civil War to World War II* (New York: Doubleday, 2008); Robert Perkinson, *Texas Tough: The Rise of America's Prison Empire* (New York: Metropolitan Books, 2010); Steve Bickerstaff, *Lines in the Sand: Congressional Redistricting in Texas and the Downfall of Tom DeLay* (Austin: University of Texas Press, 2010).

27. "The Truth about Texas Southern University & S.N.C.C."

28. Mari J. Matsuda, "Looking to the Bottom: Critical Legal Studies and Reparations Minority Critiques of the Critical Legal Studies Movement," *Harvard Civil Rights–Civil Liberties Law Review* 22, no. 2 (1987): 324–325.

29. George B. Nesbitt, "Relocating Negroes from Urban Slum Clearance Sites," *Land Economics* 25, no. 3 (1949): 275–288, https://doi.org/10.2307/3144797; "Slums Are Barrier to City's Growth"; John F. Bauman, *Public Housing, Race, and Renewal: Urban Planning in Philadelphia, 1920–1974* (Philadelphia: Temple University Press, 1987); Connolly, *A World More Concrete*; Shelton, *Power Moves*.

30. Ben Raffield, "Broken Worlds: Towards an Archaeology of the Shatter Zone," *Journal of Archaeological Method and Theory* 28, no. 3 (September 1, 2021): 871–910, https://doi.org/10.1007/s10816-021-09520-y; Wilderson, *Red, White & Black*.

31. Mary Poole, *The Segregated Origins of Social Security: African Americans and the Welfare State* (Chapel Hill: University of North Carolina Press, 2006), 7.

32. Bernadette Rabuy and Peter Wagner, "Following the Money of Mass Incarceration," *Prison Policy Initiative*, January 25, 2017, https://www.prisonpolicy.org/reports/money.html; Christian Henrichson and Ruth Delaney, "The Price of Prisons: What Incarceration Costs Taxpayers," *Federal Sentencing Reporter* 25, no. 1 (2012): 68–80, https://doi.org/10.1525/fsr.2012.25.1.68.

33. Shawn Moulton, "Does Increased Funding for Homeless Programs Reduce Chronic Homelessness?" *Southern Economic Journal* 79, no. 3 (2013): 802.

34. Melanie Hanson, "How Much Would Free College Cost? 2022 Cost Analysis," *Education Data Initiative*, December 8, 2021, https://educationdata.org/how-much-would-free-college-cost; Timothy J Bartik et al., "Economic Benefits and Costs of Tuition-Free College in Illinois" (prepared for the Joyce Foundation and the Illinois Governor's Office, 2021), 15, https://research.upjohn.org/reports/267.

35. Jeffrey T. Denning, "College on the Cheap: Consequences of Community College Tuition Reductions," *American Economic Journal: Economic Policy* 9, no. 2 (2017): 186.

36. Jason Delisle and Andrés Bernasconi, "Lessons from Chile's Transition to Free College," *Evidence Speaks Reports* 2, no. 43 (March 15, 2018).

37. House Report 117–118, "National Defense Authorization Act for Fiscal Year 2022 [Congressional Record]" (Washington, DC: Government Printing Office, September 10, 2021).

38. House Report 117–118, "Joint Explanatory Statement to Accompany the James M. Inhofe National Defense Authorization Act for Fiscal Year 2023" (United States Committee on Armed Services, December 6, 2022), https://www.armed-services.senate.gov/press-releases/sasc-and-hasc-release-text-of-fy23-ndaa-agreement.

39. Toni Cade Bambara, *Deep Sightings and Rescue Missions: Fiction, Essays, and Conversations* (New York: Knopf Doubleday Publishing Group, 2009), 249.

40. Jeremy J. Gibbs, "Religious Conflict, Sexual Identity, and Suicidal Behaviors among LGBT Young Adults," *Archives of Suicide Research* 19, no. 4 (2015): 472–488, https://doi.org/10.1080/13811118.2015.1004476.

41. Cynthia Deitle Leonardatos, "California's Attempts to Disarm the Black Panthers," *San Diego Law Review* 36, no. 4 (1999): 947–996; Michael Siegel et al., "The Impact of State Firearm Laws on Homicide and Suicide Deaths in the USA, 1991–2016: A Panel Study," *Journal of General Internal Medicine* 34, no. 10 (October 1, 2019): 2021–2028, https://doi.org/10.1007/s11606-019-04922-x; Michael Luca, Deepak Malhotra, and Christopher Poliquin, "Handgun Waiting Periods Reduce Gun Deaths," *Proceedings of the National Academy of Sciences* 114, no. 46 (November 14, 2017): 12162–12165, https://doi.org/10.1073/pnas.1619896114; A. L. Beautrais, D. M. Fergusson, and L. J. Horwood, "Firearms Legislation and Reductions in Firearm-Related Suicide Deaths in New Zealand," *Australian & New Zealand Journal of Psychiatry* 40, no. 3 (March 1, 2006): 253–259, https://doi.org/10.1080/j.1440-1614.2006.01782.x.

INDEX

Page numbers in italics refer to figures and maps.

accommodationism, 141, 145, 160
Acres Homes, 32, 42–45
Acres Homes Transit Company, 44
activism: boycotts, 44, 71, 211; community activism, 172, 201; protests, 165, 171–173, 178, 189–190, 198–200; student activism, 165, 167–168, 172–174, 189–190, 211
Adair, Christia: childhood of, 34–35, 38–39; civil rights work, 52; correspondences, 50–51; Dorcas Home for Colored Girls, 45–46; gender and, 54–55; move to Houston, 42; NAACP and, 34, 46–47; politics of, 31, 41; rape case investigations, 53–54; Sakowitz investigation, 49–50; teaching career of, 39–40; on term "black," 51; voting activism, 41–42; on womanhood, 33–34, 37, 39, 51–52; on the women's liberation movement, 38–39
Adair, Elbert, 39–42
African American Urban History since World War II (Kusmer and Trotter), 2
Afropessimism, 18–27, 69, 89, 169–170, 211
Agamben, Giorgio, 23
agency: history and, 4, 13, 220n40; humanity and, 19–21, 23, 117; lack of, 16, 18, 25, 209; presumption of, 168–169; racialization of, 221n60
Alexander, Michelle, 207
Alien Registration Act, 77
Alldred, Pam, 181

Allen, Earl, 178
American Dream, 97–98, 103–104, 156, 158
Americanism, 76–77, 99, 154, 158–159
American Rescue Plan Act, 208
An American Dilemma (Myrdal), 52–53, 124
Anderson, James, 141
annexation, 44–45, 125–126, 244n121
anti-blackness: Afropessimism and, 18; anti-nothing and, 189; black spaces and, 128; capture of, 4, 27, 117, 167, 201–202, 220n40; denialism of, 87; liberal humanism and, 218n14; manhood and, 135; reproduction of, 137–138; segregation and, 2–3, 78, 102; social structure and, 50, 52, 90, 116, 211; static nature of, 11–13, 16–17, 196, 201; subordination by, 187–188; the term, 10; tropes of, 79; urban history and, 97–98. *See also* blackness
anti-black terror, 95, 99, 164–166, 183–184, 192–197
anti-disciplinary, 4, 19, 28, 61, 89, 182
anti-ethics, 18, 26–27, 195, 202–203
anti-racism, 20–21, 89–90, 173
Archer, Charles, 65
archives, 23–25, 71, 89, 164–168, 194
armed defense, 176, 193, 196–198, 200, 202–203, 260n105
Ashanti Pioneer, 77
asset forfeiture, 207–208
Asset Forfeiture Fund, 207

assimilation, 96–97, 159
Associated Negro Press, 120, 151
Atlanta, Georgia, 2, 6–8, *7*, 47

Baker, Alvin, 61–62, 80
Bambara, Toni Cade, 214
Barnett, Claude A., 151, 153–154
Batese family, 198, 201
Bell, Derrick, 15, 17, 52
Bell, Spurgeon, 82, 250n74
Benjamin v. Bush, 210
Benskin, Don, 181
black, the term, 51, 140
black bodies, 33, 47–49, 123, 180–181, 186–187, 199
Blackburn, Robin, 95
black businesses, 43, 114–115, 125, 133–134, 155–156
black communities: communal care in, 202–203; income diversity in, 43; inner-core neighborhoods, 5–6; living conditions in, 6, 43–44, 110, 197, 205, 241n98; locations of, 6, 64; population density, 7, *10*, 43; stigmas of, 119–121; suburbs, 97–98, 124–127
black criminality, 65, 110, 128–129
blackened, the term, 253n13
blackened world, 13, 96, 203–204
black image, 33, 48–50, 61–62, 102. *See also* Negro, the
Black Lives Movement, 89–90
black male studies, 22, 85, 160, 180–183, 187–188, 199
black men, 63, 67, 74, 180–183, 186–188
black middle class, 124, 241n98
black neighborhoods. *See* black communities
blackness: capture of, 99; as criminal, 65, 110, 128–129; fungibility of, 36; as nothingness, 19, 94, 116–117; politics and, 99, 183, 201; the term, 16, 128; whiteness in relation to, 35, 86, 90–91, 111, 116–117, 188–189
black nihilism, 95, 132, 171
black optimism, 27, 170–171, 195
black ordinary, 196, 203
Black Panther Party, 215

black people: experiences of, 36, 38–39, 115, 193, 211–212; fungibility of, 21–22, 35; nonexistence of, 48, 53, 73, 101; as non-human, 59–60, 74, 116
black police officers, 61–62, 176–177
black politics, 55, 69, 166–167
Black Power Freedom Army, 191
black press, 53, 62, 119, 134, 150–151, 182
black revolutionary thought, 22, 135, 147
black spaces, 110–112, 116, 123, 126–129, 149, 173
Black Studies, 15–17, 47, 169
black women, 33–38, 40–42, 47, 49–52, 198, 214
Blair, Albert, 175
Blaylock, Robert G., 173, 175–177, 180
Bodenheimer, Billy, 63–67
bombing of Caesar home, 93–95, 107–109. *See also* Caesar home
Booker, John, 184
boycotts, 44, 71, 211. *See also* activism
Bromell, Nick, 74
Brooks, Richard, 110–111
Broussard, John, 75
Brown, Wendy, 136
Brown v. Board of Education, 3, 139, 210
Bullard, Robert D., 126, 244n124
Bullock, Henry Allen, 210–211
Burroughs, James, 187–189
Busby, Leo, 61–62
buses, 44, 51, 57, 70–71, 73, 125
Bush, George Jr., 209–210
Butler, William D., 174–176, 179
Byrd, Alex, 167–169, 196, 200–201

Caesar, Donald, 108
Caesar, Dorothy, 27–28, 100, 107, 165
Caesar, Jack, 27–28, 100, 107–108, 165
Caesar home: attempted buyout of, 104–105; bombing of, 93–94, 107–109, 165; defense of, 108–109; harassment of family, 103–104; purchase of, 100–102
capitalism, 2, 59–60, 71, 77, 96, 117, 158
Captives and Voyagers (Byrd), 167–168
capture: of anti-blackness, 4, 27, 117, 167, 201–202, 220n40; of the black

image, 49–50, 102; of blackness, 99; of democracy, 72–73, 89–90, 99, 215; disciplinary capture, 14–15, 18, 61, 88–91; of double taxation, 141; of gender, 27, 38, 54–55, 129, 133, 146, 154; of idea of the law, 60, 94, 132; of the imagination, 211; of Jim Crow, 140; of liberal humanism, 34, 61–62; of liberal individualism, 154; narrative capture, 3–4, 13, 17, 24–25, 108, 222n83; of the Negro, 48–50; of nonviolence, 211; of oral histories, 117; of race, 4, 59, 63, 99, 103–104, 117, 129; of racialization, 155; resistance and, 60–61, 103–104; subjective capture, 3–4, 13, 24, 26; sustaining, 55; the term, 3–4, 220n40; of theodicy, 14–15, 18, 155, 160
Carlson, Liane, 14
Carnegie Library, 52
Carter v. Texas, 80
Chandler, Nahum, 25
Child Safety Fund, 207
Christian democracy, 137, 155
Christianity, 51, 107, 134–135, 137, 155, 157
Christian theodicy, 14–15, 18, 155, 160
Citizens Committee of Riverside Terrace and Other Areas, 106
citizenship, 60–61, 78, 121–122, 137, 139–140, 155
civil rights: approaches to, 139–148; Civil Rights Act of 1964, 68–69; civil rights legislation, 3, 50–52, 87; civil rights movement, 27, 61, 89–90, 191, 203; individualism and, 159–160
Clayson, William, 165
Clemons, David Arthur, 65
Cleveland, Sidney E., 166
Clinton Park, 124–127
Clinton Park Development Company (CPDC), 124
clothing stores, 49–50
Cobb, Charles E. Jr., 196–197
collectivism, 155–156, 167–168
Collins, Luther, 84–86
color blind society, 51, 156–159, 206, 212–213

color line, 70
Comet Rice Company, 197
Committee on Better Race Relations (COBRR), 172
communal care, 198, 200–203
communism, 47, 76–78, 137, 151, 250n70
community survey, 195–196, 208–209
Constitution. *See* United States Constitution
context in history, 15, 90, 166
contingency, 14–15, 88, 90, 155, 160, 220n40
Cox, Oliver Cromwell, 183
Crawford, George, 86
Crawford Elementary School, 118, 143
crime, 65, 119– 121, 123–124, 158, 206
Criminal Intelligence Division, 191–192
criminal legal system, 65, 78, 81, 84, 86–87, 131
critical fabulation, 24, 66–67, 89, 168–169, 194
critical legal studies, 60, 67–68, 90, 95, 157
critical race theory, 15, 17, 27, 52, 86
cross burning, 192, 196, 198
cultural racism, 120

Daniels, Christia. *See* Adair, Christia
Davis, Carl Dewey "Red," 93–94, 98, 102, 109, 131
Davis, George, 86
Davis, Lucille, 192–196, 203
Davis, Sam W., 58, 63, 78, 80–83, 89
Deacons for Defense, 191
death penalty, 65, 82–87, 90, 211
death, threat of, 74–75, 167, 169–170, 196–199
deed covenants, 100
Delectable Negro, The (Woodward), 186
democracy: black people and, 60–61, 68–69, 77–78, 104; capture of, 72–73, 89–90, 99, 215; Christian democracy, 137; individualism and, 157; inevitability of, 159–160; raceless democracy, 3, 13, 137–138, 154–155, 160–161
democratic equality, 96, 132

Dennis v. United States, 77
Dent, Thomas H., 78–80, 82–83
desegregation, 68, 110–111, 139–148, 190, 192, 206, 209–210
Detroit, Michigan, 6–8, *7, 9, 10, 11*
Dillon, Elizabeth Maddock, 101
Dilworth, Richardson, 119
disciplinary capture, 14–15, 18, 61, 88–91
domestic labor, 46–47, *64*, 100–101, 237n21
Dorcas Home for Colored Girls, 32, 34, 42, 45–46
Dorr, Lisa Lindquist, 85
double taxation, 141–142, 148, 160
Doyle, Henry, 78–79
Du Bois, W. E. B.: on history, 25; on ignorance, 227n63; on liberalism, 60; *Philadelphia Negro, The*, 121; on race, 33, 51, 145; socialism and, 77, 157–158; *Souls of Black Folk*, 74, 157
due process, 54, 79, 82, 86–87, 192
dumps, 44, 126, 205
Dupree, Anna, 115, 149
Dupree, Clarence, 115, 149
Durham, William J., 78–79, 142

Eastex Freeway (U.S. 59), 118, 197
East Freeway (I-10), 197
economics, 1–2, 36, 39, 97, 119, 123. *See also* political economy
education: higher education, 140, 148–150, 209, 212–214; and ignorance, 227n63; inequality in, 13; level of, 6; moral education, 49, 51–52, 55, 107; schools, 113, 148–150; segregation in, 140–146, 209–210
Education of a Storyteller, The (Bambara), 214
Egerton, John, 140
Ehrenhalt, Alan, 113
El Dorado Ballroom, 115
emancipation, 40–41, 160, 169–170, 193
Emancipation Park, 113
eminent domain, 112–113
encroachment, 2, 68, 106–107, 132, 238n48
Enlightenment, 17, 49
environmental hazards, 44, 126–127, 171, 197, 205
equalization, 142, 145–146, 149, 153
Equal Protection Clause, 80, 83, 87, 136, 140
Erickson, Ansley, 13
Errante, Antoinette, 115–116
European immigrants, 43

fair trial, 75–76, 78–79, 86–88, 165
false confessions, 54, 64–66, 69–70, 75, 80
Fanon, Frantz, 16, 47–49, 104, 116–117, 147, 183, 194, 203
feminine, 33, 135, 154, 246n23
Fidelity (suburb), 124–127
Fifth Ward, 113, 118, 123, 197, 205
Floyd, George, 27, 89
Foreign Agent Registration Act, 77
forfeiture, 207–208
Foucauldian methodology, 97–98, 190
Fourteenth Amendment, 68–69, 80, 83, 87, 122, 140
Fourth Ward, *29*, 63, *64*, 112–113, 123
Fox, Nick J., 181
Franklin, Trazawell, 174, 176, 179–180, 198–200
Fredrickson, George, 48
freedom, 19, 26, 136, 156, 174–175, 193–195
Freeman, Charles, 175, 179–180
free will, 147, 170–171
Freud, Sigmund, 48
Friends of SNCC, 172, 191–192, 211
Furman v. Georgia, 65

Gatesville School for Boys, 65
gender: capture of, 27, 38, 54–55, 129, 133, 146, 154; fungibility, 246n23; gendercide, 199; gender roles, 52–53, 129, 133; as identity, 37; ideology, 32, 51, 135; meanings of, 36–37; norms, 38; race and, 38–39, 52–55, 129, 133–135; rape and, 64–66, 181
Ginsburg, Jack, 104–105
Gordon, Lewis, 13, 96
grand jury commissions, 80–82
grassroots organization, 68

Greater Riverside Terrace Homeowners' Association, 93, 104–105
Green Pond, 63–64, *64*
Green Pond Seven, 60, 63–68
Guinier, Lani, 158
guns, 176, 193, 196–198, 200, 202–203, 260n105

Haley, Sarah, 46
Hall, Clarence, 184–185
Hancock, Gordon Blaine, 120, 241n98
Harding, William, 41
Hardy, Leon, 175
Harris County, *7*
Harris County Community Action Association, 178, 191
Harris County Council of Organizations (HCCO), 86, 118, 142–143, 191, 209
Harris County Sheriff's Department, 61–62, 75
Hartman, Saidiya: on blackness, 16–17; critical fabulation, 24, 66–67, 89, 168–169; on fugitivity, 235n112; on the hold, 28, 32, 201; on humanity, 20; on individuality, 110; on mortality, 167, 196; *Scenes of Subjection*, 12; on violence, 12, 164; on white supremacy, 135–136
Hawkins, Ben, 151–152
Hawkins, Michael, 21
HBCUs (historically black colleges and universities), 38, 172, 209
Heavenly Houston, 58–59, 87–88, 96, 103, 107–108, 209
Herman, Susan N., 86
higher education, 140, 148–150, 209, 212–214
highways: construction of, 112, 118, 197, 210, 237n25; Eastex Freeway (U.S. 59), 118, 197; East Freeway (I-10), 197; I-45, 112–113; State Highway 288 (South Freeway), 111, 237n25
Hilliard, Mattie Marcher, 105
Hilliard, Sid, 47, 86, 118, 142–144, 151, 245n4
historically black colleges and universities (HBCUs), 38, 172, 209

history: as ahistorical, 20–21; antidisciplinary, 4, 22, 26; change over time, 11–17, 20, 28, 211, 220n40; creation of, 21, 22, 89, 165; disciplinary capture, 14–15, 18, 61, 88–91; discipline of, 12, 19–20, 216, 220n40; historical narration, 89, 173–174; linear chronology and, 23, 220n40; and photography, 184; realism, 88–89; structural positionality, 25
Hodge, Frederic, 102
Hofheinz, Roy, 52, 107, 109, 131
Hoggatt, Rodney, 100, 105
hold, the, 32–33, 51, 164, 167, 185, 189, 201–203
Hollins, V. J., 176, 185
Holmes Road Dump, 126, 171, 200, 205
home buyout efforts, 104–105, 108
homelessness, 208, 212
home ownership, 42–43, 102–104, 112, *118*, 132, 207
home vacancies, 7, *9*, 111–112
homoeroticism, 186–187
homoerotic violence, 187
homogenization, 68, 185
Hopson, Maurice, 174–175
House Un-American Activities Commission (HUAC), 77
housing market, 102, 245n4
Houston: census data, 5–8, *9*, *10*, *29*; city resources, 45, 207, 208, 210; community survey, 195–196, 208–209; downtown, 6, 8, 114, 116, 121, 190; narratives of, 96, 103, 192–196, 209; race relations in, 87–88, 165, 173, 188–189, 195–196, 207–209; racial structure in, 10–11, 208; segregation in, 29–30, 205–206; socioeconomic aspects, 6; socioeconomic characteristics, 8, 117; urban history and, 2
Houston, Charles Hamilton, 86, 141
Houston Chronicle, 150–153, 166, 181, 195
Houston College for Negroes, 113, 148–149. *See also* Texas Southern University (TSU)
Houston Colored Junior College, 113,

148–149. *See also* Texas Southern University (TSU)
Houston Housing Authority, 205
Houston Independent School District (HISD), 142–144, 159, 206, 209
Houston Informer: on Caesar home bombing, 104–107, 131; Carter Wesley and, 133–135, 138; on communism, 77–78; on crime, 119, 121, 158; on individualism, 159–160; on Morris case, 62–63, 71, 75–76; on police brutality, 123; on race, 103, 131, 136, 155–157; on schools, 118, 136, 142–144, 152–153; on Supreme Court Decisions, 3
Houston Police Department (HPD): attack on Texas Southern University, 166, 173–189, 210; black people in, 61–62, 207–208; charges against, 121–122; funding, 207–208; Green Pond Seven, 63–67; personnel budget, 262n12; surveillance by, 191–192
Houston Post, 50, 62, 119, 166
Houston Transit Company, 57–58
Howard, Charles, 175
Howard, William Lee, 48
Howell, George, 93–94, 98, 102, 109
HUD (US Department of Housing and Urban Development), 205–206
human consumption, 186–187
"human, the," 16, 19–25, 48, 50, 55
humanity: blackness and, 100, 124, 183, 185, 194, 218n14; concept of, 15–16, 60; redemption of, 19–20
Hunter, Tera, 47–48
Hurd v. Hodge, 102

identity, 16, 24, 37, 183
individualism, 107, 131–132, 135–137, 155–160
infrapolitics, 70–72
integration, 68, 106, 139–140, 142, 146, 160
Irvin, Walter, 75–76

Jackson, Zakiyyah Iman, 55
Jack Yates High School, 113, 144, 148–149
Jim Crow: black people under, 47, 73–75, 133–134, 170; capture by, 140; domestic labor under, 237n21; as a hold, 32; infrapolitics under, 70; political economy of, 36, 78, 87, 97, 135; racial etiquette of, 228n10; segregation after, 210–211; sexual relationships under, 59; and the term "black," 51; white people under, 139–140
Johnson, Adrian, 64–65
Johnson, Walter, 17, 23
Jones, Mack, 166, 172
Jordan, Winthrop, 180
Joseph, Benny, *190*
jury selection, 58–59, 79, 80–83, 87, 89
Justice, Blair, 178–179, 194–196, 208–209

Kazanjian, David, 66, 89, 168–169, 201
Kelley, Robin D. G., 70, 72
Kelly Courts, 197
Kern, C. V. "Buster," 61–62, 79
Kinder Institute for Urban Research, 29–30
King, Gilbert, 76
Kingsville, Texas, 39–41
Kirkpatrick, Frederick Douglass, 178–179, 200
KKK (Ku Klux Klan), 189–191, *190*, 196, 198, 200
Klarman, Michael J., 87
Kruse, Kevin, 2, 8
Kuba, Louis, 173, 175, 179–180
Ku Klux Klan (KKK), 189–191, *190*, 198, 200
Kusmer, Kenneth L., 2

Lamar Fleming Estate, 143–145
landfills, 126, 205
language, 18–19, 61, 74, 138, 154–155, 160
Lanier, Raphael O'Hara, 149–154, 250n70
Lassiter, Matthew, 2
Latinx people, 10–11, 207
Lavergne, Gary, 150
law, the: arbitrariness of, 68, 94, 189; black people and, 60, 67–68, 73, 210; capture by idea of, 60, 94, 132; criminal

legal system, 65, 78, 81, 84, 86–87, 131; critical legal studies, 60, 67–68, 90, 95, 157; due process of, 54, 79, 82, 86–87, 192; fair trial, 75–76, 78–79, 86–88, 165; jury selection, 58–59, 79, 80–83, 87, 89; meaninglessness of, 95–96; political nature of, 68, 94, 132; presumption of innocence, 58; race-blindness, 88, 155; rule of, 27, 68–69, 94–95, 131; white supremacy and, 94; zone of validity, 60, 67–68, 95
Laws, Clarence, 193
Lawson, Bill, 166, 178–179, 200
Lee, Donald P., 114, 116
Legal Defense Fund, 140, 142, 158
Lewis, Robert Jr., 181, 184–185
liberal democracy, 72, 90
liberal equality, 68, 136
liberal humanism: black people and, 33, 103, 117, 132, 218n14; capture of, 34, 61–62; codes of, 26; faith in, 91; history as, 19–21; and the law, 86–87
liberal individualism, 50–51, 124, 138, 154, 158–160
liberalism, 32–33, 55, 60, 112, 147, 158
linear chronology, 23, 220n40
lives in motion, 34, 168, 169, 189, 196, 200–201
living conditions, 43–44, 46, 110, 119–120, 125, 197, 205
Lockwood Inn, 133–134
Logan, Trevon D., 5
Lovinggood, Reuben Shannon, 38
low-income neighborhoods, 117, 119–120, 191, 205–207

MacGregor area, 100, 103, 111–112, 192
manhood, 134–135, 138, 146–147, 154, 181, 187–188, 198
Man-Not, 160
Margold, Nathan, 141
Marriott, David, 20, 67, 147, 182–184
Marshall, Thurgood, 79, 86, 122, 141–142, 145–147, 158
masculine, 135, 138, 154, 246n23
mass incarceration, 211, 213
Matsuda, Mari, 211–212
McCall, Willis, 75–76

McCleskey v. Kemp, 87
McCleskey, Warren, 87
McDonald, G., 50
McDowell, Clive, 182
McFarland, A., 50–51
McMillon, Annabelle, 115–116
McNair, Oscar, 185
meaninglessness: Afropessimism and, 18; of black suffering, 171, 189, 204; of the law, 95–97, 132–133; of the "self," 115; Western epistemology and, 48
Mexican-American Legal Defense and Education Fund, 209
Miller, Robert, 65, 67
Miller, Roy, 65, 67
miscegenation, 54, 58–59, 62–63, 80, 189
Mitchell, Mattie Louis, 66
Monell v. Department of Social Services, 95
Montrose, 63, *64*
Moody, Robert J., 178–179
moral education, 49, 51–52, 55, 107
Morris, Christine, 58, 61–63, 86
Morris, Johnnie Lee: arrest of, 58–59, 61–62; miscegenation charge, 58–59, 63; name, 228n2; Nowak stabbing, 57–58, 69–70, 73–74; press on, 62–63; trial of, 79–84, 86–88
Morrison, Frank, 70, 73–74
Mothers Clubs, 40
Movement for Black Lives, 89–90
Muhammad, Khalil Gibran, 119–120
multi-family units, 111–112, 245n4
municipal incorporation, 44
murder rate, 208
Myrdal, Gunnar, 52–53, 124

NAACP (National Association for the Advancement of Colored People): communism and, 47, 76–77; court censure of, 191; Houston Independent School District and, 209; investigations by, 49–50, 53–54; legal system and, 59, 77–78; Morris case, 62, 75, 78; on schools, 140–141; Carter Wesley and, 140–141
NAACP Houston Branch, 41, 46, 85
NAACP Legal Defense Fund, 140, 142, 158

narrative capture, 3–4, 13, 24–25, 108, 222n83
Nashville, Tennessee, 13
National Association for the Advancement of Colored People. *See* NAACP (National Association for the Advancement of Colored People)
National Equal Rights League, 41–42
Negro, the: as an object, 35, 59, 67–68, 73–74; capture of, 48–50; creation of, 120; as feminine, 33, 38, 135, 154; and manhood, 146–147; sexuality of, 110, 180
Negrophobia, 47–49, 53, 106–108
Negro problem, the, 33, 51, 145
Negro struggle, 136–137
Negro town, 39–40, 46
newspapers, 53, 62–63, 119, 134, 150–151, 182
Nichols, Floyd, 174–175, 178–180, 198, 200
nonviolence, 55, 202, 211, 260n105
Norris, James, 173, 175–176
Norris v. Alabama, 80, 87
Northwood Junior High School, 171–172, 178, 189, 197–199, 201
nothingness, 16–17, 132–133, 140, 164, 199
Novkov, Julie, 160
Nowak, Florian Antone, 57–58, 62, 73, 79–80

Oakland, California, 7–8, *9*
Odom, Brian S., 105
One Safe Houston, 208
ontology, 17, 19, 164, 201–203, 222n83
oral histories, 115–117
overreading method, 66, 168–169

Parker, John, 179–180, 186
Parks, Gordon, 160
Parks, Rosa, 52–53
Parman, John M., 5
Patterson, Orlando, 185, 187
Pavlicek, Bessie, 57–58, 73
Perry, Leon Jr., 195
Phelps, Wesley, 165–166

Philadelphia Negro, The (Du Bois), 121
Philadelphia, Pennsylvania, 95, 119
photography, 181–184
Pierce, Joseph, 153, 191
Pioneer Bus Company, 44
Pitre, Merline, 145
Pittman, Blair, 181
Pleasantville, 124–125, 127, 209, 244n121
Plessy v. Ferguson, 140, 144, 146
police: brutality by, 64, 75–76, 121–123, 164, 181–182, 199, 242n110; harassment by, 127–128; misconduct of, 66–67, 80, 189; perception of, 66, 174, 195; surveillance by, 191–192. *See also* Harris County Sheriff's Department; Houston Police Department (HPD)
polio, 126
Political Affairs, 76
political economy, 36, 78, 87, 97, 135
population density, 7, *10*, 43, 117
positivism, 14, 23, 182
poverty, 5–6, 44, 120, 196, 206–207
power, 12–15, 85, 160, 214–215
Prairie View A&M, 38, 209
prior torture, 164, 171–172, 189–202
propaganda, 24, 182, 185
property rights, 107, 110–111, 132
property values, 100–102, 106, 117, *118*, 132, 144, 205–206, 245n4
protests, 165, 171–173, 178, 189–190, 198–200. *See also* activism
public transportation, 44, 51, 57, 70–71, 73, 125

Quashie, Kevin, 115

race: capture of, 4, 59, 63, 99, 103–104, 117, 129; conceptualization of, 11, 16, 59–60, 136–137; gender and, 38, 52–54, 129, 133–135; hierarchy of, 73–74, 183; sexuality and, 180–181; study of, 97–98
Race and the Houston Police Department (Watson), 165–166
raceless democracy, 137–138, 145, 154–155, 159–161, 203

race riots, 53, 195
racial capitalism, 59–60, 71, 77, 117
racial democracy, 27, 55, 94, 99, 104
racialization: blackness and, 183; capture of, 155; of crime, 120–121; gender and, 37, 246n23; of space, 98, 116, 117, 123
racial justice, 52–55, 77, 159
racial liberalism, 52
racial purity, 10, 32, 34, 106
racism: analyses of, 48–49; cultural racism, 120; humanity and, 159; as intent, 87; permanence of, 17, 52, 203, 211; as sexual violence, 136; as terrorism, 99
rationalism, 138, 145–147, 154–155
realism, 88–89, 139, 211
Reconstruction, 34, 46, 110, 113, 122, 136. *See also* Fourteenth Amendment
Red Scare, 47, 76
relativism, 212
rental units, 111–112, 245n4
residential demolition, 111
resistance, 25, 55, 60–61, 70–71, 103, 167, 170–171, 184
Rice, Claudius William, 150–151, 250n70
River Oaks, 63, *64*
Riverside, 111
Riverside Terrace, *99*, 100–112, 237n25
Robinson, Judson Jr., 127–128
Robinson, Willie, 176
Rogers, Mary Beth, 150
Rose, Carol, 110–111
Ross, Herman Lee, 79
rule of law, 27, 68–69, 94–95, 131

Sakowitz investigation, 49–50
Salder, Ira Lee, 65
Salmi, Hannu, 88
San Antonio pool ordinance, 139
San Felipe Courts, 112–113
Saucier, P. Khalil, 72
Scenes of Subjection (Hartman), 12
schools: conditions of, 118; creation of, 113, 148–150; protests in, 171–172; segregation in, 136, 140–144, 159–160, 209
Scott, Rule, 195
Scottsboro decisions, 79, 81, 86–87

Seber, George, 108, 195
segregation: after Jim Crow, 210–211; anti-blackness and, 2–3, 78, 102; in businesses, 49–50, 190, 195, 197; cost of, 141; racism and, 211; reasons for, 2–3, 5; resources and, 208; in schools, 136, 140–146, 159–160, 209–210; separatism and, 146; sex and, 52–54; sin of, 157. *See also* anti-blackness; black communities; blackness; capture; desegregation; education; Houston; law, the; white neighborhoods
Sekhon, Nirej, 60
self-defense, 59, 72, 75, 84, 108. *See also* armed defense
Self, Robert, 2
Senate Bill 1, 211, 249n64
separatism, 146, 149
servants, 46–47, *64*, *99*, 100–101, 237n21
sex, 35, 47–48, 52–55, 59, 122
Sexton, Jared, 169
sexual assault, 50, 53–54, 63–66, 85–86, 180–181, 184, 186
sexuality, 180–181
Shabazz, Amilcar, 145
Shah, Courtney, 42
Sharpe, Christina, 116, 253n13
Sheeler, John Reuben, 192
Shelley v. Kraemer, 3, *99*, 100, 105, 110–112
Shepherd, John Ben, 81–82
Shepherd, Samuel, 75–76
Short, Herman, 173, 179–180, 186, 191
Siegel, Reva, 159
Simon, Dorothy Johnson, 75
Simon, Felogen, 75
Sithole, Tendayi, 116
slavery, 17–18, 22–23, 32, 36, 95–96, 169–170, 218n14
Smallwood, Stephanie, 17
Smiley, Sidney, 104–106, 238n48
Smith, Joe Edward, 65
Smith v. Allwright, 140, 155
Smith v. Texas, 83
SNCC (Student Nonviolent Coordinating Committee), 171, 191, 195, 201. *See also* Friends of SNCC

social death, 169–170, 185, 187, 198
social democracy, 201
socialism, 77, 158
social life of social death, 32–33, 112–117, 163–170, 197–198, 218n44
Souls of Black Folk (Du Bois), 157
sovereignty, 60, 122
space, 98, 110–112, 116–117, 123, 126–129, 149, 173
speculative work, 66, 168, 186
State Highway 288 (South Freeway), 111, 237n25
states' rights, 136
Stearns, Eldreway, 189
student movement, 171–172, 189–191
Student Nonviolent Coordinating Committee (SNCC), 171, 191, 195, 201. *See also* Friends of SNCC
subjective capture, 3–4, 13, 24, 26
subjunctive, exploitation of, 25, 67, 168, 186, 194
suburbs and suburbanization, 6–8, 97–98, 124–128, 212
suffragist movement, 40–43
Sugrue, Tom, 2, 8
Sullivan, Othello, 185, 187
Sunnyside, *29*, 126, 171, 195, 200, 205, 209
Supreme Court, 3, 77, 79, 81, 83, 87, 136
Sweatt, Heman, 140, 146–147, 160
Sweatt v. Painter, 79, 113, 140, 147–149, 159
Sweet, Gladys, 108
Sweet, Ossian, 104, 108
swimming pools, 139, 146

Texas Commission on Environmental Quality, 205
Texas Department of Transportation, 111
Texas Permanent University Fund, 148
Texas Senate Bill 1, 211, 249n64
Texas Southern University (TSU): black campus movement, 172; board of regents, 152–153, 250n74; campus map, *170*; founding of, 113–114, 148–153; funding, 160, 209–210, 249n64; 250n70; name, 249n64;

police attack, 171–189, 211; police surveillance, 191–192; Raphael O'Hara Lanier, 149–154, 250n70; TSU Five, 179–180
Texas State Constitution, 144
Texas State University for Negros (TSUN), 79, 113, 138–139, 146, 148–149, 249n64. *See also* Texas Southern University (TSU)
Texas v. NAACP, 47
theodicy, 14–15, 18, 155, 160
Third Ward, *29*, 98, *99*, 117, *118*, 123, 210
Thomas, Greg, 169
Thomas, Thelma D., 118–119
Thompson residence, 178, 197–200
Thompson, Wendell Mrs., 178, 197–198, 200
thought in motion, 169, 201–202
tobacco settlement fund, 209–210
Tollett, Kenneth S., 148
Trotter, Joe W., 2
Trouillot, Michel-Rolph, 12
TSU (Texas Southern University). *See* Texas Southern University (TSU)
TSUN (Texas State University for Negros), 79, 113, 138–139, 146, 148–149, 249n64. *See also* Texas Southern University (TSU)
Turner, Dave G., 124
Turner, Felton, 189–190, *190*, 199
Turner, Sylvester, 205–208
Turner, Thomas, 178

underbounding, 12, 45, 204
unincorporated land, 43
United States Constitution, 105, 121–122, 136–137, 156–158
United States Department of Justice, 77
University of Texas, 79, 140, 146, 148, 150
urban crisis, 97–98, 128
urban history, 2–5, 8, 12–14
urban renewal, 12, 28, 212
US Department of Housing and Urban Development (HUD), 205–206
U.S. v. Cruickshank, 95

vacant residences, 7, *9*, 111–112
Vera Institute of Justice, 213
voting, 40–42, 68–69, 155, 211
Voting Rights Act, 68–69

wages, 129, 196, 209, 213
Waller, Douglas "Wayno," 174–177, 179–180, 198–200
War on Poverty, 191
Warren, Calvin: on blackness, 16, 19, 94, 169, 189, 253n13; on humanity, 48; on ontology, 101, 164; on racism, 106, 159
Washington, Booker T., 145, 156
Washington Terrace, *99*, 100
Watson, Dwight, 165–166
Welch, Louie, 178, 191–192, 195, 208–209
Wells-Barnett, Ida B., 37, 52–53
Wesley, Carter: on the Caesars, 104; on Claudius William Rice, 250n70; on gender and race, 133–137, 146–147, 154–155; on Heavenly Houston, 109–110; on home ownership, 106; on individualism, 155–160; Thurgood Marshall and, 145–147; NAACP and, 140–141; police attack on, 122–123; rationalism of, 139–140, 145–146; on segregation, 131–132, 141–145, 150; on socialism, 165; on Texas State University (TSU), 146, 152–153
Western epistemology, 16–17, 48
Wheeler Avenue, 172–174, 176–179, 209
White, Bob, 54
White, Hayden, 89
White, Julius, 78
White, Lulu B., 47, 78, 140, 142, 145–146

white allies, 37, 187–188
white flight, 8, 97, 107, 111–112, 119–120
white neighborhoods, 5, 102, 106, 132, 238n48
whiteness: blackness in relation to, 35; as male, 129, 154; rationalism and, 154–155; relationship with blackness, 90–91, 111, 210
white power, 167, 182, 186, 196, 204
white press, 62–63, 182
white terrorism, 108–109, 171–172, 189, *190*, 192, 199, 209
Wilderson, Frank III, 17, 24, 132
Wiley College, 148–149, 248n63. *See also* Texas Southern University (TSU)
Williams, Red, 62, 80, 176
Winborn, A. C., 62, 79–81, 83
womanhood, 37, 51–52, 198
women's suffragist movement, 40–43
Woodlawn Pool, 139
Woods, Tryon P., 22, 61, 72, 97–98, 164, 169, 183
Woodward, Vincent, 186–187
"this world," 15–18, 170–171, 203, 214–216, 218n14, 220n40
worldmaking, 196, 203, 211–212
Wright Land Company, 42
Wynter, Sylvia, 12, 15–16, 19, 133

Yates, Jack, 113
Young, Iris Marion, 158
Young, James, 177, 184–185
Young, Jasmin, 198

zone of validity, 60, 67–68, 95